Introduction

CW01499935

A global brand relying on investor protec.....

UCITS stands for Undertaking for Collective Investment in Transferable Securities. UCITS is a global investment brand and the key to the success of the brand to date has been and will always be its reputation, which comes from the heavy and systematic controls carried out by all of the various fund service providers. UCITS is therefore a recognized, authorized product with all the necessary safeguards in place at all levels to provide investor protection. Despite the recent financial crisis, UCITS still remains one of the favored choices among investors. Statistics alone give an idea of how attractive this investment vehicle is. Approximately 40% of UCITS funds are sold outside the European Union (EU) – in Asia, the Middle East and Latin America – making them Europe's most successful financial service export.

The European Fund and Asset Management Association (EFAMA) releases monthly and quarterly statistics about UCITS. In its quarterly edition in November 2011, the figures were still impressive despite the financial crisis. It stated that the total net assets of UCITS were €5,472 billion at the end of September 2011.

> "The combined assets of the investment fund market in Europe reached EUR 7,667 billion at end September 2011, compared to EUR 6,171 billion at end 2008, EUR 7,154 at end 2009 and EUR 8,142 at end 2010. Equity funds are responsible for approx. 82 percent of the fall in total net fund assets over the first nine months of 2011." [1]

Chapter written by Christian SZYLAR.
1 EFAMA, Quarterly Statistical Release, November 2011, N47. The document can be downloaded on their website: www.efama.org.

By the end of January 2012, the total net assets of UCITS were €5,711 billion and the combined assets belonging to the investment fund market in Europe reached €7,941 billion.

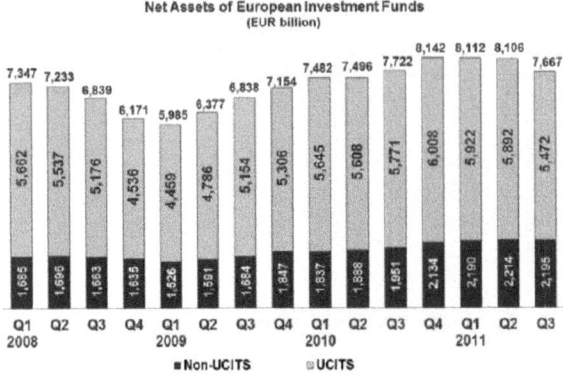

Figure I.1. *Net assets of the European UCITS investment fund*

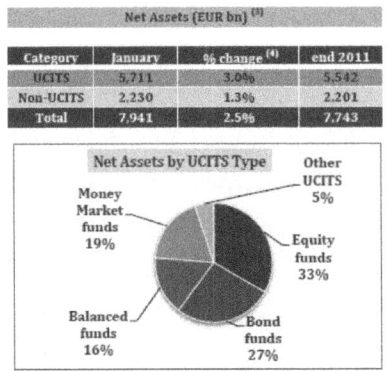

Figure I.2. *The European investment fund industry, split by the type of investment funds. Non-UCITs is a catch-all term referring to all non-harmonized funds, whether subject to national regulation or not. This comprises a wide range of investment styles and products – ranging from retail-oriented projects, such as open-ended real estate funds, to more volatile products, such as community and private equity funds²*

Luxembourg, France and Dublin are the leading places for UCITS.

---

2 EFAMA, Investment fund industry fact sheet, January 2012.

UCITS Handbook

UCITS Handbook

How to Set up, Monitor, Manage and Distribute a UCITS Fund

Edited by
Christian Szylar

First published 2012 in Great Britain and the United States by ISTE Ltd and John Wiley & Sons, Inc.

ISTE Ltd
27-37 St George's Road
London SW19 4EU
UK

www.iste.co.uk

John Wiley & Sons, Inc.
111 River Street
Hoboken, NJ 07030
USA

www.wiley.com

Library of Congress Cataloging-in-Publication Data

Szylar, Christian.
UCITS handbook / Christian Szylar. -- 1
   p. cm. -- (Iste ; 615)
  Summary: "This UCITS handbook intends to introduce systematically recent developments in different areas of UCITS through a multi-disciplinary approach. The coverage will be broad and thorough with balance in theory and applications. Each chapter covering a special aspect of UCITS is edited by leading experts and practitioners in the area and covers state-of-the-art methods and theory of the selected topic. The purpose of this UCITS handbook is to provide in a clear format a summary of the main aspects of each discipline that UCITS involves."-- Provided by publisher.
  Includes bibliographical references and index.
  ISBN 978-1-84821-349-4 (hardback)
  1. Securities--European Union countries. 2. Investments--Law and legislation--European Union countries. 3. Mutual funds--Law and legislation--European Union countries. 4. Capital market--Law and legislation--European Union countries. 5. Swaps (Finance)--Law and legislation--European Union countries. 6. Risk management--Law and legislation--European Union countries. I. Title.
  KJE2247.S99 2012
  332.6094--dc23

                                                                                    2012012680

British Library Cataloguing-in-Publication Data
A CIP record for this book is available from the British Library
ISBN: 978-1-84821-349-4

Printed and bound in Great Britain by CPI Group (UK) Ltd., Croydon, Surrey CR0 4YY

Table of Contents

Chapter 2. UCITS Management Companies   41
Jérôme WIGNY and Céline WILMET

Chapter 3. Risk Management in the Context of UCITS IV   77
Thierry LÓPEZ and Benjamin GAUTHIER

Luxembourg has a long-standing reputation as a jurisdiction for all types of alternative investment funds, mostly in the regulated sector. If we take a more detailed view of Luxembourg, which was historically the first country to specialize in UCITS fund administration and services, the increase in UCITS funds and assets under its management is really astonishing[3].

Why UCITS?

As we have seen above, the appetite for investing funds under UCITS has grown significantly over time and this trend will continue as some hedge fund managers are now considering the launch of UCITS products to enhance investor confidence or increase their distribution networks. Considering newcomers' interest in UCITS, for example hedge-fund managers, as well as increasing brand perception in countries outside the EU, the trend towards growth is expected to continue. Many hedge-fund investors are now looking to more regulated products, such as the UCITS structure, which is known for its heightened liquidity, transparency, risk management and regulatory scrutiny. UCITS is attractive for many investors because:

– it offers a wider choice of funds;

– it offers greater transparency than other products;

– its regulations are unique and strong;

– its funds usually have good returns compared to other investments;

– it is liquid; and

– it has enhanced risk controls.

UCITS was first introduced in 1985. The intent was to establish a common legislative framework for open-ended funds investing in transferable securities set up in any EU Member State, with the goal that a fund authorized in one Member State could be sold in other Member States without local authorization being required. It was developed, in effect, to establish a free pan-European market in collective investment schemes.

UCITS' history started with the UCITS Directive 85/611/EEC [EUR 85]. Its main objective was to create a harmonized legal framework to facilitate cross-border investment fund offers for the retail investor and to develop an integrated and competitive European single market for investment funds. Another key objective that followed this first European Directive established a defined level of investor protection through strict investment limits (based on the principle of risk

---

3 The well know association of the Luxembourg fund industry the ALFI (www.alfi.lu), which leads industry efforts publishes various guidelines, statements and recommendations which might prove of interest to the reader.

diversification), capital, organizational and disclosure requirements, as well as asset safe-keeping and fund oversight, usually by an independent depositary.

UCITS Directive 85/611/EEC was adopted and published in late 1985[4]. Its implementation by Member States was due by October 1, 1989. It is not surprising that the Grand Duchy of Luxembourg was one of the first Member States to translate the directive into its national law, due to taxation requirements. This helped Luxembourg to become the first country in the world with UCITS domiciliation.

At this stage, UCITS was limited to investment in transferable securities, a concept that was not properly defined by the first UCITS directive. In the absence of an agreed definition, transferable securities had been understood to mean simply listed bonds and equities. It is critical here to mention that the EU Directive of 1985 required 90% of UCITS' assets to be invested in transferable securities, while the remaining 10% could be placed in certain other financial instruments. Under the terms of the original directive, use of a UCITS did not allow fund managers to widely invest in shares of other funds, derivative products or money market instruments, among other things, for speculative purposes. Furthermore, due to diversification limitations inherent to UCITS I (i.e. generally no more than 5% of UCITS' assets could be invested in a single issuer, unless an increase on this level was authorized by an individual Member State), index and tracker funds did not qualify as a UCITS. UCITS industry did not grow as it might have done due to these inherent limitations. In the meantime, the financial industry had created evermore new financial instruments that asset managers increasingly wanted to incorporate as part of their investment strategies. These inherent limitations have also pushed the growth of hedge funds, which were subject to fewer constraints.

When the European Commission regulated the fund industry in 1985, it had three main objectives that have been partly achieved:

– to keep regulation up to speed with changes in the investment market;

– to create a level playing field for funds established in different Member States; and

– to ensure investors are well-protected by a single regulator across all EU markets.

---

4 Official definition from Directive 85/611/EEC: "Undertakings: the sole object of which is the collective investment in transferable securities of capital raised from the public and which operate on the principle of risk-spreading, and the units of which are, at the request of holders, re-purchased or redeemed, directly or indirectly, out of those undertakings' assets. Action taken by a UCITS to ensure that the stock exchange value of its units does not significantly vary from their net asset value shall be regarded as equivalent to such re-purchase or redemption."

The UCITS industry remained regulated by this first European Directive for more than 15 years. As with anything designed by committee, what was intended to be a horse ended up as a camel and the planned free market did not really take off for a number of reasons. These included the obstacles created by each Member State's own market rules, local taxation requirements and the relatively limited nature of the definition of transferable securities.

Even though UCITS I was implemented in 1985, the network of Member States' rules and local laws did not permit them to achieve the original objectives of the directive in practice. Throughout the 1990s there was much grumbling and discussion about the actions needed to ensure UCITS achieved its original objectives. This culminated in new proposals being put forward by the EU Commission in 1998 that were eventually formally adopted in December 2001. There were actually two directives published on the same day – UCITS II and UCITS III – but the two collectively are commonly known as UCITS III.

Significant amendments were made to Directives 2001/107/EC and 2001/108/EC and both were due for implementation in Member States by February 13, 2004. As we will see later, the significant amendments made by these two new European Directives are:

– the expansion of eligible assets;

– new investment techniques that required enhanced risk management capabilities;

– a simplified prospectus for investors; and

– rules on management companies.

Other amendments were made after 1985 to improve regulations and oversights in UCITS products. These amendments can be found in the following:

– Directive 88/220/EEC introducing mortgage bonds;

– Directive 95/26/EC5 following the post-Bank of Credit and Commerce International incident;

– Directive 2000/64/EC about the exchange of information with third countries;

– Directive 2004/39/EC, also known as the MiFID Directive; and

– Directive 2005/1/EC, known as the Lamfalussy Directive.

The first set of key principles is set up around what we can call the structural principles of UCITS. These principles consist of:

– the "redeemability" at net asset value, which is a key distinction versus hedge funds;

– the concept of segregation of assets; and

– the clear separation of functions to limit conflicts and abuse.

The second set of key principles can be summarized in the concept of "investment rules", which made UCITS funds so different from other investment vehicles, such as hedge funds. These principles include:

– the list of eligible assets

– the important aspect of diversification in investing;

– no borrowing/shorting; and

– in principle no commodities or real estate (exposure via indices is permitted assuming compliance with certain criteria).

The third set of key principles belongs to the UCITS passport. It is a matter of:

– EU-wide marketing once authorized in a home country;

– the notification procedure with registration in another EU Member State; and

– very limited host country involvement.

UCITS III allows more instruments and asset classes to be used within funds. This should enable experienced and skilled fund managers to enhance returns in low volatility markets. UCITS III consists of the two 2001 EU Directives, known as the Management Directive and the Product Directive.

Following the introduction of UCITS III and the capacity to use financial derivative instruments for direct investment purposes, UCITS funds gained the ability to synthetically shorten,[5] and thus allow the creation of long-short products and enhanced investment strategies in UCITS such as:

– classic long-only (equities, fixed income, balanced, etc.);

– long/short equity;

– hedge fund index product;[6]

– commodities index product;[7]

– fund-of-funds/UCITS fund-of-hedge-funds/hedge-fund index products;

– exchange traded funds;

– UCITS managed futures/commodity trading advisor products;[8]

---

5 In synthetic short selling, the security is not actually sold. A share position is created through financial derivative instruments that create an exposure to the price of the security, rather than the actual sale of the security.

6 Especially using total return swaps.

7 Commodities indices are subject to strict criteria for eligibility. Usually exposure is gained using SWAP instruments.

8 Commodity trading advisor funds relate mainly to funds trading commodities futures. It is a recently-launched UCITS product.

– UCITS absolute return funds;[9]

– 130-30 funds; and

– UCITS tactical asset allocation funds.

Using appropriate financial derivatives, the portfolio managers were able to diversify their investment strategies, improving performance.

The past few years have seen a significant increase in the number of UCITS being established that pursue what would typically be considered to be alternative investment strategies. This trend is expected to continue over the next few years.

UCITS IV was approved by the European Parliament on January 13, 2009. This recent adoption of the UCITS IV Directive constitutes another challenge for the asset management industry. UCITS IV introduces several modifications to the UCITS regulatory landscape. It offers fund managers the opportunity to undertake a strategic reflection on their product range and management structure as well as measures to enhance speed-to-market and investor protection.

To summarize, the most important enhancements of UCITS IV in comparison to the UCITS III Directive are:

– the management company passport allowing an UCITS authorized in one Member State to be managed remotely by a management company established in another Member State;

– simplification of the procedures for cross-border distribution;

– a framework for domestic and cross-border mergers of an UCITS allowing consolidation of UCITSs;

– the introduction of master-feeder structures to facilitate (mostly tax-driven) asset-pooling; and

– replacement of the simplified prospectus with a key investor information document designed to present comprehensible information that is similar for the UCITSs in each Member State. This document introduces the risk/reward indicator.

Why produce a handbook on UCITS?

The global investment appeal of the UCITS product is expected to broaden even further with the advent of UCITS IV. The most advantageous prescriptions of UCITS IV are generally perceived as removing red-tape barriers to cross-border sales,

---

9 Funds managed with the aim of delivering absolute (i.e. more than zero) returns in any market conditions. Typically funds in this sector would expect to deliver absolute (more than zero) returns on a 12-month basis. Strategies employed may be to use long positions, synthetic shorts, pair trades and a cash/top-down business cycle approach implemented through bottom-up long and short positions/multiple strategies.

simplifying the authority notification procedure (particularly with regards to documentation), permitting master-feeder structures and simplifying the procedures relating to cross-border UCITS fund mergers. For these and other reasons, the implementation of UCITS IV is likely to encourage increased investor accessibility through master-feeder structures, reduce operating and administrative costs and broaden the UCITS market.

Despite the importance of the UCITS industry, I was surprised to see that there was almost no book dealing with UCITS apart from publications issued by consulting firms, mainly the so-called Big 4. At the time I was working for a management company domiciled in Luxembourg, I was receiving a lot of requests from EU and non-EU investors to send them such documentation about UCITS – mainly on risk management as it was one of the main building-block of UCITS III. I then decided to publish a book on risk management under UCITS III/IV with the same editor as this current book[10]. This book has been a success. One weakness of this book is that it mainly focuses on risk management. UCITS is a broad topic and when discussing with some friends it came obvious than the next step would be to write a book aiming to offer a clear presentation of all themes linked with UCITS from the legal set up of a UCITS fund to the distribution of the fund as well as operational aspects, risk management, etc. In order to produce such a book, it was natural to involve experts in each field in the UCITS world (legal, fund administrations, distribution, compliance, risk, etc.). I devoted some time to finding such experts, who are considered outstanding professionals in their respective fields of qualification, and all the people contacted not only agreed but were eager to cooperate, as they saw the importance of having a publication containing all of the different aspects of UCITS. I would like to thank them again for their time and devotion on this project, considering their very busy schedules.

The goal of this handbook on UCITS is to provide a one-stop source that investors, whether institutional or retail, professionals in the fund or banking industry, service providers, students, researchers, and practitioners can use to gain the necessary knowledge and analytical skills they need when setting up, managing and monitoring a UCITS fund. The *UCITS Handbook* intends to systematically introduce recent developments in different areas of UCITS through a multi-disciplinary approach. The coverage is broad and thorough, with a balance between theory and applications. Each chapter covering a special aspect of UCITS is written by leading experts and practitioners in the area and covers state-of-the-art methods and theory of the selected topic. The purpose of this *UCITS Handbook* is to provide a summary of the main aspects of each discipline that UCITS involves in a clear format.

---

10 Christian Szylar, *Risk Management under UCITS III/IV: New Challenges for the Fund Industry*, ISTE Ltd and JohnWiley and Sons, 2010

Chapter 1 introduces the legal set-up of a UCITS fund. An Undertaking for Collective Investment in Transferable Securities (UCITS) is an investment fund that meets the criteria laid down by EU Directives to be eligible for sale in EU Member States. This chapter explains then the different legal forms a UCITS may be consist of (Société d'Investissement á Capital Variable (SICAV), Fond Commun de Placement (FCP), single fund, umbrella fund), the capital base, the authorization.

Chapter 2 presents the concept of a management company. A UCITS management company must limit its activities to the management of undertakings for collective investment in transferable securities. The activities of such a company include investment management, the marketing of units in an FCP and administrative functions, such as legal services, fund accounting, portfolio evaluation and the calculation of net asset value per share (including tax aspects), the sale and redemption of units/ shares, client administration, compliance and client servicing. Under certain conditions, a management company may also offer discretionary portfolio investment services to individual clients, including pension funds, in accordance with mandates given by those investors. This chapter clearly explains the different types of management companies and their respective responsibilities and core functions, the capital requirement, the legal forms, the management, the roles and responsibilities with regards to all stakeholders, their operating model and organizational requirements applicable to Luxembourg management companies, the CSSF supervision and taxes, and finally the key concept of the management company passport.

Chapter 3 studies risk management requirements under UCITS. Risk management is a fundamental characteristic of UCITS and one key driver of UCITS success among investors, as it sets high standards in terms of sound and proper risk management. UCITS IV contains important measures that reflect the post-crisis emphasis on investor protection and systemic risk. This chapter specifies all requirements in terms of risk management via the risk-management policy. It also outlines the key requirements around the main risk areas that UCITS needs to measure: market risk and global exposure, liquidity risk, counterparty risk and operational risk. Each specific requirement is explained and each concept is presented in a detailed way so to properly understand value-at-risk, stress testing and back-testing. While UCITS IV requires fund managers to address the issues associated with liquidity risk, it does not specify how they should do so. Readers will therefore find details of some interesting approaches that comply with this requirement. UCITS IV also adds a new area of monitoring with the operational risk. This chapter will help readers to understand how to deal with all of these challenges with the ultimate aim of reinforcing *investors'* protection.

Chapter 4 deals with counterparty risk. As a result of the financial crisis, counterparty risk has become a very sensitive topic. Due its significant importance we have decided to dedicate a specific chapter to this topic. This chapter introduces the UCITS requirements with regards to trading OTC (over-the-counter derivatives) and describes the methods used to measure and manage incumbent counterparty risk of a UCITS through limits, collateral, hedging and the quality of the counterparties. After outlining these rules and potential exceptions, the author offers some advanced techniques to implement and leverage these rules in order to improve the counterparty risk management of a UCITS fund beyond the necessary compliance with UCITS rules.

Chapter 5 summarizes and explains the investment limits applicable to a UCITS fund. A UCITS must operate on a principle of risk spreading and consequently, a UCITS must be properly diversified. There are many individual limits around the areas of asset eligibility, concentration and counterparty eligibility and the chapter explains how these limits are to be checked with an information technology (IT)/operational focus. Each rule is described in detail, highlighting any specific data requirements or peculiarities it may have. The author also focuses on the issue of consistent data provision and steps that can be taken to ensure quality data are available for restriction monitoring. Finally, the chapter ends by outlining the IT/operational process that should accompany the checking of investment limits, both *ex-ante* and *ex-post*.

Chapter 6 provides an overview of UCITS cross-border distribution. Funds that comply with UCITS are created to facilitate collective investment by the public and therefore target the full range of potential investors. The overarching objective of a UCITS is to maximize the assets under management by reaching as wide a range of investors as possible, each with their specific needs and objectives. It follows that national and cross-border distribution is a critical component of the life a typical UCITS. UCITS as a brand is seen not just as a European fund passport, but a global one. It is increasingly used in Asia, South America, Central and Eastern Europe and the Middle East. This chapter offers a complete overview of the cross-border funds industry, with a particular focus on the evolving distribution structure of UCITS funds and Luxembourg's role in its growth and future. It is also particularly important for alternative managers setting up UCITS funds and any newcomers within the UCITS world to understand the distribution process and channels that are explained in this chapter.

Chapter 7 looks at the UCITS management companies and delegation. UCITS IV introduces significant changes for UCITS management companies that need to be addressed. In particular, through the UCITS IV Implementing Directive, new Markets in Financial Instruments Directive (MiFID) – such as organizational and internal control requirements, conflicts of interest requirements and risk management requirements – apply to UCITS management companies. In addition, UCITS management companies need to comply with new rules of conduct. This chapter outlines the key changes and discusses the impact they have on UCITS management companies and how they carry on and control their activities. UCITS management companies should be able to delegate some of their activities to third parties, provided proper due diligence checks are carried out to ensure the third party is qualified. In many cases, therefore, UCITS management companies will seek to meet their obligations by ensuring that their delegates meet the requirements of the Implementing Directive. Ultimate responsibility for ensuring that they do so, however, rests with the management company. This chapter focuses on all of these aspects and provides a clear picture on how best to ensure that delegation complies with UCITS rules.

Chapter 8 deals with UCITS taxation. Tax is an important consideration for any investment. The chapter addresses the major tax issues surrounding the Luxembourg undertakings for collective investments. In order to explain these tax issues, the authors take an approach whereby they look at several "levels" of a fund (investments, the fund itself, and investors in the fund). Furthermore, they analyze the tax issues relating to the different actors/players surrounding the UCIs, such as advisory and management companies.

Chapter 9 presents alternative UCITSs. The structuring of hedge-fund strategies as UCITSs has been very popular since the 2007 financial crisis. Alternative fund managers are choosing to replicate alternative strategies under UCITS in order to access assets from retail and institutional investors that are not comfortable investing through less regulated structures, among other reasons. From an alternative manager's point of view, the primary upside of UCITS can be summarized in one word: distribution. Being an EU-regulated investment product, UCITS can be sold throughout the EU to both institutional and retail investors. This automatic passport is particularly attractive. It is therefore not surprising that the market for alternative UCITS has grown dramatically in the past five years. The author explains the development of alternative UCITS following the consequences of the financial crisis and assesses how alternative strategies can be replicated under UCITS regulations, as well as their potential limitations. The chapter analyzes the performance of these alternative UCITS compared to their hedge funds peers. It also presents the most commonly used derivatives used to gain synthetic short exposure and/or leverage.

Author biographies

Andrew Patrick White is the Founder and CEO of FundApps Ltd., a company which provides cloud-based compliance software to the fund industry. Before FundApps Andrew created the monitoring software MIG21 for Aquin Components GmbH. He went on to become the Managing Director & Head of Business Development for Aquin international. During this time he won Complinet's "Best Technology Solution" for MIG21 in 2008. Prior to joining Aquin, Andrew worked in a compliance company in Zurich and at the German Research Centre for Artificial Intelligence in Saarbruecken. Andrew holds a degree in Computer Science, Linguistics & German from Trinity College Dublin.

Thierry López has professional experience of almost 20 years. He is the partner leading the Risk Management Services at PwC Luxembourg. Thierry is coordinating a global offer to investment funds, banks, insurance undertakings, operational companies and the public sector. Thierry represents the worldwide PwC network as a member of the IIF (Institute of International Finance) Working Group on Liquidity and is the Liquidity Risk Leader of the EMEA region for the PwC network. Thierry is also a member of consultative committees for various regulators and professional bodies. Thierry is also the founder (1997) and board member of PRiM, the Luxembourg association for Risk Management Professionals. He is involved in the academic circle and research as ALM / GRC / Risk Management Professor / speaker at amongst others the HEC-Business School of the University of Liège. He has written articles and well-known books in English with John Wiley & Sons and in French with De Boeck University.

Benjamin Gauthier is Manager in the Risk Management Services team of PricewaterhouseCoopers Luxembourg. During the past 8 years, Benjamin has acquired great experience in the Investment fund industry in Luxembourg. Benjamin was an auditor at PricewaterhouseCoopers Luxembourg for nearly five years. He then served as a Risk Manager for an institutional Investment fund in Luxembourg. During that period, he qualified for the Financial Risk Manager certificate issued by GARP. He joined PwC Luxembourg as Manager in Advisory Services in 2010. His areas of expertise are: Risk Management in the context of UCITS III/IV and AIFMD, VAR: review of computation process, selection of software solutions, mappings, proxy selection, back testing, stress testing, Risk Management Governance (top down and bottom up approach, risk appetite, risk tolerance, Risk Aversion Matrix), Operational risk; Liquidity risk for investment funds; Derivatives; Process and control engineering; Risk reporting; Collateral Management for OTC derivatives.

Jérôme Wigny holds a "licence en droit belge" from the Université Catholique de Louvain-la-Neuve. He became a member of the Luxembourg Bar in 1994 and worked as an assistant with Slaughter and May (London) in 1995. He became a partner of Elvinger, Hoss & Prussen in 2001. He specializes in the field of investment funds, in particular UCITS and alternative investment funds. He is co-chairman of the Hedge Fund Working Group and a member of various other commissions of the Luxembourg Association of Investment Funds (ALFI). He is a regular speaker at conferences and seminars, in particular in relation to investment fund-related topics, and is an invited professor at Hautes Etudes Commerciales (HEC), Liège (Belgium).

Romain Berry is the EMEA and APAC representative of the Citigroup Cross Product Margining team that provides clients with seamless integration of their portfolios across cleared and uncleared products and Citi legal vehicles. In this capacity, he helps clients optimize their portfolio risk profile to realize optimal capital and operational efficiencies through advanced methodologies in monitoring market, counterparty credit, concentration and liquidity risks.

Romain has over 10 years of experience in risk management, developing and monitoring Value-at-Risk (VaR) models. More specifically, Romain has extensive experience in Market, Credit and Operational Risk, Value-at-Risk, Portfolio Management, Alternative Investments, and Emerging Markets. Prior to joining J.P. Morgan, Romain worked in Risk Management for J.P. Morgan, Morgan Stanley, Investcorp, KPMG, Ernst & Young, and the Central Bank of France. Romain earned a B.Sc. (Hons.) in Economics from the University of Montpellier, France, an M.Phil. in Operational Research from École Polytechnique, École des Mines and University of Paris-IX Dauphine, France, and an M.Sc. in Decision Sciences from the London School of Economics, UK.

Mark Evans is a partner in the Advisory Practice at PwC Luxembourg and a member of the Asset Management Group since 2001. Having worked in investment management for more than 20 years, Mark specializes in the distribution, regulation and tax aspects of investment funds. Since 1999 he has provided comprehensive advice to asset managers seeking to create and execute cross-border fund distribution strategies for the first time and also assist fund groups to maintain existing complex cross-border strategies, often on a global basis. Before joining PwC in Luxembourg he worked in London in the asset management practice of PwC and before that in Australia as a tax professional and auditor. Mark has a degree in accounting, a Masters in taxation and is a Chartered Accountant.

Killian Buckley is a Member of Kinetic Partners where he acts as a Central Bank authorized Designated Individual and MLRO for a variety of UCITS funds. He provides regulation and compliance advice to a range of UCITS clients from small boutique investment houses to larger institutions. Killian has multi-jurisdictional set up experience, with particular knowledge of the offshore domiciles and Ireland. Killian also has a broad range of experience advising public and private companies in relation to mergers and acquisitions, fundraisings and flotations. Killian is co-Chair of the Irish Funds Industry Association Marketing Committee.

Christian Szylar is currently Global Head of Risk and Performance Measurement in a leading global asset management firm. Christian worked at Kinetic Partners LLP as a Partner where he headed a risk and valuation solution to asset managers and banks, monitoring and reporting on areas such as market risk, OTC valuation, investment restrictions, liquidity, counterparty risk and performance measurement. Prior to this, he was Managing Director of RBS Portfolio Risk Services, where he developed a portfolio of risk management services tailored to worldwide asset managers and was also a conducting officer at RBS Luxembourg offering independent management company services for UCITS funds. He was also a Vice President at Mizuho Financial Group. He is an international recognized expert on risk management for banks and asset management and especially on UCITS. He has advised a number of regulators across the world on international best practices and regulations.

Christian holds a PhD in Management Science from University of Law, Economics and Management at Nancy II. He furthered his studies at MIT/Sloan School of Management and participated in a number of Harvard Economics programs as well as in the Europe Harvard participated in a number of Harvard Economics programs as well as in the Europe Harvard Model Congress. He teaches in various Masters degrees in different universities. Christian has published a lot of articles in reviews and several books with Hermes, Economica Gestion on management. His latest book with ISTE/Wiley was "Risk Management under UCITS III/IV - New Challenges for the Fund Industry".

Céline Wilmet holds a "licence en droit" from the University of Liège (Belgium). After working as an assistant at the University of Liège, she worked as a business lawyer, first in the Luxembourg office of an international law firm and thereafter at Elvinger, Hoss & Prussen. She specializes in the field of investment funds and is "collaborateur scientifique" at the University of Liège.

Ciara O'Sullivan is an Associate Director with Kinetic Partners where she provides a range of regulatory advisory services to the Dublin Funds community and most recently has been in a compliance consultant role with a large US Investment Manager in Dublin. Prior to this, Ciara worked with Brown Brothers Harriman in a number of roles, including European Compliance Officer, Head of the Trustee Group and Chairperson of their Market Initiative Group. Ciara was the Chair of the Association of Compliance Officers of Ireland Funds Working Group, and is currently an author and lecturer of Irish funds industry regulatory educational courses.

André Pesch was a co-founder of the Baker & McKenzie Luxembourg office in 2010. He has extensive experience in advising on Luxembourg tax issues related to tax efficient investment, holding, financing and IP structures. André Pesch is (or has been) a member of several expert groups from the European Commission, the Luxembourg Bankers Association (ABBL) and of the Association of Luxembourg Fund Industry (ALFI). Prior to joining Baker & McKenzie, André Pesch was leading the financial tax department of a Luxembourg Big 4 and co-headed its EMEA Asset Management tax group. He has been practicing in Luxembourg since 1993.

Ludovic Deflandre joined the Tax Group of Baker & McKenzie in 2010. He has more than 5 years' experience in indirect tax and specializes in the delivery of advisory services. He provides advice to multinational companies in various areas of indirect tax and industries, providing optimization of financial flows, tax diagnostics and advice with regard to international tax planning.

Romain Jacques joined the Tax Group of Baker & McKenzie in 2011. Prior to joining the Firm, Romain was Senior tax advisor in the International Tax Services department of a Luxembourg Big 4. He advises financial institutions and investment funds on a wide range of Luxembourg and international tax planning matters. He also provides advice on tax-related matters with regard to mergers, acquisitions, financing and corporate restructuring.

Chapter 1

Setting up a UCITS Fund

1.1. Introduction to the UCITS concept

UCITS is the acronym for Undertakings for Collective Investment in Transferable Securities. It refers to a single regulatory regime set up across the European Union[1] (EU) for the public offer of open-ended funds regards investing in transferable securities and other liquid financial assets authorized by the UCITS IV Directive (as defined under 1.1.1. below).

The key characteristics of a UCITS can be summarized as follows:

– the sole objective of the UCITS must be the collective investment of funds in transferable securities or other financial assets referred to in Article 41 (1) of the 2010 Law;

– investment must be made in accordance with the risk-spreading principle;

– the capital of the UCITS must be raised from the public;

– shares/units of the UCITS shall, at the request of their holders, be redeemed, directly or indirectly, out of the assets of the fund; and

Chapter written by Jérôme WIGNY and Céline WILMET.
1 According to the 2010 Law, non-Member States of the European Union that are parties to the agreement creating the European Economic Area are (within the limits set forth by the agreement) considered as equivalent to Member States of the European Union. For the purpose of this chapter, all references to the European Union shall (within the limits of the agreement) be construed as including all Member States of the European Economic Area.

– Luxembourg UCITS are prohibited from being transformed into investment undertakings that are not subject to the UCITS IV Directive.

1.1.1. *A half-century of legal developments*

In Luxembourg, the concept of a common fund was created in the late 1950s on the basis of the general concepts of civil law, relating in particular to undivided co-ownership, the agency relationship and the depositary contracts. In order to circumvent the civil law principle pursuant to which joint possession (*indivision*) can only be temporary, open-endedness clauses (allowing investors to leave the fund at any time) were introduced in management regulations.

At that time, there was no legal or regulatory basis for supervision. The pioneers of investment funds therefore decided to instigate a system of advanced rulings by the Ministry of Finance. This type of ruling: (i) offered tax advantages; (ii) afforded some form of control of the promoter's standard; and (iii) protected the assets of the fund by the requirement of a major bank as a depositary.

A few years later (towards the end of 1966), practitioners created the first corporate-type fund. As opposed to common funds, this type of fund could avail itself of a solid corporate framework under the Law of August 10, 1915 on commercial companies (the *Company Law*). Once again, the creation of a new kind of company required some adjustments to the existing environment. For instance, the prohibition of the redemption of shares in a Luxembourg company was overcome by allocating a large portion of the contributed assets to reserves (as opposed to capital).

The first regulation explicitly regulating investment funds was the Decree of December 22, 1972, which provided *inter alia* for forced liquidation of investment funds and required audit by an independent professional expert.

The first comprehensive legislation providing for both legal and supervisory frameworks of investment funds entered into force in 1983. The Law of August 25, 1983 (the *1983 Law*) explicitly derogated from the restrictions regarding the repurchase of shares and inaugurated a complete regulatory body of supervision for investment funds.

The 1983 Law was replaced in succession by:

– the Law of March 30, 1988 on collective investment undertakings (the *1988 Law*) incorporating the provisions of Directive 85/611/EEC (the *UCITS I Directive*) into Luxembourg law;

– the Law of December 20, 2002 regarding undertakings for collective investment (the *2002 Law*), which implemented Directives 2001/107/EC and 2001/108/EC (referred to as *UCITS III Directive* and themselves amending the UCITS I Directive) in Luxembourg law;

– the Law of December 17, 2010 concerning undertakings for collective investment (the *2010 Law*). The 2010 Law: (i) implements Directive 2009/65/EC of the European Parliament and of the Council of July 13, 2009 on the coordination of laws, regulations and administrative provisions relating to undertakings for collective investment in transferable securities (referred to as *UCITS IV Directive*); and (ii) introduces a series of other changes aimed at facilitating the day-to-day management of Luxembourg funds and introducing tax advantages to the current Luxembourg investment fund legislation.

1.1.2. *Legal/regulatory framework*

Since July 1, 2011[2], all existing or newly-created UCITS and their management companies are subject to the 2010 Law, which abrogates the 2002 Law with effect from July 1, 2012[3] (to the exclusion of Articles 127 and 129 of the 2002 Law, which were abrogated with effect from January 1, 2011).

Along with the 2010 Law, UCITS are governed by:

– regulations issued by the European Commission (which are directly applicable in Luxembourg);

– Grand Ducal regulations;

– regulations issued by the Luxembourg regulator, the *Commission de Surveillance du Secteur Financier* (the "*CSSF*"); and

– circulars whereby the CSSF (and its predecessor, the "*Institut Monétaire Luxembourgeois*" or *IML*) describe their administrative practice and interpretation of the UCITS legal framework.

Without purporting to be exhaustive, these include:

– European Commission Regulation 583/2010 of July 1, 2010 implementing the UCITS IV Directive as regards key information and conditions to be met when

---

2 For non-UCITS funds subject to the 2010 Law and their management companies, the 2010 Law entered into force on January 1, 2011. These funds, however, have until July 1, 2012 to comply with Articles 95(2) and 99 (6) sub-paragraph 2 of the 2010 Law (insofar as those Articles apply to them).

3 The difference between the date of entry into force of the 2010 Law and the abrogation of the 2002 Law is due to the transitional regime, providing for certain grandfathering measures concerning *inter alia* the implementation of the key investor information document.

providing key investor information or the prospectus in a durable medium other than paper or by means of a website (*Regulation 583/2010*);

– European Commission Regulation 584/2010 of July 1, 2010 implementing the UCITS IV Directive as regards the form and content of the standard notification letter and UCITS attestation, the use of electronic communication between competent authorities for the purpose of notification, and procedures for on-the-spot verifications and investigations and the exchange of information between competent authorities;

– Grand Ducal Regulation of February 8, 2008 relating to certain definitions of the amended law of December 20, 2002 on undertakings for collective investment, and implementing the Commission Directive 2007/16/EC of March 19, 2007 itself implementing Council Directive 85/611/EEC on the coordination of laws, regulations and administrative provisions relating to undertakings for collective investment in transferable securities (UCITS) as regards the clarification of certain definitions;

– CSSF Regulation N° 10/4 transposing Commission Directive 2010/43/EU of July 1, 2010, implementing Directive 2009/65/EC of the European Parliament and the Council as regards organizational requirements, conflicts of interest, conduct of business, risk management and content of the agreement between a depositary and a management company (*Regulation 10-4*);

– CSSF Regulation N° 10/5 transposing Commission Directive 2010/44/EU of July 1, 2010 implementing Directive 2009/65/EC of the European Parliament and the Council as regards certain provisions concerning fund mergers, master-feeder structures and notification procedure;

– CSSF Circular 11/508 regarding new provisions applicable to Chapter 15 management companies[4] and self-managed investment companies with variable capital[5];

– CSSF Circular 11/509 regarding new notification procedures to be followed by a Luxembourg UCITS wishing to market its units in another EU Member State of and by a UCITS of another EU Member State wishing to market its units in Luxembourg;

– CSSF Circular 11/512 relating to: (i) the presentation of the main regulatory changes in risk management following the publication of CSSF Regulation 10-4 and

---

4 A Chapter 15 Management Company is a management company subject to Chapter 15 of the 2010 Law (i.e. a management company whose corporate object envisages the management of at least one UCITS).

5 A self-managed investment company with variable capital is an investment company with variable capital that has not designated a Chapter 15 Management Company. For further details in this respect, please refer to section 1.2.4.2.1.

ESMA[6] clarifications; (ii) further clarifications from the CSSF on risk management rules; and (iii) definition of the content and format of the risk management process to be communicated to the CSSF; and

– IML Circular 91/75 on the revision and remodeling of the rules to which undertakings governed by the 1988 Law are subject (*Circular 91/75*). Although this circular is somehow old-fashioned and should, in some respects, be updated, it sets the basis of the Luxembourg UCITS regulatory framework.

1.1.3. *EU passport/brand*

UCITS benefit from the so-called European passport, allowing the cross-border distribution of the shares/units of any UCITS throughout the EU[7] through a simplified regulator-to-regulator notification procedure.

Although UCITS were initially intended to be marketed in the EU, the UCITS brand has been recognized as a stable and well-regulated product and, over time, has become the only investment vehicle distributed worldwide.

1.2. Legal forms and structures

Luxembourg UCITS may be established in the form of either a fund of the contractual type (a common fund) or a fund of the corporate type (an investment company).

1.2.1. *Legal forms available*

1.2.1.1. *Common fund ("fonds commun de placement")*

A *"fonds commun de placement"* (*FCP*) is not in itself a legal entity but a co-proprietorship of assets governed by the 2010 Law and the Luxembourg Civil Code.

Since an FCP has no legal personality, it cannot perform any legal act itself and needs to be managed on behalf of the joint owners (i.e. the investors/unit holders in the FCP) by a management company that has a legal personality. That management company can either be a Luxembourg company governed by Chapter 15 of the 2010 Law (a *Chapter 15 Management Company*) or a foreign company established in

---

6 ESMA is the acronym for European Securities and Markets Authority.
7 According to the 2010 Law, the non-Member States of the EU that are parties to the agreement creating the European Economic Area are (within the limits set forth by the agreement) considered as equivalent to EU Member States.

another EU Member State[8]. A management company makes all decisions relating to the investments and operations of a FCP in its own name and on behalf of the FCP. It acts in accordance with the prospectus and management regulations of the FCP in the best interests of the investors.

An FCP is created and operates on the basis of: (i) its prospectus; (ii) its management regulations[9]; and (iii) the subscription agreements executed by each investor.

Unless otherwise provided for in the management regulations, there is no relationship between the unit holders and they are not entitled to change the management regulations or replace the management company of an FCP, nor are they entitled to liquidate an FCP. Investors in an FCP are not vested with the power to manage the fund or to represent it *vis-à-vis* third parties and are only liable up to the amount contributed by them.

Unlike investors in an investment company, investors in an FCP are not, in principle, entitled to vote, unless and to the extent provided for in the management regulations. This is not usually the case, which makes the FCP a flexible vehicle that is attractive for those who wish to increase their control over the fund.

1.2.1.2. *Investment company*

Contrary to an FCP, UCITS of the corporate type do have a legal personality and can therefore perform legal acts on their own behalf. They are governed by the 2010 Law and (insofar as that law does not provide otherwise) by Company Law.

There are two kinds of corporate-type UCITS: (i) an investment company with variable capital ("*société d'investissement à capital variable*" or *SICAV*) and; (ii) an investment company with fixed capital ("*société d'investissement à capital fixe*" or *SICAF*).

1.2.1.2.1. SICAV

A SICAV may only be set up under the form of a public limited liability company ("*société anonyme*" or *SA*).

Its capital is at all times equal to its net asset value (NAV) and automatically increases each time the SICAV receives new subscriptions or decreases each time the SICAV receives redemption orders from its investors. The capital of a SICAV

---

8 In this case, it will be governed by the provisions implementing the UCITS IV Directive in the management company's home State.
9 For further details on the management regulations, please refer to section 1.5.3.2.

may therefore change at any time without complying with the provisions of Company Law, which in principle requires the holding of an extraordinary general meeting of shareholders and the intervention of a notary to change the share capital of the company.

Due to the flexibility of its capital structure, a SICAV is the most common form taken by UCITS investment companies.

1.2.1.2.2. SICAF

The 2010 Law does not limit SICAFs to any specific corporate forms. A SICAF could therefore in theory be incorporated under the form of a public limited liability company, a private limited liability company (*"société à responsabilité limitée"* or *S.à r.l.*), a partnership limited by shares (*"société en commandite par actions"* or *SCA*), a corporate limited partnership (*"société en commandite simple"* or *SCS*), a general partnership (*"société en nom collectif"*), a cooperative company (*"société cooperative"*) or a cooperative company incorporated as a public limited liability company (*"société coopérative organisée comme une société anonyme"*).

Unlike SICAVs, whose capital varies automatically, the capital of a SICAF can, in principle, only vary by virtue of a decision made at the extraordinary general meeting of shareholders (or, under certain limited circumstances, by virtue of a decision of the management body of the company[10]).

Therefore, a SICAF requires somewhat more complicated formalities to increase or reduce its share capital. It can nevertheless issue further shares or redeem its own shares in a similar manner as a SICAV by means of adequately structured capital comprising par value and premium.

1.2.1.2.3. Similar regimes

Most of the rules governing UCITS SICAVs apply *mutatis mutandis* to UCITS SICAFs. The main differences between the two regimes relate to: (i) the paid-up portion of the shares; (ii) the nominal value of the shares; (iii) the rules governing capital variations; (iv) the legal reserve; (v) the rules governing the preferential subscription right; (vi) the rules governing the distribution of the net assets of the company; (vii) the rules governing the payment of interim dividends; and (viii) the mention following the name of the company in all documents issued by the company.

---

10 This procedure is referred to as the authorized capital procedure.

1.2.2. *Capital requirements*

1.2.2.1. *Minimum capital requirements*

1.2.2.1.1. Investment company

The initial capital requirements depend on whether the investment company is self-managed or whether it has designated a management company.

While an investment company having designated a management company may be incorporated with a minimum capital of €30,986.69 (rounded up to €31,000), a self-managed investment company is required to have a minimum capital of €300,000 at the time of its authorization.

In addition, the capital of the investment company must reach €1,250,000 within a period of six months following its authorization, irrespective of whether or not it has designated a management company[11].

1.2.2.1.2. Common fund

Contrary to an investment company, an FCP is not subject to any requirement concerning the initial assets of the fund. It can therefore be set up with lower initial assets than a fund of the corporate type. This advantage, however, is of short duration as the net assets of the FCP (like the capital of an investment company) are required to reach €1,250,000 within the six months following its authorization[12].

In addition to the requirements regarding the assets of the FCP itself, the capital requirements that apply to its management company shall be taken into consideration when examining the opportunity to set up an FCP rather than an investment company. It is worth noting here that a management company can be authorized to manage several UCITS and that it is therefore not required to set up a new management company each time an FCP is created.

1.2.2.2. *Bearer versus registered shares/units*

Shares of an investment company or units of an FCP may either be issued in registered form or in bearer form.

---

11 The 2010 Law, however, provides that a CSSF regulation may raise the €300,000 and €1,250,000 minimum capital requirements up to an amount of €600,000 and €2,500,000, respectively.

12 The 2010 Law provides that a CSSF regulation (which has not been issued as yet) may increase this minimum net assets requirement up to a maximum of €2,500,000.

1.2.2.3. *Fully paid-up versus partly paid-up shares/units*

While SICAVs subject to the 2010 Law can only issue fully paid-up shares, FCPs may issue partly-paid units whose minimum percentage of payment is not prescribed by the 2010 Law.

As far as Company Law allows[13], shares of a SICAF may be fully or partly paid up. If a SICAF is set up under the form of an SA or an SCA, Company Law requires that at least 25% of each share is paid up.

1.2.2.4. *Legal reserve*

Unlike SICAFs, SICAVs are relieved of the obligation to create a legal reserve in accordance with Company Law, which requires that 5% of the net profits of a Luxembourg company[14] are allocated (each year) to the creation of a reserve until the reserve reaches 10% of the capital of the company. This allocation ceases to be compulsory as soon as the reserve reaches the 10% threshold but is again compulsory each time the reserve falls below that threshold.

As FCPs are not subject to Company Law, they are not obliged to create a legal reserve.

1.2.3. *Multicompartment/class structures*

1.2.3.1. *Multicompartment structure*

The 2010 Law specifically refers to the possibility of creating umbrella funds (i.e. funds with multiple compartments)[15].

This structure permits the creation of different compartments (that have no legal personality) within one legal entity. The different compartments shall in principle have a different investment policy and may differ as regards, *inter alia,* their target investors, fee structure, distribution policy and/or investment manager.

Although an umbrella fund constitutes one single entity, each compartment is linked to a specific portfolio of assets and liabilities that is segregated from the portfolio of the other compartments, unless its constitutional documents provide otherwise.

---

13 Company Law does not authorize the issue of partly paid-up shares in an S.à r.l.
14 This requirement does not apply to SICAFs incorporated in the form of a corporate limited partnership or a general partnership.
15 Funds that do not provide for the possibility to create different compartments are called "stand-alone funds".

This segregation principle, which is commonly referred to as the "ring-fencing principle", triggers the following consequences:

– the rights of investors or creditors concerning a compartment, or that have arisen in connection with the creation, operation or liquidation of a compartment, are limited to the assets of that compartment;

– the assets of a compartment are available exclusively to satisfy the rights of investors in relation to that compartment and the rights of creditors whose claims have arisen in connection with the operation of that compartment, unless a clause included in the constitutional documents of the UCITS provides otherwise;

– for the purpose of the relations between investors, each compartment is deemed to be a separate entity;

– the liquidation of a compartment does not trigger the liquidation of the other compartments or of the UCITS (which will only be liquidated upon liquidation of its last compartment);

– the withdrawal of the authorization of a compartment does not trigger the withdrawal of the entire fund from the CSSF official list; and

– since the adoption of the 2010 Law, a compartment may be authorized (under the conditions set forth in the 2010 Law) to invest in another compartment of the same UCITS without being subject to the requirements of Company Law with respect to the subscription, acquisition or holding by a company of its own shares.

1.2.3.2. *Multi-class structures*

The creation of different classes of shares/units does not always require the creation of a segregated portfolio of underlying investments for each class. In certain circumstances it may indeed be more appropriate to pool the subscription proceeds of different classes of shares/units and to invest them in a common portfolio in accordance with a common investment policy. Different classes may therefore be created either within one or more compartment(s) of an umbrella fund or within a stand-alone fund[16]. The different classes of a multiple class structure may differ as regards, *inter alia*, their target investors, fee structure, distribution policy, denomination currency or hedging techniques.

Although the underlying investments are the same for all classes of shares/units of a multiple class structure, the net asset value per share of each class may differ, for instance, as a result of their different fee structure, distribution policy or, in the case of hedging, upon the conclusion of hedging transactions on behalf of one class of shares/units only.

---

16 A stand alone-fund is a fund that does not contain any compartments.

Unlike compartments, there is no segregation between the assets and liabilities of the different classes of shares/units of a compartment, or of the fund in the case of a stand-alone fund.

1.2.4. *Management*

Contrary to FCPs (which shall necessarily be managed by a management company as they have no legal personality), Luxembourg investment companies can either be self-managed or designate a management company. The management body of the investment company will therefore have the choice to appoint conducting officers at the level of the investment company or to appoint a management company. In the second scenario, the conducting officers will be appointed at the level of the management company.

The rules governing Chapter 15 Management Companies are addressed in Chapter 2 of this book. Therefore, this section does not purport to present those rules but to provide the reader with an overview of the main differences regarding the governance of self-managed investment companies and externally managed investment companies (i.e. investment companies having designated a management company).

1.2.4.1. *Management body of the investment company*

1.2.4.1.1. SICAV

As indicated above, a UCITS SICAV must be incorporated under the form of a SA.

The rules governing the management of a SA are set forth in Company Law, according to which a SA shall be managed by a board of directors, composed of at least three members, who need not be shareholders of the company. The board of directors is required to choose a chairman from among its members. In the absence of any provision to the contrary in the articles of incorporation of the SICAV, the chairman has a casting vote in the case of a ballot.

The directors of the SICAV shall, in principle, be appointed by its shareholders for a renewable term not exceeding six years. By derogation from the foregoing, in the case of a vacancy in the office of a director, the remaining directors[17] are authorized to fill the vacancy on a provisional basis until the next general meeting of shareholders, which ratifies the appointment. This mechanism, which is commonly

---

17 Only directors that have been appointed by the shareholders can co-opt another director in replacement of a director him- or herself appointed by the shareholders.

called "co-option", is mandatory each time the number of board members is less than three.

Company Law does not impose any special requirements as to age, nationality or residence of directors. Nevertheless, before appointing a majority of members residing in the same (foreign) jurisdiction, it is advisable to check the potential tax consequences of that choice. Indeed, if the majority of the board members reside in the same country, that country might re-qualify the company and lead to the company being under its jurisdiction for tax purposes.

The appointment of the directors (as well as all changes to the board composition)[18] shall be: (i) approved by the CSSF; (ii) filed with the Luxembourg *Registre de Commerce et des Sociétés*; and (iii) published in the Luxembourg official gazette (the *Mémorial*). Prior to granting its approval, the CSSF checks whether the directors are of sufficiently good repute and have the experience required for the performance of their duties on the basis of the *curriculum vitae* referred to under section 1.8.1.1. below.

1.2.4.1.2. SICAF

The management body of a SICAF depends on the legal form chosen. For example, a SICAF set up under the form of a SA will be managed by a board of directors composed of at least three directors while a SICAF set up as an S.à r.l. will be managed by a board of managers composed of at least three managers[19]. A SICAF set up under the form of a SCA will be managed by its general partner (generally incorporated under the form of a SA or an S.à r.l. to mitigate the liability of the general partner, which is liable without any limitation for any and all obligations that cannot be met out of the assets of the SCA).

As is the case for SICAVs, there are no special requirements as to age, nationality or residence in the composition of the board.

All changes to the board composition shall be: (i) approved by the CSSF[20]; (ii) filed with the Luxembourg *Registre de Commerce et des Sociétés*; and (iii) published in the *Mémorial*.

---

18 The approval of the CSSF is only required in the case of the appointment of a new director, as the resignation is a unilateral act that does not need to be approved by the CSSF or even by the board itself.

19 In this respect, it is worth noting that even though Company Law authorizes the creation of an S.à r.l. managed by one single manager, in principle the CSSF requires that a UCITS SICAF is managed by at least three managers.

20 The approval of the CSSF is only required when a new director is appointed as the resignation is a unilateral act that does not need to be approved by the CSSF (or even by the board itself).

1.2.4.2. *Self-managed structures versus external management*

1.2.4.2.1. Externally-managed investment companies

If the management body of the investment company wishes to designate a management company, it will be compelled to delegate all functions listed in Appendix II of the 2010 Law to the management company.

These functions cover:

– portfolio management services;

– administration services (which cover: (i) legal and fund management accounting services; (ii) customer enquiries; (iii) valuation of the portfolio and pricing of the units (including tax returns); (iv) regulatory compliance monitoring; (v) maintenance of unit holder register; (vi) distribution of income; (vii) issue and repurchase of units; (viii) contract settlement (including certificate dispatch); and (ix) record keeping); and

– marketing activities.

It is therefore not possible for an investment company to delegate only one of these functions to a management company while remaining in charge of the others, or to delegate any of these functions directly to third parties.

If authorized to do so by the investment company, the management company will in turn be authorized to sub-delegate all or part of these duties to third parties under the conditions laid down in section 1.2.4.2.3.

1.2.4.2.2. Self-managed investment companies

Self-managed investment companies are required to appoint at least two conducting officers, who will be in charge of the day-to-day business of the company and will be required to report to the board of directors on a regular basis.

The conducting officers need not (but may) be directors or employees of the company. Where the conducting officers are employees of the company, no hierarchy link may exist between them.

Their role is described in CSSF Circulars 03/108 and 05/185. In a nutshell, they ensure that the different service providers of the company act at all times in accordance with its prospectus and articles of incorporation. They are therefore required to be independent from the custodian of the UCITS.

Contrary to the directors (who are appointed by the shareholders and whose appointment/removal will be published in the *Mémorial*), the conducting officers are appointed by the board of directors and their appointment/removal does not trigger any publication formalities[21].

Like the directors, they need to be approved by the CSSF. To this effect, they shall demonstrate: (i) their good repute; (ii) their experience in relation to the type of UCITS managed; and (iii) that they have enough capacity to devote sufficient time to their function.

There is no age or nationality requirement as regards the conducting officers, but in principle the CSSF requires that at least one of them is located on site[22].

1.2.4.2.3. Delegation of functions

The management company designated by an investment company or the self-managed investment company will be entitled to delegate its functions to third party service providers. The activities of the service providers will be supervised, on a day-to-day basis, by the conducting officers who will regularly report to the management body of the management company or of the self-managed investment company (as applicable).

The delegation of functions is subject to the conditions detailed below. For ease of reference, these conditions only refer to the delegation of functions by a management company but apply *mutatis mutandis* to self-managed investment companies:

– the CSSF shall be informed in an appropriate manner;

– the mandate shall not prevent the effectiveness of supervision of the management company, and in particular shall not prevent the management company from acting, or the UCITS from being managed, in the best interests of the investors;

– investment management functions may only be delegated to undertakings that are authorized or registered for the purpose of asset management and are subject to prudential supervision; the delegation must be in accordance with investment allocation criteria periodically laid down by the management company;

– where investment management functions are delegated to an undertaking domiciled in a third country, cooperation between the CSSF and the supervisory authority of that country must be ensured;

21 If the Conducting Officer is a "*délégué à la gestion journalière*" under the meaning of Company Law, his or her appointment will have to be published in the *Mémorial*.
22 CSSF Circular 03/108.

– a mandate with regard to the core function of investment management shall not be given to the depositary or to any other undertaking whose interests may conflict with those of the management company or the investors;

– the persons who conduct the business of the management company shall remain able, at any time, to monitor the activity of the undertaking to which the mandate is given;

– the mandate shall not prevent the persons who conduct the business of the management company to give further instructions, at any time, to the undertaking to which functions are delegated and to withdraw the mandate with immediate effect when this is in the interests of investors;

– any undertaking to which functions will be delegated must be qualified and capable of carrying out the delegated functions;

– the prospectus of the UCITS shall list the functions that the management company has been permitted to delegate;

– the liability of the management company and of the custodian shall not be affected by the fact that the management company delegated functions to third parties; and

– the delegation shall not result in the management company becoming a letterbox entity.

1.2.4.2.4. Benefits and drawbacks of the two structures

In a nutshell, promoters have two options when choosing the management structure of their investment company:

– they can set up a self-managed investment company; or

– they can designate a management company. In this case, they have the choice of:

- creating their own management company; or

- appointing an existing management company, which can either belong to the group of the depositary and central administrative agent or be independent therefrom.

a) Advantages of the management company option

The main advantage of the management company option is its increased specialization, which enables the investment company board to focus on strategic matters and high-level oversight.

(i) Dedicated management company

Although the creation of a management company dedicated to the new fund offers the advantage of avoiding the payment of fees to a third party, it has the disadvantage of requiring the creation of an additional company in Luxembourg (with capital and administration requirements).

(ii) Use of an existing management company

The choice of an existing management company avoids the creation of an additional company in Luxembourg but leads to the payment of fees to a third party. This disadvantage can be negated by the negotiation of a fee package, which is market practice when the management company belongs to the group of the depositary and the central administrative agent.

Some promoters will nevertheless prefer to appoint an independent management company (which may be more costly in terms of management and administration fees) to give their structure a maximum independent oversight.

b) Advantages of the self-managed option

The self-managed option is in line with the spirit of an investment company which, contrary to an FCP, has a legal personality and does not therefore need to be externally managed.

It offers straightforward governance but can seem weaker (than the management company option) in terms of independent oversight. This drawback can be corrected, however, by the appointment of independent conducting officers with appropriate seniority.

1.2.5. Choosing between legal forms and structures

1.2.5.1. FCP versus an investment company

The following aspects are to be considered when choosing between the different legal forms.

1.2.5.1.1. Fiscal situation of the targeted investors

Depending on their nationality or place of residence, target investors may be in a different tax situation if they own units in a contractual-type fund rather than shares in a corporate-type fund.

1.2.5.1.2. Control the promoter would like to keep over the investment fund

In principle, there are no unit holders' meetings in an FCP. As the unit holders of an FCP cannot, as a rule, replace the management company, they cannot take control over the fund by any other means whatsoever.

A hostile takeover is possible, at least theoretically, in the case of an investment company established under the form of a SA. Indeed, as the directors of a SA are to be appointed by the shareholders, a majority of shareholders could take control of the investment company, replace the board members and thereby also remove or appoint the service providers. The risk of unfriendly take-over is remote, however, where the fund is open-ended, since the bidder has no assurance that the shareholders will not leave the fund.

1.2.5.1.3. Habits and customs of the targeted investors

In certain jurisdictions, investors are more familiar with the contractual-type fund (which, in terms of structure, is somewhat similar to an English unit trust or a US mutual fund), while in other jurisdictions they are more familiar with the corporate-type fund.

1.2.5.2. *Variable versus fixed capital*

As to the difference between an investment company with variable capital and an investment company with fixed capital, the usual choice would be the one with variable capital which, from an administrative standpoint, is easier to handle. An investment company with fixed capital is only used in specific circumstances, such as where there is the need to issue partly paid-up shares[23].

1.2.5.3. *Self-managed structure versus external management*

For details regarding the benefits and drawbacks of these two options, please refer to section 1.2.4.2.4.

1.3. Issue/redemption of shares/units

1.3.1. *Investors*

Since UCITS are meant to be publicly distributed, shares/units of a UCITS cannot, in principle, be restricted to a specific category of investors (such as institutional investors). This general rule does not preclude the UCITS from limiting certain classes of shares/units to a specific category of investors. It is therefore

---

23 Unlike a SICAV governed by the 2010 Law, a SICAF may issue partly paid-up shares.

common to reserve certain classes of shares/units to retail investors while limiting others to institutional investors and to adapting the minimum subscription/holding requirements and fee structure of the relevant class accordingly (it being understood that a class reserved to institutional investors will usually have higher holding requirements and lower fees).

1.3.2. *Open- versus closed-ended*

UCITS shall necessarily be open-ended since the 2010 Law provides for the obligation to redeem their shares/units upon request from their investors.

Notwithstanding the above, the constitutional documents of the UCITS may, subject to adequate justification, authorize the management body to delay the settlement of redemption requests during a determined period of time, or proportionally reduce redemption requests exceeding a certain level of shares/units outstanding on the relevant dealing day. In this case, any portion of a redemption not having been honored would have to be treated as though the request had been made for the next dealing day or days until full settlement of the original request.

1.3.3. *Issue/redemption price*

The 2010 Law provides for the obligation to issue/redeem shares/units at a price arrived at by dividing the net asset value of the UCITS by the number of shares outstanding. According to Circular 91/75, issue/redemption prices of the shares/units of a UCITS must be determined at sufficiently close and fixed intervals and at least twice a month (subject to the possibility that the CSSF will grant derogations from this requirement on the basis of adequate justification).

By derogation from the foregoing, it is generally accepted that shares or units of a UCITS are issued at a fixed price during an initial offering period.

The subscription price may be increased (and the redemption price decreased) by expenses and commissions (the maximum of which shall be disclosed in the prospectus).

1.3.4. *Valuation of assets*

Unless otherwise provided for in the constitutive documents of the UCITS (i.e. the articles of incorporation of the investment company or the management regulations of the FCP), the valuation of the fund's assets, in the case of officially listed securities, will be based on the last known stock exchange quotation, unless that quotation is not representative. For securities not listed as such and for securities that are so listed, but for which the latest quotation is not representative, the valuation will be based on the probable realization value, estimated with care and in good faith.

1.3.5. *Suspension of issues/redemptions*

UCITS shall, in principle, issue and redeem shares at the frequency provided for in their prospectus and at least twice a month[24]. The CSSF or, as the case may be, the management body of the UCITS may, however, suspend the issue or redemption of the shares/units of the fund in the following circumstances:

– the CSSF is authorized to suspend the issue and redemption of the shares/units of a UCITS in the interests of shareholders (or unit holders), particularly where the provisions of laws, regulations or agreements concerning the activity and operation of the relevant UCITS are not complied with.

– The board of directors of an investment company (or the management company of an FCP) may decide to suspend the issue and redemption of shares/units in all cases provided for in the constitutional documents or management regulations of the fund. The CSSF (and, if the fund is distributed in another jurisdiction, the regulator of that jurisdiction) shall be informed without delay.

The 2010 Law automatically suspends the issue of shares/units of a UCITS (be it an FCP or an investment company) as soon as an event giving rise to the liquidation of the UCITS occurs[25]. As regards FCPs, the 2010 Law provides that as from that time, redemptions remain possible provided that the equal treatment of unit holders is ensured. The 2010 Law does not specify whether redemptions remain possible or not for an investment company. It is worth noting in this respect that in most cases, the articles of incorporation of a SICAV authorize the board of directors to suspend the calculation of the net asset value as well as the redemption of the shares of the company from the date on which the shareholders are convened to the extraordinary general meeting of shareholders called to put the company into liquidation. Redemptions of shares are therefore usually suspended from the date of the convening notice.

---

24 The CSSF may (in principle) authorize a UCITS to issue/redeem shares less than twice a month on the basis on a motivated request.
25 According to Article 181 (6) of the 2010 Law the issue of shares in an investment company remains possible for the purpose of liquidation.

In addition to the above, the issue and redemption of the units in an FCP are automatically suspended:

– during any period where the FCP has no custodian or management company;

– when its custodian or management company is put into liquidation, declared bankrupt, seeks an arrangement with creditors, there is a suspension of payment or controlled management or is the subject of similar proceedings.

1.4. Parties involved

1.4.1. *Promoter*

The CSSF requires all UCITS to be established on the initiative of a promoter. This concept (which might evolve or even disappear in the near future[26]) has been created entirely by the CSSF, which defines the promoter as the entity that has originated or brought impetus to the creation of the UCITS, who effectively determines its policies and activity and who benefits therefrom.

---

26 There have been discussions about the fact that capital requirements currently imposed on promoters of Luxembourg funds are inconsistent with the following provisions of the UCITS IV Directive:

– Article 16 (1) of the UCITS IV Directive provides that: "Member States shall ensure that a management company, authorized by its home Member State, may pursue within their territories the activity for which it has been authorized, either by the establishment of a branch or under the freedom to provide services";

– Article 16 (3) of the UCITS IV Directive provides that: "Subject to the conditions set out in this Article, a UCITS shall be free to designate, or to be managed by a management company authorized in a Member State other than the UCITS home Member State in accordance with the relevant provisions of this Directive (...)";

– Article 19 (8) of the UCITS IV Directive provides that: "Member States shall ensure that any management company authorized in a Member State is not subject to any additional requirement established in the UCITS home Member State in respect of the subject matter of this Directive, except in the cases expressly referred to in this Directive)";

– whereas clause 20 of the UCITS IV Directive provides that: "(...) authorization of a UCITS should not be subject to an additional capital requirement at the level of the management company (...)".

The CSSF might therefore not remain in a position to impose its current capital requirements on management companies authorized in another Member State managing Luxembourg UCITS. Although it is difficult to foresee the evolution at this stage, it has been envisaged: (i) to reduce the capital requirement applying to the promoter; or even (ii) to suppress the concept, it being understood that such a solution would be likely to go hand in hand with an increase of the requirements applying to the management body of the UCITS (for instance as regards the seniority of the directors) and an increase in its liability.

In order to be approved by the CSSF, the promoter shall:

– be a regulated entity;

– have sufficient financial resources[27] (in general, minimum own funds[28] of about €7.5 million) to indemnify the UCITS and its investors for losses resulting from the possible failure, irregularities or insufficiencies identified in the management or administration of the fund; and

– be of good repute and have sufficient expertise.

If the main promoter has insufficient resources, it can request the support of a so-called co-promoter (who will have similar responsibilities to those of the main promoter).

The CSSF's position regarding the indemnification obligations of the promoter is based on the fact that the promoter is considered a director of the UCITS under the meaning of Article 129 (5) of the 2010 Law (as it effectively determines the policies and activities of the fund in its setting-up phase) and must, in its capacity as such, be the last resort of investors.

The position of the CSSF has always been debated as the role, duties and liabilities of the promoter are neither defined in the law nor in any agreement (as no agreement is signed between the UCITS and the promoter).

By referring to the liability of the promoter in the case of non-performance or improper performance of its duties, the CSSF created a liability in tort of the promoter (the appreciation of which, in principle, is the reserve of the courts).

From a practical standpoint, it is relatively difficult to anticipate what the CSSF would consider as wrongdoing by the promoter. In the case of a loss resulting from a lack of communication between different service providers located abroad (such as the investment adviser/manager or distributor), the CSSF could, for example, ask the promoter to indemnify the UCITS without trying to determine the respective responsibilities of the service providers involved. The CSSF would thereby avoid never-ending discussions as regards to the responsibilities of the relevant parties, it being understood that the promoter being required to indemnify the UCITS would, at a second stage, be entitled to seek reimbursement against the service providers that effectively caused the loss. It is worth noting here that if it seems clear to the CSSF that the error was committed by a service provider located in Luxembourg (such as the custodian and, in most cases, the central administrative agent of the

---

27 In practice, this means that the promoter is not required to be a Luxembourg entity.
28 The "own funds" will be construed as referring to the capital plus the reserve of the relevant entity.

UCITS), the CSSF would presumably directly require the defaulting service provider to indemnify the UCITS.

In light of the promoter's role, the CSSF generally requires the promoter to have a majority representation on the management body of the UCITS. The CSSF nevertheless often grants derogations from the majority requirement principle, but on a case-by-case basis and on the understanding that the promoter will never be entitled to take the argument of non-representation to sidestep its indemnification obligations.

1.4.2. *Central administration*

According to Circular 91/75, the duties of a central administration agent include:

– keeping the accounts and other accounting documents;

– issuing redemptions of shares/units of the fund;

– keeping the register of share/unit holders in the fund;

– co-operating in the establishment of the prospectus, financial reports and other documents to be distributed to investors;

– dispatching and receipt of correspondence, dispatching of financial reports and all other documents to shareholders or unit holders; and

– calculating the net asset value.

UCITS are not obliged to (and as a matter of fact usually do not) perform the tasks connected to the central administration themselves but are entitled to delegate them to a third party, commonly called the central administrative agent. In theory, a UCITS could even be authorized to organize the division of the tasks connected to the central administration duties among various service providers provided that: (i) the division is not detrimental to the satisfactory performance of the central administrative duties; and (ii) the UCITS (or a duly qualified agent) is in a position to co-ordinate and supervise the execution of such tasks. In this respect, domiciliary duties are sometimes entrusted to an entity that does not carry out the other central administration duties.

Contrary to the 2002 Law, the 2010 Law no longer requires the central administration of Luxembourg UCITS[29] to be based in Luxembourg[30]. This means

---

29 The central administration of a Chapter 15 Management Company is, however, required to be located in Luxembourg. This requirement (which only applies to the management company itself and not to the central administration of the UCITS it manages) implies that the presence of the management company in Luxembourg must not be restricted to a legal or statutory head office. As a consequence, there shall be an infrastructure at the registered office

that the central administrative agent does not, in theory, need to be a Luxembourg service provider and that central administration duties might be carried out abroad. It is difficult, however, to foresee how the CSSF (which needs to be informed of and approve any delegation of functions) will interpret this legislative change and to what extent it will be ready to approve the delegation of all central administrative duties of a Luxembourg UCITS abroad. In this respect, it is worth noting that Company Law requires that the registered office of a Luxembourg investment company is located in Luxembourg. As a result, the domiciliary duties of a Luxembourg investment company will have to be entrusted to a Luxembourg service provider, even though the other central administrative duties are entrusted to a foreign entity.

In any case, if the service provider to which central administrative duties are delegated is a Luxembourg-based entity, it needs to be authorized as a financial sector professional under the Law of April 5, 1993 on the financial sector (the *1993 Law*).

1.4.3. *Depositary*

The assets of any UCITS must be entrusted to the custody of a depositary approved by the CSSF. The depositary may (but need not) be the same entity as the central administrative agent.

1.4.3.1. *Eligibility requirements*

The activity of a depositary is limited to credit institutions with their registered office in Luxembourg or that are established in Luxembourg through a Luxembourg branch if the registered office of the credit institution is located in another EU

---

that permits a centralized view of the activities of the management company and, where applicable, its delegates. To this effect, the management company shall:
– have human and technical resources available, which are necessary and sufficient to undertake and control its activities. Management companies shall be able to show that they have enough skilled staff members with the necessary knowledge and expertise for the discharge of the tasks they perform, and for an efficient monitoring of the delegated activities;
– have IT access to and/or hold, the complete documentation relating to their operations and those taken by their delegates on behalf of the management company.
30 It is worth noting that even under the 2002 Law, this obligation did not prevent the UCITS from outsourcing certain tasks relating to the central administration abroad. Although the CSSF has (under certain conditions) already authorized the outsourcing of non-core central administrative duties abroad, it has always required that the core central administrative duties (such as the physical keeping of the shareholder register, the finalization of the net asset value calculation, the dispatching of all notices and correspondence to investors) are performed in Luxembourg.

Member State[31]. Therefore, Luxembourg branches of a foreign banking institution that do not have their registered office in an EU Member State may not act as depositary for a UCITS.

1.4.3.2. *Duties*

The duties of the depositary are twofold: custody duties and monitoring duties.

1.4.3.2.1. Custody duties

According to CSSF administrative practice (which is similar to that of other European regulators), the mission of the depositary shall not be interpreted in terms of a safekeeping obligation but in terms of supervision duties. In practice, this means that the assets of the UCITS shall not necessarily be in the custody of the depositary but the depositary must have knowledge of how the assets of the UCITS have been invested and where and how these assets are available at all times.

1.4.3.2.2. Monitoring duties

Besides this general principle, the 2010 Law imposes certain specific monitoring duties on the depositary of a UCITS. The scope of these duties varies depending on the legal status of the UCITS and is broader for an FCP than for an investment company, as investors in an FCP are deemed to need additional protection due to their passive role in management.

According to the 2010 Law, the depositary of any UCITS must:

– ensure that the sale, issue, redemption and cancellation of shares or units are carried out in accordance with the law and the constitutive documents of the UCITS;

– ensure that in portfolio transactions the considerations are remitted to it within usual time limits; and

– ensure that the income of the UCITS is applied in accordance with the constitutive documents of the UCITS.

In addition, the depositary of a FCP must:

– carry out the instructions of the management company unless they are in conflict with the law or the management regulations; and

---

31 According to the 2010 Law, the non-Member States of the European Union that are parties to the agreement creating the European Economic Area are (within the limits set forth by the agreement) are considered equivalent to EU Member States. For the purpose of this note, all references to the EU shall (within the limits of the agreement) be construed as including all Member States of the European Economic Area.

– ensure that the value of an FCP's units is calculated in accordance with the law and the management regulations.

1.4.3.3. *Liability*

The depositary shall, in accordance with Luxembourg law, be liable to the investment company, the management company and the share/unit holders of the UCITS for any loss suffered by them as a result of its unjustifiable failure to perform its obligations or its improper performance thereof.

In the case of a FCP, the 2010 Law provides that the liability of the depositary *vis-à-vis* unit holders of the FCP shall, in principle, be invoked indirectly through the management company. By derogation from the foregoing, the 2010 Law authorizes the unit holders to directly invoke the liability of the depositary if the management company fails to act within a timeframe of three months after receipt of a written notice to that effect from a unit holder. It is worth noting here that Luxembourg case law refuses the right of the shareholders of an investment company to directly sue the depositary of the UCITS if they are not able to demonstrate a personal damage that is distinct from that of the company.

The liability of the custodian shall not be affected by the fact that it has entrusted a third party with the safekeeping of the assets of the UCITS. However, this does not mean that the depositary will in any event be liable if assets have disappeared through an act (or omission) of a correspondent. The rule will be interpreted in light of the duties of the depositary that will only be liable for losses which have been incurred as result of a lack of supervision.

1.4.3.4. *Cooperation agreement with the management company*

If the home Member State of the management company of: (i) a FCP; or (ii) an investment company having designated a management company, is not the same as that of the FCP or the investment company, the depositary must sign a written agreement with the management company. This agreement regulates the flow of information deemed necessary to allow it to perform its functions under the 2010 Law and other applicable laws and regulations. The content of this agreement is detailed in Regulation 10-4.

1.4.4. *Auditor*

Shareholders of Luxembourg UCITS must appoint an approved statutory auditor (*réviseur d'entreprises agréé*). This appointment is subject to the approval of the CSSF, which is conditional on the auditor having appropriate professional experience.

The auditor is in charge of auditing the accounting information contained in the UCITS annual report. His/her/its intervention, however, goes beyond the financial aspects as the auditor must report any fact or decision of which it has become aware while carrying out its duties concerning a UCITS to the CSSF, where any such fact or decision is likely to:

– constitute a material breach of the UCITS legislation or the regulations adopted for its execution;

– affect the continuous functioning of the UCITS or of an undertaking contributing towards its business activity; or

– lead to a refusal to certify the accounts or to the issue of a so-called "qualified opinion" whereby the auditor makes reservations regarding the accounts.

The scope of the mandate given to the auditor of a Luxembourg UCITS is governed by CSSF Circulars 02/77[32], 02/81[33] and 04/146[34]. CSSF Circular 02/81 introduces the so-called "long-form report" to be issued by the auditor, which encompasses a critical description of the UCITS' organization and a review of the way the UCITS operates, including its procedures and relationships with the central administration, the depositary, management company and other intermediaries, such as investment managers and distributors.

1.4.5. *Investment manager*

Under the conditions laid down in section 1.2.4.2.3., the asset management functions of a UCITS may be delegated to an investment manager, which needs to be approved by the CSSF. Unless the proposed manager is already known to the CSSF, the application file submitted to the CSSF will have to contain a detailed description of the activities of the investment manager, a copy of its articles of incorporation, a description of its management expertise and licenses as well as copies of its accounts (relating to the past three years).

---

32 Circular 02/77 on the protection of investors in case of net asset value calculation error and correction of the consequences resulting from non-compliance with the investment rules applicable to undertakings for collective investment.
33 Circular 02/81 providing guidelines concerning the task of auditors of undertakings for collective investment.
34 Circular 04/146 on the protection of undertakings for collective investment and their investors against late trading and market timing practices.

1.4.6. *Investment adviser*

The board of directors, management company or investment manager of an investment company (or the management company or investment manager of an FCP) may appoint an investment adviser to advise the board of directors, the management company or the investment manager on investment decisions. Contrary to the investment manager, the investment adviser is not entitled to make investment decisions and, therefore in principle, does not need to be approved by the CSSF (unless disclosed in the prospectus).

1.4.7. *Distributor*

The shares/units of a UCITS may be distributed to the public, either:

– directly by the UCITS (or its management company);

– by the intermediary of a distributor; or

– through stock exchanges.

UCITS may therefore choose to appoint one or more distributor(s) to market their shares and, as the case may be, to receive subscription and redemption orders as the agent for the UCITS[35].

The distributor may (but is not required to) act as nominee. When it does, it acquires the shares/units of the UCITS in its name but on behalf of its clients. The nominee is inscribed in the register of shareholders/unit holders of the UCITS, which might not be aware of the identity of the underlying investors. It is worth noting here that the nominee structure is not usually put in place by the fund, but when it is a series of rules (laid down in Circular 91/75) apply.

The distributor does not need be approved by the CSSF, unless disclosed in the prospectus.

1.5. Legal documentation

1.5.1. *Prospectus*

The prospectus is the offering document of the UCITS. It must contain the information necessary to enable investors to make an informed judgment as regards

---

35 For further details regarding the distribution of a UCITS, please refer to Chapter 5 of this book.

the investment proposed and, in particular, the risks attached thereto. The prospectus, which will be approved (and visa-stamped) by the CSSF, shall include at least the information provided for in Schedule A of Appendix I of the 2010 Law, insofar as that information does not already appear in the articles of incorporation of the investment company or the management regulations of the FCP.

According to the 2010 Law, the management regulations of the FCP or the articles of incorporation of the investment company shall form an integral part of the prospectus and must be appended thereto unless the unit holders of the FCP or the shareholders of the investment company are informed that, on request, they will either be sent those documents or be apprised of the place where they may consult them.

The essential elements of the prospectus must be kept up to date and any change to the prospectus is subject to the approval of the CSSF. If the proposed change is considered to be "material" by the CSSF, the UCITS will be required to offer all affected investors the right to leave the fund without fees for a period of one month starting from notification of the change. In such a case, the change will only enter into force on the expiry of the one-month redemption period, unless all investors in the UCITS agree to waive their redemption right in writing.

1.5.2. *Key investor information document*

The key investor information document (*KIID*) is intended to replace the simplified prospectus. While UCITS created since July 1, 2011 are already subject to the obligation to publish a KIID, UCITS created before July 1, 2011[36] have until July 1, 2012 to replace their simplified prospectus with a KIID. Contrary to the simplified prospectus, the KIID will not be visa-stamped by the CSSF.

In a nutshell, the KIID is a two-A4 page[37] pre-contractual information document intended to provide investors with information about the essential characteristics of the UCITS concerned. It purports to enable them to understand the nature and the risks of the proposed product and to make their investment decision on an informed basis.

The KIID will be written in a concise manner and in non-technical language. It shall be drawn up in a common format allowing for comparison between different UCITS and will be presented in a way that is likely to be understood by retail investors.

---

36 In fact, UCITS created before January 1, 2011 and UCITS created between January 1, 2011 and July 11, 2011 that have chosen to be subject to the 2002 Law until July 1, 2011.
37 Three for structured UCITS.

The content of the KIID (and order of disclosure of information) is laid down in Regulation 583/2010, which is directly applicable under Luxembourg law.

Where the UCITS is established in Luxembourg or markets its shares/units in Luxembourg pursuant to Chapter 7 of the 2010 Law, the words "key investor information" shall be clearly stated in the document in Luxembourgish, French, German or English.

In a nutshell, it will include:

– an identification of the UCITS;

– a short description of its investment objectives and policy;

– a presentation of its past performance or, where relevant, performance scenarios;

– the costs and associated charges; and

– the risk/reward profile of the investment, including appropriate guidance and warnings in relation to the risks associated with investments in the relevant UCITS. This will take the form of a synthetic risk and reward indicator, which will need to be accompanied by a narrative explanation detailing its main limits, as well as a narrative presentation of the material risks that are not captured by the indicator.

The KIID, whose essential elements shall be comprehensible to the investor without any reference to other documents, will clearly specify where and how investors can obtain additional information relating to the proposed investment including:

– where and how the prospectus and the annual and semi-annual reports can be obtained on request and free of charge; and

– the language in which such information is available to investors.

On December 20, 2010, the Committee of European Securities Regulators (*CESR*) published a template of the KIID document. This template, which is commonly used as a base by the investment fund industry, can be downloaded from the website of CESR's successor, ESMA[38].

---

38 http://www.esma.europa.eu/index.php?page=document_details&from_title= Documents &id=7336.

1.5.3. *Articles of incorporation/management regulations*

1.5.3.1. *Articles of incorporation*

According to Company Law, the articles of incorporation of any Luxembourg public limited liability company shall contain the following particulars:

– the identity of the founders;

– the form and name of the company;

– the location of the head office;

– the corporate object;

– the amount of the subscribed and authorized capital (if any). It is worth noting here that, due to the variable nature of the capital of a SICAV, the authorized capital procedure never applies to Luxembourg SICAVs;

– the amount paid in upon subscription;

– a description of the categories of shares composing the subscribed and the authorized capital;

– the form of shares (registered or bearer) and the limitations to conversion rights (if any);

– a description of any contribution other than in cash together with the conditions of that contribution and the name of the contributor[39];

– the reasons for and description of any particular rights or privileges granted to any of the founders;

– a description of shares (if any) that do not represent a fraction of the capital;

– the rules concerning the election of the directors and approved statutory auditors, if these rules derogate from the law and the description of the competence of those bodies;

– the duration of the company; and

– the estimated expenses and remunerations of any kind charged to the company or that it becomes liable to pay upon or by reason of its incorporation.

---

39 Recent amendments to Company Law allow increases in capital by contributions in kind without requiring an approved statutory auditor's report in the case of the contribution of eligible transferable securities and money market instruments that are traded on a regulated market. However, in practice the CSSF still insists on such a report for undertakings of collective investment.

In addition to the provisions that are required by virtue of Company Law, the articles of incorporation of a SICAV must include:

– a provision specifying that the capital of the SICAV is at all times equal to its net assets;

– a description of the valuation method of the SICAV's assets;

– an indication of the maximum time for payment of the issue and redemption prices;

– the conditions under which the issue and redemption of shares may be suspended;

– an indication of the frequency of calculation of the redemption and issue prices; and

– the nature of the fees to be borne by the SICAV.

They may also provide:

– instances where the appointment of the custodian or of the management company will cease;

– whether existing shareholders have preferential subscription rights. In the absence of any provision in this respect in the articles, no preferential subscription rights will be granted to existing shareholders; and

– restrictions regarding the distribution of dividends.

1.5.3.2. *Management regulations*

The management regulations, which form the constitutive documents of the FCP, are drafted and signed by the management company after CSSF approval.

Although this is not legally required, the management regulations are usually countersigned by the custodian, which needs to be aware of their content at all times in order to be in a position to perform its monitoring duties (as detailed in section 1.4.3.2.).

Investors in the FCP do not sign the management regulations but are deemed to have accepted them by the mere execution of their subscription agreement. Upon acceptance of their subscription agreement by the management company, investors subscribe for units in the FCP, each representing a portion of the net assets of the fund.

The minimum content of the management regulations is set forth in the 2010 Law, according to which they shall contain at least:

– the name and duration of the fund;

– the name of the management company and of the depositary;

– the investment policy of the fund;

– the dividend policy;

– the remuneration and expenses that the management company is empowered to charge to the fund and the calculation method thereof;

– the provisions governing publications;

– the closing date of the accounts of the fund;

– the cases where, without prejudice to legal grounds, the fund shall be dissolved;

– the procedures to be followed to amend the management regulations,

– the procedure governing the issue of units; and

– the procedure governing the redemption of units and the conditions under which the redemptions are carried out and may be suspended.

1.5.4. *Agreements with service providers*

The material agreements of the UCITS (i.e. the central administration agreement, depositary agreement and investment management agreement) are subject to approval of the CSSF, which requires that all agreements entered into between a Luxembourg fund and Luxembourg service provider are subject to Luxembourg law. In addition, the CSSF may request (and as a matter of fact usually does) any other agreement of the UCITS such as any prime brokerage or investment advisory agreement, where applicable.

It should be noted that the CSSF tends to request the executed version of all material agreements to be entered into by the UCITS before visa-stamping the prospectus. This enables the CSSF to check that the depositary and central administration agreement(s) effectively enter into force on the day of: (i) incorporation of the investment company; or (ii) the execution of the management regulations of the FCP.

1.5.5. *Other documents*

According to the 2010 Law, a series of documents (such as the risk management process and the periodic reports of the UCITS) have to be kept at the disposal of the investors requesting them. In addition, Regulation 10-4 requires information be kept at the disposal of investors by Chapter 15 Management Companies and, to a certain extent, self-managed investment companies. This is typically the case with any voting strategies or the company's conflicts of interest policy.

1.6. Reporting obligations

UCITS are required to provide monthly and annual financial information to: (i) the CSSF (which uses them for statistical and supervisory purposes) and to the STATEC[40] (which uses them to draw up the Luxembourg national accounts and balance of payments).

In practice, the reporting obligations are met by the central administrative agent of the UCITS. The content of the reports is detailed in CSSF Circular 97/136 of June 13, 1997, according to which:

– Monthly reports include:

- information on month-end net asset value;

- details on the value of the portfolio of the UCITS compared to total net assets at the month end;

- information on the number of shares or units issued and redeemed during the relevant month;

- information on investment income received during the relevant month; and

- information on distributions made during the relevant month.

– Annual reports include:

- a statement of net assets (summarizing the total assets, total liabilities and net assets at the end of the financial year);

- a statement of operations (including details on the total incomes, total charges, net investment income and profits or losses on operations);

- information on changes in the net assets of the UCITS; and

- information on changes in the portfolio of the UCITS (including details on the total purchases and sales of transferable securities and other investments).

---

40 The "*Service Central de la Statistique et des Etudes Economiques*".

1.7. Expenses

The expenses to be borne by a UCITS are:

– formation expenses; and

– ongoing expenses.

1.7.1. *Formation expenses*

The formation expenses (which may be amortized over a period not exceeding five years[41]) cover all of the costs involved in setting up a UCITS. They include:

– the legal and advisory fees relating to the structuring of the fund and, as the case may be, to the drafting of its documentation;

– the fees relating to the distribution of the shares/units and printing of the documentation of the fund;

– the notary fees; and

– the CSSF fixed fee for instructing the application file (equal to €2,650 for stand-alone funds and €5,000 for umbrella funds).

1.7.2. *Ongoing expenses*

The ongoing expenses (which cover the expenses incurred by the UCITS in the conduct of its business) include:

– the central administrative agent fee;

– the depositary fee;

– the management company fee (if applicable);

– the investment management/advisory fee (if applicable);

– the auditor's fee;

– the legal adviser's fee;

– the directors'/conducting officers' fees;

– the distribution fees (if any);

---

41 Please note that amortization is only possible if the accounting of the fund is drawn up in accordance with generally accepted Luxembourg accounting principles (Lux GAAP) but not under international financial reporting standards (IFRS).

– all taxes payable by the fund[42];

– stock exchange maintenance fee (if applicable);

– CSSF annual fees, which amount to:

   - €2,650 for stand-alone FCP and stand-alone investment companies having designated a management company, and

   - €5,000 for umbrella funds and for stand-alone self-managed investment companies).

1.7.3. *Prospectus disclosure*

All fees payable out of the assets of the UCITS shall in principle be disclosed in its prospectus.

1.8. CSSF authorization

1.8.1. *Approval process*

Before starting their activities, UCITS need to be approved by the CSSF[43]. To this end, UCITS have to follow a five-step procedure, which can be summarized as follows:

– initial submission;

– acknowledgment of receipt of the application file;

– transmission of comments and possible request for further information;

– advice after completion of examination and invitation to submit the final version of the compulsory documents; and

– entry on the official list.

1.8.1.1. *Initial submission*

UCITS have to file the documents and information below with the CSSF in French, German or English. This information and documentation is not exhaustive

---

42 For further details about this, please refer to Chapter 8 of this book.

43 The 2010 Law provides that a UCITS is only authorized if the CSSF approves its constitutive documents and the choice of the depositary. If the UCITS is set up under the form of an FCP or of a SICAV having designated a non-existing management company, the CSSF shall also approve the application filed by the management company.

as the CSSF reserves the right to request any additional information it may deem necessary to complete its analysis of the file:

– CSSF application questionnaire relating to the setting up of an undertaking for collective investment. This questionnaire can be downloaded from the CSSF website[44] and contains, *inter alia*:

- the proposed name of the UCITS,

- the identity of its promoter, auditor, board members, depositary, central administrative agent, investment manager/adviser

- information on the proposed marketing method, on the countries of marketing and the targeted investors, as the case may be, and

- the name of its management company;

– draft articles of incorporation of the investment company or management regulations of the FCP;

– draft prospectus;

– draft key investor information document;

– draft custody agreement;

– draft central administration agreement;

– draft investment management agreement (if any);

– engagement letter or letter of intent of the auditor;

– for each of the directors and of the conducting officers (if any):

- a copy of his/her/their passport/identity card(s),

- an up-to-date curriculum vitae, dated and signed, containing at least: (i) the date and place of birth; (ii) academic records/credentials; and (iii) information allowing an assessment of his/her experience in the performance of his/her functions,

- a recent extract of the criminal records bureau (*certificat de bonnes vie et moeurs*);

- dated and signed CSSF sworn statement (*"déclaration sur l'honneur"*) that can be downloaded from the CSSF website[45].

– the risk management process of the UCITS; and

– in addition to the above, the application for authorization of a self-managed investment company must contain information on the human and technical resources at the disposal of the investment company and describe the manner in which the management, administration and distribution functions will be monitored.

---

44 http://www.cssf.lu/fileadmin/files/Formulaires/FormulaireSetupUCI_V_2011_03_23.dot.
45 http://www.cssf.lu/fileadmin/files/Formulaires/Decl_hon_LPeng.pdf (for legal entities) and http://www.cssf.lu/fileadmin/files/Formulaires/Decl_hon_NPeng.pdf (for individuals).

1.8.1.2. *Acknowledgment of receipt of the application file*

Within approximately two business days[46], the CSSF acknowledges receipt of the file and informs the applicant of the name of the case officer in charge.

1.8.1.3. *Transmission of comments and possible request for further information*

The CSSF tries to provide the applicant with initial feedback within 10 business days of receipt of the file. At this time, the case officer may ask questions and/or request further information/documents he/she deems appropriate to complete the file.

1.8.1.4. *Advice after completion of examination and invitation to submit the final version of the compulsory documents*

The CSSF informs the applicant of the completion of the examination phase and authorizes the applicant to send the prospectus for a visa[47]. From this moment, applicants are not, in principle, authorized to amend the documents on the basis of which the examination has been completed but can, in principle, launch the UCITS and offer its shares/units to investors.

A copy of the articles of incorporation (or management regulations) and of the executed version of the agreements[48] will be filed with the CSSF together with the prospectus.

1.8.1.5. *Entry on the official list*

All approved UCITS are included in the CSSF official list of undertakings for collective investment in transferable securities. According to the 2010 Law, the inclusion on the list will be tantamount to authorization. The relevant UCITS will be notified by the CSSF. Entry and maintenance on the list is subject to the observance of all of the provisions of laws, regulations or agreements relating to the organization and operation of UCITS and the distribution, placing or sale of its shares/units. Inclusion on the list will not, however, be construed as a positive assessment made by the CSSF of the quality of the shares/units offered for sale. The list (and any amendments made to it) is available on the CSSF website[49].

---

46 All timeframes provided for in this section are indicative and are not binding for the CSSF.
47 It is worth noting that, contrary to the simplified prospectus, the KIID will not be visa-stamped by the CSSF.
48 The depositary and central administration agreement will become effective on the date of incorporation of the company (or, in the case of an FCP, on the date of the execution of its management regulations).
49 http://www.cssf.lu/fileadmin/files/Listes/Entites_surveillees/Liste_opc10_130911.pdf.

For members of the management body of the management company or, where applicable, of the investment company, authorization of the CSSF implies an obligation to notify the CSSF in writing in a complete, coherent and comprehensible manner of any changes regarding substantial information on the basis of which the CSSF examined the authorization request. Written notification as to any change in respect of the directors is also required.

1.8.2. *Timing*

The length of the approval process depends on various factors, including the quality of the file presented to the CSSF and its degree of standardization. If no particular difficulty arises, experience shows that the review of a complete file usually takes around four to eight weeks, even though the CSSF usually provides its first comments within 10 business days.

1.8.3. *Withdrawal of CSSF approval*

The entering and the maintaining on the CSSF official list is subject to observance of all the provisions of laws, regulations or agreements relating to the organization and operation of the UCITS and the distribution, placing or sale of its shares/units. The CSSF may therefore withdraw its authorization, should UCITS no longer comply with the relevant conditions.

The 2010 Law however restricts the conditions under which the CSSF may withdraw the authorization issued to an investment company or to a Chapter 15 Management Company.

1.8.3.1. *Investment company/Chapter 15 Management Company*

According to the 2010 Law, the CSSF may withdraw the authorization issued to an investment company only where that company:

– does not make use of the authorization within 12 months, expressly renounces the authorization or has not participated in the activity covered by the 2010 Law for more than six months;

– has obtained the authorization by making false statements or by any other irregular means;

– no longer fulfills the conditions under which authorization was granted;

– has seriously and/or systematically infringed the provisions of the 2010 Law or of the regulations adopted pursuant thereto; or

– falls within any of the cases where the 2010 Law provides for withdrawal.

The grounds for withdrawing the authorization of a Chapter 15 Management Company are the same as those referred to above. In addition, the CSSF is also authorized to withdraw the authorization issued to a Chapter 15 Management Company authorized to provide the discretionary portfolio management services referred to in Article 101, paragraph (3), point a) of the 2010 Law if the management company no longer complies with the provisions of the 1993 Law.

1.8.3.2. *Common fund*

The 2010 Law does not contain any provision concerning the withdrawal of the authorization of a FCP.

1.9. Incorporation process

Depending on the legal form chosen, the UCITS shall either be incorporated before a Luxembourg notary (for UCITS of the corporate type) or by a private seal document (in the case of a FCP)[50].

1.9.1. *Investment company*

Once approved by the CSSF, the articles of incorporation of the company will have to be notarized[51]. It is worth noting that the 2010 Law provides that applications for entry on the list referred to under section 1.8.1.5 must be filed with the CSSF within the month following the constitution or formation of the UCITS. This means that an investment company could (at least in theory) be incorporated before the approval of the CSSF (provided it is not offered to investors before its approval). For obvious practical reasons, however, this theoretical possibility is never applied and UCITS are never incorporated before CSSF clearance.

Incorporation is a straightforward process as it only requires that the initial shareholder(s) (or its/their duly appointed agent) appear(s) before a Luxembourg notary to sign the incorporation deed. In order to avoid unnecessary and time-consuming travel for the initial shareholder(s) (who may not necessarily be Luxembourg residents), the initial shareholder(s) usually give proxy to him/her/their legal adviser (or any other person professionally residing in Luxembourg) to

---

50 A general partnership, a corporate limited partnership, a cooperative company and a cooperative company incorporated as public limited liability company may be incorporated by a private seal document and therefore do not necessarily require the intervention of a notary.

51 Since the adoption of the 2010 Law, the articles of incorporation of a UCITS can be drafted in French, German or English (and the English version does not need to be followed by a French or German translation).

represent him/her/them at the incorporation of the company and to sign the incorporation deed of the company on his/her/their behalf. This incorporation deed includes: (i) the articles of incorporation of the company; and (ii) the minutes of the first general meeting of shareholders, whereby the initial shareholder(s) of the company appoint the directors and auditor of the company and determine its registered office.

The incorporation deed is deposited with the Luxembourg Trade and Companies Register (which grants a number to the company) and is published in the *Mémorial* by the notary.

Any subsequent change to the articles of incorporation have to be approved by the CSSF, notarized, deposited with the Luxembourg Trade and Companies Register and published in the *Mémorial*.

1.9.2. *FCP*

Once approved by the CSSF, the management regulations are signed by the management company and are deemed to have been accepted by investors subscribing for units in the FCP. It goes without saying that the management regulations have to be signed by an existing management company[52]. Hence, if the FCP does not use an existing management company but requires the incorporation of a new management company, the management company will need to be incorporated prior to the execution of the management regulations of the FCP. As indicated under section 1.5.3.2, it is not legally required that they are signed by the depositary. However, considering the depositary's supervisory duties, the management regulations are often countersigned by it.

The management regulations and any change to them will be approved by the CSSF and filed with the Luxembourg *Registre de Commerce et des Sociétés*. Notice thereof (*"mention du dépôt"*) will be published in the *Mémorial*.

---

52 Contrary to an investment company, which could in theory be incorporated before the approval of the CSSF, a Chapter 15 Management Company may only be incorporated after notification of its authorization by the CSSF.

Chapter 2

UCITS Management Companies

2.1. Introductory comment

There are two kinds of management companies under Luxembourg law:

– management companies subject to Chapter 15 of the Law of December 17, 2010 on undertakings for collective investment (the *2010 Law*), which can manage both UCITS and non-UCITS funds; and

– management companies subject to Chapter 16 of the 2010 Law, which can only manage non-UCITS funds.

Depending on the Chapter to which they are subject, Luxembourg management companies are referred to as "Chapter 15 Management Companies" or "Chapter 16 Management Companies".

This chapter purports to provide the reader with an overview of the rules governing the setting up and operations of Luxembourg UCITS management companies. Unless the context requires otherwise, all references to management companies shall therefore be construed as referring to Chapter 15 Management Companies.

Chapter written by Jérôme WIGNY and Céline WILMET.

It is worth noting, however, that insofar as the 2010 Law is broadly based on a European Directive, most of the provisions governing Luxembourg management companies have been implemented in other European Union (EU) Member States[1].

2.2. Luxembourg legal/regulatory framework

As indicated above, Luxembourg UCITS management companies are subject to Chapter 15 of the 2010 Law. Without purporting to be exhaustive, they are also subject to:

– Luxembourg Law of August 10, 1915 on commercial companies (the *Company Law*);

– *"Commission de Surveillance du Secteur Financier"* (*CSSF*) Regulation No. 10-4 transposing Commission Directive 2010/43/EU of July 1, 2010 implementing Directive 2009/65/EC of the European Parliament and of the Council with regard to organizational requirements, conflicts of interest, conduct of business, risk management and content of the agreement between a depositary and a management company (*Regulation 10-4*);

– *CSSF Circular 03/108* relating to Luxembourg management companies subject to Chapter 13 of the Law of December 20, 2002 concerning undertakings for collective investment (the *2002 Law*), and Luxembourg self-managed investment companies subject to Article 27 or Article 40 of the 2002 Law (*CSSF Circular 03/108*)[2];

– *CSSF Circular 05/185* relating to Luxembourg management companies subject to Chapter 13 of the 2002 Law, as well as Luxembourg self-managed investment companies subject to Article 27 or Article 40 of the 2002 Law (*CSSF Circular 05/185*);

– *CSSF Circular 11/508* regarding new provisions applicable to Chapter 15 Management Companies and self-managed investment companies with variable capital [3]; (*Circular 11/508*);

– *CSSF Circular 11/512* relating to: (i) the presentation of the main regulatory changes in risk management following the publication of CSSF Regulation 10-4 and

---

1 According to the 2010 Law, the non-EU Member States that are contracting parties to the agreement creating the European Economic Area are considered equivalent to an EU Member State within the limits set forth by this agreement and related acts.

2 The name of the Circular refers to the 2002 Law, which has since been replaced by the 2010 Law.

3 A self-managed investment company with variable capital is an investment company with variable capital that has not designated a Chapter 15 Management Company. For further details in this respect, please refer to section 1.2.4.2.1.

ESMA[4] clarifications; (ii) further clarifications from the CSSF on risk management rules; and (iii) the content and format of the risk management process to be communicated to the CSSF (*Circular 11/512*).

2.3. Conditions for setting up a Chapter 15 Management Company

The setting up of a Luxembourg Chapter 15 Management Company is subject to the following requirements.

2.3.1. *CSSF approval*

Access to the business of a Chapter 15 Management Company is subject to the prior approval of the Luxembourg regulator (the *CSSF*).

Before authorizing a Chapter 15 Management Company, the CSSF will, among other things:

– Make sure that all requirements detailed under sections 2.3.2. to 2.3.8. are complied with.

– Verify the reputation and experience of the auditor.

– Verify the reputation and experience of the directors, shareholders holding a qualifying participation and persons who effectively conduct the business of the management company. To this effect, the proposed directors, conducting officers and important shareholders shall submit the documents listed in section 2.5.1.3. to the CSSF.

– Where close links exist between the Chapter 15 Management Company and other legal entities or individuals, the CSSF will only grant its authorization if these links do not prevent the effective exercise of its supervisory functions. Likewise, the CSSF will refuse to give authorization if the laws, regulations or administrative provisions of a third country governing one or more legal entities or individuals with which the Chapter 15 Management Company has close links prevent the effective exercise of its supervisory functions.

The authorization procedure (and documents to be filed with the CSSF in this context) aims to enable the CSSF to verify that all of the conditions provided for by Luxembourg laws and regulations regarding access to the business of a Chapter 15 Management Company and the operations of the management company are complied with. For ease of reference, we have therefore chosen to present all

---

4 ESMA is the acronym for European Securities and Markets Authority.

conditions governing: (i) the setting-up; and (ii) the operations of the management company before; (iii) summarizing the authorization procedure (which we will detail in section 2.5.).

2.3.2. *Functions*

In order to be approved by the CSSF, a Chapter 15 Management Company has to be the designated management company of at least one UCITS. This means that the relevant UCITS has to entrust the performance of the three core functions (listed in section 2.3.2.1.) to the management company. The management company has the choice to either (i) perform these functions itself or (ii) sub-delegate one or more of these functions to a third party under the conditions provided for in section 2.3.2.3. In the first scenario, the management company will have to demonstrate that it has sufficient resources to manage, administer and distribute the shares/units of the UCITS. In the second scenario, it will have to demonstrate that it has sufficient resources to oversee and supervise the activities that have been delegated.

In addition to those functions, Chapter 15 Management Companies may (but are not required to) be authorized to provide:

– any of the core functions referred to below to one or more other UCITS;

– any of the core functions referred to below to one or more non-UCITS; and

– other services (listed in section 2.3.2.2). This possibility, however, is not often used by Chapter 15 Management Companies as the authorization to carry out these functions triggers additional requirements (detailed in section 2.3.2.2.1).

2.3.2.1. *Core functions*

The three core functions of a Chapter 15 Management Company are:

a) portfolio management services;

b) administration services that cover:

- legal and fund management accounting services,

- customer enquiries,

- valuation of the portfolio and pricing of the units (including tax returns),

- regulatory compliance monitoring,

- maintenance of the unit-holder register,

- distribution of income,

- issue and repurchase of units,

- contract settlement (including certificate dispatch), and

- record keeping); and

c) marketing activities.

2.3.2.2. *Other functions*

In addition to the core functions listed above, Chapter 15 Management Companies may be authorized to provide the following services, it being understood that under no circumstances shall they be authorized to provide the functions listed in this section if they do not also perform the core functions listed in section 2.3.2.1:

– discretionary management; and

– ancillary services.

2.3.2.2.1. Discretionary management

Management companies may be authorized to manage investment portfolios, including those owned by pension funds, in accordance with mandates given by investors on a discretionary, client-by-client basis, where such portfolios include one or more of the instruments listed in section B of Annex II of the amended Law of April 5, 1993 on the financial sector (the *1993 Law*)[5]. In that case, the management

---

5 The instruments that are listed in section B of Annex II of the 1993 Law are:
   (i) transferable securities;
   (ii) money-market instruments;
   (iii) units in collective investment undertakings;
   (iv) derivative instruments for the transfer of credit risk;
   (v) financial contracts for differences;
   (vi) options, futures, swaps, forward rate agreements and any other derivative contracts relating to:
      (a) securities, currencies, interest rates or yields, or other derivative instruments, financial indices or financial measures that may be settled physically or in cash,
      (b) commodities that must be settled in cash or may be settled in cash at the option of one of the parties (other than by reason of a default or other termination event),
      (c) commodities that can be physically settled provided that they are traded on a regulated market or a Multilateral Trading Facilities (*MTF*),
      (d) commodities that can be physically settled not otherwise mentioned under (c), and not being for commercial purposes, which have the characteristics of other derivative financial instruments, having regard to whether, *inter alia*, they are cleared and settled through recognized clearing houses or are subject to regular margin calls,
      (e) climatic variables, freight rates, emission allowances or inflation rates or other official economic statistics that must be settled in cash or may be settled in cash at the option of one of the parties (other than by reason of a default or other termination event), as well as any other derivative contracts relating to assets, rights, obligations, indices and measures not otherwise mentioned in Section B of Annex II, which have the characteristics of other

company will be required to get the prior approval of its clients (such approval may be global) before investing their assets in funds managed by the management company.

Management companies whose authorization covers discretionary portfolio management services are subject to additional requirements. These include the obligation to:

– comply with the organizational requirements laid down in Article 37-1 of the 1993 Law;

– comply with the rules relating to the conduct of business when providing investment services to clients, as laid down in Article 37-3 of the 1993 Law;

– comply with the relevant implementing measures set forth in the Grand-Ducal Regulation of July 13, 2007 relating to organizational requirements and rules of conduct in the financial sector;

– comply with the relevant provisions of CSSF Circular 07/307 regarding MiFID[6] conduct of business rules in the financial sector;

– participate in a scheme for the compensation of investors that is established in Luxembourg and recognized by the CSSF. For such management companies, membership of the Deposit Guarantee Association, Luxembourg (*Association pour la Garantie des Dépôts, Luxembourg* or *AGDL*) is therefore compulsory; and
– comply with the Luxembourg regulations implementing Directive 2006/49/EC of the European Parliament and the Council of June 14, 2006 on the capital adequacy of investment firms and credit institutions (recast); and

– have at least two conducting officers in Luxembourg.

2.3.2.2.2. Ancillary services

Management companies authorized to provide discretionary management services may be authorized to provide the ancillary services listed under items (i) and (ii) below. This means that Chapter 15 Management Companies may in no case be authorized to provide the ancillary services listed below without also providing discretionary management services:

– *Investment advice*: The 2010 Law defines investment advice as the provision of personalized recommendations[7] on one or more transactions concerning financial

---

derivative financial instruments, having regard to whether, *inter alia*, they are traded on a regulated market or an MTF, are cleared and settled through recognized clearing houses or are subject to regular margin calls.
6 MiFID is the acronym for Markets in Financial Instruments Directive.

instruments referred to in section B of Annex II of the 1993 Law. Recommendations may be provided either upon request of the client or at the management company's initiative. They have to be adapted to the client or based on examination of the client's individual circumstances and have to recommend the operation of the following categories:

- the purchase, sale, subscription, exchange, repayment, holding or underwriting of a particular financial instrument;

- the exercise or non-exercise of the right conferred by a particular financial instrument to purchase, sell, subscribe, exchange or reimburse a financial instrument.

– Safekeeping and administration services in relation to units of undertakings for collective investment.

2.3.2.3. *Delegation of functions*

Chapter 15 Management Companies are authorized to delegate their duties to third parties under the conditions detailed below:

– the CSSF shall be informed in an appropriate manner;

– the mandate shall not prevent the effectiveness of supervision over the management company, and in particular shall not prevent the management company from acting, or the UCITS from being managed, in the best interests of the investors;

– investment management functions may only be delegated to undertakings that are authorized or registered for the purpose of asset management and are subject to prudential supervision; the delegation must be in accordance with investment allocation criteria periodically laid down by the management company;

– where investment management functions are delegated to an entity domiciled in a non-EU Member State, cooperation between the CSSF and the supervisory authority of that country must be ensured;

– a mandate with regard to the core function of investment management shall not be given to the depositary or to any other undertaking whose interests may conflict with those of the management company or the unitholders;

---

7 A personalized recommendation is a recommendation which is addressed to a person by reason of his capacity as investor or potential investor or its capacity as agent of an investor or of a potential investor. A recommendation is not a personalized recommendation if it is exclusively disseminated by distribution channels within the meaning of Article 1, point 18) of the Law of 9 May 2006 on market abuse or if it is intended for the public.

– the persons who conduct the business of the management company shall remain able, at all times, to effectively monitor the activity of the undertaking to which the mandate is given;

– the mandate shall not prevent the persons who conduct the business of the management company from giving further instructions, at any time, to the undertaking to which functions are delegated. The mandate may be withdrawn with immediate effect when this is in the interests of investors;

– any undertaking to which functions will be delegated must be qualified and capable of carrying out the functions in question;

– the prospectus of the UCITS shall list the functions that the management company has been permitted to delegate;

– the liability of the management company and of the custodian shall not be affected by the fact that the management company has delegated functions to third parties; and

– the delegation shall not result in the management company becoming a letterbox entity.

The delegation of discretionary portfolio management activities is subject to stricter conditions, such as the laid down Grand-Ducal Regulation of July 13, 2007 relating to organizational requirements and rules of conduct in the financial sector.

2.3.3. Capital requirements

2.3.3.1. *Minimum capital requirement*

The initial capital of a Chapter 15 Management Company shall be at least equal to €125,000. If the value of the portfolios of the management company[8] exceeds €250,000,000, the management company will be required to provide its additional

---

8 The portfolio of the management company is composed of:

(i) the portfolio(s) of the common funds managed by the management company (including portfolios for which it has delegated the management function but excluding portfolios that it is managing under delegation);

(ii) the portfolio(s) of the investment companies for which the management company is the designated management company; and

(iii) the portfolio(s) of the other UCIs managed by the management company (including portfolios for which it has delegated the management function but excluding portfolios that it is managing under delegation).

own funds[9] (equal to 0.02% of the amount by which the value of the portfolios exceeds €250,000,000). The total of the initial capital and of its own additional funds is capped at €10,000,000.

Irrespective of these requirements, the management company's own funds shall in principle never be inferior to one-quarter of its preceding year's fixed overheads (or of the fixed overheads provided for in its business plan if the management company has not completed a year's business from its start). The CSSF may, however, adjust that requirement in the event of a material change in the management company's business since the preceding year[10].

Up to 50% of the additional own funds referred to above may be provided by way of a guarantee given by a credit institution or an insurance undertaking with its registered office in a Member State or a non-Member State subject to prudential rules considered by the CSSF as equivalent to those laid down in European Community law.

It is worth noting here that as indicated in section 2.3.2.2.1, management companies authorized to carry out discretionary portfolio management services will be required to comply with additional capital requirements. This is because they will have to comply with the Luxembourg regulations implementing Directive 2006/49/EC of the European Parliament and the Council of June 14, 2006 on the capital adequacy of investment firms and credit institutions (recast).

2.3.3.2. Registered shares

All the shares of a Chapter 15 Management Company shall be issued in registered form.

2.3.3.3. Fully paid-up versus partly paid-up shares

To the extent authorized by Company Law[11], shares of a Chapter 15 Management Company may either be fully or partly paid up. If the management company is set up under the form of a SA or SCA, Company Law requires that at least 25% of each share is paid up.

---

9 According to the 2010 Law, the term "own funds" has the meaning ascribed to it in title 5, Chapter 2, section 1 of Directive 2006/48/EC. For the purpose of this definition, Articles 13 to 16 of Directive 2006/49/EC apply *mutatis mutandis*).
10 Article 21 of Directive 2006/49/EC.
11 Company Law does not authorize the issue of partly paid-up shares in an S.à r.l.

2.3.3.4. *Legal reserve*

Chapter 15 Management Companies are required to create a legal reserve in accordance with Company Law, which requires that 5% of the net profits of a Luxembourg company are allocated (each year) to the creation of a reserve until the reserve reaches 10% of the capital of the company. This allocation ceases to be compulsory as soon as the reserve reaches the 10% threshold, but is again compulsory each time the reserve falls below that threshold.

2.3.4. Legal forms

According to the 2010 Law, Luxembourg Chapter 15 Management Companies may be incorporated under the form of a public limited liability company (*"société anonyme"* or *SA*), a private limited liability company (*"société à responsabilité limitée"* or *S.à r.l.*), a cooperative company (*"société cooperative"*), a cooperative company incorporated as a public limited liability company (*"société coopérative organisée comme une société anonyme"*) or a partnership limited by shares (*"société en commandite par actions"* or *SCA*).

2.3.5. Management

2.3.5.1. *Management body*

The management body of the management company depends on the legal form chosen. For example, a management company set up under the form of a SA will be managed by a board of directors composed of at least three directors[12], while a management company set up as a S.à r.l. will be managed by a board of managers composed of at least three managers[13]. A management company set up under the form of a SCA will be managed by its general partner (generally incorporated under the form of a SA or a S.à r.l. to mitigate the liability of the general partner, which is liable without any limitation for any and all obligations that cannot be met from the assets of the SCA).

In practice, the SA is the most frequent form of Luxembourg management companies. There are no age, nationality or residence requirements for the directors. The directors of an SA shall in principle be appointed by its shareholders for a

---

12 It is worth noting here that even though Company Law provides that a management company having one single shareholder may be managed by one single director, the CSSF requires that a management company is managed by at least three directors.

13 In this respect, it is worth noting that even though Company Law authorizes the creation of an S.à r.l. managed by one single manager, the CSSF in principle requires that a management company is managed by at least three managers.

renewable term not exceeding six years. By derogation from the foregoing, in the case of a vacancy in the office of a director, the remaining directors[14] are authorized to fill the vacancy on a provisional basis until the next general meeting of shareholders. This mechanism is commonly called "co-option".

The appointment of the directors (as well as all of the changes to the board composition)[15] shall be: (i) approved by the CSSF; (ii) filed with the Luxembourg *Registre de Commerce et des Sociétés*; and (iii) published in the Luxembourg official gazette (the *Mémorial*).

Prior to granting its approval, the CSSF checks whether the directors are of sufficiently good repute and have the experience required for the performance of their duties. To this effect, the proposed directors shall submit the documents listed in section 2.5.1.3 to the CSSF.

2.3.5.2. *Conducting officers*

The business of a Chapter 15 Management Company shall be conducted by at least two conducting officers. Like the conducting officers of a self-managed investment company, the conducting officers of a management company are in charge of the day-to-day business of the company and are required to report to the board of directors of the management company on a regular basis. They are appointed by the board of directors of the management company after prior approval of the CSSF. Their appointment/removal does not trigger any publication formalities[16].

The conducting officers of a management company may (but are not required to) be directors or employees of the management company (provided that if the conducting officers are employees of the company, there is no hierarchy link between them). They may not be employees of the custodian of the UCITS.

There is no age or nationality requirement for the conducting officers but the CSSF, in principle, requires that one of the conducting officers be on site. When discretionary portfolio management is performed, both – or at least two – of them will be on site.

---

14 Only directors that have been appointed by the shareholders can co-opt another director in replacement of a director him- or herself appointed by the shareholders.

15 The approval of the CSSF is only required in the case of the appointment of a new director, as the resignation is a unilateral act that does not need to be approved by the CSSF or even by the board itself.

16 If the day-to-day manager is a "*délégué à la gestion journalière*" under the meaning of Company Law, its appointment will have to be published in the *Mémorial.*

Their role (which is similar to that of the conducting officers of a self-managed investment company) is described in Regulation 10-4 as well as in CSSF Circulars 03/108 and 05/185.

According to Regulation 10-4, the conducting officers shall:

(i) be responsible for the implementation of the general investment policy of each managed UCITS;

(ii) supervise the adoption of investment strategies of each managed UCITS;

(iii) ensure that the management company has a permanent and effective compliance function, even if this function is performed by a third party;

(iv) ensure and regularly verify that the general investment policy, the investment strategies and the risk limits of each managed UCITS are properly and effectively implemented and complied with, even if the risk management function is performed by third parties;

(v) approve and regularly review the adequacy of the internal procedures regarding the adoption of investment decisions for each managed UCITS so as to ensure that such decisions are consistent with the approved investment strategies;

(vi) approve and regularly review the risk management policy and arrangements, processes and techniques relating to the implementation of that policy (including the risk limit system for each managed UCITS);

(vii) receive, on a frequent basis (and at least annually), written reports on compliance, internal audit and risk management matters. These reports shall in particular indicate whether appropriate remedial measures have been taken in the event of any deficiencies;

(viii) regularly receive reports on the implementation of investment strategies and of the internal procedures for taking investment decisions referred to under items (ii) to (v) above;

(ix) assess and regularly review the effectiveness of the policies, arrangements and procedures put in place to comply with the obligations laid down in the 2010 Law and take appropriate measures to remedy any deficiencies.

2.3.6. *Auditor*

Chapter 15 Management Companies shall entrust the audit of their annual accounting documents to one or more auditors (*réviseurs d'entreprises agréés*), which may but are not required to be the same entity as the one auditing the accounts of the UCITS under management. The appointment and change of auditor is subject to the prior approval of the CSSF. Like the management company and the UCITS under management, the auditor is subject to supervision by the CSSF.

The duties of the auditor of a Chapter 15 Management Company are similar to those that apply to the auditor of the UCITS. The auditor shall therefore:

– audit the financial statements included in the annual report;

– prepare a long form report;

– report promptly to the CSSF any fact or decision which s/he has become aware of while carrying out the audit of the accounting information contained in the annual report of a management company or while carrying out any other mission concerning (i) the management company, (ii) a UCI or (iii) another undertaking with close links resulting from a control relationship with this management company or an undertaking contributing towards its business activity where any such fact or decision is likely to:

- constitute a material breach of the 2010 Law or the regulations adopted for its execution; or

- impair the continuous functioning of the management company, or of an undertaking contributing towards its business activity; or

- lead to a refusal to certify the accounts or to the expression of reservations thereon.

– inform the CSSF forthwith if, in the discharge of its duties, the auditor becomes aware that the information provided to investors or to the CSSF in the reports or other documents of the management company does not truly describe the financial situation and the assets and liabilities of the management company;

– provide the CSSF with all of the information or certificates that it may require on any matters of which the auditor has or ought to have knowledge in connection with the discharge of his/her/its duties; and

– comply with the obligations laid down in CSSF Circulars 02/77[17] and 04/146[18].

The auditor's good faith disclosure to the CSSF does not constitute a breach of professional secrecy or any restriction on disclosure of information imposed by contract and will not result in any kind of liability on the part of the auditor.

---

17 Circular 02/77 on the protection of investors in case of NAV calculation error and correction of the consequences resulting from non-compliance with the investment rules applicable to undertakings for collective investment.

18 Circular 04/146 on the protection of undertakings for collective investment and their investors against late trading and market timing practices.

The CSSF may request the auditor to control one or more particular aspects of the activities and operations of a management company. This control is performed at the expense of the management company concerned.

2.3.7. Shareholders

Both legal entities and individuals may acquire shares in a management company but the 2010 Law requires that the CSSF is informed of the identity of any legal or natural person(s) directly or indirectly holding at least 10% of the capital or the voting rights or that have any other possibility to exercise a significant influence over the management of the company. This holding is referred to as a "qualifying participation". The CSSF must be notified of the extent of the participation, as well as any changes in it.

The CSSF is entitled to refuse the management company authorization if, taking into account the need to ensure the sound and prudent management of the company, it is not satisfied as to the suitability of the shareholder(s) or member(s) with a qualifying participation. The notion of sound and prudent management will be assessed on the basis of the following criteria: (i) the professional standing and financial soundness of the proposed shareholder; (ii) the professional standing and experience of each person responsible for managing the activities of the management company; (iii) compliance with prudential and supervisory requirements at the level of the group to which the proposed shareholder belongs; and (iv) the risks related to money laundering or the financing of terrorism.

2.3.8. Registered office and central administration

The registered office and central administration of a Luxembourg management company shall be located in Luxembourg.

This requirement (which only applies to the management company itself and not to the central administration of the UCITS it manages) implies that the presence of the management company in Luxembourg cannot be limited to a legal or statutory head office. In practice, this means that a management company must have an infrastructure allowing a centralized view of its activities and, where applicable, its delegates. To this effect, the management company shall:

– have human and technical resources available that are necessary and sufficient to undertake and control its activities. The management company shall be able to show that it has enough skilled staff with the necessary knowledge and expertise to discharge the tasks it performs, and for efficient monitoring of the delegated activities; and

– have computer access to, and/or hold, the complete documentation relating to its operations and those undertaken by its delegates on behalf of the management company.

2.4. Operating conditions applicable to Luxembourg management companies

2.4.1. *Organizational requirements*

The 2010 Law requires Chapter 15 Management Companies to have:

– sound administrative and accounting procedures,

– control and safeguard arrangements for electronic data processing; and

– adequate internal control mechanisms including, in particular, rules regarding:

   - personal transactions carried out by their employees,

   - the holding or management of investments in financial instruments in order to invest for their own account.

These mechanisms shall at least:

– enable the management company to be in a position to reconstruct each transaction involving the UCITS according to its origin, the parties to it, its nature, and the time and place at which it was effected; and

– guarantee that the assets of the UCITS managed by the management company are invested according to the management regulations or to the instruments of incorporation and the legal provisions in force.

These requirements are specified in Regulation 10-4. Without going into too much detail, it is worth noting that Regulation 10-4 lays down the following principles:

– general requirements on procedures and organization;

– human resources of the management company;

– complaints handling;

– electronic data processing;

– accounting procedure;

– internal control mechanism;

– personal transactions;

– recording of portfolio transactions;

– recording of redemption and subscription orders; and

– record-keeping requirements.

2.4.1.1. *General requirements on procedures and organization*

Chapter 15 Management Companies are required to:

– establish decision-making procedures and an organizational structure, which clearly documents reporting lines and allocates functions and responsibilities;

– ensure that the relevant persons are aware of the procedures, which must be followed for the proper discharge of their responsibilities;

– establish, implement and maintain adequate internal control mechanisms designed to secure compliance with decisions and procedures at all levels of the management company;

– establish: (i) effective internal reporting and communication of information at all relevant levels of the management company; as well as (ii) effective information flows with any third party involved;

– maintain adequate and orderly records of their business and internal organization;

– establish, and maintain systems and procedures that are adequate to safeguard the security, integrity and confidentiality of information, taking into account the nature of the information concerned;

– establish an adequate business continuity policy;

– establish accounting policies and procedures that enable them to deliver financial reports to (and upon request of) the CSSF that reflect a true and fair view of their financial position and complying with all applicable accounting standards and rules; and

– monitor and, on a regular basis, evaluate the adequacy and effectiveness of their systems, internal control mechanisms and arrangements.

2.4.1.2. *Human resources of the management company*

Management companies are required to employ personnel with sufficient skills, knowledge, expertise and time to properly discharge their responsibilities.

According to CSSF Circular 03/108, the members of staff must in principle be employees of the management company. The CSSF may, however, grant an exemption and allow that all or some of the personnel are either on secondment (i.e. a temporary transfer) or are made available through an undertaking belonging to the same group as the management company or by a non-affiliated company. In this case, the contract governing this secondment or availability (which must stipulate rules concerning the management of conflicts of interests between the persons concerned and the undertaking, if the latter belongs to the same group) must be submitted to the CSSF.

2.4.1.3. *Complaints handling*

Management companies are required to implement effective and transparent procedures for the reasonable and prompt handling of complaints received from investors. Such procedures must be available to investors free of any charge. Each complaint and the measures taken for their resolution shall be recorded.

2.4.1.4. *Electronic data processing*

Management companies shall put suitable electronic systems in place that permit a timely, secure and proper record of each portfolio transaction or subscription/redemption order.

2.4.1.5. *Accounting procedure*

The accounts of each UCITS shall be kept in such a way that all of its assets and liabilities can be directly identified at all times. In the case of umbrella UCITS, separate accounts shall be maintained for each compartment.

Furthermore, management companies shall put accounting policies and procedures in place that are in line with the accounting rules of the UCITS Member State so as to ensure that the calculation of the net asset value of the UCITS is accurately effected on the basis of its accounts and that subscription and redemption orders can be properly executed at that net asset value.

2.4.1.6. *Internal control mechanism*

Chapter 15 Management Companies are required to put internal control mechanisms in place including: (i) a senior management supervisory function; (ii) a compliance function; (iii) an internal audit function; and (iv) a risk management function.

2.4.1.6.1. Senior management and supervisory function

The term "senior management" refers to the persons who effectively conduct the business of the management company (i.e. the conducting officers). For further details as to their role, please refer to section 2.3.5.2.

The term "supervisory function" refers to the persons/body that are/is responsible for supervising the conducting officers. This also includes the assessment and periodic review of the adequacy and effectiveness of the risk management process and the policies put in place to comply with the management company's obligations under the 2010 Law.

2.4.1.6.2. Permanent compliance function

Management companies are required to establish a permanent and effective compliance function that shall, under the responsibility of a compliance officer:

– monitor and, on a regular basis, assess the adequacy and effectiveness of the measures, policies and procedures put in place by the management company to detect any risk of failure by the management company to comply with its obligations under the 2010 Law, and the actions taken to remedy any deficiencies in the management company's compliance with its obligations; and

– where necessary, assist any person with regard to compliance matters.

The compliance function shall have the necessary resources, authority, expertise and access to all of the relevant information. In order to preserve its independence, the persons involved in that function cannot, in principle, be involved in the performance of the services or activities they monitor. The CSSF can, however, authorize a management company to depart from this requirement if the management company is in a position to demonstrate that this requirement is not proportionate in light of the nature, scale and complexity of its business.

2.4.1.6.3. Permanent internal audit function

Where appropriate and proportionate in light of the nature, scale and complexity of their business as well as the nature and range of collective portfolio management activities undertaken in the course of that business, management companies shall establish an internal audit function that is separate and independent from their other functions and activities. The internal audit function shall:

(i) implement an audit plan to examine and evaluate the adequacy and effectiveness of the management company's systems, internal control mechanisms and other arrangements;

(ii) issue recommendations based on the result of work carried out in accordance with point (i);

(iii) verify compliance with the recommendations referred to in point (ii); and

(iv) report to senior management in relation to internal audit matters.

2.4.1.6.4. Permanent risk-management function

Management companies shall establish and maintain a permanent risk-management function that, in principle, shall be hierarchically and functionally independent from operating units (it being understood that the CSSF may derogate from this requirement where it appears that it is not proportionate to its business and the UCITS it manages).

A management company shall be able to demonstrate that appropriate safeguards against conflicts of interest have been adopted so as to allow an independent performance of risk-management activities, and that its risk-management process satisfies the requirements of Article 42 of the 2010 Law.

The permanent risk-management function shall:

– implement the risk-management policy and procedures;

– ensure compliance with the UCITS' risk limit system;

– provide advice to the board of directors regarding the identification of the risk profile of each managed UCITS;

– provide regular reports to the board of directors and, where it exists, the supervisory function, on:

- the consistency between the current levels of risk incurred by each managed UCITS and the risk profile agreed for that UCITS,

- the compliance of each managed UCITS with relevant risk limit systems,

- the adequacy and effectiveness of the risk management process, indicating in particular whether appropriate remedial measures have been taken in the event of any deficiencies;

– provide regular reports to the senior management outlining the current level of risk incurred by each managed UCITS and any actual or foreseeable breaches of their limits, so as to ensure that prompt and appropriate action can be taken;

– where appropriate, review and support the arrangements and procedures for the valuation of over-the-counter derivatives; and

– have the necessary authority and access to all of the relevant information that is necessary to fulfill its duties.

2.4.1.7. *Personal transactions*

In a nutshell, management companies shall ensure that the persons (i) who are involved in activities that may give rise to a conflict of interest or (ii) who have access to inside information or to other confidential information regarding a UCITS do not use that information for their benefit or disclose it to a third party likely to use the information for its own benefit.

2.4.1.8. *Recording portfolio transactions*

Management companies shall be in a position to reconstruct the details of each order and of each transaction relating to the UCITS they manage. To this effect, they shall ensure that the following information is recorded:

– the name of the UCITS and of the person acting on its behalf;

– the details necessary to identify the relevant instrument;

– the quantity;

– the type of order or transaction;

– the price;

– for orders, the date and exact time the order was transmitted and the name or other designation of the person to whom the order was transmitted, or for transactions the date and exact time of the decision to deal and execute the transaction;

– the name of the person transmitting the order or executing the transaction;

– where applicable, the reasons for the revocation of an order; and

– for executed transactions, the identification of the counterparty and execution venue (i.e. the regulated market, multilateral trading facilities, systematic internalizer, market maker or other liquidity provider, or any entity providing similar functions in a third country).

2.4.1.9. *Recording of redemption and subscription orders*

Management companies shall take all reasonable steps to ensure that the subscription and redemption orders are centralized and recorded upon receipt.

The record shall include the following information:

– the relevant UCITS;

– the person giving or transmitting the order;

– the person receiving the order;

– the date and time of the order;

– the terms and means of payment;

– the type of the order;

– the date of execution of the order;

– the number of units subscribed or redeemed; and

– the subscription or redemption price for each unit.

2.4.1.10. *Record-keeping requirements*

Management companies shall in principle keep their records for a period of at least five years. They are subject to the possibility that the CSSF will require records to be kept for a longer period of time in certain circumstances. The records shall be maintained through a medium that allows the storage of information in a way that is accessible for future reference by the CSSF.

2.4.2. Conflicts of interest

Management companies are required to minimize the risks that conflicts of interest arise between the management company and its clients as well as between two of its clients, if it adversely affects the interests of clients.

Where conflicts cannot be avoided, management companies shall ensure that all the UCITS they manage are fairly treated. To this effect, Chapter 15 Management Companies are required to implement an effective conflicts of interest policy. The policy shall be laid down in writing.

The conflicts of interest policy shall include:

– the identification of the circumstances that constitute or may give rise to a conflict of interest entailing a material risk of damage to the interests of the UCITS or one or more other clients; and

– the procedures to be followed and measures to be adopted in order to manage such conflicts.

If the management company belongs to a group, the policy shall also take into account any circumstances that may give rise to a conflict of interest resulting from the structure and business activities of other members of the group.

The persons engaged in activities involving a conflict of interest shall carry on these activities at a level of independence appropriate to the size and activities of the management company and the group to which it belongs, and to the materiality of the risk of damage to clients' interests. To this effect, Regulation 10-4 states that it might be appropriate to have separate supervision of the persons whose principal functions involve the performance of collective portfolio management activities or the provision of services to clients with different interests that may conflict with each other or with the interests of the management company.

Management companies are required to keep and regularly update a record of the types of collective portfolio management activities undertaken by or on behalf of the management company: (i) in which a conflict of interest entailing a material risk of damage to the interests of one or more clients has occurred; or (ii) in the case of an ongoing collective portfolio management activity, which may arise.

In order to minimize conflicts of interests, management companies are also required to put in place strategies determining when and how voting rights attached to instruments held in the managed portfolios are to be exercised, to the exclusive benefit of the UCITS concerned. A summary of the strategy shall be made available to investors and details on the actions taken shall be made available free of charge upon request. The strategy shall determine measures and procedures for:

– monitoring relevant corporate events;

– ensuring that the voting rights are exercised in accordance with the investment objectives and policy of the relevant UCITS; and

– preventing or managing any conflicts of interest that arise from exercising voting rights.

It is worth noting here that these rules apply *mutatis mutandis* to self-managed SICAVs.

2.4.3. *Rules of conduct*

Regulation 10-4 lays down a series of rules of conduct for Chapter 15 Management Companies. Most of these rules aim at ensuring such companies:

– Act in the best interests of the UCITS they manage and their share/unitholders. To this effect, management companies are required to treat all share/unitholders of the UCITS they manage equally and shall refrain from placing the interests of a group of share/unitholders above those of another group.

– Ensure a high level of diligence in the selection and ongoing monitoring of investments in the best interests of the UCITS and the integrity of the market. Management companies shall establish written policies on the due diligence applied and ensure that all investment decisions are carried out in compliance with the objectives, investment strategy and risk limits of the UCITS.

– Inform the share/unitholder of the execution of his/her/its subscription or redemption orders.

– Take all reasonable steps to obtain the best possible result for the UCITS, taking into account price, costs, speed, likelihood of execution and settlement, order size and nature, and any other consideration relevant to the execution of the order. The policy put in place in this respect shall be approved by all SICAVs managed by the management company and shall be available to share/unit holders of the UCITS. The policy shall be reviewed annually or each time a material change affecting the management company's ability to continue to obtain the best possible result occurs. Similar rules apply when the management company places its orders with other entities. In such a case, the policy put in place will have to identify, the entities with which the orders may be placed for each class of instrument.

– Put in place procedures enabling it to promptly, sequentially and fairly execute all portfolio transactions on behalf of the UCITS.

– Do not mix up orders from different clients or orders placed on its behalf with orders placed for clients without complying with the conditions laid down in Regulation 10-4.

– Avoid any undue cost for the UCITS they manage and its share/unitholders. To this effect, Regulation 10-4 provides for a series of rules as regards inducements. In addition to this, CSSF Circular 10/437[19] lays down guidelines for variable component of the remuneration policy of the management body of the management company and of the persons whose professional activities have a material impact on the risk profile of the company.

2.4.4. *Risk management*

Chapter 15 Management Companies shall employ a risk-management process that enables them to monitor and measure the risk of the positions and their contribution to the overall risk profile of the portfolio at all times. They shall employ a process for accurate and independent assessment of the value of over-the-counter derivatives. In accordance with the detailed rules defined by the CSSF, they shall regularly inform the CSSF of the types of derivative instruments, underlying risks, quantitative limits and methods that are chosen to estimate risks associated with transactions in derivative instruments regarding each managed UCITS.

For further details on risk management, please refer to Chapter 3 of this book.

2.5. CSSF supervision

2.5.1. *Approval process*

In order to obtain the approval of the Luxembourg regulator, the applicant is required to submit a file containing at least the documents and information listed under sections 2.5.1.1 to 2.5.1.7. The applicant is authorized to add any further information deemed useful for a good understanding of the file and the CSSF

---

19 CSSF Circular 10/437 providing guidelines concerning remuneration policies in the financial sector.

reserves the right to request any further information it would deem necessary to complete its analysis of the application file.

2.5.1.1. *Structure and organization of the management company*

The request for authorization shall include[20]:

– a presentation of the management company (including the denomination, legal form and initial capital of the company) and the reasons for establishing its business in Luxembourg;

– a program of activities describing:

- the scope of the proposed services for the next three financial years (this description shall include information regarding the number of UCITS managed directly or by delegation, the law under which the UCITS concerned have been set up, their net assets as well as the number and net assets of the UCITS created at the initiative of a company not belonging to the same group as the management company),

- the investment policies of the managed UCITS, as well as the instruments and financial markets concerned, and

- the risk management method;

– the provisional three-year budget of the management company;

– draft articles of incorporation of the management company;

– description of the administrative, accounting and technical infrastructure of the management company, including a functional organization chart that indicates the number of people working for the management company and, where possible, their names;

– designation of the person within the management company responsible for the provision of information on the financial situation of the management company;

– a detailed description of the activities performed internally by the management company and those that are delegated to professionals (a list of the delegates indicating their name, address and, where applicable, the name of the supervisory authority to which they are subject, is to be enclosed);

– draft agreements concluded with the delegates;

– detailed description of the monitoring performed by the management company on the delegates;

---

20 Additional clarifications regarding the above points can be found in CSSF Regulation No. 10-4 and Circulars CSSF 11/508 and 03/108.

– designation of a person responsible for the accounting administration of the undertakings for collective investment (*UCIs*) within the management company;

– information on the distribution network put in place by the management company: countries of distribution, intermediaries, those in charge of the distribution, target client base;

– where the management company intends to perform the central administration for the UCIs, the information available under the section "PFS – Procedure/FAQ on PFS statuses – List of additional information for authorization as central administration of UCIs" is to be provided[21];

– explicit confirmation concerning compliance with the provisions of Articles 109(1) and 111 of the 2010 Law as regards: (i) the conflict of interests policy; and (ii) the rules of conduct and the related procedures as laid down by Circular CSSF 11/508;

– details on the proposed investment of the initial capital indicating, where applicable, the name of the financial institution at which the initial capital is deposited;

– name of the auditor;

– where applicable, the name of the company responsible for maintaining the management company's accounting records;

– a description of the remuneration policy put in place by the management company in accordance with Circular CSSF 10/437;

– details of the person responsible for the compliance function, including his/her *curriculum vitae*. The compliance function and internal audit function cannot be undertaken concurrently by the same person;

– details of the person responsible for the internal audit function (who cannot be an employee of the auditor), including his/her *curriculum vitae*;

– details on the person responsible for risk management, including his/her *curriculum vitae*. The risk management function and the compliance function cannot be undertaken concurrently by the same person;

– the name of the person responsible for the processing, centralization and follow-up of complaints, including a description of the procedure put in place to handle complaints; and

– the draft anti-money laundering procedures put in place.

---

21 This list can be downloaded from the following website: http://www.cssf.lu/en/psf-en/procedure-faq/.

2.5.1.2. *Description of the shareholders*

The applicant shall describe the structure of the direct and indirect shareholding of the management company. The documents to be filed with the CSSF in this respect depend on whether the shareholder is an individual or a legal entity.

Both kinds of shareholders shall provide the CSSF with the following information:

– the name of the shareholder and the number of shares he/she/it holds in the company;

– identification of the beneficial owner of the shares;

– confirmation that the initial capital has not been sourced from a loan or other cash advance and that the shares of the management company are unsecured; and

– in order to evaluate the financial soundness of the proposed shareholders, the application for authorization shall also contain the information laid down in Appendix II of the "Guidelines for the prudential assessment of acquisitions and increases in holdings in the financial sector required by Directive 2007/44/EC" appended to Circular CSSF 09/392.

In addition to the above, each legal entity acquiring a qualifying participation in the management company shall file the following documents:

– a presentation of the group to which the shareholder belongs;

– an organization chart of the direct and indirect ownership of the shareholder, specifying which entities are subject to prudential supervision and indicating their respective regulatory authorities;

– an identification of the beneficial owner(s) of the shares of the shareholder;

– the last three audited annual reports of the shareholders, the most up-to-date non-audited balance sheet in the case where the first financial year of the shareholder has not yet finished, or the opening balance sheet for those shareholders in the process of being established;

– articles of incorporation;

– information about the consolidated supervision that may be instigated by a regulatory authority on the group to which the shareholder belongs.

Each individual acquiring a qualifying participation in the management company shall provide the CSSF with:

– a dated and signed *curriculum vitae*;

– a recent extract of the criminal records bureau;

– a declaration of honor by the shareholder, a template of which may be downloaded from the CSSF's website (http://www.cssf.lu/en/forms/);

– proof that the shareholder has sufficient financial resources to ensure sound and prudent management of the management company;

– confirmation that the shareholder holds the shares on its own account and not on that of a third party; and

– an indication as to whether the shareholder is subject to regulation as an individual by a supervisory authority.

2.5.1.3. *Information regarding the directors and conducting officers*

For each of the directors and conducting officers, the following documents have to be submitted to the CSSF:

– in the case of individuals:

- a sworn statement (*déclaration sur l'honneur*), which can be downloaded from the CSSF's website[22];

- a copy of his or her identity card/ passport;

- a dated and signed *curriculum vitae*. In the case where tasks are divided between the conducting officers, the *curriculum vitae* will have to provide evidence of the individual's experience in his or her respective areas of responsibility; and

- a recent extract from the criminal records bureau;

– in the case of legal entities:

- a declaration of honor, which can be downloaded from the CSSF website[23];

- a copy of their articles of incorporation;

- an extract from the trade and companies register; and

- the annual accounts for the past three years.

– in addition to the above, the conducting officers are required to provide the CSSF with a copy of their employment contract and the convention regulating their availability, respectively. In the case where they work for several companies, the CSSF might require proof that each of these persons is able to fulfill the tasks for which they are responsible at all times. Furthermore, to the extent applicable, the

---

22 http://www.cssf.lu/fileadmin/files/Formulaires/Decl_hon_NPeng.pdf.
23 http://www.cssf.lu/fileadmin/files/Formulaires/Decl_hon_LPeng.pdf.

management company will have to provide the CSSF with a description of the division of tasks[24] between the conducting officers.

2.5.1.4. *Description of the risk management process*

The application for authorization shall include a description of the risk-management process applied by the management company to the UCIs that it manages. The risk-management process shall be in line with Circular 11/512, CSSF Regulation 10-4 and "CESR's guidelines on risk measurement and the calculation of global exposure and counterparty risk for UCITS (CESR/10/788)".

2.5.1.5. *Extended scope of activity*

Management companies wishing to be authorized to carry out the functions referred to in section 2.3.2.2. have to provide the CSSF with:

– a program of activities that includes information with respect to: (i) discretionary management; (ii) investment advice; and (iii) safekeeping and administration information in relation to units of undertakings for collective investment;

– confirmation of membership of the AGDL;

– a template of the discretionary management/investment advisory services contracts that the management company intends to ask its clients to sign; and

– confirmation that the MiFID provisions[25] are complied with.

2.5.1.6. *Capitalization of the management company*

To the extent that part of the additional amount of own funds referred to in section 2.3.3.1. is provided through a guarantee, the management company will be required to provide the CSSF with the draft guarantee arrangement to be issued by the credit institution or insurance company.

---

24 The requirement to appoint at least two conducting officers can be viewed as an application of the "four eyes are better than two" principle in management companies. As a result, it is not possible for the conducting officers to split the tasks so that certain powers are reserved for one to the exclusion of the other. The division of tasks will therefore only be authorized if the conducting officer is in a position to supervise the tasks generally carried out by the other and to replace him or her in the case of absence.

25 Articles 37-1 and 37-3 of the amended Law of April 5, 1993 on the financial sector, completed by the provisions of Grand-Ducal Regulation of July 13, 2007 relating to the organizational requirements and rules of conduct in the financial sector.

2.5.1.7. *Miscellaneous*

Management companies are required to inform the CSSF of the name of the promoter/initiator of the UCIs it intends to manage (and to let the CSSF know whether the promoter/initiator belongs to the management company's group).

In addition, the management company has to let the CSSF know whether it intends to manage foreign UCIs. In this case, the CSSF will need to be informed of:

– the country of origin of the UCI(s) to be managed by the management company;

– their investment policy;

– the services offered (i.e. portfolio management, administration or distribution) by the management company on behalf of the UCI(s) concerned;

– the service level agreement.

2.5.2. *CSSF approval and inclusion on the list*

Authorized management companies are entered on a list by the CSSF. This entry is tantamount to authorization and the CSSF notifies the management company concerned. Applications for entry on the list must be filed with the CSSF before the incorporation of the management company, which can only be undertaken after notification of the authorization by the CSSF.

2.5.3. *Reporting to the CSSF*

Once approved by the CSSF and entered on the official list, the management company will be subject to ongoing supervision by the CSSF. In this context, it will be required to report to the CSSF on a quarterly basis. The content of the reports is laid down in the appendices of CSSF Circular 03/108. Without going into too much detail, the information to be provided to the CSSF can be divided into two categories:

– the first applies to all UCITS management companies and relates to:

  - the financial situation of the management company,

  - the profit and loss account, and

  - the identification of the UCIs managed by the management company; and

– the second only applies to management companies authorized to carry out "other functions" (as detailed in section 2.3.2.2.).

2.5.4. *CSSF taxes*

A lump sum of €2,650 is payable for the assessment of each application of a new Chapter 15 Management Company whose activity is limited to the collective management of undertakings for collective investment. This tax is increased to €3,250 if the activities of the Chapter 15 Management Company include wealth management services as provided in Article 101(3) a) of the 2010 Law.

In addition, an annual fee of €5,000 will have to be paid by a Chapter 15 Management Company whose activity is limited to the collective management of undertakings for collective investment. This tax is increased to €12,000 if the activities of the Chapter 15 Management Company include wealth management services, as described in Article 101(3) a) of the 2010 Law.

2.5.5. *Withdrawal of CSSF authorization*

The CSSF may withdraw the authorization issued to a management company subject to Chapter 15 of the 2010 Law only where that company:

– does not make use of the authorization within 12 months, expressly renounces the authorization or has not exercised the activity covered by Chapter 15 of the 2010 Law for more than six months;

– has obtained the authorization by making false statements or by any other irregular means;

– no longer fulfills the conditions under which the authorization was granted;

– no longer complies with the 1993 Law if its authorization also covers the discretionary portfolio management service referred to in Article 101 (3) a) of the 2010 Law;

– has seriously and/or systematically infringed the provisions of the 2010 Law or of regulations adopted pursuant thereto; or

– falls within any of the other cases where the 2010 Law provides for withdrawal.

In the case where a management company pursues collective portfolio management activities on a cross-border basis, the CSSF shall consult the competent authorities of the UCITS home Member State before withdrawing the authorization of the management company.

2.6. Management company passport

The UCITS IV Directive introduced a full[26] management company passport, whereby a management company authorized by its home Member State may carry out the activities for which it has been authorized in all Member States, either through the establishment of a branch or under the freedom to provide services. In practice, this means that a management company that is authorized in one Member State is not only authorized to manage UCITS domiciled in that Member State but also UCITS domiciled in any other Member State.

2.6.1. *Notification procedure*

A Luxembourg management company wishing to provide services in another Member State will be required to inform the CSSF of its intention. The notification sent to the CSSF shall be accompanied by the following information and documents:

– the Member State within the territory of which the management company plans to provide services;

– a program of operations setting out the activities and services envisaged and the organizational structure of the branch, including a description of the risk-management process put in place by the management company; and

– a description of the procedures and arrangements taken to properly deal with investors' complaints.

In the case of a branch, the notification shall also include:

– the address from which documents may be obtained in the management company's host Member State; and

– the name of the persons responsible for the management of the branch.

This information will then be communicated by the CSSF to the host Member State's supervisory authority within one month if the management company wishes to use the freedom to provide services, and within two months where a branch is established. Where a management company wishes to pursue the activity of

---

26 It is worth noting here that the UCITS III Directive already provided for a theoretical passport, which has not shown its potential due to the wording of the Directive, which defined the home Member State of a common fund as the Member State in which the common fund management company has its registered office, thus requiring that a common fund and its management company are both situated in the same Member State. With investment companies, the UCITS III Directive enabled the provision of cross-border management services by management companies to investment companies but this possibility has never been implemented in practice by the EU Member State authorities.

collective portfolio management, along with the documentation sent to the competent authorities of the management company's host Member State the CSSF shall enclose confirmation that the management company has been authorized pursuant to the provisions of the 2010 Law. This will include a description of the scope of the management company's authorization and details on any restriction on the types of UCITS that the management company is authorized to manage.

The management company will be authorized to start its business:

– upon informing the host Member State in the case of freedom to provide services; and

– upon receipt of a communication from the host Member State (or, within a timeframe of two months following the provision of information by the CSSF) when a branch is established.

2.6.2. *Cooperation agreement*

If the home Member State of the management company of an FCP or an investment company with a designated management company is not the same as that of the FCP or the investment company, the supervisory authority of the host Member State needs the cooperation agreement entered into between the management company and the depositary of the UCITS.

The minimum content of the agreement is defined in Regulation 10-4 and relates to the following topics:

– services provided by and procedures to be followed by the parties;

– exchange of information and obligations on confidentiality and money laundering;

– appointment of third parties;

– amendments and the termination of the agreement; and

– miscellaneous.

2.6.2.1. *Services provided by and procedures to be followed by the parties*

The agreement shall include:

– a description of the procedures to be adopted for each type of asset of the UCITS entrusted to the depositary, including those related to safekeeping;

– a description of the procedures to be followed where the management company envisages a modification of the management regulations or instruments of incorporation or prospectus of the UCITS. The agreement should specify when the depositary should be informed, or where a prior agreement from the depositary is needed to proceed with the modification;

– a description of the procedures through which the depositary has the ability to enquire into the conduct of the management company and to assess the quality of information transmitted, namely by way of site visits;

– a description of the procedures by which the management company can review the performance of the depositary in respect of the depositary's contractual obligations;

– a description of the means and procedures through which the depositary will inform the management company of all the relevant information needed to perform its duties. This should include a description of the means and procedures related to the exercise of any rights attached to financial instruments, and the means and procedures applied to allow the management company and the UCITS to have timely and accurate access to information relating to the UCITS accounts; and

– a description of the means and procedures through which the depositary will have access to all of the relevant information it needs to perform its duties.

2.6.2.2. *Exchange of information and confidentiality and anti-money laundering obligations*

The agreement shall include:

– a list of all the information that needs to be exchanged between the UCITS, its management company and the depositary regarding the subscription, redemption, issue, cancellation and repurchase of units of the UCITS;

– the confidentiality obligations applicable to the parties to the agreement; and

– information on the tasks and the responsibilities of parties to the agreement in respect of obligations relating to the prevention of money laundering and the financing of terrorism, where applicable.

2.6.2.3. *Appointment of third parties*

The agreement shall include:

– an undertaking by both parties to provide details, on a regular basis, of any third parties appointed by the depositary or management company to carry out their respective duties;

– an undertaking that, upon request by one of the parties, the requested party will provide information on the criteria used to select the third party and the steps taken to monitor it ; and

– a statement that a depositary's liability, as referred to in Article 19 or Article 35 of the 2010 Law, shall not be affected by the fact that it has entrusted all or some of the assets in its safekeeping to a third party.

2.6.2.4. *Amendments and termination of the agreement*

The agreement shall detail:

– the period of validity of the agreement;

– the conditions under which the agreement may be amended or terminated; and

– the conditions that are necessary to facilitate transition to another depositary and, in the case of such a transition, the procedure through which the depositary will send all relevant information to the new depositary.

2.6.2.5. *Miscellaneous*

The agreement shall indicate:

– the applicable law (being the law of the UCITS Member State);

– whether the parties to the agreement agree to the use of electronic transmission for part or all of the information that flows between them. The agreement shall contain provisions ensuring that a record is kept of such information; and

– the scope of the agreement (i.e. the list of UCITS concerned).

2.6.3. Supervision

The 2010 Law allocates the supervisory duties between the supervisory authority of the home Member State of the management company and that of the host Member State.

2.6.3.1. *Competence of the management company's home Member State authority*

The management company's home Member State authorities are the competent authorities for authorizing the management company and supervising its compliance with the rules and applicable provisions in the management company's home Member State. These rules comprise those relating to the authorization (authorized services; minimum capital and own fund requirements; shareholder requirements; authorization of conducting officers) and organization of the management company (including delegation arrangements, risk-management procedures, prudential rules and supervision, the requirement to have administrative, accounting and control procedures, and the management company's reporting requirements).

2.6.3.2. *Competence of the UCITS' home Member State authority*

The rules of the UCITS' home Member State apply to the constitution and functioning of the UCITS. The competent authorities of the UCITS' home Member State are responsible for supervising compliance with these rules. In an effort to distinguish between the scope of the management company's home Member State rules (and consequent competence of the management company's home Member State authority) and the UCITS' home Member State rules (and consequent competence of the UCITS' home Member State authority), the 2010 Law specifically lists the rules that relate to the constitution and functioning of the UCITS as those rules that cover:

a) the setting up and authorization of the UCITS;

b) the issue and redemption of units;

c) investment policies and limits, including the calculation of total exposure and leverage;

d) restrictions on borrowing, lending and uncovered sales;

e) the valuation of assets and the accounting of the UCITS;

f) the calculation of the issue or redemption price, and errors in the calculation of the net asset value and related investor compensation;

g) the distribution or reinvestment of income;

h) the disclosure and reporting requirements of the UCITS, including the prospectus, key investor information and periodic reports;

i) the arrangements made for marketing;

j) the relationship with unitholders;

k) the merging and restructuring of the UCITS;

l) the dissolution and liquidation of the UCITS;

m) where applicable, the content of the unitholder register;

n) the licensing and supervision fees regarding the UCITS; and

o) the exercise of unitholders' voting rights and other unitholders' rights in relation to points a) to m).

Chapter 3

Risk Management in the Context of UCITS IV

3.1. Introduction

"What is risk management?" Even though the concept may sound obvious, properly defining it can be complex. More than being a limited and defined approach; it is more about a global concept. It is so broad that summarizing it in one single sentence will probably only give a flavor of the related challenges.

Risk management is about identifying all risks to which an entity is exposed (which can be either financial or non-financial) and defining and implementing measures that will help to monitor, limit or eliminate these risks.

It is therefore a complete and complex exercise starting from the identification of risks and including the definition of controls that help to mitigate them.

In the context of the asset management industry, and especially for regulated funds such as UCITS, for several years now the regulator has requested specific risk management analysis on top of compliance limitations in order to reinforce the protection of investors.

This chapter, dedicated to risk management for UCITS funds, guides the reader through the requirements requested by the regulator through the use of illustrative examples and methods to enhance them. We will cover the areas of risk to which investment funds are exposed:

Chapter written by Thierry López and Benjamin Gauthier.

– market risk;

– liquidity risk;

– counterparty risk; and

– operational risk.

For all these topics, the methodologies are described, as are the best practices currently observed in the market.

3.2. Regulator expectations

3.2.1. *From European directives to local regulation*

As we will continuously refer to guidelines, laws and circulars, before going straight into details we need to clarify the global process from European decisions and the publication of directives to the implementation within local risk management guidelines and regulations.

In the context of Securities markets, following the recommendation of the Wise Men on the Regulation of European Securities Markets (a committee chaired by Baron Alexandre Lamfalussy)[1], in order to quickly react to innovation and changes in the financial market, the development and implementation of new regulations follow a four-level regulatory approach.

At the first level, the European Parliament and Council adopt a global framework that includes the definition and first level of guidelines that need to be implemented in a directive/regulation.

At the second level, the European and Securities Committee (ESC) and the Committee of European Securities Regulators (CESR) provide a first set of measures to be implemented.

At the third level, CESR provides detailed recommendations, guidelines and common standards.

At the fourth level, the European Commission checks Member State compliance with EU law.

---

1 Final Report of the Committee of Wise Men on the Regulation of European Securities Market, Brussels, February 15, 2001. This report is available at the following web address: http://ec.europa.eu/internal_market/securities/docs/lamfalussy/wisemen/final-report-wise-men_en.pdf

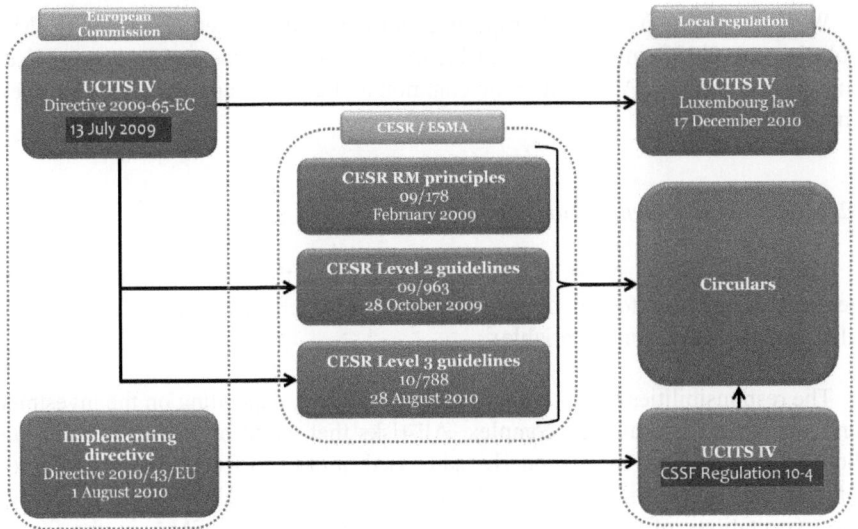

Figure 3.1. *From level 1 to level 3*

As it can be seen on figure 3.1 that the starting point of UCITS IV is the publication of Directive 2009-65-EC (the *UCITS IV Directive*) issued on July 13, 2009. This constitutes the first step in the regulation process (level 1). CESR, in connection with the ESC, then prepared and communicated more detailed guidelines (CESR/09-963[2]) finalizing level 2. The level 3 guidelines (CESR/10-788[3]) giving detailed methods to be implemented – areas not covered by European Union (EU) legislation – were issued in August 2010. At that stage, all of the information required to start the transposition into local regulations (level 4) was available.

In Figure 3.1, we have illustrated the case in Luxembourg[4] where UCITS IV was transposed into local law before the end of 2010. After this, the Commission de Surveillance de Sectuer Financier (CSSF) issued dedicated circulars relating to the consideration of CESR guidelines.

---

2 CESR's technical advice to the European Commission on the level 2 measures related to the UCITS management company passport. The full text is available at: http://www.esma.europa.eu/popup2.php?id=6150

3 CESR's *Guidelines on Risk Measurement and the Calculation of Global Exposure and Counterparty Risk for UCITS.* The full text is available at: http://www.esma.europa.eu/popup2.php?id=7000

4 The *Commission de Surveillance du Secteur Financier* is the local regulator for the Financial industry.

With the creation of the European Securities and Market Authority (ESMA) replacing the CESR in January 1, 2011, the Lamfalussy process has been revised, empowering the ESMA to ensure the common and uniform application of European Union law.

3.2.2. Risk management requirements

The responsibility of risk management pertains to the management company of the fund or pertains to the fund in the case of a self-managed SICAV (Société d'Investissment A Capital Variable)[5].

The responsibilities in this area are quite broad and, depending on the investment fund's structure, can also be complex. All risks that could be material to the fund should be considered and properly addressed in the procedures set up by the company and summarized in a key document termed the Risk Management Policy. The expectations of the regulator are summarized by the ESMA in the 09-963 guidelines as follows:

> "Management companies shall establish, implement and maintain an adequate and documented risk management policy which identifies the risks the UCITS they manage are or might be exposed to. In particular, the risk management policy shall comprise procedures which enable the management company to assess the exposure to market risks, liquidity risks, counterparty risks and to all other risks, including operational risks, which might be material to each UCITS it manages."[6]

Based on that last paragraph, we perceive that the tasks and expectations coming from the regulator relating to risk management are quite high. However, they are necessary to meet the investor protection levels claimed by the UCITS brand.

Having to cope with high expectations from the regulator, some management companies or self-managed SICAVs are willing to delegate the task of risk management. This opportunity is considered and accepted by the regulator[7] but it is

---

5 Committee of European Securities Regulator, 2009 technical advice to the European Commission on the level 2 measures related to the UCITS management company passport, CESR/09-963, Section I, paragraph 9.
6 Committee of European Securities Regulator, 2009 technical advice to the European Commission on the level 2 measures related to the UCITS management company passport, CESR/09-963, Section IV, Chapter 1, Box 1, paragraph 1.
7 Committee of European Securities Regulator, 2009, technical advice to the European Commission on the level 2 measures related to the UCITS management company passport, CESR/09-963, Section IV, Chapter 1, Box 3.

important to stress the fact that only the task is delegated; the responsibility remains entirely with the board of directors or senior management of the entity delegating risk management tasks. Furthermore, when delegating such a function, the management company (or self-managed SICAV) will need:

– to ensure that the third party has the necessary skills to perform such activities;

– to perform on-going assessment of the standard of third-party performance; and

– to retain the necessary resources and expertise to effectively supervise the risk management activities carried out by the third party.

These obligations to be met by management companies delegating risk management functions lead the delegates to ask for third-party validation of their procedures, allowing them to quickly demonstrate that their policies and computation processes are aligned with the regulations that are in place.

3.3. Market risk

3.3.1. *Definition*

The market risk is the potential loss that will be incurred by investors following changes on the market.

The main factors of market risk, are among, others:

– changes in equity prices;

– changes in interests rates;

– changes in foreign exchange rates;

– changes in commodity prices;

– etc.

3.3.2. *How to measure market risk*

Several indicators exist and are commonly used to assess market risk, for example:

– commitment[8]: this consists of the computation of the equivalent funded exposure of derivatives exposure;

---

8 We will return to this concept (see section 5.3.5).

– value at risk (VaR)[9]: this estimates the maximum loss level for a defined time horizon and defined level of confidence;

– tracking error: this is a relative measure assessing the volatility of the difference between the performance of the portfolio and the performance of the benchmark;

– performance volatility: this measures the volatility of the returns without the consideration of whether these returns are positive of negative;

– duration: this assesses the sensitivity of bonds valuation in relation to changes in interest rates; and

– conditional VaR (CVaR or expected shortfall)[10]: this focuses on loss levels beyond the VaR (tail risk).

With current regulator expectations, the commitment and VaR approaches are the methods recommended for measuring market risk, where other measures (even though they are relevant) are not linked to any defined requirements. The only recommendation of the regulator regarding other measurement methods concerns the opportunity to use other indicators as well as commitment/VaR to enable a more complete assessment of risks taken (i.e. the use of CVaR or other methods that are able to detect the potential impact of low-probability market events[11]).

3.3.3. Regulator expectations

As a first step, in the context of UCITS IV, depending on the fund's risk profile[12], the risk manager's will have to define the method that is best adapted – either the commitment approach or the value at risk (VaR) approach – to measure market risk[13] (i.e. the global exposure in the context of UCITS IV guidelines). It is worth noting that under UCITS III[14], the choice between the commitment and VaR approaches was based on whether the fund was classified as "sophisticated" or "unsophisticated". However, since Member States did not agree on a common

---

9 We will return to this concept (see section 5.3.6).
10 We will return to this concept (see section 5.3.6).
11 Committee of European Securities Regulator, 2010, Guidelines on Risk Measurement and the Calculation of Global Exposure and Counterparty Risk for UCITS, CESR/10-788, paragraph 74.
12 Types of risks and the related levels to which the fund is exposed.
13 Committee of European Securities Regulator, 2010, Guidelines on Risk Measurement and the Calculation of Global Exposure and Counterparty Risk for UCITS, CESR/10-788, Box 1.
14 *Commission de Surveillance du Secteur Financier*, 2007, Rules of conduct to be adopted by undertakings for collective investment in transferable securities with respect to the use of a method for the management of financial risks, as well as the use of derivative financial instruments, CSSF Circular 07/308, III.1.1.

definition of "sophisticated" and "unsophisticated" funds there was confusion among market participants and this classification has since been abandoned[15].

The commitment approach focuses on exposures taken through derivatives and limits the related additional exposure by converting derivatives' exposures in fully funded equivalent positions. The maximum level of commitment is set at 100% of the fund's total net assets (TNAs)[16].

The VaR approach (taking into account the assumptions of the model selected for computation) estimates the maximum level of loss the fund will suffer over a defined time horizon and give a defined interval of confidence. Two types of limits exist regarding VaR. On one hand, if the VaR is computed on an absolute basis, the VaR level cannot be above 20% for a 20 days' holding period and there is a 99% confidence interval[17]. On the other hand, if the VaR is computed on a relative basis, the fund's VaR (same parameters in terms of interval of confidence and holding period) cannot exceed 200% of the representative portfolio VaR[18].

The global exposure (terms used by the regulator to cover market risk) needs to be computed at least on a daily basis (where less frequent computations were authorized under UCITS III for "unsophisticated" funds)[19].

3.3.4. *Risk profiling*

The fund's classification of "unsophisticated" and "sophisticated" has been abandoned. Risk profiling is now the recommended approach for selecting the computation method for the measurement of global exposure. This is probably better

---

15 Committee of European Securities Regulator, 2009, technical advice to the European Commission on the level 2 measures related to the UCITS management company passport, CESR/09-963, Section IV, Chapter 1, paragraph 55.

16 *Official Journal of the European Union*, 2009, Directive on the coordination of laws, regulations and administrative provisions relating to undertakings for collective investment in transferable securities (UCITS), Directive 2009/65/EC, Article 51, paragraph 3.

17 Committee of European Securities Regulator, 2010, Guidelines on Risk Measurement and the Calculation of Global Exposure and Counterparty Risk for UCITS, CESR/10-788, Box 12.

18 Committee of European Securities Regulator, 2010, Guidelines on Risk Measurement and the Calculation of Global Exposure and Counterparty Risk for UCITS, CESR/10-788, Box 15.

19 *Commission de Surveillance du Secteur Financier*, 2007, Rules of conduct to be adopted by undertakings for collective investment in transferable securities with respect to the use of a method for the management of financial risks, as well as the use of derivative financial instruments, CSSF Circular 07/308, II.1.

adapted to a risk management approach where the starting point is a proper understanding of the fund's strategy and related risks.

Based on ESMA guidelines, the main steps to consider when approaching the risk profile of a fund in order to select the global exposure computation method are as follows[20]:

– it engages in complex investment strategies that represent a non-negligible part of the UCITS' investment policy;

– it has a non-negligible exposure to exotic derivatives; or

– the commitment approach does not adequately capture the market risk of the portfolio.

Even though the regulator is providing a defined path by which to assess the level of sophistication of the fund, a lot of the points to be considered still leave room for interpretation. Terms like "complex", "negligible part" and "exotic" are not factually based and need to be interpreted, defined and adapted to each fund by the management company taking into consideration both the concepts of risk appetite[21] and risk tolerance[22]. Probably, the most important point in analyzing and defining the fund's risk profile is the last on in the above list. Unfortunately, it is also probably the least tangible aspect of the recommended approach, since the perception of capturing the market risk can dramatically differ from one actor to another.

Through the following chapters, we will present computation methods used for global exposure measurement in greater detail. For all of these sections, we do not just focus on regulator guidelines, but try to improve the picture by adding analysis and comparison, allowing the reader to better assess the advantages and drawbacks of the two main approaches (i.e. commitment and VaR).

3.3.5. *The commitment approach*

With the market risk and commitment approach, we have to emphasize a key aspect of the approach before going into greater detail: the commitment approach principally focuses on derivatives and not on the total market risk level of the portfolio.

---

20 Committee of European Securities Regulator, 2010, Guidelines on Risk Measurement and the Calculation of Global Exposure and Counterparty Risk for UCITS, CESR/10-788, Box 1, point 4.
21 The COSO (Committee of Sponsoring Organizations) framework defines risk appetite as "the amount of risk, on a broad level, an entity is willing to accept in pursuit of value".
22 Risk tolerance is the acceptable level of variation relative to the achievement of objectives.

Derivatives instruments derive their value from the value of the underlying security or basket to which they are related. These instruments are not fully funded instruments and so they can generate leverage. To make this concept comprehensible, let us take an example.

When buying one share of Company X, you have to fully finance it. If the current market value of one share is €100, then you will have to pay that amount in order to own one share of Company X. After a certain period of time (let us consider a six-month timeframe) the security value has increased by 5% and you decided to sell your shares. You then have a gain on Company X of 5%[23].

Another way of having the same level of exposure could be to buy a future on Company X, giving you the opportunity to buy one Company X share at €100 at the maturity date (six months later). Let us now consider that at the maturity date, the value of Company X is €105. This means that, thanks to your future contract, you are allowed to buy Company X shares at €100 where the market value at the maturity date is €105. Should you sell at that position in the market[24], you have gained 5%[25]. This means that you have synthetically replicated the purchase of Company X shares by buying a derivatives contract.

Currently, these two investment approaches look very similar in terms of performance (with a 5% gain). However, the level of money invested in these two cases is very different.

In the first scenario this transaction is fully funded, meaning that you had to invest the related amount of cash to buy the security and gain the performance exposure. In the second scenario, the amount invested will no longer be the price of the shares but the amount of margin to be paid to the broker in order to enter the transaction. Let us consider that the margin is 10% of the total exposure (one share of Company X with an initial value of €100). The amount that will initially be financed for a similar performance exposure to the fully-funded one will be €10. So even though, as described before, the performance exposure remains similar (fully funded/synthetic exposure), the funding is really different. As, in the example taken, €10 will result in similar performances for the investor, that also means that with

---

23 Here we are not considering any transaction costs to make the example easier to understand.
24 We are here considering that there is a physical settlement, as it makes the example easier to understand.
25 Here we are voluntarily ignoring any transaction costs to make our example easier to understand.

€100 the investor could potentially multiply its exposure to the performances of the underlying starting price by 10 with the same initial amount of cash[26].

The use of the commitment approach for market risk computation in the context of UCITS funds has clearly been imposed to limit the leverage opportunities. The commitment approach is actually converting any derivatives exposures into fully funded values. In our example, if we look at the cash invested for the exposure gained through the future, we will have €10 while the equivalent fully-funded exposure (commitment approach) is €100 (the equivalent value of the underlying funded exposure).

From a regulatory standpoint, the total commitment of the UCITS fund is required to be lower than 100% of the TNAs of the fund. In other words, the total market exposure (and so the leverage) of the fund is limited to twice the TNAs.

3.3.5.1. Conversion methods

The conversion methods are defined by the regulator for most derivatives[27] and described here.

Futures can be of different types depending on the underlying instrument (bonds, currency, index, equity etc.) but the global approach will remain similar. All futures give exposure to a certain number of underlying items. This is the contract size. This factor is really important to take into consideration when computing the commitment, since the goal is to compute the fully funded equivalent amount. As an example, the commitment formula for equity futures is the following.

Number of contracts * notional contract size * market price of underlying equity share, where:

– number of contracts: number of futures contracts purchased,

– notional contract size: number of underlying linked to each future contract,

– market price of underlying equity: current value of the underlying.

---

26 The exposure is then said to be leveraged, since in a fully-funded environment the final exposure is equivalent as having borrowed 10 times the initial cash amount and having invested it in Company X.
27 Committee of European Securities Regulator, 2010, Guidelines on Risk Measurement and the Calculation of Global Exposure and Counterparty Risk for UCITS, CESR/10-788, Box 12.

Let us now make it more tangible with a concrete example and take one long position on a future (buying the future contract) on a well-known index: the Euro STOXX 50. The formula given by the ESMA is very similar to that of equity future except that the market price of the underlying equity share is replaced by the index level:

– number of contracts * notional contract size * index level.

Based on information obtained from the data provider (see Figure 3.2), we can then compute the commitment for the selected future:

- numbers of contracts: 1 (purchase of one future contract on Eurostoxx50),

- notional contract size: €10,

- current index level (as at September 21, 2011 – see Figure 3.3): 2,122.03.

$\Rightarrow$ the total commitment on the selected future is then: 1*10*2,122.03 = €21,220.3

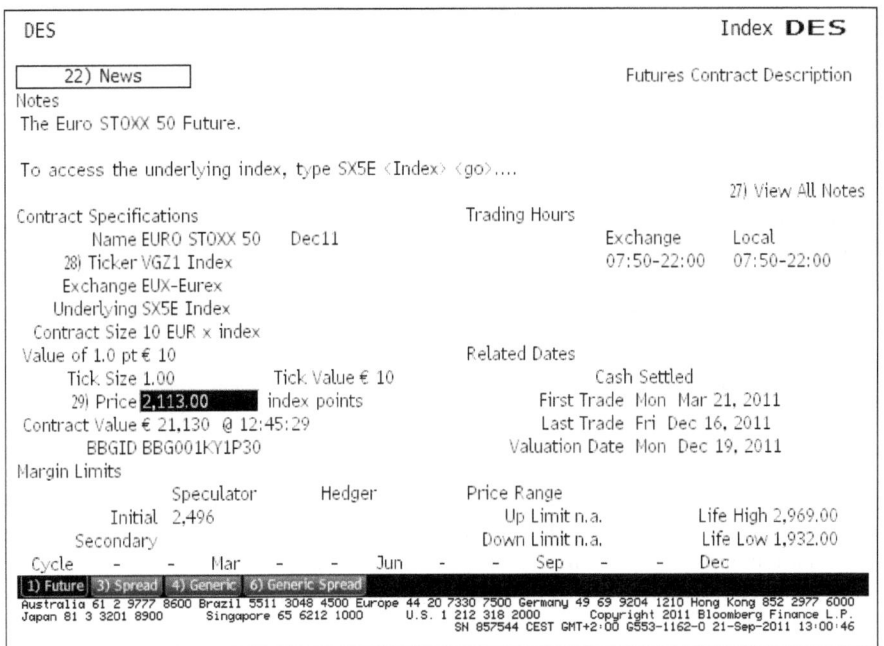

Figure 3.2. *Euro STOXX 50 future December 2011 (Source: Bloomberg)*

```
<HELP> for explanation, <MENU> for similar functions.        Index HP

CLOSE/PRICE                                               Page  1 / 3
SX5E      Euro Stoxx 50 Pr              PRICE 2122.03
                                                  HI 3011.25   ON  4/29/11
Range  3/21/11  to  9/21/11    Period D Daily     AVE 2662.32
                        EUR    Market M mid/trd   LOW 1995.01   ON  9/12/11
    DATE   PRICE  VOLUME     DATE   PRICE  VOLUME     DATE   PRICE  VOLUME
F                         F   9/ 2  2220.72 1.03BLN F  8/12  2307.33 1.58BLN
T                         T   9/ 1  2305.75  944MLN T  8/11  2215.45 2.54BLN
W   9/21  2122.03         W   8/31  2302.08 1.07BLN W  8/10  2153.77 2.46BLN
T   9/20  2140.41 1.08BLN T   8/30  2239.14  734MLN T  8/ 9  2294.24 2.69BLN
M   9/19  2096.10  924MLN M   8/29  2239.30  528MLN M  8/ 8  2286.91 2.57BLN

F   9/16  2159.28 2.38BLN F   8/26  2190.44  935MLN F  8/ 5  2375.15 2.69BLN
T   9/15  2155.62 1.51BLN T   8/25  2216.70 1.15BLN T  8/ 4  2412.29 1.72BLN
W   9/14  2083.38 1.51BLN W   8/24  2238.70  866MLN W  8/ 3  2497.83 1.84BLN
T   9/13  2036.64 1.68BLN T   8/23  2199.98  997MLN T  8/ 2  2544.89 1.79BLN
M   9/12 L1995.01 1.79BLN M   8/22  2183.39 1.04BLN M  8/ 1  2593.34 1.84BLN

F   9/ 9  2073.67 1.14BLN F   8/19  2159.07 1.63BLN F  7/29  2670.37 1.24BLN
T   9/ 8  2163.40  980MLN T   8/18  2206.61 1.33BLN T  7/28  2692.76 1.42BLN
W   9/ 7  2151.16  992MLN W   8/17  2331.12  911MLN W  7/27  2693.71 1.28BLN
T   9/ 6  2080.10 1.45BLN T   8/16  2323.67 1.06BLN T  7/26  2739.65 1.51BLN
M   9/ 5  2107.27 1.06BLN M   8/15  2324.48  349MLN M  7/25  2742.70 1.79BLN
Australia 61 2 9777 8600 Brazil 5511 3048 4500 Europe 44 20 7330 7500 Germany 49 69 9204 1210 Hong Kong 852 2977 6000
Japan 81 3 3201 8900       Singapore 65 6212 1000      U.S. 1 212 318 2000      Copyright 2011 Bloomberg Finance L.P.
                                                  SN 857544 CEST GMT+2:00 G553-1162-0 21-Sep-2011 13:01:27
```

Figure 3.3. *Euro STOXX historical price (Source: Bloomberg)*

The other conversion methods considered by the regulator for futures are the following:

– bond future: number of contracts * notional contract size * market price of the cheapest-to-deliver[28] reference bond;

– interest rate future: number of contracts * notional contract size; and

– currency future: number of contracts * notional contract size.

Plain vanilla options (bought/sold puts and calls): it is important to note that compared to what was used under UCITS III, under UCITS IV the commitment computation approach remains the same for both the buyer and seller. Under UCITS III, for buyer positions, it was allowed to only consider the adjusted premium for buying positions[29]. This is no longer the case under UCITS IV. In the context of

---

28 Futures on bonds are not linked to a defined underlying bond but more on bonds criteria (maturity, issuer, credit risk, etc.). Therefore several underlying bonds can exist that match the required criteria. Among these bonds, the least expensive is called the cheapest-to-deliver.
29 *Commission de Surveillance du Secteur Financier*, 2007, Rules of conduct to be adopted by undertakings for collective investment in transferable securities with respect to the use of a

open-ended funds (which is always the case for UCITS funds), only considering the adjusted premium could potentially lead to unidentified leveraged performances, with an impact on investors subscribing and redeeming their shares at any time. When using the full commitment approach for all options traded, this will always be taken into account.

The conversion methods considered by the regulator for plain vanilla options are the following:

– plain vanilla bond option: notional contract value * market value of underlying reference bond * delta[30];

– plain vanilla equity option: number of contracts * notional contract size * market value of underlying equity share * delta;

– plain vanilla interest rate option: notional contract value * delta;

– plain vanilla currency option: notional contract value of currency leg(s) * delta;

– plain vanilla index option: number of contracts * notional contract size * index level * delta;

– plain vanilla options on futures: number of contracts * notional contract size * market value of underlying asset * delta;

– plain vanilla swaptions: reference swap commitment conversion amount * delta; and

– warrants and rights: number of shares/bonds * market value of underlying referenced instrument * delta.

For *swaps*, the exposure is no longer related to the contract size or delta but mainly to the notional of the contract. The conversion methods considered by the regulator for swaps are the following:

– plain vanilla fixed/floating rate interest rate and inflation swaps: the notional value of the fixed leg;

– currency swap: notional value of currency leg(s);

– cross-currency interest rate swaps: notional value of currency leg(s);

– basic total return swap: underlying market value of the reference asset(s);

---

method for the management of financial risks, as well as the use of derivative financial instruments, CSSF Circular 07/308, Appendix 1.
30 Options are nonlinear instruments; therefore, to convert them we need to use their current sensitivity to changes in value of the underlying given by the delta.

– non-Basic total return swap: cumulative underlying market value of both legs of the total return swap,

– single name credit default swap:

- protection of the seller: the higher of the market values of the underlying reference asset or the notional value of the credit default swap,

- protection of the buyer: the market value of the underlying reference asset,

- contract for the differences: number of shares/bonds * market value of the underlying referenced instrument.

As for swaps, the exposure related to *forwards* is computed based on the notional contract. The conversion methods considered by the regulator for forwards are the following:

– FX forward: notional value of currency leg(s); and

– Forward rate agreement: notional value.

On top of direct exposures on derivatives, the regulator is also considering conversion methodologies for instruments embedding derivatives. Some of the instruments considered by the regulator (a non-exhaustive list has been provided by the ESMA) are:

– convertible bonds: number of referenced shares * market value of the underlying reference shares * delta;

– credit linked notes: market value of the underlying reference asset(s);

– partly-paid securities: number of shares/bonds * market value of the underlying referenced instruments; and

– warrants and rights: number of shares/bonds * market value of underlying referenced instrument * delta.

Further to what has been described here and could be considered common derivatives instruments, the ESMA is also considering non-standard or exotic derivatives. Here[31], instruments such as variance swaps, barrier options, etc., are considered. Even though, methods exist and are proposed by the regulator to determine the level of commitment on these instruments, we should bear in mind that the starting point in the selection of the method for computing global exposure is a risk profile analysis. In this respect, and as long as exotic instruments are

---

31 Committee of European Securities Regulator, 2010, Guidelines on Risk Measurement and the Calculation of Global Exposure and Counterparty Risk for UCITS, CESR/10-788, Box 2, section 8.

considered, it is likely that the fund's strategy will start to reach a level of sophistication where the commitment approach will no longer be adapted. The fund manager will therefore have to take the decision as whether or not to use the commitment approach for such instruments.

Based on what has been explained in the previous pages, we could be tempted to consider the commitment approach as being a straight-forward method, as for each type of derivatives a conversion method has been defined by the regulator. The picture is not yet complete, however, as hedging, netting, interest rate sensitivity, etc., still need to be considered.

3.3.5.2. *Exclusion from global exposure computation*

Two types of situations, when respecting a certain number of criteria, mean that the fund does not have to include derivatives in global exposure.

The first one relates to derivative instruments totally swapping the performance of financial assets held in portfolio for the performance of other reference financial assets. For this specific situation it may seem obvious that the related derivative exposure can be excluded from the global exposure computation since no additional exposure has been added to the fund. The fund is not exposed to market risk from more than the invested amount; in fact it is only the market exposure that has been modified, not the total exposure.

However, additional criteria need to be met in order to exclude certain derivatives from global exposure computation[32]:

– it must totally offset the market risk of the swapped assets held in the UCITS portfolio so that the UCITS performance (e.g. the performance of the net asset value) does not depend on the performance of the swapped assets; and

– it must not include additional optional features leverage clauses or other additional risks compared to a direct holding of the reference financial asset.

The second point relates to derivatives exposure that is fully cash-backed. As illustrated at the beginning of this chapter, derivatives are unfunded instruments that lead to potential leverage. However, should the fund hold cash (or cash-equivalent instruments) in a portfolio for amounts that are equivalent to the exposure levels taken through derivatives, it is not true to say that the derivatives are generating additional exposure for the portfolio. As this concept is probably less obvious than the first case described (the total swap of one market exposure for another), let us take an example to illustrate this concept.

---

32 Committee of European Securities Regulator, 2010, Guidelines on Risk Measurement and the Calculation of Global Exposure and Counterparty Risk for UCITS, CESR/10-788, Box 3.

For this example we first consider a fund investing all of its capital (e.g. €1,000,000) in a basket of securities replicating the Euro STOXX 50 index. In terms of performance, the fund will be perfectly correlated[33] with the Euro STOXX 50. We now keep the same performance objectives but synthetically replicate that performance by investing in derivatives. The fund is fully investing its capital in cash and cash equivalents (risk-free assets) and, at the same time, buying futures on Euro STOXX 50for a total exposure of the total capital size (€1,000,000, as mentioned earlier). From a performance perspective, the fund will, as in the previous example, again have the Euro STOXX 50 evolution as the driver for performance.

From this example, we learn that having an exposure on derivatives and at the same time having the equivalent amount of cash in the portfolio does not add any market exposure to the portfolio.

To make full use when excluding derivatives from global exposure computation, we have to respect another criterion[34]: the financial derivative instrument is not considered to generate any incremental exposure and leverage or market risk.

3.3.5.3. *Hedging and netting*

On top of exposures that can be excluded from the global exposure computation, hedging and netting arrangements may be taken into account to reduce global exposure.

Hedging involves combinations of trades that do not necessarily refer to the same underlying, having the sole aim of offsetting risks. Strategies that used to be considered as eligible in the context of the commitment computation (i.e. under UCITS III) could potentially now be unacceptable since additional criteria have been added by the ESMA[35]. To be considered as hedging, the following criteria have to be met:

– investment strategies that aim to generate a return should not be considered hedging arrangements;

– there should be a verifiable reduction of risk at the UCITS level;

– the risks linked to financial derivative instruments, i.e. general and specific, if any, should be offset;

---

33 For the purpose of this example, and to limit its complexity, we are not considering trading costs or any other fees that could have an impact on the performance of the fund compared to the related index. We apply the same approach for margin payments.
34 Committee of European Securities Regulator, 2010, Guidelines on Risk Measurement and the Calculation of Global Exposure and Counterparty Risk for UCITS, CESR/10-788, Box 4.
35 Committee of European Securities Regulator, 2010, Guidelines on Risk Measurement and the Calculation of Global Exposure and Counterparty Risk for UCITS, CESR/10-788, Box 8.

– they should relate to the same asset class; and

– they should be efficient in stressed market conditions.

Notwithstanding the above criteria, financial derivative instruments used for currency hedging purposes (i.e. instruments that do not add any incremental exposure, leverage and/or other market risks) may be netted when calculating the global UCITS exposure. As clearly mentioned in the ESMA guidelines, however, no market-neutral or long/short investment strategies will comply with all the criteria given above[36].

To illustrate the increase in eligibility criteria for hedging, let us take the following example. Let us consider the situation where the exposure of a very well diverse portfolio is hedged by a short position on one derivative having an underlying index that is highly correlated with the initial portfolio. These conditions are meeting all the hedging criteria and therefore can be considered as hedging and so deducted from the global exposure computation.

Let us now keep the same scenario and slightly modify it. Instead of a very diverse portfolio on one hand and a highly correlated index on the other, we now have a long position on one security and a short position on a derivative having another security (but highly correlated in terms of performance) as the underlying. This specific structure will no longer be considered as hedging and therefore the total global exposure cannot be reduced. The reason for this is that in that the portfolio composition and, in comparison with the previous example, the specific risk of the invested share is not hedged. The purpose here is also to avoid the temptation to try to hide long/short strategies that are specifically rejected from hedging by the regulator.

The concept of netting concept is similar to hedging but gives less room for interpretation, since the underlying should refer to the same asset (ignoring the derivatives' maturity date). Derivatives exposures can be netted provided that they refer to the same underlying. The same netting opportunities also apply between derivatives and portfolio investments as long as the underlying derivative is held in the portfolio. Additional netting opportunities are also considered for interest rate derivatives using duration-specific rules. These duration netting rules solve an issue with netting as interest rates derivatives' underlying may only differ by the maturity and so be rejected from netting opportunities. To solve this specific limitation, the ESMA proposed an *optional* approach. As the use of this approach is not a requirement and, taking into account that the defined method is very specific, we

36 Committee of European Securities Regulator, 2010, Guidelines on Risk Measurement and the Calculation of Global Exposure and Counterparty Risk for UCITS, CESR/10-788, Box 8, point 2 and 3.

decided not to include the description of the full process in this chapter. For further details, readers can go to the dedicated section of the ESMA guidelines (CESR/10-788, Box 7).

3.3.6. *Value at risk (VaR)*

The concept of VaR was introduced by JP Morgan in the early 1990s when the Chairman Dennis Weatherstone asked his staff to provide him with a daily page indicating the potential losses over the next 24 hours based on the bank's entire portfolio[37]. The one-page report was supposed to be handed to him at 4:15 PM (soon after market closing) and was called the "4:15 report".

In order to properly meet the requirements of JP Morgan's Chairman, both the computation approach, all of its underlying assumptions as well as the development of the related tool (risk metrics) were launched and quickly started to be used as a best practice in measuring market risk within banks. This tool was included in the Basel II regulation.

With regards to investment funds, the implementation of UCITS III gave more room for "alternative strategies" and more opportunities concerning derivatives trading, leading to the regulator starting to consider the obligation of implementing risk management techniques on top of compliance limits. With part of these new obligations relating to market risk, specific limits have been put in place based on the VaR approach for funds exposed to more sophisticated asset management.

3.3.6.1. *VaR definition*

One of the strongest aspects of VaR is the ease of interpretation of the final results, as VaR is the estimation of the maximum loss a portfolio will suffer during a defined future period with a defined confidence interval.

As an illustrative example, a 10% VaR computed with a 95% confidence interval and a 20-day holding period means that 95% of time the maximum loss the fund will suffer over the coming 20 days will be 10% (i.e. 5% of the time this loss will be higher).

---

37 Dowd, Kevin, Section 1.3.1 "The Origin and Development of VaR" in *An Introduction to Market Risk Measurement*, Wiley Finance, 2002.

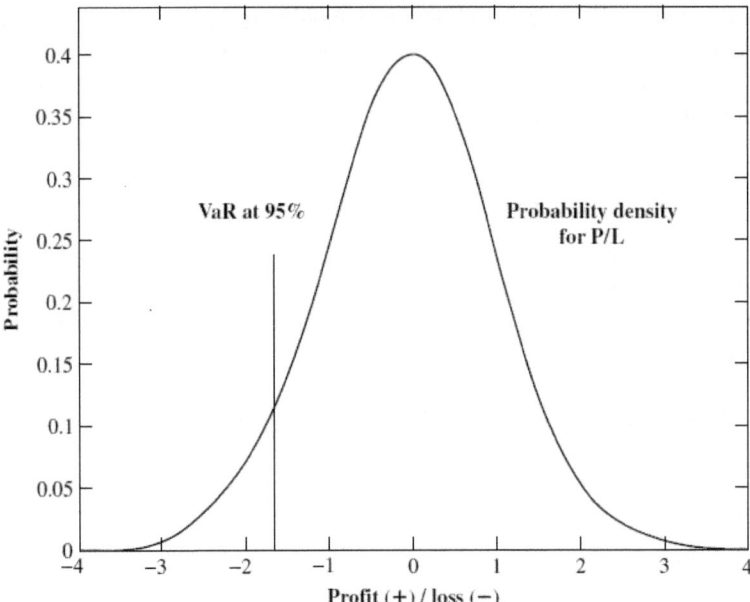

Figure 3.4. *Returns distribution (Source: An introduction to Market Risk Measurement, Kevin Dowd, 2002, Wiley Finance, 2002)*

To better illustrate this concept, we will use a probability density function of returns. As is shown in Figure 3.4, 40% of the time (the probability of 0.4 on the Y axis) the profit will be 0%. As soon as we start to move away from the average level, the frequency of occurrence starts to decrease quite quickly. In this case, the VaR (computed with a confidence interval of 95% for the example) will be the profit level at which we have 95% of the profit/loss events on the right-hand side and the remaining 5% on the left-hand side. Therefore, starting from that specific example (considering the assumption of the model), you know that 95% of the time your level of loss will not be above 1.65 (approximation of the VaR level of the chart in Figure 3.3).

3.3.6.2. Limitations

The main strength of the VaR (easy interpretation of results) is also what is probably its main drawback.

The VaR computation needs to be considered as an indicator. Even though different methods can be used for the computation of VaR (from really basic to very advanced methods[38]), it is not perfect and should not be considered a guarantee of limited losses. However, this is a strong and advanced indicator that will (as long as tools and models are properly implemented) give clear and easy to interpret information to the risk managers and any related parties of the current portfolio risk levels.

3.3.6.3. Computation methods

Based on what has been described above, VaR can sound as though it is a "simple" indicator. From an interpretation point of view, we can agree with this statement; however, from a computation standpoint, we must be more careful in our judgment.

Three main approaches are currently used to compute the VaR:

– the parametric approach;

– the historical approach; and

– the Monte Carlo approach.

To quickly describe them before going into greater detail, let us concentrate on the main assumptions of these approaches.

From a general standpoint, as the VaR is giving the potential level of the maximum loss you will suffer in the coming day(s) – the length of time will depend on the time horizon used for the computation – we need to make some assumptions on how market will behave in the coming periods. This is basically what differentiates the methods mentioned above.

For the parametric approach, the assumption made is that future returns will follow a defined distribution frequency. This really simplifies the computation as we have a defined path for future returns; however, this is also a strong hypothesis.

The historical approach is based on the main assumption that what happened in the past provides a good estimation of what will happen in the future.

Finally, for the Monte Carlo approach future returns will be simulated based on a stochastic approach.

3.3.6.4. Parametric VaR

As previously described, the VaR is an expectation of the future maximum loss; we then need to find ways to reasonably forecast the future returns levels. One way

---

38 These methods will be described in greater detail in the coming pages.

of doing this would be to consider that future returns follow a standardized distribution. In this context, the most commonly used distribution is the normal distribution. The main reason this distribution is preferred is that only two parameters are required to define it: the mean and the standard deviation where normally four moments are considered to define the distribution:

– the mean;

– the standard deviation;

– the skewedness; and

– the kurtosis.

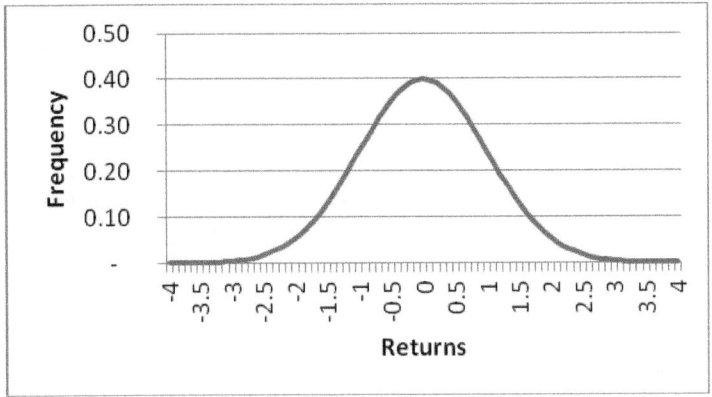

Figure 3.5. *Normal distribution*

As far as the normal distribution is concerned, the skewedness is 0 (the peak of the distribution is equal to the mean and there is no departure from the symmetry) and the kurtosis is equal to 3 (i.e. there is no excess kurtosis). From a technical standpoint, and more specifically from an implementation standpoint, having only two parameters to define the distribution instead of four provides a strong advantage as it simplifies the computation process. Therefore, considering the central limit theorem[39] the assumption of the normal distribution of returns is generally made in order to simplify and accelerate the computation process.

In order the better describe the concepts of skewedness and kurtosis, we will use charts.

---

39 This theorem states that if Sn is the sum of n mutually-independent random variables, then the distribution function of Sn is well approximated by a certain type of continuous function known as a normal density function.

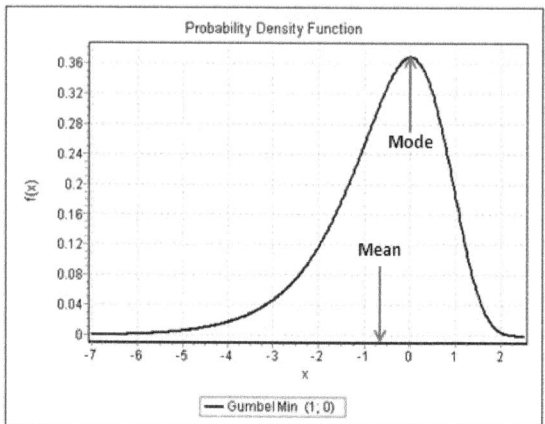

Figure 3.6. *Left-skewed distribution[40] (Source: Easifit from Mathwave)*

In Figure 3.6, the distribution shows a negative skew meaning that we have a fat tail on the left-hand side. From a risk standpoint, should this distribution show the returns distribution it means that the levels of loss levels tend to be higher than the levels of profit.

Figure 3.7 shows a positive skew where we have a fat tail on the right-hand side. From a risk standpoint, should this distribution show the returns distribution it means that profit levels tend to be higher than loss levels.

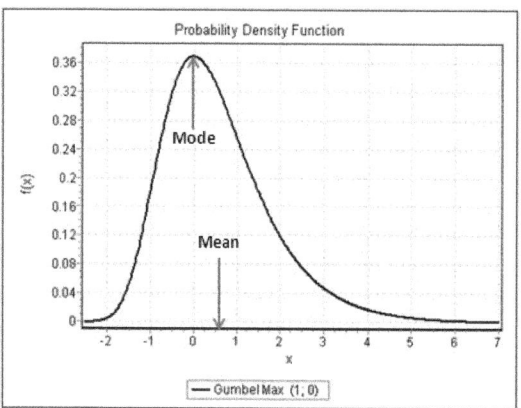

Figure 3.7. *Right-skewed distribution (Source: Easifit from Mathwave)*

---

40 The mean is the average value of returns (x being the returns in Figure 3.5), and the mode is the value that appears the most frequently. For the normal distribution (see Figure 3.4) the mean and the mode are equivalent.

The fourth moment of the distribution is the kurtosis. The kurtosis qualifies the shape of the distribution. A distribution is said to be leptokurtic[41] (see Figure 3.8) when the occurrence of events is more concentrated around the mean, leading to a higher peak level compared to the normal distribution. From a risk standpoint, this implies that rare events are also appearing more frequently than for the normal distribution. In contrast, platykurtic[42] distributions refer to distributions with a lower concentration around the mean (leading to a flatter peak compared to the normal distribution) implying fatter tails compared to the normal distribution. From a risk standpoint, this means that potential losses are higher and more frequent compared to normal distribution.

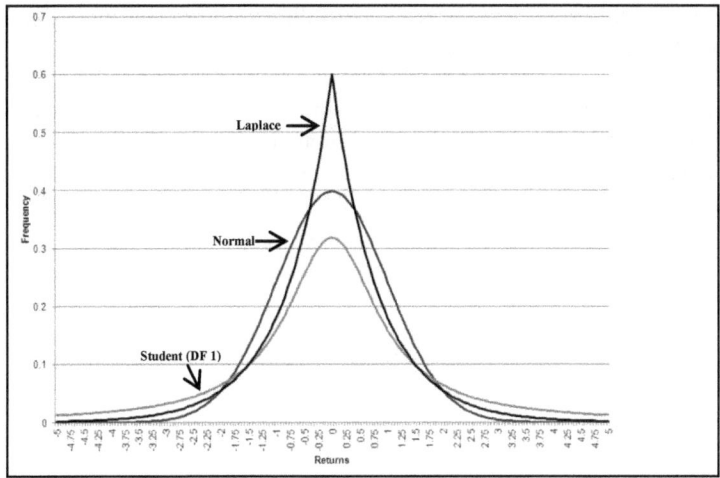

Figure 3.8. *Normal distribution, Student distribution (platykurtic), Laplace distribution (leptokurtic)*

Having described the potential impact of simplifying the returns distribution by using the normal distribution as an assumption of returns distribution, we will now link the normal distribution to the VaR calculation concept and show how VaR is computed using a parametric approach.

As described in Figure 3.3, and by referring to the concept of probability density functions illustrated in Figures 3.4 to 3.8, by knowing the returns distribution and assuming that it follows a normal distribution, we can easily determine the distance from the mean that must be used to determine the VaR. To illustrate this, let us consider a VaR at 95%. In this context, we would like to know where on the chart

41 The kurtosis level is above 3 here and excess kurtosis is above 0.
42 The kurtosis level is below 3 here and excess kurtosis is below 0.

(in Figure 3.4) the limit between the 95% highest returns and the remaining 5% is. By making the assumption of a normal distribution of returns, and by using the related statistical tables, we know that at a distance of 1.65 times the standard deviation (1.65 * σ^{43}) 95% of occurrence in the distribution is covered. In other words, in this specific context, by only measuring the standard deviation of the actual returns and, considering that future returns will follow a normal distribution, we will be able to determine the VaR.

However, computing the VaR of a portfolio can be a bit more complex. As portfolio composition changes over time, using a portfolio of past returns to determine the returns standard deviation will lead to a major bias, as the only situation where this is acceptable is for portfolios with an unchanging composition over time. This is very improbable.

Therefore, the current portfolio composition needs to be considered for VaR computation. From a standard deviation computation point of view, this means that on one hand the historical returns of the instruments in portfolio will need to be considered and, on the other hand, the covariance[44] between the returns will also need to be integrated in the computation. The easiest way of integrating this concept in the computation process is to use matrix notation, as described in equation [3.1]:

$$\left| \sigma \frac{2}{p} \right| = \begin{bmatrix} w_1 \cdots w_n \end{bmatrix} \begin{bmatrix} \sigma_{11} \cdots \sigma_{1n} \\ \vdots \quad \vdots \\ \sigma_{n1} \cdots \sigma_{nn} \end{bmatrix} \begin{bmatrix} w_1 \\ \vdots \\ w_n \end{bmatrix} = w' \sum w \qquad [3.1]$$

Even though this approach allows portfolio risk computation on an *ex-ante*[45] basis, the size of the variance/covariance matrix can dramatically increase with the number of securities in a portfolio. As an example, the number of factors to consider in the variance/covariance matrix for a portfolio containing of five securities will be 15 and will reach 5,050 for a portfolio containing 100 securities[46]!

Considering this quickly-increasing number of factors that will slow down the computation process, different methods can be used such as index mapping, beta mapping, diagonal mapping, etc. Although these methods simplify the complexity of the computation as well as the time required, their impact on the VaR computed needs to be assessed as it will impact the results. In his book *Value-at-Risk* Philippe

---

43 The Greek letter "σ" is commonly used in statistics to describe standard deviation.
44 Covariance is the measure of how much two variables change together.
45 *Ex-ante* means that the current portfolio allocation is considered.
46 The number of factors included in the variance/covariance matrix is estimated using the following formula: N*(N+1)/2, with N being the number of securities in the portfolio.

Jorion[47] carried out an analysis for three types of portfolio and the results are very illustrative of the importance of considering the potential impact of the use of mapping methods on final results.

Position	Portfolio		
	Diversified	High tech	Long-Short
	$1,000,000	$1,000,000	$0
VaR			
Index mapping	$63,634	$63,634	$0
Beta mapping	$70,086	$84,008	$298
Industry mapping	$69,504	$90,374	$7,388
Diagonal model	$81,238	$105,283	$41,081
Individual mapping (exact)	$78,994	$118,955	$32,598

Table 3.1. *Impact of mapping methods on results of parametric VaR computation (Source: Value-at-Risk, P. Jorion)*

The parametric approach for computing VaR is very efficient in terms of computation. However, as the future returns distribution follow a defined distribution, the impact of both the distribution and the mapping process used on the VaR results will need to be carefully assessed in order to guarantee relevant results.

3.3.6.5. *Historical VaR*

Compared to the approach previously described, the historical approach does not rely on any defined statistical distribution but states that past events are a good prediction of future trends.

The main challenge here lies in the computation of the past returns, taking into account current portfolio composition as the portfolio will go through a full valuation process for a past period of an average of one to three years. Since all the securities included in the portfolio will be valued at each past day over the defined past period, the computation process of the historical VaR is quite intense. The past returns of the portfolio will be recreated considering the current portfolio investments. The implied challenge of this process lies in the valuation tool and the valuation of securities that have recently been launched (since their past returns do

47 Jorion, Philippe, *Financial Risk Manager Handbook*, Fourth edition, Wiley Finance, Part 2, Table 7-7 2007.

not exist and will need to be simulated). Situations where a few major decreases have appeared on the market at a defined point in time are also important to consider. These events will push down the VaR as long as they remain part of the range of dates included in the past window used to estimate future returns. Taken the other way around, if the past years were quite stable and no major market events took place, this will imply a potential underestimation of market risk, as higher risk levels are likely to appear.

Once the past returns distribution is recomposed based on the process described here, the distribution quartile corresponding to the selected confidence interval is measured and the VaR is determined. Let us use a simplified example to illustrate this.

Let us consider that we have 30 weekly past returns (in percentages): 2, 4, 7, 10, 24, 15, -3, -6, -10, -12, 6, 13, 3, 17, -5, 1, -11, - 16, 1, 1, 3, -1, -7, -22, -30, -13, -9, -8, -1, 4. By simply rearranging them from the smallest to the highest and considering that our goal is to compute a weekly VaR at 90% of confidence, by looking at the losses and isolating the 3 lowest returns (10% * 30 = 3), we have identified our VaR which is -16.

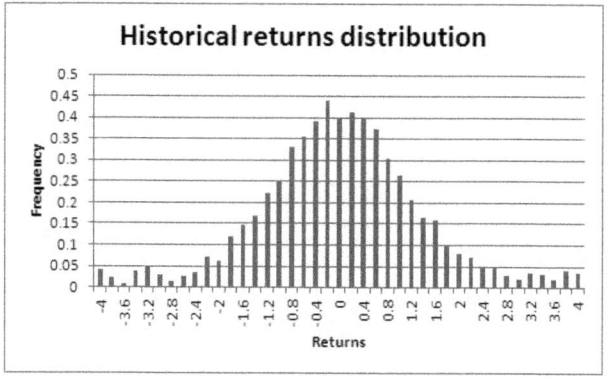

Figure 3.9. *Example of historical returns distribution*[48]

3.3.6.6. *Monte Carlo VaR*

As for historical computation, Monte Carlo computation does not rely on defined returns distribution to estimate future returns but instead oo using past returns they will be simulated.

---

48 This distribution clearly shows the difference from the normal distribution, especially in the tails where high frequency appears from some of the very low and very high levels of returns.

The Monte Carlo approach (as long as the selected model is reliable and appropriate) is the most advanced method of VaR computation, since the portfolio will be fully evaluated a higher number of times by using different (randomly generated) values for the main valuation factors of the instruments in the portfolio.

More than being a model, the Monte Carlo approach is an algorithmic approach that is applied to the assessment of the VaR. The Monte Carlo concept can be used to evaluate many different types of measures by using a loop generating a high number of different random values that aim to evaluate a specific output.

Starting from an initial portfolio value, a high number of paths (usually several thousand) are simulated in order to generate the distribution of simulated returns that will finally be used to assess the VaR, as done for historical computation.

Figure 3.10 illustrates how the returns distribution is obtained from a high number of simulations.

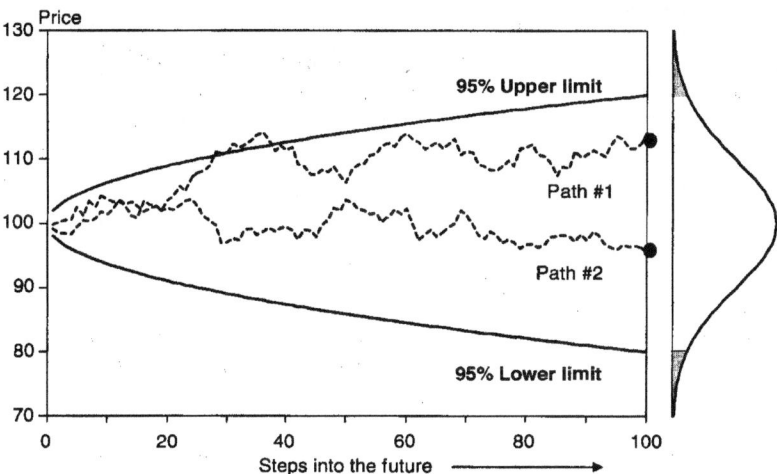

Figure 3.10. *Monte Carlo returns simulation (Value-at-Risk, P Jorion[49])*

3.3.6.7. *Advantages and drawbacks of the different VaR computation methods*

Table 3.2 identifies the main advantages and drawbacks of each VaR computation method.

49 Jorion, Philippe, *Financial Risk Manager Handbook*, Fourth edition, Wiley Finance, Part 3, Figure 12-1 2007.

Method	Advantages	Drawbacks
Parametric	• Easy to implement • Fast and efficient method for measuring VaR where optionality is not a dominant factor • Provides a useful tool for understanding and analyzing the risk driver of a portfolio	• Nonlinear payments (options) are not captured • Normality assumptions may produce inaccurate data sets
Historical	• No distribution assumptions required • Only returns must be calculated • Accommodates market behavior that is not statistically explicable • Deals with optionality	• Requires an adequate set of data for each instrument held • Calculation are much more intensive than with parametric approach • Forecasting based on historical data excludes the possibility of accounting for new risks not inherent in historic data • Relies on a model for valuation of securities for which historical returns do not exist (recently launched)
Monte Carlo	• Powerful and forward-looking method to compute VaR • Accounts for a wide range of risks (including nonlinear risk) • Ideal for complex and exotic positions • Does not assume history will repeat itself	• Most expensive to implement • Relies on a specific stochastic model and factors implying model risk • Non-intuitive and can be difficult to explain

Table 3.2. *Advantages and drawbacks of the main VaR computation methods*

3.3.6.8. *Time scaling*

As mentioned in the section 3.3.3, the regulator expects a 20-day VaR at 99%. That means that rescaling could be necessary if the final user is interested in having an equivalent VaR level for a different timeframe. In the context of UCITS IV, the use of the square root of time is accepted by the regulator even though this implies a strong hypothesis, being that the returns of the distribution are i.i.d[50].

To illustrate this concept let us consider the following case: we have a 20-day VaR (5%) and we would like to compute a corresponding daily VaR. By simply

---

50 Identically and independently distributed.

dividing the 20-day VaR by $\sqrt{20}$ we obtain 1.12%, which is the related one-day VaR. Should the situation be the other way around, multiplying the one-day VaR (1.12%) by $\sqrt{20}$ gives the related 20-day VaR.

3.3.6.9. Back testing

Another regulatory obligation related to VaR computation is back testing. As the VaR corresponds to the estimation of the maximum loss and the portfolio will suffer in an approaching defined time horizon it makes sense to assess *ex post* whether or not the estimation was correct.

As an example, in T, we have computed the portfolio 99% one-day VaR for T+1. The VaR level was 5% (i.e. the maximum expected loss for the confidence interval and holding period) in T. In T+1, the fund's actual return was -4%. Therefore, the back test confirms that the estimation was reliable and so the quality of the model parameters and factors appears to be adequate. Should the actual returns in T+1 have been -6%, then we would have identified a breach in our back test. However, to be properly performed, this analysis needs to be done over a longer timeframe. In the context of UCITS IV, a period of 250 days needs to be considered. Furthermore, VaR will be back-tested based on daily VaR results and analysis needs to be performed at least on a monthly basis[51]. Also if more than four breaches have been identified in the last 250 days (2.5% being the expectation, as the VaR is computed with a confidence interval of 99%[52]) a specific report must be made to the board describing why such levels have been reached and whether this implies a review of the model calibration is required.

In our example, we described what we call "dirty" back testing, by focusing on actual returns and we have not considered the impact of changes in the portfolio (purchase and sale of securities). As the expectation made by the VaR is based on the current portfolio composition, it would then be more adequate to assess the quality of the expectations by comparing the actual performance of the same portfolio by performing "clean" back testing. However, due to additional technical implications linked to "clean" back testing, "dirty" back testing commonly appears in risk management in practice.

3.3.6.10. Stress testing

Part of the risk manager's responsibility involves the consideration of the impact of rare but potentially serious events on portfolio performance.

---

51 Committee of European Securities Regulator, 2010, Guidelines on Risk Measurement and the Calculation of Global Exposure and Counterparty Risk for UCITS, CESR/10-788, Box 18.
52 Normal expectations then means that actual returns breach VaR levels 1% of the time.

In the context of UCITS IV, there is a also an obligation for the risk manager to supplement the risk computation by stress testing that needs to be performed at least on a monthly basis[53]. Stress scenarios can be arbitrary or historical (9/11, the 1987 market crash, the 1998 Russian crisis, etc.) but, at least the main factors that may impact the fund performance need to be considered. The regulator also focuses on the impact of leverage by asking the manager to consider a potential situation leading to a net asset value (NAV) below 0[54]. This is clearly emphasizing the regulator's expectation of seeing practitioners carefully selecting their factors in order to properly assess the level of unexpected events.

3.3.7. *Global exposure: VaR versus commitment*

As both commitment and VaR can be used to assess a fund's global exposure, we need to better understand the value they provide before being able to make the right choice between these two methods.

In order to clearly illustrate the difference in information provided by the two methods, we decided to analyze the information given by two indicators for two different portfolios with a similar structure.

Portfolios A and B are exposed to benchmark performances through synthetic exposure gained through performance swaps that are cash-backed by cash in the fund.

As can be seen in Figure 3.11, a quick analysis of the underlying swaps gives a rough idea of the relative risk levels of these two portfolios. This quick assessment is mainly due to their very straightforward structure.

However, by looking at the computed results, we can see that the commitment levels are exactly the same while their market risk levels actually differ strongly. This is reinforced when we consider that by being cash-backed, the commitment on the swap is compensated for by the level of cash leading to a commitment of 0 for both portfolios A and B. Even though from a leverage standpoint the commitment approach gives some information, from a market risk point of view we have demonstrated that absolutely no information is given by the commitment levels.

---

53 Committee of European Securities Regulator, 2010, Guidelines on Risk Measurement and the Calculation of Global Exposure and Counterparty Risk for UCITS, CESR/10-788, Box 19, 20 and 21.

54 Committee of European Securities Regulator, 2010, Guidelines on Risk Measurement and the Calculation of Global Exposure and Counterparty Risk for UCITS, CESR/10-788, Box 20.2. Here the regulator is taking a "reverse" stress-testing approach since the starting point is not the shock but the result of the stress scenario.

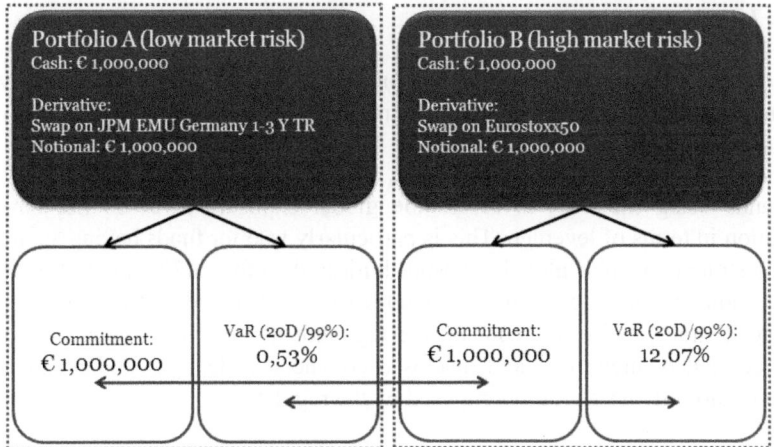

Figure 3.11. *VaR versus commitment*

By only looking at the VaR levels[55] we see (without spending time analyzing the portfolio composition) that the market risk level of portfolio B is much higher than A.

Furthermore, the VaR level will change over time giving a dynamic aspect to the measurement of the market risk, while the commitment will remain stable as long as the swaps' notionals are not modified. This is illustrated in Figure 3.10. Here we can see that while the VaR is increasing dramatically in periods of higher market risk (end of 2008 – Lehman's default), the commitment remains stable. Also, even though the VaR of the two benchmarks are increasing during the same period of time, their levels are different. The commitment remained stable and exactly the same throughout the period for both portfolios A and B.

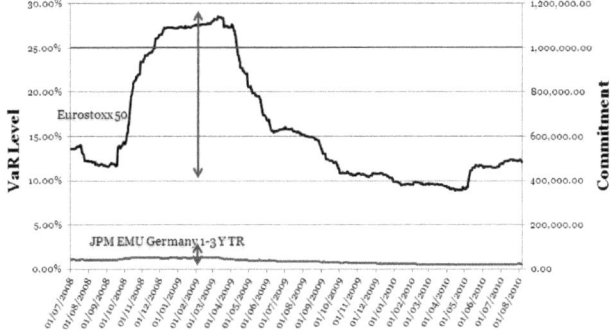

Figure 3.12. *VaR versus commitment in change over time*

---

55 As long as the computation method is the same.

3.3.8. *Leverage*

For funds using commitment as the measure for global exposure, their leverage is limited to a ratio of two as the maximum additional exposure is 100% of the TNAs, as described in Section 3.3.5.

Funds using the VaR to assess the global exposure level do not have any limitation in terms of leverage. This is particularly true for funds having an absolute returns strategy as their global exposure limit is therefore a 20-day VaR at 99% of 20%. Funds running low volatility strategies are then indirectly allowed to run leveraged strategies. In this context, the regulator now wants to have the leverage level computed, monitored and disclosed (financial statements and prospectus[56]). There is currently no limitation imposed by the regulator[57].

As illustrated in Figure 3.13, applying a two-for-one leverage ratio on a fund exposed to a low volatility market will not be identified by VaR measurement, even though low internal limits have been put in place[58].

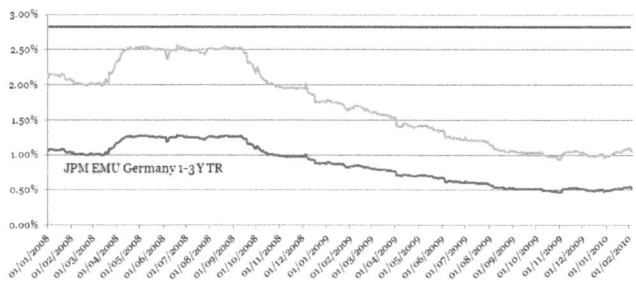

Figure 3.13. *Leverage and VaR*

The methods recommended by the ESMA (the method to be used for disclosure purposes in financial statements and prospectus) are simple and could potentially be misleading, as the leverage is measured by summing all derivatives' notionals[59]. Any reinvestment of collateral or other guarantees leading to additional market

---

56 This will be covered in greater detail in the disclosure section.

57 This could potentially change in the light of AIFMD (Alternative Investment Fund Manager Directive where leverage limitations are considered.

58 The internal limit used for the example is 2.8%. This is actually much lower than the 20% limit imposed by the regulator leading to a potentially high level of leverage.

59 Committee of European Securities Regulator, 2010, Guidelines on Risk Measurement and the Calculation of Global Exposure and Counterparty Risk for UCITS, CESR/10-788, Boxs 24 and 25.

exposure must also be considered in the computation. As this method can generate a very high level of leverage, part of which might not be relevant from a financial standpoint[60], in its dedicated circular[61] the Luxembourg financial regulator (CSSF) has decided to also allow the use of the commitment approach to assess the level of leverage[62].

3.4. Counterparty risk

As a chapter of this book will be dedicated to counterparty risk, we will limit this chapter to the regulator's expectations. For more details and advanced methods, we recommend referring to Chapter 4 by Romain Berry, which is dedicated to the subject.

3.4.1. *Definition*

Counterparty risk is the risk to each party linked by a contract default.

It defers from credit risk[63] by being two-sided. Parties entering in over-the-counter (OTC) contracts are, depending on the market trends, exposed from one period to another to the potential impact of a counterparty default.

As an illustration, let us consider two parties (A and B) entering a performance swap maturing in three months where A is betting that the market will go up and B that it will go down. In T, the market is going up. A is currently exposed to B's default since A has an unrealized gain on the transaction. In T+3, the market is plummeting, implying an unrealized gain for B who is therefore exposed to the potential default of A.

3.4.2. *Regulator expectations*

Compared to UCITS III, where the computation of the counterparty risk included a lot of arbitrary levels and where the results of the computation were not giving the expected information (i.e. the amount of loss should the counterparty default), in the

---

60 As an example, derivatives exposure covered by the equivalent cash amount in the portfolio would be considered as generating leverage while it is a pure synthetic replication of funded instruments (see section 3.3.5.2 on the exclusion from global exposure computation).
61 CSSF Circular 11/512.
62 CSSF Circular 11/512, section IV.5.2.
63 The risk that a borrower does not make the payments as promised.

context of UCITS IV the regulator is going a step back and recommend focusing on the level of unrealized gain[64] adjusted by the collateral received[65].

According to Article 52(1) of the UCITS Directive[66] the risk exposure of a UCITS to counterparty on an OTC derivative may not exceed 5% of assets. This limit is raised to 10% in the case of credit institutions[67].

As opposed to UCITS III requirements, UCITS IV also considers the initial margin posted to and variation margin receivable from a broker relating to exchange-traded instruments[68].

The total sum of one counterparty's exposure (including direct investments, bank deposit, counterparty net exposure, etc.) must not exceed 20% of the fund's TNAs[69].

3.5. Liquidity risk management

3.5.1. *Definition*

In the context of investment funds, liquidity risk must be seen from two sides: assets (portfolio) and liability (investor's behavior).

Liquidity risk on the asset side arises when securities cannot be sold, liquidated or closed at a minimum cost in an adequately short timeframe.

Liquidity risk on the liability side arises when the fund cannot meet redemption payments or is able to do so but with such an investment deviation that it could generate claims from the investors.

---

64 Committee of European Securities Regulator, 2009, technical advice to the European Commission on the level 2 measures related to the UCITS management company passport, CESR/09-963, Section IV, Chapter 2, Box 12.

65 A set of high-level principles must be met in order to be considered in the counterparty risk computation. Committee of European Securities Regulator, 2010, Guidelines on Risk Measurement and the Calculation of Global Exposure and Counterparty Risk for UCITS, CESR/10-788, Box 26.

66 *Official Journal of the European Union*, 2009, Directive on the coordination of laws, regulations and administrative provisions relating to undertakings for collective investment in transferable securities (UCITS), Directive 2009/65/EC.

67 For more information on the definition and criteria of credit institutions, please refer to article 50.1(f) of the UCITS IV Directive.

68 A set of high-level principles must be met in order to be considered in the counterparty risk computation. Committee of European Securities Regulator, 2010, Guidelines on Risk Measurement and the Calculation of Global Exposure and Counterparty Risk for UCITS, CESR/10-788, Box 27.1.

69 Article 52.2 of the UCITS IV Directive.

3.5.2. *Regulator expectations*

In the context of UCITS IV, the regulator is expecting to see liquidity risk monitoring incorporated into the risk manager's tasks[70]. However, compared to what is done for counterparty risk and market risk, no recommendations are provided in terms of implementation but the expectations are challenging.

As UCITS funds are open-ended, they are supposed to be able to pay redemptions at any time. Therefore, the regulator is putting a focus on that aspect by asking the risk managers to ensure that the portfolio risk profile is aligned with the redemption policy[71] and, where appropriate, that stress tests are conducted to assess the liquidity risk of the UCITS under exceptional circumstances[72].

This lack of information and guidelines from the regulator probably makes liquidity risk management one of the main risk management challenges of UCITS IV.

3.5.3. *How to approach liquidity risk in the context of investment funds*

Having securities in a portfolio that are not liquid or that present low liquidity levels is not an issue as such. It only starts to be a concern when investors start to leave the fund, as the fund manager will need to be able to meet the cost of these redemptions that could trigger the sale of investments should cash levels not appear to be sufficient.

Also, as investment funds have to comply with a set of rules (UCITS law and investment policy), positions cannot be liquidated without considering the potential impact it could have on the limits they have to respect. Furthermore, investors who are not leaving the fund should not be financing the cost of the redemptions of investors leaving the fund. Therefore, fairness for the remaining investors is also a key point to consider while starting selling positions to meet redemption payments.

---

70 Committee of European Securities Regulator, 2010, Guidelines on Risk Measurement and the Calculation of Global Exposure and Counterparty Risk for UCITS, CESR/10-788, Box 1, explanatory text 1.

71 Commission Directive 2010/43/EU of July 1, 2010 implementing Directive 2009/65/EC of the European Parliament and of the Council as regards organizational requirements, conflicts of interest, conduct of business, risk management and content of the agreement between a depositary and a management company, Chapter IV, section 2, art. 40.4.

72 Commission Directive 2010/43/EU of July 1, 2010 implementing Directive 2009/65/EC of the European Parliament and of the Council as regards organizational requirements, conflicts of interest, conduct of business, risk management and content of the agreement between a depositary and a management company, Chapter IV, section 2, Art. 40.3.

A structured process then needs to be followed when analyzing liquidity risk within the investment industry.

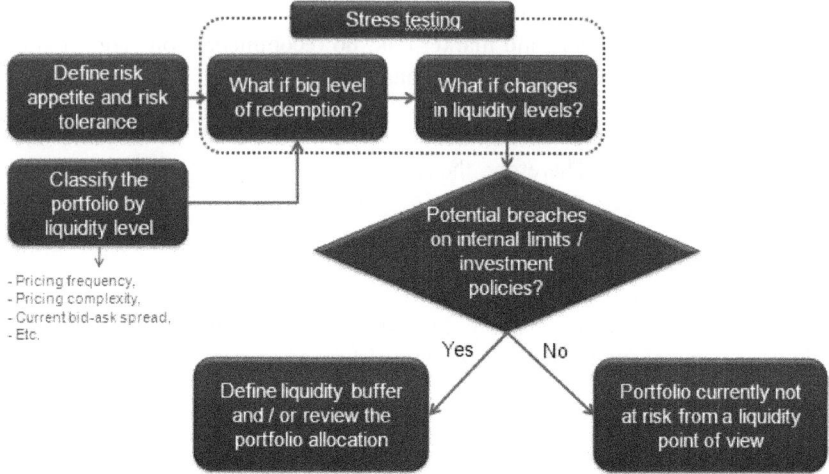

Figure 3.14. *Liquidity risk for investment funds – a decision tree*

As illustrated in Figure 3.14, the first step to consider when approaching liquidity risk for investment funds whether the expected and accepted level of liquidity risk exposure of investors is understood. While this is not totally relevant for UCITS (broad range of investors), it may be different for less widely distributed funds. Should the investors know from the launch of the fund that the selected investments are showing low liquidity levels, and so decide to invest in these instruments on purpose? Performing a deep liquidity analysis may not appear to be relevant, since the output of such analysis will be aligned with the investor's first expectations. However, in a context of a wide range of investors of different types (as it is for UCITS funds), knowing the current liquidity levels of invested instruments and going through a defined framework ensuring that the fund will be able to meet redemption payments (even in stressed conditions) will, to a certain extent, limit the potential impact of liquidity events on the fund.

3.5.4. *Methods and techniques to measure and monitor liquidity risk (asset side)*

As mentioned in the definitions, in the context of investment funds, liquidity risk must be seen and analyzed from two sides: assets (portfolio) and liabilities (investor behavior).

Of the common indicators to measure liquidity risk of investments, the average traded volume, the bid-ask spread and the liquidity VaR (LVaR) are probably the most well-known.

3.5.4.1. *Average traded volume*

Using the average traded volume to assess the capacity to sell a portion (or the total amount) of equities in a portfolio is probably one of the easiest ways to assess the liquidity level of equities. The method is quite simple and the interpretation of the final results is easy.

As equities are traded on regulated markets, it is really easy to obtain the number of securities traded during the past days, weeks or months. Therefore, the quantity held in portfolio can be compared to the average volume traded on the market. If the quantity the portfolio manager wants to sell on the market is really low compared to the average volume, we can than consider that it is very unlikely that the trade will have an impact on the market price. Should that quantity be high compared to the average volume, however, the portfolio manager will more than probably want to sell the positions over a longer period of time and trading prices will probably be effected by that trade.

As an illustration, let us consider the case where the trader would like to sell 100 shares (a) of company X. By gathering market information on these shares, he knows that during the past 20 days the average traded volume was 10,000 shares (b). By comparing the quantity held in the portfolio to the average quantity traded on the market, you can easily calculate the ratio between (a) and (b), giving a ratio of 0.01 that, in simple words, means that the 100 shares of the portfolio could be liquidated within one day with a very low probability of it having an impact on the price.

However, this computation implies that we are not considering that other market players could also decide to liquidate their positions at the same time. Therefore, "haircuts" are commonly applied to the average traded volume to compare portfolio positions to a portion of the average traded volume[73].

The results of our previous computation (applying a percentage of 20%) would then have been $100/2,000 = 0.05$.

The computation results are easy to interpret as they represent the number of days required to liquidate the positions. Furthermore, it is really easy to implement

---

73 10, 20 or 30% of the average traded volume are commonly used.

since the average traded volume can easily be obtained from a market data provider and some of them provide interfaces and tools to facilitate this analysis[74].

This indicator can, however, be misleading in some cases. If we consider the situation where the large quantity traded is due to the fact that the related company is currently not behaving well and that high volumes are due to people disinvesting, this will lead to good levels for the selected liquidity risk indicators while the trading price will probably be affected at some point.

3.5.4.2. Bid-ask spread

When talking about bonds, the ratio previously described will no longer be applicable. Bonds are generally traded OTC, meaning that the information related to the quantity traded will not be as available as it is for equities. Therefore another indicator will need to be used.

It is quite common to see the bid-ask spread[75] used to assess the liquidity of bonds. The wider the bid-ask, the higher be the liquidity risk will be as this would mean that market makers and, more globally, buyers are considering that by buying that security they are taking a risk of not being able to sell it on the market for a good price.

Even though this approach seems to be relevant and adequate, it suffers from some drawbacks. First, market information could be difficult to gather. Second, what does a wide bid-ask mean exactly? Is 1% high or do we have to consider higher levels?

3.5.4.3. Liquidity VaR

Compared to the VaR that has been previously described, the VaR level is adjusted by the bid-ask spread here. The formula that is commonly used is:

$$LVaR = VaR + \left(\frac{1}{2}\right)(bid - ask\ spread)$$

Therefore, the liquidity VaR is an adjusted VaR. The main advantage of this is the interpretation, as the LVaR will be the maximum loss that will impact the portfolio in a defined timeframe at a defined interval of confidence (e.g. LVaR $_{20d-95\%}$ = 5% means that 95% of time the maximum loss will be 5% in the coming 20 days). On the other hand, as it is an adjusted value of market risk it does not directly

---

74 E.g. The LRSK function on Bloomberg stations.
75 The difference in price between the highest price that a buyer is willing to pay for an asset and the lowest price at which a seller is willing to sell it.

give an assessment of the liquidity risk and, by being adjusted based on the bid-ask spread, it will suffer from the same drawbacks.

3.5.4.4. *Other liquidity risk indicators*

As seen earlier, the indicators that are commonly used suffer from some drawbacks; therefore, we need to go a step further if we want to properly assess the liquidity risk of the portfolio. We decided then to explore less well-known liquidity indicators:

– *Percentage of outstanding shares*: as for bonds, the average traded volumes are not available and the notional of the bond held in the portfolio can be compared to the total outstanding size giving information on the percentage of the total issue represented by the portfolio holdings. A high percentage suggests a low liquidity.

– *Stressed bid-ask*: volatility between the different bid-asks provided by the different contributors for one security. A high level suggests low liquidity.

– *Number of market-pricing providers*: having a high number of market-pricing providers suggests a high liquidity.

– *Kyle's lambda*: this indicator, based on Albert Kyle's research[76], can be used in a simple form. It represents the ratio between the stressed bid-ask spread and the volume exchanged. This indicator helps to account for bid-ask spreads related to significantly different traded volumes.

– *Credit ratings – LOT*[77]: Lesmond, Ogden and Trzcinka analyzed the link between liquidity and credit ratings. This indicator was calculated based on an analysis (by LOT) of 4,000 bonds, indicating a liquidity score for each credit rating.

– *Stale prices*: having prices of investments that remain unchanged for a consecutive period of time is also an indicator of a potential liquidity issue.

Having a broader set of indicators can be considered a good start when performing relevant liquidity risk analysis. However, it does not solve the key issues risk managers face when assessing their portfolio liquidity, which can be summarized as follows:

– how to interpret the results of each indicator;

– how to aggregate the liquidity levels within a balanced portfolio; and

– how to communicate computation results in an efficient way.

---

76 Kyle, Albert (November 1985), *Continuous Auctions and Insider Trading*.
77 Lesmond D., Ogden J., Trzcinka C., "A new estimate of transaction costs", *Review of Financial Studies*, vol. 12, pp. 1113-1141.

These points probably summarize the main practitioners' questions regarding liquidity when indicators have been identified and selected.

One way of addressing these is the use of relative measures to qualify instruments' liquidity levels. By being compared to a broad and representative set of results, each liquidity measure will then be considered as being high or low. They will probably better support analysis and decisions because the value of any of the indicators that have been described here will probably be difficult to interpret on an absolute basis. Furthermore, to have the broadest view of the liquidity level of an investment not one indicator but a set of indicators need to be used that will then be aggregated to give a composite liquidity score.

Creating a relative liquidity measure by comparing securities results (each indicator's value or a score aggregating the results of a selection of indicators) to a representative benchmark will allow the creation of a liquidity score based on a limited scale (e.g. a liquidity scale going from 1 to 5). This kind of approach will more than probably ease the communication as having a simple indicator (e.g. 1–5, with 5 being highly liquid) giving a quick idea of the liquidity of the instrument traded is easier to communicate than a bid-ask spread of 133 bps (basic points). Finally, a liquidity score based on a defined and common scale will also allow the aggregation of results by simply weighting the final scores of each instrument and summing them.

So, investments' liquidity levels will probably be more interpretable and easier to manage when defined on a relative basis compared to an absolute basis.

3.5.5. *Methods and techniques to measure and monitor liquidity risk (liability side)*

As described earlier, the regulator expects a strong focus on the liability side as redemption payments may trigger the sale of a portion of the securities held in a portfolio should the cash levels be too low. Determining the potential level of redemptions based on the information available and estimating the impact of different levels of stress will definitely be a strong tool for managing liquidity risk for investment funds. Furthermore, this is also a clear and defined expectation of the regulator in the context of UCITS IV[78].

---

78 Commission Directive 2010/43/EU of July 1, 2010 implementing Directive 2009/65/EC of the European Parliament and of the Council as regards organizational requirements, conflicts of interest, conduct of business, risk management and content of the agreement between a depositary and a management company, Chapter IV, section 2, Art. 40.3.

This can be a difficult challenge as a lot of investments in investment funds are done through nominee accounts leading to a serious lack of transparency about the investors. Therefore the country of origin and any other information that could potentially help the risk manager to carry out a deep analysis on potential redemptions will probably be difficult to gather.

Should that statement lead to the conclusion that nothing can be performed to determine the potential trends in future redemptions? We do not think so.

Risk managers and investment managers will be impacted by the net level of redemption rather than by the behavior fund investors could have on a separate basis. Therefore, past trends in subscriptions and redemptions could constitute a reliable basis on which to determine potential future trends in redemptions as well as defining plausible[79] and relevant stress tests.

A simple approach could be computing the average past levels of redemptions, identifying the maximum levels of redemptions that have happened in the past as well as the standard deviation of past subscriptions and redemptions. These two indicators will give an idea of the normal trend (average) of redemption as well as the level of deviation that could be expected. This approach could potentially be sufficient to meet the regulator's expectations. However, the information remains quite limited as results are expressed in numbers of shares and the link with the liquidity of the portfolio could be quite difficult to make.

More advanced methodologies could then be used to provide risk managers and board members with information that is easier to gather and offering clear link with the liquidity at portfolio level.

Typically, as we are looking at past trends (see Figure 3.15) a time series model can be used to model future trends based on past trends. By applying a time series analysis framework like the Box-Jenkins approach[80] to model past time series and then using the level of random errors of the time series model to define potential future stress scenarios plausible based on the analyzed past periods (see Figures 3.16 and 3.17).

---

79 I.e. unlikely to occur but not impossible. Committee of European Securities Regulator, 2010, Guidelines on Risk Measurement and the Calculation of global Exposure and Counterparty Risk for UCITS, CESR/10-788, explanatory text 62.
80 Régis Bourdonnais, Michel Terraza, *Analyse des Séries Temporelles – Applications à l'Économie et à la Gestion*, 3rd edition, Dunod, Chapter 3, Figure 7.2 2010.

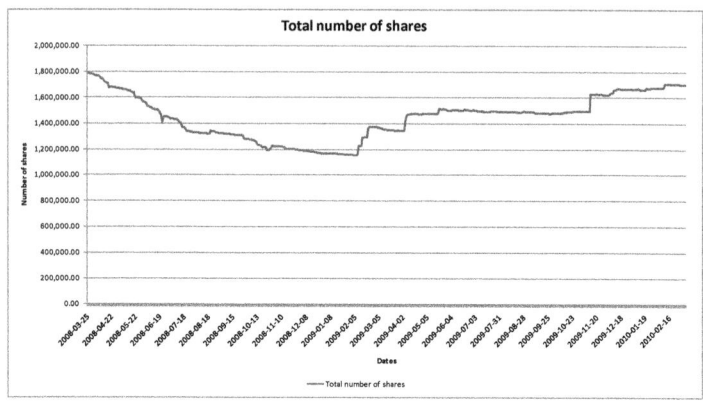

Figure 3.15. *Past trends of numbers of shares*

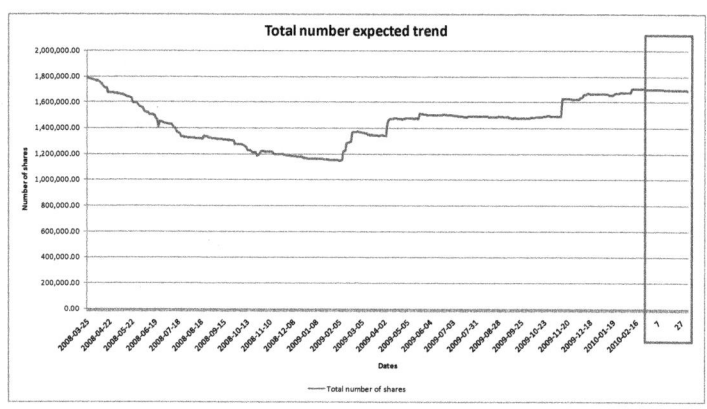

Figure 3.16. *Expected trend (average) for the next 30 days*

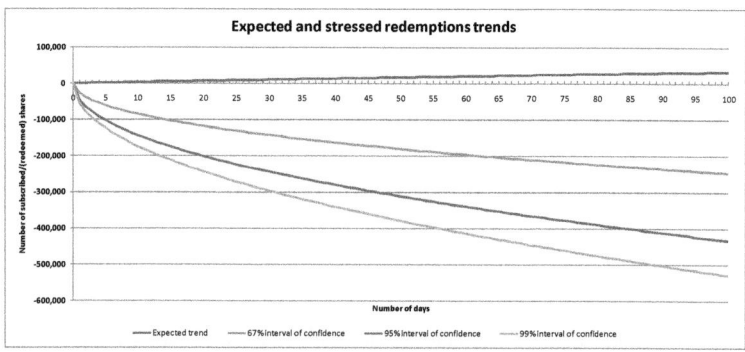

Figure 3.17. *Redemption scenarios using different level of stress*

The results taken from Figure 3.17 are potentially very useful for the end user as they give an assessment of levels of redemptions using different intervals of confidence for the coming days, giving a reasonable prospective approach with regards to potential future levels of redemptions.

This is not complete, however, and it potentially insufficient as trends in the number of shares do not give sufficient information to the report reader and do not give information allowing a clear link with the liquidity level of investments in a portfolio. As the asset manager will need to start selling securities when cash levels appear to be too low compared to the amount of redemption that needs to be repaid, replacing the number of shares by their equivalent value[81] will provide the opportunity to determine the number of days the fund will survive by to redemptions considering the amount of cash available, as shown in Figure 3.18.

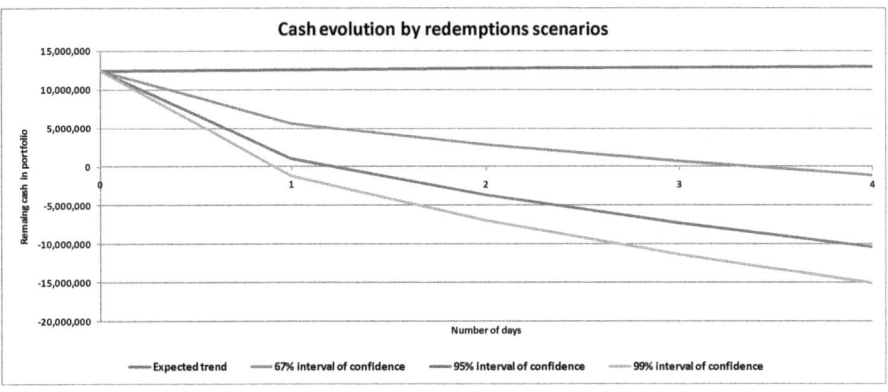

Figure 3.18. *Linking redemption scenario to cash – the number days to redemption payments using the cash available in the funds*

As the number of days before the fund runs out of cash will also give the asset manager a prospective view of how many days s/he would potentially have before being required to sell a portion of the fund's investments, that final step in the approach will link redemption trends with portfolio liquidity. To illustrate this concept, should a fund determine that the number of days before such a sale as being less than two of three, as long as portfolio investments are highly liquid, this will probably not be a concern for the asset manager. Should the investment's liquidity levels appear to be low, however, additional analysis and discussions will be

---

81 By multiplying the number of shares by the NAV per share.

required to determine how this would be managed and what cushions[82] should be determined to limit the potential impact of redemptions on portfolio management.

3.5.6. *Limiting redemptions*

UCITS funds are by definition open-ended. Therefore the opportunities for these funds to limit redemptions reducing their potential impact on portfolio management are not numerous.

We could consider adding a certain level of fees on redemption to try and limit the level and frequency of redemptions where the actual limits on redemptions will only be accepted on a case-by-case basis by the regulator (the same types of acceptance on limitations will apply to temporary suspension of NAV and side pockets).

3.6. Operational risk

3.6.1. *Definition*

Operational risk is defined as the risk of loss resulting from inadequate or failed internal processes, people and systems or from external events. This definition includes legal risk but excludes strategic and reputational risk[83].

Operational risk therefore appears to be much broader in terms of scope compared to the other risks that have already been covered.

3.6.2. *Regulator expectations*

In the context of UCITS funds, the regulator expects to assess UCITS exposure to all material risks. This includes all the risks covered earlier in this chapter dedicated to risk management, but also operational risk[84].

---

82 E.g. increasing cash levels, rebalancing of average portfolio liquidity levels by investing in more liquid instruments, etc.

83 *Basel II: International Convergence of Capital Measurement and Capital Standards: A Revised Framework*, Part 2, Chapter V.A.

84 A set of high-level principles must be met in order to be considered in the counterparty risk computation. Committee of European Securities Regulator, 2010, Guidelines on Risk Measurement and the Calculation of Global Exposure and Counterparty Risk for UCITS, CESR/10-788, explanatory text 1.

Despite this, and as was the case for liquidity risk, the regulator has not provided any recommendations or guidelines regarding operational risk. Therefore, each risk management team will have to properly identify the operational risks to which they are exposed and their potential impacts on the UCITS and their investors.

3.6.3. *How to approach operational risk for UCITS*

UCITS management compagny's (Manco) are in charge of the following functions:

– investment management;

– marketing and distribution;

– legal services;

– fund accounting;

– portfolio evaluation;

– NAV calculation;

– sale and redemption of units/shares;

– client administration; and

– compliance (including risk management).

All of these functions could potentially generate operational risks that could impact the UCITS and its investors. As an example, a mistake in the NAV computation will directly impact the investors and more specifically those who will redeem with a wrong NAV.

All of the processes therefore need to be analyzed and all of the risks that are identified will need to be reviewed to put the potential impact they could have on the fund investors into perspective.

3.6.3.1. *Main types of operational risk*

Operational risk can be split into four main categories:

– failed internal process;

– people (risks linked to human errors and fraud);

– systems (IT issue and potentially related impacts); and

– external events.

For all of these types of operational risk we have both high frequency low severity (HFLS) events. These are well known but their impacts are not material.

We also have low frequency high severity (LFHS) events, which are the most challenging to identify but also those that need to be avoided as much as possible.

3.6.3.2. *Main approaches to measure operational risk*

Two main approaches coexist:

– the "top-down" approach where the analyses are based on a macro view (like the history of past events and their related impacts); and,

– the "Bottom-up" approach where analyses are based on a very detailed view of the individual processes.

In the context of investment funds, even though the "top-down" approach could appear to be more attractive from a technical standpoint (e.g. computing an operational VaR), the "bottom-up" approach (which could be really time consuming) appears to be better adapted.

The reason for this is that, with some of the issues that can potentially impact the wealth of the investors, a lot of the operational responsibilities of the Manco are delegated to other entities. More importantly, investors benefit from a certain level of protection imposed by the regulator (more specifically for NAV errors and where investment policy and/or UCITS law are not respected).

Therefore, instead of going for detailed and intense computation, it will probably be more relevant to identify all the risk areas and ensure that they will not have material impact on the investor.

A first step would be to document the different processes by using the flowchart approach allowing the clear identification of potential risk areas (see Figure 3.19).

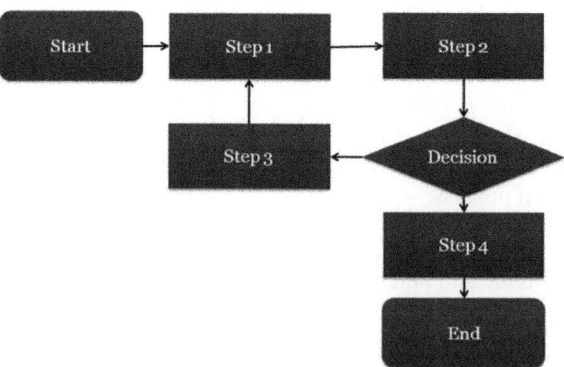

Figure 3.19. *Process flowchart example*

Then, in a second step, the different risks identified will need to be qualified using a likelihood/impact approach (taking into account controls already put in place). By using a matrix approach as illustrated in Figure 3.20, locating the different risks (adjusted by the related controls) will allow risk managers to define the key focus areas in terms of operational risk. This approach will allow time to be spent on areas that require it.

LIKELIHOOOD	IMPACT			
Very probable 0.85	8 500 €	51 000 €	127 500 €	1 275 000€
Probable 0.50	5 000 €	30 000 €	75 000 €	750 000€
Possible 0.20	2 000 €	12 000 €	30 000 €	300 000 €
Nearly impossible 0.05	500 €	3 000 €	7 500 €	75 000 €
	Very low	Low	High	Very high
FINANCIAL	[0€ - 20K€] 10 K€	[20 K€ - 100K€] 60 K€	[100K€ - 200K€] 150 K€	[> 200K€] 1 500 K€

Figure 3.20. *Example of a likelihood/impact matrix*

3.6.3.3. *Operational risk within an UCITS environment*

The main areas of risk from an operational standpoint include the NAV calculation, the portfolio valuation, sales and redemptions of units. These responsibilities of the Manco are often outsourced to other entities (within or outside the group). The Manco will therefore have the opportunity to first rely on the results of the controls that are performed (e.g. internal audit results, controls reports issued by third parties, etc.) and, more than probably, in the case of errors, the final investor will be reimbursed for the impacts it had. Furthermore, with NAV computation, issues will probably be identified by auditors. Controls in place will identify the issue and, depending on local regulation and the supervisor, specific impact analysis and reporting will need to be considered[85]. Based on this description, we can say that

---

85 As an example, the reader can refer to CSSF Circular 02/77 for Luxembourg.

even though operational risk will need to be carefully monitored, the main risks have probably already been identified and covered. Regarding the potential impact on the investor, by taking into account the potential impact of problems relating to reputation compared to the cost of reimbursing investors due to errors, the final impact on investors is expected to be quite limited.

As data management is quite intensive within the asset management industry, issues with an IT system could potentially be very high. The adequate disaster recovery plan and business continuity plan should, however, have already been put in place and tested to ensure the continuity and safety of operations, even in stressed conditions (including external events).

Based on what has been discussed in the context of UCITS funds, a lot of controls are already in place. This enables a basic but sound analysis of operational risk exposure by listing all the risks identified and the related responses for the limitation of such risks. Although this could be time-consuming, this is currently deemed as worth being adopted and relevant.

3.7. Internal risk limits

The regulator clearly expects to see internal limits set regarding risk management[86]. As risk management is not there to predict the future but more to ensure that it will happen, setting internal limits that trigger additional analysis and decisions before things go a step too far is key.

Therefore, on top of regulatory limits, internal limits adapted to the fund's risk profile as well as to board and management expectations are more than recommended – they are essential.

3.8. Disclosure

With UCITS IV, some risk information is now required to be given to investors through the prospectus and financial statements[87].

---

86 A set of high-level principles must be met in order to be considered in the counterparty risk computation. Committee of European Securities Regulator, 2010, Guidelines on Risk Measurement and the Calculation of Global Exposure and Counterparty Risk for UCITS, CESR/10-788, explanatory text 40.

87 A set of high-level principles must be met in order to be considered in the counterparty risk computation. Committee of European Securities Regulator, CESR's Guidelines on Risk Measurement and the Calculation of Global Exposure and Counterparty Risk for UCITS, CESR/10-788, Boxes 24 and 25.

For the prospectus, it is required to publish the following information:

– the method used to compute global exposure (i.e. the commitment approach, VaR or relative VaR);

– for funds using the VaR approach: the level of leverage expected; and

– for funds using a relative VaR approach: information on the reference portfolio must be disclosed.

For financial statements, the requirements are approximately the same, except that for the funds using VaR, the utilization level of the VaR limits will need to be disclosed (including at least the lowest, highest and average levels), as well as the actual average level of leverage for the past period.

Chapter 4

Counterparty, Issuer and Concentration Risk Management for UCITS funds

4.1. Introduction: no institution is "too big to fail"

4.1.1. *Background and definitions*

Many articles and books have been written about the causes of the recent (credit) crisis that started in 2007 in an effort to genuinely draw from the lessons that needed to be learnt or even relearnt in some instances (rehypothecation and quality of collateral, underestimation of exposure, miscalculation of default probability and wrong-way risk) as much as finding someone to blame[1]. From a counterparty risk standpoint, the main lesson that needed to be learnt was that there is no such institution in the world that is "too big to fail". The bankruptcy of Lehman Brothers, the sudden and in extremis acquisition of Bear Stearns and Merrill Lynch by JP Morgan and Bank of America, respectively, and the government bailouts of the Royal Bank of Scotland, AIG, Fannie Mae and Freddie Mac will forever remind us of that very fact! A second lesson would be that a AAA rating (Triple A) is not a guarantee that an institution bearing this rating encompasses no counterparty risk at all. Doing business with such an institution is indeed not risk free. Finally, like other risk types (market, credit, etc.), one can mitigate counterparty risk but cannot fully remove it.

Chapter written by Romain BERRY.
1 Sir Howard Davies's book, *The Financial Crisis: Who is to Blame?* (Polity, 2010) lists an impressive number of plausible causes as there is still no consensus on who or what caused the recent crisis.

Counterparty risk is one of the oldest financial risks. It has existed since the first financial contract was written, and despite its obvious presence in most financial transactions it was widely underestimated until the recent credit crunch reminded us of our blunder. *Counterparty risk can be defined as the risk that an organization does not pay out on a derivative trade or transaction when it is supposed to.* Some may claim that counterparty risk does not relate to exchange-traded instruments as it is the role of a clearing house to guarantee every participant of the payments of their contracts. This statement only stands as long as you can believe that a clearing house is too big to fail... It is impressive and reassuring to some extent that the London Clearing House utilized only 35% of the margins it held against Lehman Brothers after it collapsed in September 2008; but considering the push from worldwide regulators towards central clearing, it is fair to say that systemic risk has increased as a result. There are still not enough clearing houses in the world to spread more efficiently the various risks attached to running such tangled operations. If any of these houses were to collapse, the consequences would be catastrophic.

Counterparty risk can obviously be bilateral (swaps, forwards, etc.). For example, if a UCITS fund buys an equity put option on the over-the-counter (OTC) market and markets were to plunge as they have done in recent times, then the mark-to-market (MtM) value of the put option will increase sharply, introducing significant counterparty risk to the fund. Similar risks exist in swaps, swaptions and inflation-linked swaps. Counterparty risk differs from credit risk due to the uncertainty of the exposure that is determined by market movements. The magnitude of this risk is measured by *counterparty credit exposure*. Counterparty credit exposure represents the cost of replacing a transaction or a set of transactions with a counterparty if that counterparty defaults (today or in the future) under the assumption of no recovery. Even if intertwined, it is important to dissociate the two concepts of counterparty risk and counterparty exposure. In other words, exposure is conditional on counterparty default.

Counterparty risk was inappropriately measured, monitored and managed in most financial institutions before the subprime meltdown. We elusively relied on external parties to carry out the analysis (credit rating agencies [CRAs], research analysts, media, regulators, governments, etc.). The UCITS regulations on counterparty risk deal with measuring and mitigating it (mainly through credit limits, netting and legal agreements, collateral, and hedging). After listing these rules and potential exceptions, we offer some more advanced techniques to improve the counterparty risk management of a UCITS fund beyond the sufficient compliance with the UCITS rules.

Issuer risk belongs to the universe of credit risks but differs from counterparty risk in the sense that it is the risk that the issuer (or borrower) of securities defaults and is not able to fulfill its obligation (generally making payments on coupons, dividends, etc.). Simply put, it is a probability of loss resulting from the issuer of a security defaulting. It is generally included in measuring *market risk* (more or less implicitly within a bond and CDS price, for instance) and/or credit risk (through PD, EAD, LGD estimates at a fund's level[2]). UCITS regulations mainly imposed limits to manage issuer risk. After describing the rules that apply to managing issuer risk in a UCITS fund, we dissociate between corporate and sovereign issuer risk and highlight the importance of stress testing in managing it.

Concentration risk is the risk of loss due to an adverse movement in the mark-to-market value of a large exposure to a counterparty or product, industry or country proportional to the fund's overall assets. Similarly to issuer risk, UCITS regulations impose concentration limits but do not account for the correlations between the various exposures. It is therefore a qualitative rather than a quantitative risk metric. Alternatively, the Basel Committee on Banking Supervision defines a risk concentration as "any single exposure or group of exposures with the potential to produce losses large enough (relative to a bank's capital, total assets, or overall risk level) to threaten a bank's health or ability to maintain its core operations. Risk concentrations (or abrupt changes in concentrations) are arguably the single most important cause of major problems in banks"[3]. The main challenging issue with managing concentration risk effectively lies in how one can monitor stochastic risk exposures with deterministic limits as set in UCITS regulations. We offer some ways to measure and manage concentration risk at the end of this chapter.

---

2 These concepts are not mentioned in UCITS regulations but are widely used in the risk management community when dealing with credit risk. For instance the Basel Committee on Banking Supervision defines them as follows:

– *probability of default* (PD) is the likelihood of a default over a particular time horizon. It provides an estimate of the likelihood that a client of a financial institution will be unable to meet its debt obligations. The PD is an estimate of the likelihood that the default event will occur over a fixed assessment horizon, usually taken to be one year. The PD can be estimated for a particular obligor that is the usual practice in wholesale banking, or for a segment of obligors sharing similar credit risk characteristics, which is the usual practice in retail banking.

– *exposure at default* (EAD) can be defined as the gross exposure under a facility upon default of an obligor. In general, EAD can be seen as an estimation of the extent to which a bank may be exposed to a counterparty in the event of, and at the time of, that counterparty's default. EAD is equal to the current amount outstanding in case of fixed exposures like term loans.

– *loss given default* (LGD) is the credit loss incurred if an obligor defaults. LGD is facility-specific because such losses are generally understood to be influenced by key transaction characteristics, such as the presence of collateral and the degree of subordination.

3 Basel Committee on Banking Supervision, *International Convergence of Capital Measurement and Capital Standards*, paragraph 770, page 214, June 2006

4.1.2. *Managing counterparty risk within a UCITS framework*

As has been described in Chapter 1, the legal framework for UCITS funds is composed of European and national legislative texts. European legislation is itself formed of three levels: level 1 directives, level 2 regulations and level 2 directives. Level 1 directives, such as Directive 2009/65/EC (referred to as UCITS IV in this chapter), provide a legal framework for UCITS funds. Level 2 regulations are legislative texts that are directly applicable into law. Finally, level 2 directives have to be transposed into national law. National legislations translate the European legislative texts into national law.

Among this profusion of legislative documents, very few actually pertain to counterparty, issuer and concentration risk. They are:

– *Directive 2009/65/EC* commonly called the UCITS IV Directive sets guidelines on the coordination of laws, regulations and administrative provisions relating to UCITS. This text is actually a recast of the UCITS Directive 85/611/ECC that was repealed with effect from July 1, 2011.

– *Commission Directive 2010/43/EU* of July 1, 2010 implements the UCITS IV Directive produced by the European Parliament and Council. This Directive provides rules on organizational requirements, conflicts of interest, conduct of business, risk management and content of the agreement between a depositary and a management company.

– the *Law of 17 December 2010* implements UCITS IV Directive into Luxembourg Law.

– *CSSF Regulation 10-04* transposes Commission Directive 2010/43/EU into Luxembourg Law.

– *CSSF Circular 11/512* presents the main regulatory changes in risk management following the publication of CSSF Regulation 10-04 and ESMA clarifications, mainly bringing further clarification from the CSSF on risk management rules and defining the content and format of the risk management process to be communicated to the CSSF.

– *CSSF Circular 07/308* regulates the risk management of a UCITS but was replaced by CSSF Circular 11/512.

We will refer to these texts in this chapter to define and calculate counterparty risk for a UCITS fund.

4.2. Measuring counterparty risk for a UCITS fund

As defined in Article 3 of the Commission Directive 2010/43/EU, *counterparty risk means the risk of loss for the UCITS resulting from the fact that the counterparty to a transaction may default on its obligations prior to the final settlement of the transaction's cash flow.*

Article 43 of the Commission Directive 2010/43/EU stated that:

> 2. When *calculating the UCITS exposure to a counterparty* in accordance with the limits as referred to in Article 52(1) of Directive 2009/65/EC, management companies shall use the *positive mark-to-market value of the OTC derivative contract with that counterparty.*[4]

Paragraph III.5.1 on *OTC financial derivative instruments* of CSSF Circular 11/512 further clarified that the consideration of potential future credit risk (using add-on factors) and of the weighting factor depending on the credit quality of the counterparty (typically 20% or 50%) is no longer permitted[5]. This is an important change from UCITS III.

The CESR/10-108 paper mentioned that:

> The following exposure must also be calculated within the OTC counterparty limits specified in Article 52(1):
>
> − Any exposure with a central clearing house whereby exposure with the OTC counterparty is novated to the clearing house. In this case the risk exposure is with the clearing house and not the OTC counterparty.
>
> − Initial and variation margin posted to a broker for the use of exchange-traded derivatives which is not protected by client money or other similar arrangements to protect the UCITS against the insolvency of the broker.
>
> − Any net exposure to a counterparty generated though a stock-lending or repurchase agreement, net exposure being understood as the amount receivable by the UCITS less any collateral provided to the UCITS custodian. Exposures created through the reinvestment of

---

4 OTC derivative transactions with negative mark-to-market values do not attract counterparty risk to a UCITS fund since these amounts represent what its counterparty should claim against the fund. They lie in the counterparty risk of the counterparty that deals with the UCITS fund.
5 Like it was previously required by CSSF Circular 07/308 and European Directive 2000/12/EC.

collateral must also be taken into account in the issuer-concentration calculations.

Furthermore, when calculating the UCITS' exposure to a counterparty, management companies may focus on the net derivative positions, provided that they have the means to legally enforce *netting arrangements* with the counterparty on behalf of the UCITS and reduce exposure through the receipt of *collateral*.

4.3. Controlling and mitigating counterparty risk of a UCITS fund

Over the years, risk managers have developed a few tools to control and mitigate counterparty risk but none of them are perfect and they all have their pitfalls. A combination of tools is thus recommended by UCITS regulations, mainly limits, netting and collateral.

4.3.1. *Limits*

Determining and enforcing limits was probably the first way to manage risk in general as this basic concept can be applied to all risk types (maybe with the exception of operational risks where occurrence and impact are very much unpredictable). As the old adage says: *"do not put all your eggs in one basket"* because if you drop it, you will lose everything. The core idea behind fixing limits relates to a primary principle of financial theory: *diversification.*

Determining the maximum amount of exposure a UCITS fund should be prepared to take on with one single counterparty seems to make perfect common sense. Indeed, what can possibly be easier than deciding not to overexpose a fund to the same counterparty in order to limit the impact in the case it defaults? Here we have the issue of determining what too much exposure is. So the next task concerns the methodology by which to establish and maintain these limits. A UCITS fund could carry out an exhaustive due diligence analysis on the counterparty prior to an adequate limit but this best practice comes at a cost and it may require some time to gather enough relevant information, conduct interviews, scrutinize the legal terms of the agreement, etc. A fund can rely on external ratings from CRAs but even they appear to have done all the work for you, it may still be some time before they dare to make the difficult decision to downgrade a company. There is also the danger of receiving very favorable terms when negotiating an agreement. Counter-intuitively, this should raise red flags when a counterparty seems too eager to deal with you. Ultimately, paragraph IV.1.2., *Quality of the counterparty to OTC derivatives*, of CSSF Circular 11/512 provides some guidelines:

The counterparties to OTC derivative transactions shall be institutions subject to prudential supervision and belonging to the categories approved by the CSSF in accordance with Article 41(1)(g) of the 2010 Law (i.e. credit institutions, investment firms). Moreover, they shall be specialized in this type of transactions.

Interestingly, Lehman Brothers met these requirements before collapsing in September 2008. The credit limits a UCITS fund must respect are clearly stated in Article 52 of the UCITS IV Directive:

1. The risk exposure to a counterparty of the UCITS in an OTC derivative transaction shall not exceed either:

"(a) 10% of its assets when the counterparty is a credit institution referred to in Article 50(1)(f); or

"(b) 5% of its assets, in other cases.

The UCITS IV Directive then introduced some exception rules to the aforementioned limits:

2. Member States may raise the 5% limit laid down in the first subparagraph of paragraph 1 to a maximum of 10%. If they do so, however, the total value of the transferable securities and the money market instruments held by the UCITS in the issuing bodies in each of which it invests more than 5% of its assets shall not exceed 40% of the value of its assets. That limitation shall not apply to deposits or OTC derivative transactions made with financial institutions subject to prudential supervision.

Notwithstanding the individual limits laid down in paragraph 1, a UCITS shall not combine any of the following where this would lead to the investment of more than 20% of its assets in a single body:

(a) investments in transferable securities or money market instruments issued by that body;

(b) deposits made with that body; or

(c) exposures arising from OTC derivative transactions undertaken with that body.

3. Member States may raise the 5% limit laid down in the first subparagraph of paragraph 1 to a maximum of 35% if the transferable securities or money market instruments are issued or guaranteed by a Member State, by its local authorities, by a third country or by a public international body to which one or more Member States belong."

4. Member States may raise the 5% limit laid down in the first subparagraph of paragraph 1 to a maximum of 25% where bonds are issued by a credit institution which has its registered office in a Member State and is subject by law to special public supervision designed to protect bond-holders. In particular, sums deriving from the issue of those bonds shall be invested in accordance with the law in assets which, during the whole period of validity of the bonds, are capable of covering claims attaching to the bonds and which, in the event of failure of the issuer, would be used on a priority basis for the reimbursement of the principal and payment of the accrued interest.

Where a UCITS invests more than 5% of its assets in the bonds referred to in the first subparagraph which are issued by a single issuer, the total value of these investments shall not exceed 80% of the value of the assets of the UCITS.

Member States shall send to the European Commission a list of the categories of bonds referred to in the first subparagraph together with the categories of issuers authorised, in accordance with the laws and supervisory arrangements mentioned in that subparagraph, to issue bonds complying with the criteria set out in this Article. A notice specifying the status of the guarantees offered shall be attached to those lists. The European Commission shall immediately forward that information to the other Member States together with any comments which it considers appropriate and shall make the information available to the public. Such communications may be the subject of exchanges of views within the European Securities Committee referred to in Article 112(1).

5. The transferable securities and money market instruments referred to in paragraphs 3 and 4 shall not be taken into account for the purpose of applying the limit of 40 % referred to in paragraph 2.

The limits provided for in paragraphs 1 to 4 shall not be combined, and thus investments in transferable securities or money market instruments issued by the same body or in deposits or derivative instruments made with this body carried out in accordance with paragraphs 1 to 4 shall not exceed in total 35 % of the assets of the UCITS.

Companies which are included in the same group for the purposes of consolidated accounts, as defined in Directive 83/349/EEC or in accordance with recognised international accounting rules, shall be regarded as a single body for the purpose of calculating the limits contained in this Article.

Member States may allow cumulative investment in transferable securities and money market instruments within the same group up to a limit of 20 %.

Paragraph III.5.1. *OTC financial derivative instruments and Paragraph III.5.2. Securities lending and reverse repurchase agreement transactions/repurchase agreement transactions* of CSSF – 11/512 paper further added that:

Exposure in relation to the initial margins posted by UCITS to a broker and with variation margins to be received by UCITS from the broker within the context of financial derivative instruments dealt in on a regulated market or OTC derivatives, shall be included within the limits of 10% and 5% respectively of the counterparty risk provided for in Article 43(1) of the 2010 Law if there are no arrangements that protect UCITS against the risk of insolvency of the relevant broker (point 1 of Box 27 of ESMA Guidelines 10-788).

"The net exposure of UCITS to counterparties in respect of securities lending or reverse repurchase agreement transactions/repurchase agreement transactions shall be taken into account within the limit of 20% provided for in Article 43(2) of the 2010 Law pursuant to point 2 of Box 27 of ESMA Guidelines 10-788.

Paragraph IV.3. *Counterparty risk associated with efficient portfolio management transactions* concluded that:

The net exposures (i.e. the exposures of the UCITS less the collateral received by the UCITS) to a counterparty arising from securities lending transactions or reverse repurchase/repurchase agreement transactions shall be taken into account in the 20% limit provided for in Article 43(2) of the 2010 Law pursuant to point 2 of Box 27 of ESMA Guidelines 10-788.

Consequently, the specific limits of 5%/10%, as indicated in CSSF Circular 08/356 are no longer applicable.

The last issue with enforcing limits relates to their monitoring and regular update. Again, it is easy to draw a graph similar to Figure 4.1 that matches the current risk exposure of a UCITS fund to its various counterparties with their assigned limit.

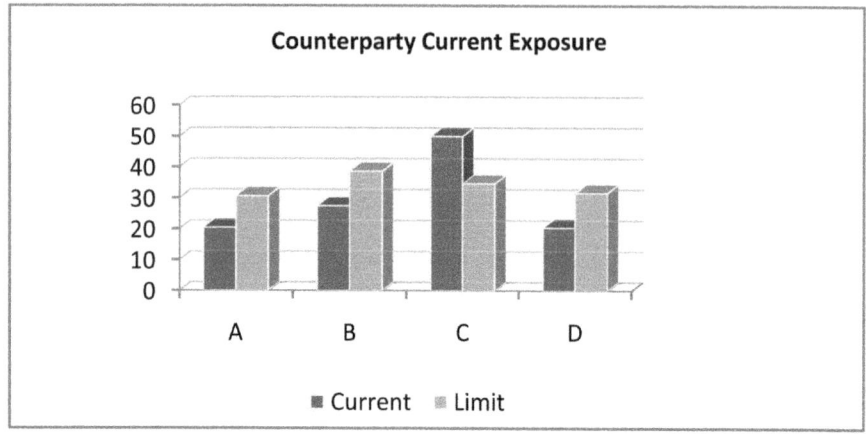

Figure 4.1. *Basic backward-looking illustration of the monitoring of credit limits across a few counterparties*

Updating these limits may seem to be a quick exercise, but since these limits may not change for a little while – as it may take time and money to update the original analysis that led to their initial determination – the same focus and rigor should be applied in moving them up or down on a periodic basis. It has not been sufficiently highlighted in risk management manuals that maintaining a close but independent tie with a UCITS fund's counterparties is also part of managing the risk of dealing with them. Let us remember that the trading fraud at Société Générale (which ultimately cost the bank €4.9bn) perpetuated by one of its junior traders, Jérôme Kerviel, was uncovered when an abnormally large counterparty risk was detected by a large bank that did not recognize the transactions booked against it.

Box 4.1. *Due diligence and pre-trade analysis*

Prior to the start of trading with a new counterparty, a UCITS fund should carry out a due diligence analysis on the counterparty and update its findings on at least a yearly basis.

Both qualitative and quantitative factors should be taken into account. Qualitative factors may include the counterparty's financial statements and annual reports, maturity profile of its debt, exception items, provisions, credit rating, quality of its assets (split and diversity), board and senior management, and operational processes. Quantitative factors can comprise CDS spread, share volatility and volume, profit trends, and equity growth.

In order to illustrate that credit rating should not be viewed as the single summary of the credit worthiness of a company, Figure 4.2 shows the CDS spreads of various banks prior to the collapse of Lehman Brothers. A CDS to protect against a credit event at Lehman Brothers had been traded at twice the amount of the average CDS on its competitors for over a year before it filed for bankruptcy.

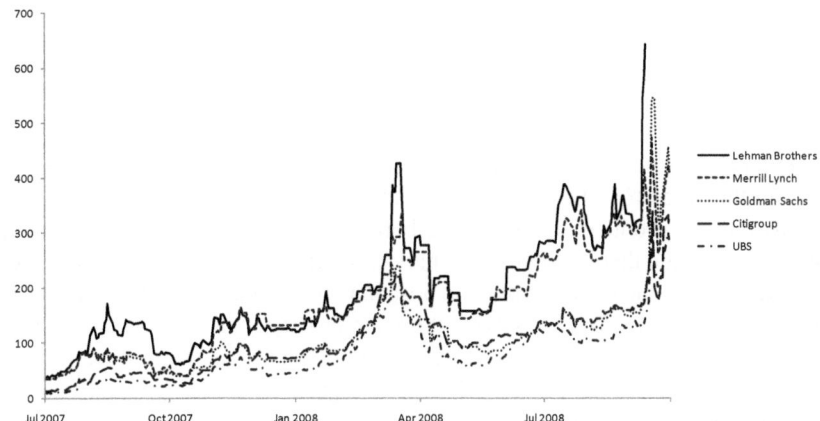

Figure 4.2. *CDS spreads in basis points of various banks prior to Lehman Brothers' collapse in September 2008*

Similarly, prior to placing a trade, a UCITS fund should also conduct a pre-trade analysis to assess what the impact of this trade or set of trades will be on the fund's overall risk profile. Market, counterparty, issuer, concentration and liquidity risks should be analyzed and the fund could also perform some stress testing to estimate the impact on the future performance of the fund.

The main problem with credit limits is that from a quantitative risk management perspective they are not easily comparable because potential future exposure (PFE) is generally calculated at different confidence levels to expected exposure (EE) and root mean square exposure (RMSE)[6]. The difference in the credit scoring of two counterparties is also generally a qualitative assessment with very few quantitative inputs. Finally, correlations between default across counterparties and between default and exposure are ignored.

---

6 As this is not a part of the UCITS regulation, it goes beyond the scope of this book to extensively describe how to calculate these three very important metrics in order to manage counterparty risk, but at a high level:

– PFE is the credit exposure at a given future date with a specified confidence interval (generally at least 95%);

– EE is the expectation credit exposure at a given future date; and

– RMSE measures the amount of volatility/error in calculating EE at a given future date. It is the square root of the expectation of exposure squared at a given future date.

Fortunately, there are other mitigants in the control of counterparty risk that are at a UCITS fund's disposal, namely *netting agreements* and *collateral*. Both have been well documented in the UCITS regulations, and CSSF Circulars 11/512 and 07/308 offered some helpful guidance.

4.3.2. *Netting*

Netting aims to set all of the trades a UCITS fund has with one single counterparty on a net basis as opposed to a gross amount so the fund manager knows (and can thus monitor) the current fund exposure to this counterparty. This method pertains only to products that can have both positive and negative mark-to-market values. Each trade that has a positive mark-to-market value would represent a claim the fund has with the counterparty and a trade with a negative mark-to-market value represents a debt the fund has with the counterparty. On a daily basis, the fund should consolidate all these trades and determine what is its current exposure is to each counterparty. By doing so with all of its counterparties, the fund manager is thus able to know exactly which counterparty it has the largest exposure to and ensure it respects paragraph 1 of Article 52 of the UCITS IV Directive which states that a UCITS fund shall invest no more than 5% of its assets in transferable securities or money market instruments issued by the same body. More importantly, in case of one of its counterparties defaulting, the fund manager will know the fund's exposure at risk.

In order to enter a netting agreement with a counterparty, a UCITS fund has to sign a legally-binding agreement with this counterparty that will allow some trades to be netted out. As always when signing an agreement, special care must be taken to review its entirety to ensure that there are no restrictive clauses, that it is appropriate to the strategy and the instruments traded by the fund and will protect the fund if the counterparty defaults. If a fund does not have an in-house legal counsel, it is generally recommended a law firm be used to review the document on behalf of the fund. Contract management is generally an aspect of risk management that is not sufficiently considered by risk managers but is one of the most efficient ways of mitigating risk prior to the start of trading. Netting agreements are generally bespoke contracts but it is usually feasible for a fund to add some netting language in its ISDA Credit Support Annex (CSA). Most brokerage firms can offer both options to a UCITS fund. A fund manager should be aware that a netting agreement generally provides privileged rights to the counterparty to the detriment of other fund creditors (such as shareholders or bondholders) in case the fund defaults. The fund manager should therefore ensure where it fits in the cascade in the case a counterparty defaults.

It is easy to see the benefits for a fund to enter a netting agreement. Let us assume that a fund has a set of trades with a given counterparty amounting to a total positive mark-to-market value of +€10 million and a set of trades with the same counterparty that have a negative mark-to-market value of -€5 million. Without a netting agreement, the UCITS fund has an exposure of +€10 million. If it has signed a netting contract, however, the fund now has a positive exposure to this counterparty of +€5 million. It has reduced its exposure by half. The counterparty has also reduced its exposure to the fund from +€5 million (the opposite side of the fund's negative position) to zero (since if the fund goes bankrupt, the counterparty will not have to pay for the +€5 million it owes the fund). Netting therefore genuinely benefits both parties and it is the reason why, in practice, a lot of netting agreements are bilateral.

The CESR/10-788 paper illustrates how the netting process works.

A UCITS portfolio contains:

– 10 DAX-listed shares X, whose combined market value is 100;

– a short position through futures on that same share X whose market value is -20;

– a long position through futures on the FTSE, with a market value of 30; and

– a short position through futures on the DAX with a market value of -10.

The commitment of each individual derivative is:

– derivative on share X: -20;

– derivative on the FTSE: 30; and

– derivative on DAX: -10.

Without any netting or hedging arrangement, the global exposure would be equal to the sum of the absolute values of each individual derivative commitment and would therefore be 60.

The combined long position and short position on share X constitutes a netting arrangement.

The gross commitment of that netting arrangement is -20. However, the position in shares X (100) can be offset against this -20. This leads to a net commitment of nil.

> Global exposure is equal to the sum of:
>
> – the absolute value of the commitment of the derivative on FTSE: 30;
>
> – the absolute value of the commitment of the derivative on DAX: 10; and
>
> – the absolute value of the net commitment of the netting arrangement: 0.
>
> It is not permitted to net the DAX short exposure against share X. Global exposure is thus equal to 40.

It is also possible for a UCITS fund to run some simulations on the future values of these trades in order to anticipate how its exposure to one counterparty could evolve. This would be very helpful to a fund that trades illiquid or very volatile instruments, not only to ensure it that it will not breach Article 52 of the UCITS IV Directive, but also to ensure that it can foresee what its exposure to a given counterparty will be in a few days/weeks/months/years.

In practice, a UCITS fund can trade with more than one legal entity of a given counterparty and therefore could enter into a multi-entity netting agreement that will enable the fund to net all of its trades with the same counterparty across various legal entities of the counterparty. These types of contract are more complex but could increase the benefits to the fund by expanding the number of asset classes (OTC derivative instruments) it can net with the same counterparty. A fund should be especially careful to ensure that the agreement will be fully enforceable in the jurisdiction it has been signed, despite the fact that trades have been booked with various legal entities that cover more than one jurisdiction.

The Commission Directive 2010/43/EU recalls that:

> Management companies may net the derivative positions of a UCITS with the same counterparty, provided that they are able to legally enforce netting agreements with the counterparty on behalf of the UCITS. Netting shall only be permissible with respect to OTC derivative instruments with the same counterparty and not in relation to any other exposures the UCITS may have with that same counterparty.

The CESR/10-788 paper offered additional guidance on the netting agreements and its implication in calculating global exposure as highlighted in the previous chapter.

Box 5

1. When calculating global exposure using the commitment approach, netting and hedging arrangements may be taken into account to reduce global exposure.

2. Netting arrangements are defined as combinations of trades on financial derivative instruments and/or security positions that refer to the same underlying asset, irrespective – in the case of financial derivative instruments – of the contracts' due date; and where the trades on financial derivative instruments and/or security positions are concluded with the sole aim of eliminating the risks linked to positions taken through other financial derivative instruments and/or security positions.

Box 6

A UCITS may net positions:

– between financial derivative instruments, provided they refer to the same underlying asset, even if the maturity date of the financial derivative instruments is different;

– between a financial derivative instrument (whose underlying asset is a transferable security, a money market instrument or a collective investment undertaking) and that same corresponding underlying asset;

– a UCITS that invests primarily in interest rate derivatives may make use of specific duration netting rules in order to take into account the correlation between the maturity segments of the interest rate curve.

Box 7. Duration-netting rules:

1. The duration-netting rules cannot be used if it would lead to an incorrect assessment of the risk profile of the UCITS. A UCITS using these netting rules should not include other sources of risk (e.g. volatility) in their interest rate strategy. Therefore, for example, interest rate arbitrage strategies may not apply these netting rules.

2. The use of these duration netting rules cannot generate any unjustified level of leverage through investment in short-term positions. Thus, for example, short-dated interest rate derivatives cannot be the main source of performance for a UCITS with medium duration if it makes use of this netting methodology.

3. A UCITS interest rate derivative should be converted into its equivalent underlying asset position according to the following methodology:

1. Allocate each interest rate financial derivative instrument to the appropriate range ('bucket') of the following maturity-based ladder:

Bucket	Maturity range
1	0 - 2 years
2	2 – 7 years
3	7 – 15 years
4	> 15 years

2. Calculate the equivalent underlying asset position of each interest rate derivative instrument as its duration divided by the target duration of the UCITS and multiplied by the market value of the underlying asset:

$$Equivalent\ underlying\ asset\ position = \frac{duration_{FDI}}{duration_{target}} \times MtM_{underlying}$$

where:

– $duration_{FDI}$ is the duration (sensitivity to interest rates) of the interest rate derivative instrument;

– $duration_{target}$ is in line with the investment strategy, the directional positions and with the expected level of risk at any time and will be regularized otherwise. It is also in line with the portfolio duration under normal market conditions.

– $MtM_{underlying}$ is the market value of the underlying asset.

3. Net the long and short equivalent underlying asset positions within each bucket. The amount of the former that is netted with the latter is the netted position for that bucket.

4. Net the amount of the remaining un-netted long (or short) position in the bucket (i) with the amount of the remaining short (long) position remaining in the bucket (i+1).

5. Net the amount of the un-netted long (or short) position in the bucket (i) with the amount of the remaining short (long) position remaining in the bucket (i+2).

6. Calculate the netted amount between the un-netted long and short positions of the two most remote buckets.

7. The UCITS calculates its total global exposure as the sum of:

(a) 0% of the netted position for each bucket;

(b) 40% of the netted positions between two adjoining buckets (i) and (i+1);

(c) 75% of the netted positions between two remote buckets separated by another one, meaning buckets (i) and (i+2);

(d) 100% of the netted positions between the two most remote buckets; and

(e) 100% of the remaining un-netted positions.

4. A UCITS making use of the duration netting rules, which are optional, can still make use of the hedging framework further to Box 8. However, only the interest rate derivatives that are not included in hedging arrangements can still make use of duration netting rules.

4.3.3. *Collateral management*

A UCITS fund can use collateralization to reduce its counterparty risk as it provides an additional layer of protection in case of a counterparty defaulting. *Collateralization is a risk reduction technique associated with derivatives transactions by providing the UCITS fund with some protection in the event of a default on a transaction because the fund (if it is the collateral receiver) would recourse to the collateral to make up for some or all of the loss suffered.* Collateralization has a few benefits for a UCITS fund:

– it acknowledges the difference in creditworthiness between parties;

– it may increase the number of investment opportunities due to reducing collateral required to pledge;

– it may translate into better transaction pricing by reducing the credit spread that the counterparty may charge the portfolio manager; and

– it removes the need to fund derivative receivables if the underlying derivative becomes an asset (i.e. has a positive net present value).

Let us assume that after netting a UCITS fund still has a large exposure that, as we have just seen, is a positive mark-to-market value of all of the trades it has with a given counterparty. In order to further reduce its exposure to this counterparty, the fund can ask the counterparty to post some collateral that represents a portion of the mark-to-market value of all its trades with the counterparty. If the counterparty defaults, the fund will seize the collateral to make up for the loss incurred. The amount of collateral is valued on a daily basis to reflect the changes in the netting arrangement. It may well happen that one day a fund may have to post some collateral only to see it returned the next day if its net exposure with this counterparty has become negative. In order to limit the recurrent operational burden, a minimum transfer amount (MTA) can be defined. Despite all of its benefits, collateralization can give rise to market (valuation of collateral) and operational risks (mainly legal and linked to the operational processes of valuing and transferring the collateral) that may require an adequate framework to be in place (systems, team, and policies).

Article 43 of the Commission Directive 2010/43/EU states that:

> 3. Member States may allow management companies to reduce the UCITS exposure to a counterparty of an OTC derivative transaction through the receipt of collateral. Collateral received shall be sufficiently liquid so that it can be sold quickly at a price that is close to its pre-sale valuation.

> 4. Member States shall require management companies to take collateral into account in calculating exposure to counterparty risk as referred to in Article 52(1) of Directive 2009/65/EC when the management company passes collateral to OTC counterparty on behalf of the UCITS. Collateral passed may be taken into account on a net basis only if the management company is able to legally enforce netting arrangements with this counterparty on behalf of the UCITS.

Paragraph III.5.1. *OTC financial derivative instruments* of the CSSF Circular 11/512 paper states that:

> Regarding collateral, ESMA Guidelines 10-788 only set out in Box 26 the general principles related thereto (e.g. in respect of liquidity, valuation and issuer credit rating).

Further, in Paragraph IV.2 on Limitation of the counterparty risk associated with OTC derivatives through the receipt of *collateral*, we can read that:

> The CSSF would like to clarify that the list referred to in Section II (b) ("Receipt of an appropriate guarantee") of CSSF Circular 08/356, which includes the types of collateral which are eligible for the purpose of limiting the counterparty risk linked to efficient portfolio management transactions also applies within OTC derivative transactions. Notwithstanding the above, the rules outlined in point 1 of Box 26 of ESMA Guidelines 10-788 shall also be complied with.

The CSSF would like to draw your attention to points 2 and 3 of Box 26, and in particular to the need to define and to apply appropriate and prudent discounts.

Moreover, collateral received by a UCITS, other than cash, cannot be sold, reinvested or pledged. Cash collateral can only be reinvested in risk-free assets which are eligible under the 2010 Law, i.e. eligible assets which do not provide a yield greater than the risk-free rate.

The CESR/10-788 paper also offers some additional guidelines about collateral management in paragraph 4:

1. Collateral may be used to reduce counterparty risk exposure provided it complies with the following set of high-level principles at all times:

- *Liquidity*: any collateral posted must be sufficiently liquid in order that it can be sold quickly at a robust price that is close to pre-sale valuation. Collateral should normally trade in a highly liquid marketplace with transparent pricing. Collateral with a short settlement cycles is preferable to long settlement cycles as assets can be converted into cash more quickly.

- *Valuation*: collateral must be capable of being valued on at least a daily basis and the possibility of "stale prices" should not be allowed. An inability to value collateral through independent means would clearly place the UCITS at risk, and this would also apply to "mark-to-model" valuations and assets that are thinly traded.

- *Issuer credit quality*: as collateral provides secondary recourse, the credit quality of the collateral issuer is important. This may involve the use of haircuts in the event of a less than "very high grade" credit rating. It should be reasonable to accept collateral on assets that exhibit higher price volatility once suitably conservative haircuts are in place.

- *Correlation*: *correlation* between the OTC counterparty and the collateral received must be avoided.

- *Collateral diversification* (asset concentration): there is an obvious risk if collateral is highly concentrated in one issue, sector or country.

- *Operational and legal risks*: collateral management is a highly complex activity. As such, the existence of appropriate systems, operational capabilities and legal expertise is critical.

- Collateral must be held by a third party custodian that is subject to prudential supervision, and that is either unrelated to the provider or is legally secured from the consequences of the failure of a related party.

- Collateral must be fully enforced by the UCITS at all times without reference to or approval from the counterparty.

- Non-cash collateral cannot be sold, re-invested or pledged.

- Cash collateral can only be invested in risk-free assets.

2. UCITS may disregard the counterparty risk on the condition that the value of the collateral, valued at market price and taking into account appropriate discounts, exceeds the value of the amount exposed to risk at any given time.

3. For the valuation of collateral presenting a significant risk of value fluctuation, a UCITS should apply prudent discount rates.

Finally, in paragraph 4.1 on *Collateral* the CESR/10-108 paper mentioned that:

82. It should be noted that collateral in the form of cash deposits in a currency other than the currency of exposure should also be the subject to an adjustment for currency mismatch.

4.3.4. *Hedging*

As risk cannot be fully removed, one of the first tools developed by risk managers was hedging. The CESR/10-788 paper defined hedging agreements as:

... combinations of trades on financial derivative instruments and/or security positions which do not necessarily refer to the same underlying asset and where the trades on financial derivative instruments and/or security positions are concluded with the sole aim of offsetting risks linked to positions taken through the other financial derivative instruments and/or security positions.

Without going over what was discussed in Chapter 3 again, the paper further clarified in Box 5 that:

4. If the UCITS uses a conservative calculation rather than an exact calculation of the commitment for each financial derivative instrument, hedging and netting arrangements cannot be taken into account to reduce commitment on the derivatives involved if it results in an underestimation of the global exposure.

Box 8

1. Hedging arrangements may only be taken into account when calculating global exposure if they offset the risks linked to some assets and, in particular, if they comply with all the criteria below:

(a) investment strategies that aim to generate a return should not be considered as hedging arrangements;

(b) there should be a verifiable reduction of risk at the UCITS level.

(c) the risks linked to financial derivative instruments, i.e., general and specific if any, should be offset;

(d) they should relate to the same asset class; and

(e) they should be efficient in stressed market conditions.

2. Notwithstanding the above criteria, financial derivative instruments used for currency hedging purposes (i.e. that do not add any incremental exposure, leverage and/or other market risks) may be netted when calculating the UCITS global exposure.

3. For the avoidance of doubt, no market neutral or long/short investment strategies will comply with all the criteria laid down above.

As we can see, these guidelines only pertain to market risk. What about counterparty risk – can/should it be hedged? The answer is "yes" but then the problem is how. Let us assume that a UCITS fund has an €10m net exposure with counterparty A that represents almost all of the 10% of the assets it is allowed to invest with counterparty A (A here is a credit institution referred to in Article 50(1)(f)). Clearly, the fund cannot increase its dealing with A without breaching the aforementioned limit, but if the UCITS can buy a CDS on counterparty A with a notional of €10m this should hedge the counterparty exposure to zero, thus enabling the UCITS to continue trading with counterparty A. Hedging counterparty risk with CDS comes at a cost that can depend on the maturity, the credit quality of the counterparty, etc. These terms must be weighted when deciding to hedge the full amount or a portion of it.

The main drawback of hedging credit exposure with CDS is that it will not hedge any future exposure to this counterparty. So if the net exposure decreases to substantially less than €10m, the fund would be paying for a level of hedge it no longer needs. Similarly, if its assets grow, its limit with counterparty A will grow proportionally. Therefore, €10m may not fully cover the net exposure with counterparty A at some points in time. One solution could be to terminate the CDS and enter a new one on a periodic basis to account for change in the credit exposure of the fund to counterparty A. Not only will this hedging strategy be expensive, however, but it will also always be sub-optimal as at some times the fund will be over-protected while at other times it will be under-protected. A more optimal solution would be for the fund to be able to hedge its future credit exposure to counterparty A instead of its current exposure[7]. Such instruments that enable this do exist; they are called *contingent credit default swaps* (CCDS). CCDS have the same features as CDS with the difference that the notional is not a fixed amount but rather the mark-to-market value of a specific transaction. The underlying transaction could be any product (including derivatives), since the terms of the contract can be tailored to the fund's needs. CCDS therefore seem to offer the perfect hedge to derivative instruments as they can protect the fund to any current and future credit exposure to a given counterparty. In practice, however, the hedge is not perfect because the fund now has some counterparty risk with the CCDS provider... Remember that most risks cannot be eliminated – they can only be mitigated. In this case, using CCDS would only make sense if the CCDS provider had a higher credit quality than counterparty A. A UCITS fund manager should also consider the correlation between counterparty A and the CCDS provider. A high correlation signals that the hedge will not be worthwhile if counterparty A was to default as this could trigger a default at the CCDS provider too.

4.3.5. *Early termination and other legal tools*

Another way to control counterparty risk lies in negotiating tight legal agreements with the fund's counterparties. Netting and collateral agreements form parts of a broader legal document, such as an ISDA or a more bespoke agreement that an UCITS fund could sign with its counterparties. Among the many clauses embedded in these agreements, a seemingly important clause addresses early termination in which the trigger, timeline, impact and execution should be well defined and negotiated. These break clauses allowed the fund to exit a relationship under certain conditions, and generally at pre-determined dates and at limited or no cost (transactions being executed at market rates). Such conditions may be that the counterparty's credit worthiness has deteriorated (measured by its credit rating, for instance) or that some readily-observable parameters like the counterparty CDS spread has widened from the CDS spread of a reference entity or has broken a fixed level beyond which the UCITS fund does not feel comfortable bearing the risk any longer. Break clauses are often bilateral so each party can exercise this type of *Bermudan option* in disguise.

An early termination clause is not as nuclear as a credit event wherein the counterparty is deemed to be in default (failing to meet its part of the agreement, such as meeting daily margin calls for instance) or is deemed to be in bankruptcy. Once the counterparty is in default, it is generally too late to avoid problems and

---

7 In section 4.5 we discover the necessity and means by which UCITS funds can measure and monitor future exposure.

there is a good chance that the fund will suffer some losses due to the counterparty default; therefore, including early termination clauses is an effective method to control counterparty risk.

In practice, though, we should point out that termination clauses are barely used. Break clauses are generally not exercised when they should have been to preserve a good relationship with the counterparty (another proof, if needed, that risk management must act independently of any business concern at times) and collateralization through the daily margin seems to offer a continuous framework that is more flexible and close to real time. Without the daily margining of collateral, the counterparty risk increases as the time window to terminate a transaction approaches. If an UCITS fund has signed a collateral agreement, however, its counterparty risk is monitored through the daily posting of collateral adjustments that reflect the evolution of the mark-to-market value of the collateral initially posted.

Besides exercising early termination clauses, a UCITS fund possesses other legal tools that can help it to manage counterparty risk. It can enter into a contract to segregate its initial margins (IM), variation margins (VM) or both via a custodian or fund administrator. A cap amount can also be agreed on IM or VM that can be either a fixed amount or calculated using some static or risk-adjusted rules that are replicable by both parties. A cap will limit the amount of IM or VM that can be collected by the fund's counterparties or that the fund would have to give to its counterparties. The UCITS fund should also feel comfortable with the dispute mechanism in the agreement and make sure there are clauses that clearly define the timeline, an additional external quote, penalties and the outcome of the analysis to avoid being considered in default, whereas it is only disputing the call.

Finally, a fund can determine the MTA to the level that feels comfortable with its counterparties. MTA is the amount of unsecured credit risk that two counterparties are willing to accept before a collateral demand will be made. If the difference between the mark-to-market and the actual value of the collateral is in excess of the MTA, extra collateral needs to be posted. MTA can be linked to a counterparty's credit rating or to other more responsive indicators of creditworthiness. Let us assume a UCITS fund (A) has entered into an OTC trade with counterparty B that requires IM posting. On a daily basis, they reconcile the VM (MtM of the collateral) which results in Figure 4.3.

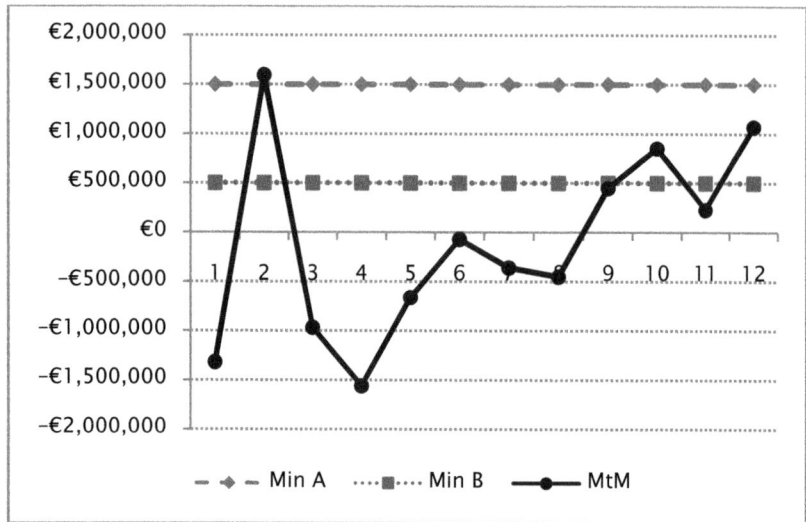

Figure 4.3. *Variation margin monitoring*

Min A is the MTA of the UCITS fund to counterparty B and is equal to €1.5m. Min B is the MTA of counterparty B to the UCITS fund and amounts to €0.5m. Therefore, Min A = 3 × Min B. In order to illustrate the importance of fixing reasonable MTA, let us discuss two instances:

– if a default occurs beyond Min A (as shown at time 2): both parties will be affected and will incur loss of the difference between the mark-to-market of the outstanding trades and the minimum transfer amount;

– if a default occurs between Min A and Min B (at times 10 and 12): only the UCITS fund will experience losses in the total amount of the MtM of the outstanding trades. Counterparty B incurs a loss of the difference between the MtM of the outstanding trades and Min B.

A UCITS fund can also decide to close out some trading positions with the counterparty, or initiate new trading positions that have the effect of reducing the risk. It can novate a contract, i.e. reassign the contract to a different counterparty. It can finally "book out" a trade if it finds that it has identical and offsetting trades to two different counterparties.

4.3.6. *Recouponing*

An alternative risk mitigation technique to collateralization consists of periodically adjusting the coupon of a trade or a set of trades so that the actual mark-to-market value is zero. Recouponing is particularly useful when there are some issues regarding the collateral eligibility or when a counterparty does not want to post an initial margin. The first issue has been addressed by UCITS regulations by listing criteria that must be met for the collateral of a fund to be received. So far, however, nothing obliges a counterparty not to post an initial margin to a UCITS fund. Therefore, recouponing could prove a viable option if it is well defined and monitored by the fund.

Let us look at an example to illustrate how recouponing works. Let us assume that a UCITS fund has bought a CDS on company X on September 3, 2012 with a three-year maturity and a 50 bps coupon.

Notional	Buy/sell	Maturity	Coupon	Restructuring	Cash flow
€100 m	Buy	September 2, 2015	250 bps	Modified	€2.5 m

We can convert this trade into two long CDSs with a 100 and 500 bps coupon each. In order to keep the same annual cash flow and net notional exposure and maintain the jump-to-default risk and DV01 identical, we can have the following two trades:

Notional	Buy/sell	Maturity	Coupon	Restructuring	Cash flow
€62.5 m	Buy	September 2, 2015	100 bps	No	€0.625 m
€37.5 m	Buy	September 2, 2015	500 bps	No	€1.875 m
€100 m	**Total**			**Total**	**€2.5 m**

The main benefits of recouponing for a UCITS fund are simplification and standardization. First, recouponing helps risk managers keep the complexity of managing CDS on different names or indices to a limited and more manageable number. A UCITS fund could have traded many CDS that have different coupons, maturity dates, durations, and convexity but may also contain different restructuring clauses, effective look-back credit event dates, roll dates and accrual periods. Recouponing some of its CDS into CDS with either 100 bps or 500 bps can harmonize the portfolio without incremental risk. Second, unwinding its CDS into more standardized fixed 100 bps and 500 bps terms increases the liquidity of the fund's basket of CDS.

Thus, reducing the number of CDSs an UCITS fund holds will actually contribute to managing counterparty risk (by reducing the number of counterparties it deals with[8]) but may give rise to a risk of credit concentration. In practice, recouponing generally comes at an extra spread cost and the UCITS fund should conduct a cost–benefit analysis before recouponing its CDS.

4.3.7. *Guarantees*

Guarantees are provided by counterparties with a higher credit rating than the original counterparty and offer the double advantage of decreasing the credit risk associated with the original counterparty, since the UCITS fund can have access to funds from a counterparty with a more remote probability of default and decreasing the risk of loss as both counterparties must be in default for the fund to experience a loss. The joint probability of both counterparties defaulting will be far less than the probability of the original probability of a default. This would not be as true if there was a significant correlation between the two counterparties, in which case this joint probability would be ignored as this sort of insurance would be deemed ineffective.

4.3.8. *Central counterparty clearing house*

Does counterparty risk arise only from OTC transactions? In other words, is it correct to presume that moving the uncleared trades of a UCITS fund to a clearing house will completely remove the counterparty risk attached to these trades? The answer is "no", because clearing houses do fail. This has been the case with the Caisse de Liquidation in Paris in 1974, the Kuala Lumpur Commodities Clearing House in 1983 and the Hong Kong Futures Exchange in 1987. A UCITS fund can reduce its market risk on a particular position by entering into an offsetting transaction. This will always give rise to counterparty risk, however, if the counterparty is different from the one the original trade was entered with. It is worth pointing out that Basel 3 requires clearing members to hold capital against both their exposure to central clearers and any residual exposure to cleared clients.

A further consequence of hedging away could lead to the fund having to post more collateral to the new counterparty that it would have if it had traded with the original counterparty (having a netting agreement in place). This illustrates the fact that multilateral netting is superior to bilateral netting. In a CCP (Central Counterparty) framework, the CCP will absorb the market risk as it holds both sides of the trade: with the fund and with the fund's counterparty. Ultimately, the fund will still bear the market risk of the position but it will have added some

---

8 As far as the fund respects the limits set in Article 52 of the UCITS Directive.

counterparty risk to the CCP itself. The fund now needs to monitor the credit quality of the CCP instead of the counterparty (as the counterparty may and does not need to be known through the CCP).

Trading through clearing houses may therefore seem to mitigate the counterparty risk of a UCITS fund. UCITS regulations do reward a UCITS fund that employs CCPs as stated in paragraph IV.1.1. of the CSSF Circular 11/512:

> The CSSF would like to clarify that OTC derivative transactions negotiated on a regulated market whose clearing house complies with the three following conditions may, in principle, be excluded from the calculation of the use of the counterparty risk limitations:
>
> – backing by an appropriate completion guarantee;
>
> – daily valuation of the market values of the positions on financial derivative instruments; and
>
> – making margin calls at least once a day.
>
> As already mentioned in Section III.5.1, exposure in relation to the initial margin posted by a UCITS to a broker, and the variation margin to be received by a UCITS from the broker relating to financial derivative instruments dealt in on a regulated market or OTC derivatives, shall be included in the counterparty risk limits of 10% and 5% respectively, as set out in Article 43(1) of the 2010 Law if there are no arrangements that protect UCITS against the insolvency risk of the relevant broker (point 1 of Box 27 of ESMA Guidelines 10-788).

4.4. Policy and corporate governance guidelines to monitor counterparty risk

As highlighted in the previous section, any due diligence to establish a relationship with a new counterparty should include a review of their corporate governance structure and their risk-management policies and procedures. However, a UCITS fund must also abide by a code of ethics and standards as set in Section 3 of Chapter II of the Commission Directive 2010/43/EU.

> Article 12 - Permanent risk management function
>
> a) implement the risk management policy and procedures;
>
> b) ensure compliance with the UCITS risk limit system, including statutory limits concerning global exposure and counterparty risk in accordance with Articles 41, 42 and 43;

c) provide advice to the board of directors as regards the identification of the risk profile of each managed UCITS;

d) provide regular reports to the board of directors and, where it exists, the supervisory function, on:

i. the consistency between the current levels of risk incurred by each managed UCITS and the risk profile agreed for that UCITS;

ii. the compliance of each managed UCITS with relevant risk limit systems;

iii. the adequacy and effectiveness of the risk management process, indicating in particular whether appropriate remedial measures have been taken in the event of any deficiencies;

e) provide regular reports to the senior management outlining the current level of risk incurred by each managed UCITS and any actual or foreseeable breaches to their limits, so as to ensure that prompt and appropriate action can be taken;

f) review and support, where appropriate, the arrangements and procedures for the valuation of OTC derivatives as referred to in Article 44.

Section 2 of Chapter VI of the same directive reinforced guidelines on measuring and managing risk.

Article 40 - Measurement and management of risk

1. Member States shall require management companies to adopt adequate and effective arrangements, processes and techniques in order to:

a) measure and manage at any time the risks which the UCITS they manage are or might be exposed to;

b) ensure compliance with limits concerning global exposure and counterparty risk, in accordance with Articles 41 and 43.

Those arrangements, processes and techniques shall be proportionate to the nature, scale and complexity of the business of the management companies and of the UCITS they manage and be consistent with the UCITS risk profile.

2. For the purposes of paragraph 1, Member States shall require management companies to take the following actions for each UCITS they manage:

a) put in place such risk measurement arrangements, processes and techniques as are necessary to ensure that the risks of taken positions and their contribution to the overall risk profile are accurately measured on the basis of sound and reliable data and that the risk measurement arrangements, processes and techniques are adequately documented;

b) conduct, where appropriate, periodic back-tests in order to review the validity of risk measurement arrangements which include model-based forecasts and estimates;

c) conduct, where appropriate, periodic stress tests and scenario analyses to address risks arising from potential changes in market conditions that might adversely impact the UCITS;

d) establish, implement and maintain a documented system of internal limits concerning the measures used to manage and control the relevant risks for each UCITS taking into account all risks which may be material to the UCITS as referred to in Article 38 and ensuring consistency with the UCITS risk-profile;

e) ensure that the current level of risk complies with the risk limit system as set out in point (d) for each UCITS;

f) establish, implement and maintain adequate procedures that, in the event of actual or anticipated breaches to the risk limit system of the UCITS, result in timely remedial actions in the best interests of unit-holders.

With regards to counterparty risk, the CSSF Circular 11/512 brought additional guidelines.

4. Determination and monitoring of the counterparty risk arising from OTC derivatives.

4.1. The counterparty risk management policy in respect of OTC derivatives shall be described.

4.2. The process for selecting counterparties (criteria, etc.) shall be described.

4.3. The method for calculating the counterparty risk shall be confirmed.

4.4. The policy in connection with mitigation techniques (netting, definition of eligible collateral, collateral management, discounts, monitoring of collateral, allocation of responsibilities with respect to management and monitoring of collateral, etc.) relating to the counterparty risk shall be described.

5. Determination and monitoring of the counterparty risk arising from techniques and instruments (efficient portfolio management).

5.1. The counterparty risk management policy in respect of techniques and instruments shall be described, in particular with reference to the provisions of Circular 08/356 and ESMA Guidelines.

5.2. The process for selecting counterparties (criteria, etc.) shall be described.

5.3. The policy in relation to the collateral (definition of eligible collateral, collateral management, discounts, monitoring of collateral, allocation of responsibilities with respect to management and monitoring of collateral, etc.) used for mitigating counterparty risk linked to these transactions shall be described.

4.5. Measuring future counterparty credit exposure

The UCITS regulations are probably the most restrictive and conservative regulations in the investment industry. This could explain the fact that the UCITS brand is one of the most respected. There are risk limits, required independent and daily valuation of OTC derivatives, a separation between investment management and risk management functions, periodic reporting to regulators and investors, etc. We may therefore think that risks in a UCITS vehicle are well under control – and rightly so – but as we saw earlier, risk can only be mitigated, not completely removed. In order to have no risk, we should not have taken any risk in the first place. This is a common issue for risk managers who generally intervene once a trade has been placed. As computers are becoming increasingly powerful, it should no longer be an issue of running simulations on the potential incremental risk a single trade may add to a portfolio. The UCITS regulations tried to acknowledge the need to carry out some pre-trade analysis, such as assessing the quality of the counterparty and its collateral, setting risk limits, ensuring the enforceability of netting agreements, etc., but these guidelines are rather qualitative and static. Marking-to-market OTC derivatives is an essential part of managing counterparty risk, but without some forward-looking tools the fund realize in sufficient time when one of its counterparties is about to default. For instance, there is no mention in these regulations of widely-accepted and measured concepts such as *expected exposure* (EE), *potential future exposure* (PFE) or *credit value adjustment* (CVA). Without delving too much into the details that an inquisitive reader can find in books dedicated to counterparty risk, this section intends to give the risk manager of a UCITS fund some basic knowledge to incorporate in the monitoring and mitigation of future exposure in his or her daily tasks.

4.5.1. *Definitions*

The (credit) exposure of a UCITS fund to a counterparty corresponds to the loss that the fund would incur if the counterparty were to default. As described in section 4.3.2, a UCITS fund owes money to its counterparty if the value of an OTC derivative is negative and is owed money if the mark-to-market value is positive. In most instances, a UCITS fund owes the mark-to-market value of the derivative contract to the counterparty even if it defaults. The key focus in monitoring and managing counterparty risk therefore relates to assessing the positive mark-to market value of the derivatives contracts, since this is the money it may never see again (depending on the recovery rate) if the counterparty defaults. We can thus define exposure as

$$\text{Exposure} = \text{Max (MtM, 0)}$$

where MtM represents the mark-to-market value of the OTC derivative contract.

Measuring exposure is crucial to quantify counterparty risk since only the cost of replacement is at risk in a derivative transaction, not the notional. This illustrates the fact that any static risk measure expressed as a small percentage of the notional of a derivative contract is not very helpful on its own and does not characterize the riskiness of the transaction at all. Measuring the exposure on a derivative contract should incorporate both the present and future mark-to-market value of the derivative contract. It is important to know what the current exposure is in case the counterparty were to default now, but it is even more useful to know what the exposure would be in the future before the counterparty defaults, as it would still be possible for the UCITS fund to take appropriate action to avoid or reduce this risk to a minimum. Exposure should therefore be seen as conditional on the counterparty defaulting. The fund should also estimate the probability of its counterparties defaulting at different points in time over the life of the trade. The concept of the PFE is an attempt to take account of the future value of the derivative contract. PFE is the credit exposure (or positive mark-to-market value) at a given future date with a specified confidence interval (generally at least 95%). In order to estimate the PFE, we need to simulate future (mark-to-model) values of the contract at different points in the future at a given confidence interval. Figure 4.4 illustrates the fact that PFE is deduced from running simulations on the future value of the derivative contract.

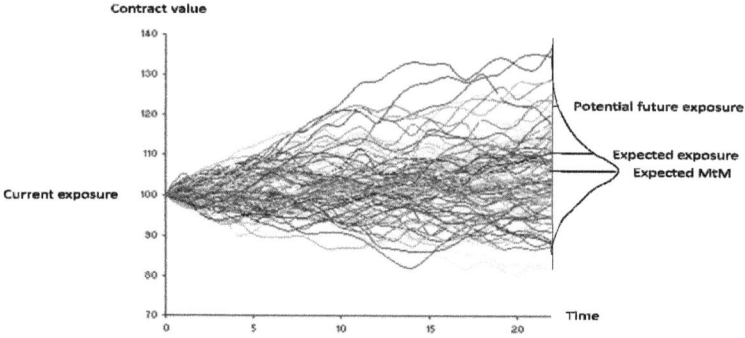

Figure 4.4. *Potential future exposure of a derivative contract*

Methodology to estimate future credit exposures using Monte Carlo simulations[9]:

– Step 1: *Determining the risk factors*: one can either run a *principal component analysis[10]* (PCA) or a multiple regression analysis on a set of fixed risk factors (such as spot prices, interest rates, FX rates, implied volatilities, etc.).

– Step 2: *Generating the scenarios*: once we have identified the risk factors, we need to run some simulations on their joint realizations at various points in time. We recommend running at least 5,000 simulations if not 10,000 in order to cover a wide set of possible future values and minimize tail events.

– Step 3: *Revaluing the positions*: at each point in time, we then revalue each trade using appropriate pricing models. This step is probably the most time-consuming. Let us assume that an UCITS fund trades with 20 counterparties, has on average 30 trades with each counterparty over a one-year (250-day) period and runs 10,000 simulations. In order to determine its future credit exposure at the fund level (and assuming a fixed long-term correlation matrix among all of these products), the

---

9 Despite their complexity and time consumption, Monte Carlo simulations are to be favored over MtM + add-ons or semi-analytical methods when estimating future credit exposure because they take account of path dependency patterns in the asset prices, correlations, netting and collateral in a more efficient and automated way. This methodology is rather similar to running a Monte Carlo value-at-risk on the fund.
10 Principal component analysis (PCA) is a statistical method that converts variables (possibly correlated) into new uncorrelated variables, called principal components. It enables the practitioner to reduce the amount of information to a more manageable set of values. This approach represents the original variables in a new geometrical space according to their maximum distance to inertia and searches for independent axes that best explain the dataset's variance.

risk manager of this fund will have to run $20 \times 30 \times 250 \times 10{,}000 = 1.5$ billion simulations in total!

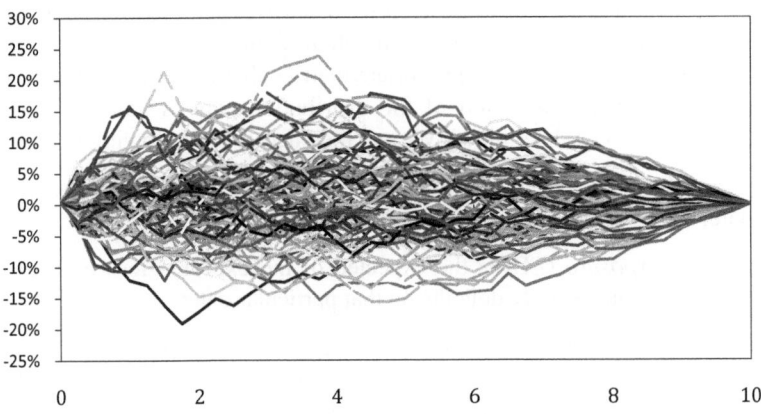

Figure 4.5. *Simulations of the future values of a financial product*

– Step 4: *Aggregating the positions and reading the future credit exposure*: after revaluing each transaction, we need to incorporate any correlations (ideally through copulas) and reflect netting and collateral agreements before reading the fund's future credit exposure at a high confidence level (95% or 99%).

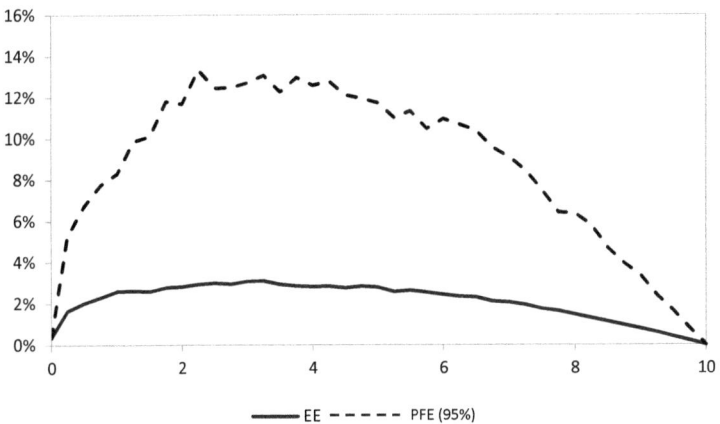

Figure 4.6. *The EE and PFE of a financial product*

At maturity, for instance, we can attempt to characterize the PFE with some probability distribution functions as shown in Figure 4.4. We can see from this figure that the exposure (positive mark-to-market value) of this trade is the area above 100 (assuming the current exposure of 100 represents the situation where the trade has a profit and loss of 0). Therefore, quantifying the future credit exposure will require the probability distribution function of the PFE to be characterized at some future dates and the most appropriate metrics that could be deduced, such as the mean and standard deviation of the distribution and its value at some high confidence levels, to be determined. We can then derive the following terms:

– *expected mark-to-market* (EMtM) is the expected value of a transaction at a future date;

– *expected exposure* (EE) is the expected of the expected loss on a trade at a future date if the counterparty defaults on that particular date;

– *potential future exposure* (PFE) is the credit exposure of a derivative contract at a given future date with a specified confidence interval. We note that PFE seems very similar to value-at-risk (VaR) but differs in the fact that market VaRs are estimated over shorter time horizons (generally daily, weekly or twice-monthly) while PFE is estimated at different points in time until maturity (up to 30 years). Also unlike VaR that represents an estimated loss, the PFE represents an estimated gain (positive MtM of the derivative contract thus in favor of the fund);

– *expected positive exposure* (EPE) is the average EE through time and could represent the future exposure of a derivative trade with a single number.

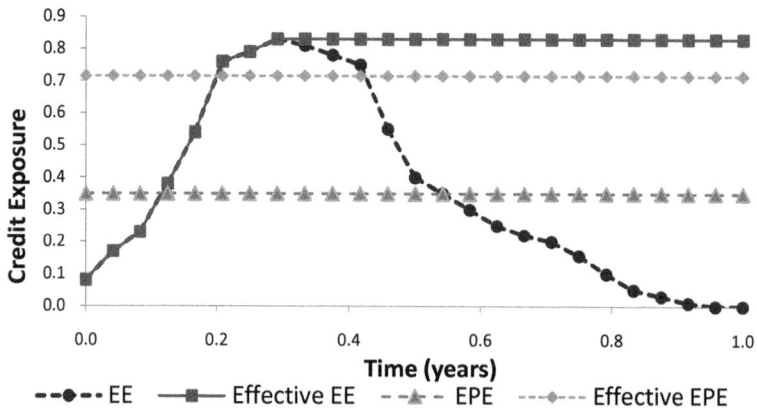

Figure 4.7. *Metrics for credit exposure*

It is interesting to identify the usual shape of the expected exposure that starts by increasing as the underlying risk factors migrate until reaching a point in time where it decreases until maturity as cash flows are paid off.

4.5.2. Formulation

Let us now look at the formulation using a normal distribution for the PFE for simplicity characterized by its mean μ (expected MtM or mean) and standard deviation σ (error term in estimating it)[11].

$$EMtM = \mu + \sigma \times Z$$

where Z represents the standard normal distribution with a 0 mean and a standard deviation of 1.

The PFE is the exposure that will only be exceeded with a probability of less than $1-\alpha$.

$$PFE = \mu + \sigma \times \Phi^{-1}(\alpha)$$

where $\Phi^{-1}(\alpha)$ is the inverse of a cumulative normal distribution function at a confidence level of α. In Microsoft Excel[TM], this is achieved using the function NORMSINV(). For instance, $\Phi^{-1}(95\%) = 1.645$. In other words, PFE is a number $(\Phi^{-1}(\alpha))$ of standard deviations σ away from the mean, μ.

Recall that exposure is expressed as:

$$Exposure = Max\,(MtM,\,0)$$

The EE is the expected value of the positive MtM values of the derivative contract.

$$EE = \int_{-\frac{\mu}{\sigma}}^{\infty} (\mu + \sigma x)\varphi(x)dx = \mu\Phi\left(\frac{\mu}{\sigma}\right) + \sigma\varphi\left(\frac{\mu}{\sigma}\right)$$

where $\Phi(\bullet)$ is a normal distribution function (using NORMDIST() in Microsoft Excel[TM]). If we look at the special case where $\mu = 0$, this yields to:

---

11 This example is taken from Jon Gregory, *Counterparty Credit Risk*, Wiley Finance, 2010.

$$EE_0 = \sigma\varphi(0) = \frac{\sigma}{\sqrt{2\pi}} \approx 0.4\,\sigma$$

In order to calculate the EPE, we need to formulate what the MtM would be over the life of the trade (as opposed to one single point in time as before). Let us redefine the exposure at various times, t, by using the annual standard deviation as:

$$EMtM_t = \mu + \sigma \times \sqrt{t} \times Z_t$$

Still assuming a mean of 0, we deduce the EPE by integration over time:

$$EPE_0 = \frac{1}{\sqrt{2\pi}}\sigma \int_0^T \sqrt{t}\,\frac{dt}{T} = \frac{2}{3\sqrt{2\pi}}\sigma T^{\frac{1}{2}} = 0.27\sigma\,T^{\frac{1}{2}}$$

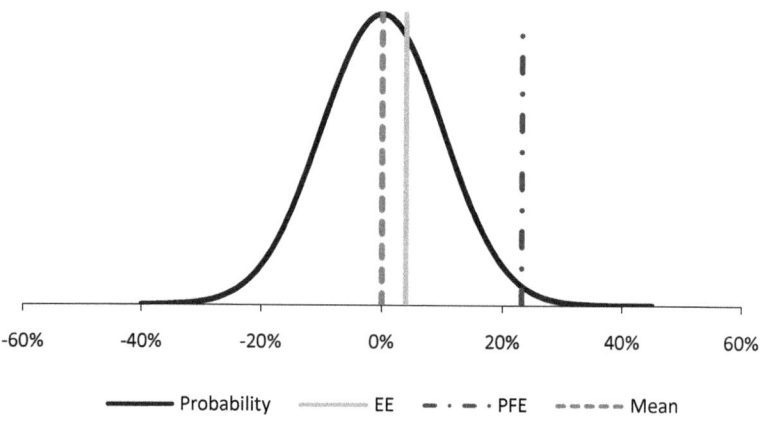

-60%   -40%   -20%   0%   20%   40%   60%

———— Probability   ········ EE   — · — · PFE   ----- Mean

Figure 4.8. *EE and PFE for a normal distribution*

How can we incorporate the impact of netting in calculating EE and PFE? Netting occurs when two trades are in opposite directions. Unfortunately, we cannot add or subtract exposures while running Monte Carlo simulations at the portfolio level. As a result, netting needs to take place at the trade level and before simulations are run.

How can one incorporate the impact of collateral in estimating EE and PFE? UCITS regulations require daily margining of the collateral but in practice, it may be that the collateral a UCITS fund is entitled to take more than one day to reach its account. This could stem from the time it takes to calculate or agree on the margin account. This could stem from the time it takes to calculate or agree on the margin call (in the case of a potential dispute), the time it will take the collateral to be transferred and settled in the fund's account, any "grace" period (time granted to the counterparty to meet the margin call after the deadline has passed) that may exist in the legal documentation or the time it takes to liquidate positions in case of a credit event. As we can see, daily margining does not always imply an effective daily remargin period.

In order to account for the collateralized exposure during the remargin period, we can consider the uncertainty of the exposure with this simple formula[12] that represents the volatility of exposure over the remargin period:

$$\text{PFE}_\alpha = \Phi^{-1}(\alpha) \times \sigma_{CE} \times \sqrt{T_{RM}}$$

where σ_{CE} is the annualized volatility of the collateralized exposure and T_{RM} is the remargin period expressed in number days over a year (250 days).

As an example, suppose an exposure has an annual volatility of 6% over three days. At the 95% confidence level, the worst change in the value of the exposure is estimated at:

$$\text{PFE}_{95\%} = -1.645 \times 6\% \times \sqrt{\frac{3}{250}} = -1.08\%$$

This formula only applies to cash collateral in a single currency. So how can we take account of multiple currencies or even multiple assets in collateral, as there may be a correlation between the nature of the collateral and the exposure? The answer is by incorporating the inter-relationships (correlations) between these various assets as follows:

$$\sigma_{CE} = \sqrt{\sum_{i=1}^{N} \sigma_{CE}^2 + 2 \sum_{i=1,j>i}^{N} \rho_{ij}\sigma_i\sigma_j}$$

where ρ_{ij} is the correlation matrix among the mark-to-market values of the N different products in collateral.

---

12 Assuming that changes in the netted exposure follow a normal distribution with zero mean and σ_{CE} volatility.

For illustration, let us assume that a UCITS fund can receive both € and US Treasury bills (expressed in USD) as collateral with a respective annual volatility of 3% and 7% and a correlation of 0.50. The volatility of the collateral is then:

$$\sigma_{CE} = \sqrt{3\%^2 + 7\%^2 - 2 \times 3\% \times 7\%} = 4\%$$

and the relevant PFE is given by:

$$PFE_{95\%} = -1.645 \times 4\% \times \sqrt{\frac{3}{250}} = -0.72\%$$

As we can see, the uncertainty of the collateralized exposure has decreased because using two types of collateral that are correlated to some extent may decrease the volatility of its mark-to-market values. This corresponds to hedging the collateral by diversification.

At the fund level, the mathematics becomes much more complex as we need to account for the independent amount, threshold, minimum transfer amount and rounding at every netting point of the Monte Carlo simulations along each path.

The logic required to calculate the amount of collateral (*Coll*) that can be called at the current time, assuming rounding down, should be as follows:

$$Coll = (1 - mod\ r) \times Q \times \{[Max(MtM_{fund} - T, 0) - Max(-MtM_{fund} - T, 0)] - C\}$$

where $Q = \dfrac{\{[Max(MtM_{fund}-T,0)-Max(-MtM_{fund}-T,0)]-C-MTA\}^{+}}{[Max(MtM_{fund}-T,0)-Max(-MtM_{fund}-T,0)]-C-MTA}$

where *r* is the block rounding of the collateral amount, MtM_{fund} is the mark-to-market value of the fund, *T* is the collateral threshold, *C* is the collateral currently held by the fund, and *MTA* is the minimum transfer amount.

Figures 4.9 and 4.10 illustrate the impact of collateral on EE and PFE using a normal distribution.

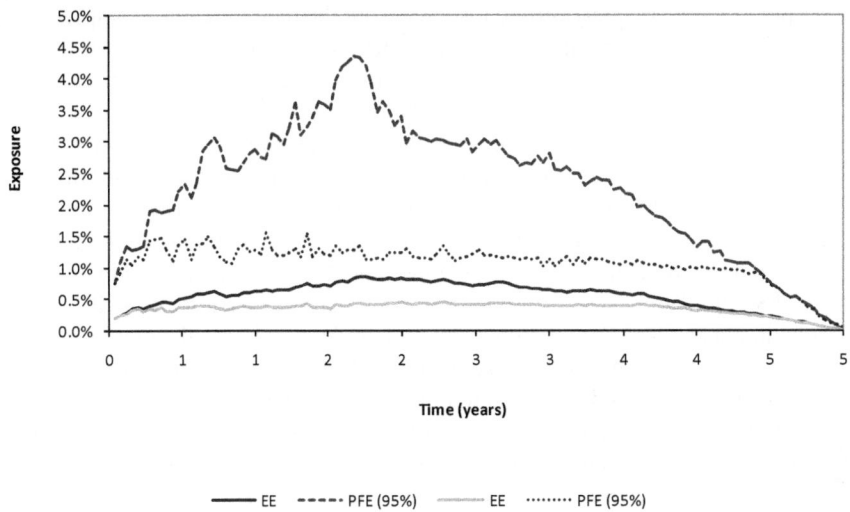

Figure 4.9. *Impact of collateral on EE and PFE for a normal distribution*

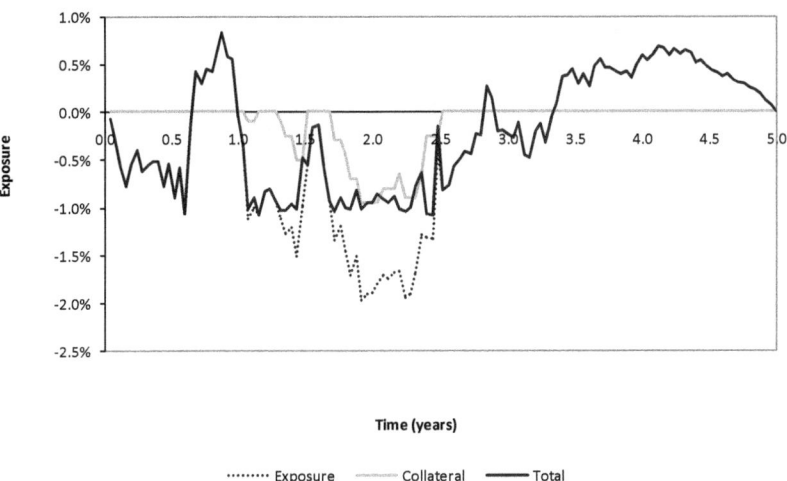

Figure 4.10. *Evolution of exposure and collateral over five years*

Box 4.2. *Wrong-way risk*

Wrong-way risk refers to a particular situation whereby the exposure to a counterparty increases as the credit worthiness of this counterparty decreases, and is therefore more likely to default. Wrong-way risk is generally difficult to spot as there are many different sources, but the more obvious example would be for a UCITS fund to short the stock of a counterparty or buy a "put option" on the counterparty. The fund will make money if the stock price goes down, which would increase the likelihood of it defaulting. Another example would be a UCITS fund investing in a derivative whose underlying asset is linked to a counterparty. For example, a UCITS fund could sell oil futures or buy oil swaps (paying floating and receiving fixed prices) to an oil company. Clearly, the main revenues of the counterparty stem from the oil price, but the lower the price gets, the more profits can be generated by the UCITS fund. Wrong-way risk does not imply that the counterparty will default, but captures the possibility that if a trade is well into the money, a UCITS fund may never see the payoff if that leads to such a dramatic gain the counterparty would be forced to default on its payments.

There are few ways to account for wrong-way risk. The first one would be to recommend increasing the error term when estimating the EE or estimating the PFE at a higher confidence level. This method is very easy to implement but has little scientific justification other than adding a buffer to the estimated values making them more conservative. Unfortunately, only when the counterparty defaults would this add-on have proven itself appropriately priced in. It would be too late if it was not. A second solution would be to incorporate a correlation factor between the value of the contract (on a given counterparty) and the likelihood of this counterparty defaulting when calculating the EE. Not only is this correlation factor difficult to estimate, it has also very limited economic justification. A third solution would be to include a devaluation factor to the value of the contract in the event that the counterparty defaults.

4.6. Managing issuer risk

4.6.1. *UCITS regulations on issuer risk*

The only authorized tool by which an UCITS fund can mitigate its issuer risk is through the compliance with credit limits. The sheer number of exceptions, however, demonstrates their limited efficiency to mitigate this type of risk.

The first restriction relates to the list of eligible investments a UCITS is allowed to invest in. These restrictive categories do indeed prevent a UCITS fund from investing in instruments where the issuers are not of the highest credit quality. Events can evolve very quickly in the markets, however, and these constraints may not prove sufficiently reactive for a UCITS fund to realize that some of its instruments no longer meet these criteria.

Article 50 of the UCITS IV Directive lists these eligible instruments. A UCITS fund can invest in instruments issued by issuers meeting specific criteria as stated in Paragraph (h):

(h) money market instruments other than those dealt in on a regulated market, which fall under Article 2(1)(o), if the issue or issuer of such instruments is itself regulated for the purpose of protecting investors and savings, provided that they are:

(i) issued or guaranteed by a central, regional or local authority or central bank of a Member State, the European Central Bank, the Community or the European Investment Bank, a third country or, in the case of a Federal State, by one of the members making up the federation, or by a public international body to which one or more Member States belong;

(ii) issued by an undertaking any securities of which are dealt in on regulated markets referred to in points (a), (b) or (c);

(iii) issued or guaranteed by an establishment subject to prudential supervision, in accordance with criteria defined by Community law, or by an establishment which is subject to and complies with prudential rules considered by the competent authorities to be at least as stringent as those laid down by Community law; or

(iv) issued by other bodies belonging to the categories approved by the competent authorities of the UCITS home Member State provided that investments in such instruments are subject to investor protection equivalent to that laid down in points (i), (ii) or (iii) and provided that the issuer is a company whose capital and reserves amount to at least EUR 10 million and which presents and publishes its annual accounts in accordance with Fourth Council Directive 78/660/EEC of 25 July 1978 based on Article 54(3)(g) of the Treaty on the annual accounts of certain types of companies, is an entity which, within a group of companies which includes one or several listed companies, is dedicated to the financing of the group or is an entity which is dedicated to the financing of securitisation vehicles which benefit from a banking liquidity line.

The CESR/10-788 paper adds that:

Issuer credit quality – as collateral provides secondary recourse, the credit quality of the collateral issuer is important. This may involve the use of haircuts in the event of a less than 'very high grade' credit rating. It should be reasonable to accept collateral on assets that exhibit higher price volatility once suitably conservative haircuts are in place.

Let us recall that Article 52 of the UCITS IV Directive requires that:

1. A UCITS shall invest no more than:

(a) 5% of its assets in transferable securities or money market instruments issued by the same body; or

(b) 20% of its assets in deposits made with the same body.

4. […] Where a UCITS invests more than 5% of its assets in the bonds referred to in the first subparagraph which are issued by a single issuer, the total value of these investments shall not exceed 80% of the value of the assets of the UCITS.

Article 53 of the UCITS IV Directive also specifies that:

2. Member States may raise the limit laid down in paragraph 1 to a maximum of 35% where that proves to be justified by exceptional market conditions in particular in regulated markets where certain transferable securities or money market instruments are highly dominant. The investment up to that limit shall be permitted only for a single issuer.

Finally, Article 43 of the Commission Directive 2010/43/EU points out that:

5. Member States shall require management companies to calculate issuer concentration limits as referred to in Article 52 of Directive 2009/65/EC on the basis of the underlying exposure created through the use of financial derivative instruments pursuant to the commitment approach.

4.6.2. *Measuring issuer risk*

Issuer risk may be measured by the adverse impact of credit spread, credit mitigation and default risk on the MtM value of fixed-income instruments and similar securities. We need to differentiate issuer risk if it stems from a corporate as opposed to sovereign issuers as both types of issuer have very different characteristics.

4.6.2.1. *Corporate issuer risk*

A corporate bond, for instance, is a financial debt instrument that forces the issuer to pay the investor (bondholder) on a regular basis (usually quarterly or twice yearly) a coupon (a fixed percentage of the bond's par value) and to repay the bond's par or principal value in full at maturity. We can therefore see that the ability of the bond issuer to pay the interest and principal on his or her bonds constitutes an issuer risk problem that is generally taken into account when pricing and managing bonds.

From a market risk perspective, a UCITS fund should perform some dedicated analysis on credit default risk and credit spread risk on top of the normal market risk metrics.

Credit default risk represents the risk that a bond issuer is unable to meet its financial contractual obligations. Exclusively relying on credit rating agencies may seem an easy way to monitor bond positions but this does not constitute the optimal credit analysis that a fund should conduct on a regular basis on its holdings and prior to investing in a new issue or buying some on the secondary market. We would rather refer to Frank Fabozzi's excellent, *Handbook of Fixed Income Securities*[13], which lays down a few techniques that can be used to measure and manage issuer risk.

A credit spread is the spread between a corporate bond's yield and the yield on a sovereign security, such as a US Treasury security, which is the most common reference credit spread that is monitored in the markets. Credit spread risk is therefore the risk of loss in the MtM value of a fixed income instrument due to a change in the quality of the credit spread. Credit spread risk is generally split into two components: issuer specific or macro-economic and industry-specific factors. The former factors may include factors such the issuer's creditworthiness and financial position as a whole, or the future financial state of the issuer. The latter factors can be the level and slope of the US Treasury yield curve, the current and future states of the sector, industry or economy.

A common measure used to assess credit spread risk lies in spread duration analysis. This technique calculates the spread duration as the approximate percentage change in a bond's price for a 100 bps change in its credit spread, assuming that the US Treasury yield remains unchanged. For instance, a bond with a spread duration of 5 means that if a 100 bps change occurs in the credit spread, the bond's price will increase by 5%. This reflects the fact that as the credit spread widens, so does the risk of holding that corporate bond. Therefore, the bondholder should be rewarded for holding an instrument that has increased in risk.

---

13 McGraw Hill Professional Editions, 7th Edition, May 2005.

widens, so does the risk of holding that corporate bond. Therefore, the bondholder should be rewarded for holding an instrument that has increased in risk.

When a UCITS fund invests in a corporate bond, it is like investing in the issuer's country or the country from which the bond's issuer extracts the majority of its revenues – such as the particular case of companies involved in the extraction, refining, distribution and/or sale of commodities that may have headquarters in one country but extract their inputs or sell their outputs in others. As country risk represents a greater risk than issuer-specific risk, a UCITS fund should always carry out the same analysis it normally conducts when investing in a sovereign bond.

4.6.2.2. *Sovereign issuer risk*

A UCITS fund can invest in bonds issued by governments. In this instance it should thus assess the financial, economic, political and exogenous factors that may reduce a country's ability to meet its financial obligations. For instance, a fund could monitor a country's debt repudiation or rescheduling as a negative indicator that the state is weakening.

A UCITS fund should not only follow the analyses carried out by specialized institutions, such as the Economist Intelligence Unit or Political Risk Services, but should also develop its own statistical models that capture the fund's view on the dynamics driving the economy of a particular country. For instance, a UCITS fund could measure the debt service ratio, the import ratio, the investment ratio, the variance of export revenue, or the domestic money supply growth of a country[14]. On top of this, a fund could also incorporate some other factors in its model to account for political, legal and other sources of risk.

4.6.3. **Stress testing issuer risk**

In order to comply with the UCITS regulation, a fund must perform scenario analysis or stress testing on its fund.

Sensitivity analysis assesses the impact of a small change in a risk factor on the MtM values of the instruments across the maturity buckets that span the lifespan of the trades. Examples are DV01 or CR01 (the impact of one basis point in a credit spread). A fund must also perform stress testing by shocking the different underlying factors by a higher amount than in the sensitivity analysis.

---

14 Definition and measurement of these indicators can be found in Chapter 15 of Saunders and Cornett, *Financial Institutions Management: A Risk Management Approach*, McGraw-Hill Companies, Inc., 2008.

Methodology	Forms	Pros	Cons
Sensitivity Analysis			
	Incremental	Flexibility, automation	Local exploration
Stress Testing			
	Historical	Actual events	Limited relevance
	Customized	Flexibility, automation	Resources and time requirements
	Reverse	How to break down the house	Difficult to implement

Table 4.1. *Stress testing methodologies*

4.6.3.1. *Sensitivity analysis*

Sensitivity analysis consists of shocking various risk factors of the portfolio with small upward or downward increments. It is very simple to implement and can quickly be automated in a systematic way. Examples of shocks involve modeling a fall in all bond prices in the portfolio or parallel shifting the yield curve to shock the bonds included in the portfolio. In the former example, we reduce all bonds by 10% compared to their current price. We rerun our VaR calculation and compare it with the VaR without the 10% bond shock. That may give us a rough idea of the "sensitivity" of the equities compared to the other asset classes in the portfolio.

From here, it is possible to determine the effects of a range of larger increments to determine how sensitivity evolves as the risk factors are more dramatically shocked. Monte Carlo simulation VaR is sometimes seen as a "black box" as it is difficult to predict the outcome of simulations. Sensitivity analysis can provide some information on how the VaR reacts to shocks of various amplitudes on various risk factors. Furthermore, it is feasible to shock various factors at the same time within the same scenario. Without running individual shocks first, however, it will be hard to interpret which factor explains most of the new VaR estimate as correlations might have changed. In this instance, the risk manager needs to think more like an economist more than a quantitative analyst or needs to work with his/her colleagues in the research department to integrate the view on various asset classes, regions, currencies, etc.

It is also interesting to shock these risk factors over a longer period of time than the end of the analysis horizon (generally one day or one month). This way, we can generate different shocks that will apply to some risk factors over a few time horizons. For instance, we can recalculate a VaR on a portfolio where we have amended the exchange rates among the two main currencies with the following shocks: -10%, +5%, and -15%. Studying the historical movements of these two currencies can provide some information that can be used to project various scenarios on how the market could evolve over the next few time intervals. This is where sensitivity analysis meets with stress tests, as this last approach could be seen as a customized stress test.

Despite its simplicity, this methodology also has some pitfalls. The risk manager needs to exercise some judgment in determining the optimal size of each shock which may differ from one asset class to another. These shocks must also be reassessed on a regular basis to avoid missing a change in the pattern of one specific asset (e.g. a sudden and brief increase in volatility) or a correlation increasing between two assets. Also, since we only shock one factor at a time and with a very small change, the analysis is very local.

4.6.3.2. Stress testing

Stress testing aims to identify extreme events that could trigger catastrophic losses in a given portfolio. As its definition suggests, the shocks that are applied to the portfolio are of much greater amplitude than those used in a standard sensitivity analysis. There are three main types of stress testing: historical, customized and reverse stress testing.

Historical stress tests or scenarios intend to test the healthiness of a portfolio by analyzing what would happen to the portfolio if particularly adverse and unexpected movements that have occurred in the past hit the portfolio in the near future. Some well-known examples of historical scenarios are the Russian crisis, the attacks of 9/11, and more recently the subprime mortgage crisis. Some of these historical scenarios have only lasted a few days, like the Black Monday (October 19, 1987) scenario. Some others, like the Dotcom Bubble, spanned several months. The main advantage of these types of scenarios is that they really have happened! Even though the temptation to use these historical scenarios off-the-shelf and to systematically apply them on any type of portfolio is great, the risk manager should choose his/her historical scenarios very carefully and review them on a regular basis as the composition of the portfolio changes. This is also important because there are a few dangers.

First, we need to select the historical stress tests that are the most relevant to the portfolio. Recreating the shocks that occurred during the Russian crisis in a portfolio that does not contain any bonds will produce results of limited interest. Second, we should determine the start and end dates of the historical scenario. This is not as easy as it seems as there may be different interpretations on what these two dates are. Third, what do we do with the instruments that will reach maturity during the re-enactment of these events? You can roll them over or not, depending on your strategy or on the size of these positions. In either case, cash flows need to be appropriately taken into account. Fourth, do you apply an absolute or a relative shock to the risk factors? Generally, we perform relative shocks but that depends on the risk factor (for instance, it is better to shock volatility on a relative basis). Fifth, what do we do about missing instruments? What is the point of applying the Black Monday scenario to a portfolio of CDSs? Further, if historical data are not available on all risk factors, we should either proxy them or proceed to an interpolation (more relevant to fixed income instruments where the term structure may need to be filled in and out throughout). Finally, we should point out that historical stress tests produce a loss estimate and not a VaR. Therefore, the likelihood of seeing a historical stress test come true remains unknown.

In order to fix some of these drawbacks, we can design some specific stress tests based on historical stress tests or on areas of vulnerability in the portfolio. These stress tests are termed "customized" tests since they respond to a particular purpose, such as shocking correlations, stressing a liquidity squeeze, or creating a scenario that is more likely to impact a portfolio than historical stress tests would. These scenarios can be economic, political or financial. The complexity of the scenario depends on various factors, such as the number of risk factors taken into account, period of time the pre-defined scenario is expected to last, complexity of the portfolio, number of positions in the portfolio, running time, staff, cost, etc. In a nutshell, there must be a trade-off between the constraints of establishing a complete program of customized stress tests and the desired outcome.

Reverse stress tests try to identify the risks that would lead an institution to fail. This is an appealing idea in the sense that instead of starting from the existing standpoint and seeing how close we can go towards the ridge of the cliff without falling, reverse stress testing tells you what risks you could take that would lead you to directly fall off the cliff. This makes so much sense that you may wonder why we have not carried out reverse stress tests for ages. Well, the main problem with reverse stress testing is "how" to do it. There are so many reasons why an institution could fail that it may take some time to determine meaningful stress tests. When we conduct other types of stress testing, we always start from the known: the portfolio itself and its VaR and try to progress more or less in the dark to gauge the risks ahead. With the reverse stress test, we start from the unknown and try to figure out how we became lost on the way home. This intellectually challenging thought could soon become tedious is we try to assess which events could have triggered the failure and how this event has effected the entire system. There is no easy answer to this problem, but since contagion is the result of increasing correlation, working with copula statistical analysis could be a starting point.

4.6.4. *Hedging issuer risk*

The most obvious way to hedge issuer risk is through the use of CDS (a single name or sovereign according to the underlying name). A UCITS fund can employ index CDS to hedge its credit exposure to an industry or sector.

In light of the recent events surrounding the negotiations of Greek debt, investors in CDS should be aware that the European Union (EU) seemed keen to avoid any action that credit rating agencies would classify as a "default", since European Central Bank rules forbid the bank from accepting any debt from a bankrupt sovereign as collateral. In order to share the cost of a new bailout with private investors, the EU was considering asking bondholders to voluntarily roll over their bonds, or to maintain their exposure by buying new bonds as their holdings mature. Some CDS issuers may therefore consider that given that it was voluntary it should not trigger CDS under current (industry) documentation. Depending on what exact formulation Brussels uses, CDS holders could receive a payout or could find themselves out of pocket.

Finally, as we have highlighted on many occasions, risk can generally be mitigated but not completely removed. If a UCITS fund is holding CDSs that hedge some of its bonds, for instance, but it may give rise to incremental counterparty risk on the CDS issuers.

4.7. Concentration risk management

As stated earlier, concentration risk can be defined as the probability of loss arising from a lack of diversification. This lack of diversification may occur in a fund's set of counterparties, geographic locations, or other identifiable risk scenarios.

In June 2006, Basel II[15] stated that *"Risk concentrations are arguably the single most important cause of major problems in banks."* We can argue that one of Lehman Brothers' mistakes in the 2000s was to build a concentrated portfolio of mortgage back securities and commercial real estate. Similarly, American International Group (AIG) made the same mistake in CDS. Concentration risk in a

---

15 Basel Committee on Banking Supervision, *International Convergence of Capital Measurement and Capital Standards*, Paragraph 770, page 214, June 2006 (http://www.bis.org/publ/bcbs128.htm).

UCITS fund can arise in the building of an overall large exposure in a single security (market risk) or the recurrent reliance on the same group of counterparties (credit risk). In this section, we introduce the UCITS framework to manage concentration risk and then we delve into these two aspects of concentration risk and propose a methodology to closely monitor this risk.

4.7.1. *Concentration risk within the UCITS framework*

Similarly to issuer risk, concentration risk is monitored by risk limits. Paragraph 42 of the UCITS IV Directive highlights that:

> (42) For prudential reasons it is necessary to avoid excessive concentration by a UCITS in investments which expose it to counterparty risk to the same entity or to entities belonging to the same group.

As stated earlier, the credit limits a UCITS fund must respect are clearly stated in Article 52 of the UCITS IV Directive:

> 1. The risk exposure to a counterparty of the UCITS in an OTC derivative transaction shall not exceed either:
>
> (a) 10% of its assets when the counterparty is a credit institution referred to in Article 50(1)(f); or
>
> (b) 5% of its assets, in other cases.

The Commission Directive 2010/43/EU also mentions in its introductory paragraphs that:

> (25) As an essential element in the criteria for assessing the adequacy of risk management processes, proportionate and effective risk measurement techniques should be adopted by management companies in order to measure at any time the risks which the UCITS they manage are or might be exposed to. These requirements are based on common practices agreed by competent authorities of Member States. They include both quantitative measures, as regards quantifiable risks, and qualitative methods. Electronic data processing systems and tools used for the computation of quantitative measures should be integrated with one another or with the front-office and accounting applications. Risk measurement techniques should allow for an adequate measurement of risks in periods of increased market turbulence and be reviewed whenever necessary in the interest of unit-

holders. They should also allow adequate assessment of the concentration and interaction of relevant risks at the portfolio level.

Further, Article 43 of the same Directive specifies that:

5. Member States shall require management companies to calculate issuer concentration limits as referred to in Article 52 of Directive 2009/65/EC on the basis of the underlying exposure created through the use of financial derivative instruments pursuant to the commitment approach.

In addition, paragraph 4.2 of the CESR/10-788 explains that:

1. According to Article 52(1) of the UCITS Directive the risk exposure of a UCITS to a counterparty to an OTC derivative may not exceed 5% of assets. This limit is raised to 10% in the case of credit institutions. The following exposure must also be calculated within the OTC counterparty limits specified in Article 52(1):

Initial margin posted to and variation margin receivable from a broker relating to exchange-traded or OTC derivatives which is not protected by client money rules or other similar arrangements to protect the UCITS against the insolvency of the broker.

2. The following exposure must also be included when calculating the issuer concentration limit of 20% specified in Article 52(2):

Any net exposure to a counterparty generated through a stock-lending or repurchase agreement, net exposure being understood as the amount receivable by the UCITS less any collateral provided to the UCITS. Exposures created through the reinvestment of collateral must also be taken into account in the issuer-concentration calculations.

3. When calculating exposure for the purposes of Article 52 of the UCITS Directive a UCITS must establish whether its exposure is to an OTC counterparty, a broker or a clearing house.

4. Position exposure to the underlying assets of financial derivative instruments (including embedded financial derivative instruments) in transferable securities such as money market instruments or collective investment undertakings, combined where relevant with positions resulting from direct investments, may not exceed the limits set out in Articles 52 and 55.

5. When calculating issuer-concentration risk, the financial derivative instrument (including embedded financial derivative

instruments) must be looked through in determining the resultant position exposure. This position exposure must be taken into account in the issuer concentration calculations. It must be calculated using the commitment approach when appropriate or the maximum potential loss as a result of default by the issuer if more conservative. It must also be calculated by all UCITS, regardless of whether they use VaR for global exposure purposes.

6. This provision does not apply in the case of index-based financial derivative instruments provided the underlying index is one which meets with the criteria set out in Article 53(1).

Further, we can read in Box 27 that:

2. The following exposure must also be included when calculating the issuer concentration limit of 20% specified in Article 52(2):

– Any net exposure to a counterparty generated through a stock-lending or repurchase agreement, net exposure being understood as the amount receivable by the UCITS less any collateral provided to the UCITS. Exposures created through the reinvestment of collateral must also be taken into account in the issuer-concentration calculations.

5. When calculating issuer-concentration risk, the financial derivative instrument (including embedded financial derivative instruments) must be looked through in determining the resultant position exposure. This position exposure must be taken into account in the issuer concentration calculations. It must be calculated using the commitment approach when appropriate or the maximum potential loss as a result of default by the issuer if more conservative. It must also be calculated by all UCITS, regardless of whether they use VaR for global exposure purposes.

The explanatory text that follows Box 27 finally provides additional clarification:

85. The commitment approach should be used in the issuer concentration calculations where appropriate. For instance, if the use of the commitment approach leads to an infinite value (binary option), the position exposure should be equal to the maximum potential loss as a result of default by the issuer.

The UCITS IV Directive is entirely based on limit monitoring and does not truly differentiate between the various types of concentration risk based on market, credit, industry, sector or country specifics. Nevertheless, the CESR 10-788 paper[16] did mention that a UCITS fund must carry out a stress testing program that covers all risks (and therefore includes concentration risk) even if no great details have been provided.

4.7.2. *Identifying concentrations in a fund*

Concentration risk is a very easy concept to grasp but its monitoring may reserve some subtleties to risk managers. Concentration risk usually arises from:

1. *Significant* individual (market or credit) exposures. Exposures between two or more underlying securities may actually be connected through, for instance, a common parent company, suppliers, customers, management, or even creditors and guarantors. This kind of concentration called for data mining techniques to find any connections between the securities present in the fund.

2. *Large* exposures to sets of counterparties whose probabilities of default are driven by shared underlying factors, for instance:

- economic sector;

- geographical location;

- currency;

- credit risk mitigation measures (including, for example, risks associated with large indirect credit exposures to a single collateral issuer).

Concentration risk actually has different facets defined according to its source: market or credit exposure, and within these two categories at an industry or sector level or even at a country or zone level (where the same currency is used or where local currencies are relatively well correlated).

Market concentration risk can be defined as the potential loss arising from positions held for trading in securities and other obligations in tradable form because of large price movements due to credit events (such as a default or the insolvency of an issuer or obligator) that as a result significantly impair the values of their issued securities (share, bonds, CDS, etc.). Correlations between the individual transactions are generally estimated using a market risk model.

Credit concentration risk can be defined as the risk arising from corporate (or sovereign) default resulting in a significant loss due to a bankruptcy or failure to pay off a borrower or a group of borrowers. It can also be a result of bankruptcies in

---

16 Boxes 19, 20 and 21.

cascades or failure to pay in the same industry or geographic area over a period of time in response to cyclical industry factors or country risk events. It is also important to measure correlations between the counterparties.

Industry/sector concentration risk can be defined as the risk of substantial deterioration of market conditions for all counterparties within one industry sector due to macroeconomic developments, changes in law or other stress events affecting the entire industry/sector. In periods of stress, correlations between firms within the affected industry/sector will dramatically increase, posing a serious problem in terms of diversification and the liquidity of the fund. The main difficulty resides in accurately describing the boundaries and characteristics of an industry/sector, not only because they may be blur at times but also because they can mutate (shrink, expand or transform) over time.

Similarly, *geographical* (country or area-specific) concentration risk arises from common exposure to country-specific macroeconomic factors, events and government policies that may result in an inability to transfer funds from a country as a result of government policy, such as the suspension of payments imposed by the Russian Federation in 1998[17]. *Country* concentration risk can alternatively be described as the risk that a country may be unable or unwilling to honor its cross-border foreign currency obligations.

Tools used to monitor country concentration risk include drawing a watch list of countries representing the highest risk of defaulting on their debts, susceptible of amending their policies or other economic, political, financial and legal events. The internal security of its citizens would also most likely prevent a country from functioning normally (in countries at war or undermined by terrorism and corruption). A UCITS fund can also use limits with their pros and cons, as previously discussed. Finally, a fund can determine its appetite for risk towards countries and have them approved at the most senior level. This appetite for risk can be deduced from various factors: the size of the country, gross domestic product, import–export balances, level of indebtedness, reliance on international trade, level of industry concentration (such as being dependent on oil price, other natural resources or even tourism), LGD, etc.   Finally, we can also run stress testing/scenario analyses on country-specific parameters such as FX spreads, prices of bond and equity indices, etc. to assess the performance of their economy.

---

17 *Managing Concentration Risk – A Review of Industry Practice*, ISDA, BBA, LIBA, August 2006.

4.7.3. *Tools to manage concentration risk*

A UCITS fund can monitor concentration risk by actively managing (selling, reallocating, securitizing and hedging) its exposures to these risks but also through different techniques such as limits, stress testing and other credit risk mitigations (mostly legal, which we covered in section 4.3.5).

4.7.3.1. *Limit setting*

The determination and monitoring of risk limits lies in the simplest and most widespread methods of managing concentration risk. First, an UCITS fund must define its risk appetite to these different concentration risks and get it approved by the board of directors. This risk appetite depends on the fund's risk profile and trading strategy and is described in its prospectus. It can be defined as the level of risk a fund is prepared to bear before it is deemed necessary to reduce the risk. It represents a trade-off between the potential returns of the fund and the risk inherent to trading these financial products. The risk appetite relies on the fund's desired portfolio composition and benchmark (when there is one).

Limits can be based on internal and external criteria, such as notional, Assets Under Management (AUM), or even overall risk exposure, to name a few. Limits are derived at various levels within the fund: asset class, currency, industry, sector, country, etc. A UCITS fund can determine these risk limits as a percentage of the notionals and of the MtM values with or without add-ons and using a more exhaustive methodology inspired by the one described in section 4.5.

Pre-trade analyses can also be employed to assess the impact of incremental trades in these categories and to ensure the UCITS fund will respect the limits set in the UCITS regulations.

A range of qualitative and quantitative factors are generally combined to establish a heat map or an internal rating across these various categories. These include the following that are widely encountered in practice:

– purpose of the credit and sources of repayment;

– current counterparty risk profile and its sensitivity to economic and market developments;

– compliance with any applicable credit risk policy requirements, risk appetite statements and dealing assessment guidelines;

– compliance with affordability tests;

– counterparty's repayment history and ability to repay;

– the counterparty's position within a sector and the outlook for the sector;

– proposed terms and conditions embedded in the legal documentation;

– credit risk measures appropriate to the type of counterparty, such as credit grade, probability of default (PD), exposure at default (EAD) and loss given;

– default (LGD), and expected loss (EL)

– risk-adjusted return;

– adequacy and enforceability of any risk mitigation;

– portfolio loss distribution profile versus risk appetite (i.e. portfolio effects recognized as part of a multi-faceted approach to limits);

– the legal and reputational risks associated with the proposed relationship;

– size of the counterparty;

– the existence of any legal agreements or credit risk-mitigation arrangements in place (whether netting, collateral, guarantees or other);

– types of product;

– country/jurisdiction (whether there were transfer concerns or volatility issues, such as in emerging markets);

– sovereign risk rating;

– past experience with the country; and

– current political and economic environment.

4.7.3.2. Stress testing

Stress testing is widespread throughout the industry. Stress tests are increasingly becoming embedded in firms' risk management measurement and reporting. Funds' risk management reports are likely to include the results of stress tests covering a variety of risks, such as market and credit risk, but increasingly they could also cover other risks such as issuer, concentration and liquidity risk. A UCITS fund can run stress tests on macroeconomic scenarios on top of the usual sensitivity analysis present in market risk.

A UCITS fund can identify the top 10 or 25 investment-grade and non-investment-grade exposures in each country according to a defined set of parameters on a monthly basis. The factors of these scenarios can range from foreign exchange rates, interest rates, equity prices and credit spreads, to multi-factor scenarios combining more than one criterion. For instance, a UCITS fund could measure the impact of the recent subprime crisis, a drop in asset prices, a low or high economic activity, a drop or rise in interest and FX rates, a widening or tightening of credit spreads, an increased rate of inflation and unemployment or other factors that describe the state of an economy.

These scenario analyses will enable the fund manager to identify the transactions, counterparties, sectors and countries with significant sensitivity under different situations. It is also recommended that the correlations between the trades as well as between counterparties, industries, sectors and countries are stress tested because in periods of stress, correlations tend to the unity with the cohort of devastating consequences not only on the performance of the fund but also on its risk and compliance management. This could be a drop in diversification with the potential threat of breaching the regulatory limits set in the UCITS IV Directive, a reduction of the hedging efficiency of the fund, liquidity squeeze, fire sales affecting the performance, etc. An UCITS fund could also monitor the performance of the funds of its counterparties.

It would be advisable for an UCITS fund manager to run stress tests on at least a weekly basis. The manager should engage in a thorough analysis of their implications for the performance of the fund, discuss with the portfolio managers the potential areas of weakness of the fund that may have been identified through this exercise, and take appropriate action not only to remain within the regulatory limits but more importantly to mitigate the actual or future counterparty risk the fund is or will be exposed to.

4.8. Conclusion: What lies in the future?

We exposed in this chapter the rules a UCITS fund must comply with to measuring and managing counterparty, issuer and concentration risks in accordance with the UCITS IV Directive. The pillar of these regulations stands on the widespread usage of limits which in turn have their limits: fixed, not forward-looking and difficult to aggregate across these three risk types. In some instances, it is difficult to isolate market from credit risk within a single trade. Therefore, it appeared to us that we needed to go beyond the UCITS framework and should offer the risk managers with practical techniques to measure counterparty credit exposure and discuss of the best practices in measuring issuer and concentration risks.

These best practices encompass the daily measurement and monitoring of these risk types by using a risk system that can run Monte Carlo simulations, compute VaR calculations and perform generic and customized stress testing at the trade level as well as the fund level and across asset classes, currencies, industries and countries. When we look back at the initial requirements for risk management in UCITS I, we can realize we have come a long way. What was considered as Compliance has mutated into an independent risk management function that requires a wider and more quantitative skill set which reflects the increased complexity present in the financial products and the financial markets in which these are traded.

We highlighted in this chapter the frustration of the removal of the add-ons suggested in the CSSF Circular 07/308 to measure counterparty risk, which even if they were not dynamic were at least adding a buffer for safety. Simply measuring counterparty risk by the positive mark-to-market value of the OTC derivatives contracts gives the false impression these risks are being adequately managed. But valuing a UCITS fund's credit exposure to a group of counterparties is quite different from managing these exposures. A UCITS fund needs to conduct some pre-trade analysis and run some forward-looking calculations in order to take corrective actions prior to a credit event or a sudden increase of volatility that may impact the netting, collateral, and hedging ability of a UCITS fund.

New regulations around the world (Dodd-Frank Act, European Market Infrastructure Regulation, Basel III) are being shaped to push even more derivatives contracts onto dedicated clearing houses and we can only welcome this trend. But we wish to warn that without the appropriate safeguards and regulators' oversight one could assist to the concentration of counterparties that may dramatically increase systemic risk and lead to a crisis which dramatic consequences would most likely not be captured in any scenario analysis. These new regulations could also potentially reduce the liquidity in the financial markets, which could lead to increased transaction cost due to lower levels of trading activity. The risk/reward profiles of some financial products could also be negatively impacted due to a decreased mark-to-market value or higher interest rates paid as investors will want to be compensated for the lack of liquidity. Maybe, should we start back testing regulations...

So what new requirements will UCITS V and further avatars bring to the risk management profession in the future? We cannot say for now but can only hope that it will recommend more forward-looking/pre-trade analyses and allow for enhanced versions of the current tools that risk managers possess in their toolbox: dynamic hedging, wider collateral eligibility and (intra-day) cross product netting.

4.9. Bibliography

[BAS 06] Basel Committee on Banking Supervision, International Convergence of Capital Measurement and Capital Standards, BCBS, June 2006.

[BER 09] BERRY R., *Stress Testing Value-at-Risk*, J.P. Morgan Investment Analytics & Consulting Quarterly Newsletter, June 2009.

[COM 07] COMMISSION DE SURVEILLANCE DU SECTEUR FINANCIER, CSSF Circular 07/308, CSSF, August 2, 2007 [CSSF 07/308].

[COM 10a] COMMISSION DE SURVEILLANCE DU SECTEUR FINANCIER, Regulation No. 10-4, December 24, 2010.

[COM 10b] COMMISSION DE SURVEILLANCE DU SECTEUR FINANCIER, Law of 17 December 2010, CSSF, 2010.

[COM 10c] COMMITTEE OF EUROPEAN SECURITIES REGULATORS, Guidelines on Risk Measurement and the Calculation of Global Exposure for *Certain Types* of *Structured* UCITS, CSSF, November 18, 2010 [CESR/10-1253].

[COM 10d] COMMITTEE OF EUROPEAN SECURITIES REGULATORS, Guidelines on Risk Measurement and the Calculation of Global Exposure and Counterparty Risk for UCITS, 28 July 2010 [CESR/10-788].

[COM 10e] COMMITTEE OF EUROPEAN SECURITIES REGULATORS, Guidelines on Risk Measurement and the Calculation of Global Exposure and Counterparty Risk for UCITS, CSSR, April 19, 2010 [CESR/10-108].

[COM 11] COMMISSION DE SURVEILLANCE DU SECTEUR FINANCIER, *CSSF Circular* 11/512, May 30, 2011 [CSSF 11/512].

[DAV 10] DAVIES H., *The Financial Crisis: Who is to blame?*, Polity, 2010.

[EUR 09] EUROPEAN PARLIAMENT AND COUNCIL, Council Directive of 13 July 2009 [2009/65/EC].

[EUR 10] EUROPEAN COMMISSION, Commission Directive of 1 July 2010 [2010/43/EU].

[EUR 85] EUROPEAN PARLIAMENT AND COUNCIL, Council Directive of 20 December 1985.

[FAB 05] FABOZZI F., *Handbook of Fixed Income Securities*, 7th Edition, McGraw Hill Professional Editions, May 2005.

[GRE 10] GREGORY J., *Counterparty Credit Risk*, Wiley Finance, 2010.

[ISD 06] ISDA, BBA, LIBA, Managing Concentration Risk – A Review of Industry Practice, ISDA, BBA, LIBA, August 2006.

[SAU 08] SAUNDERS A., CORNETT M.M., "Sovereign risk", *Financial Institutions Management: A Risk Management Approach*, McGraw-Hill Companies Inc., 2008.

Chapter 5

UCITS – The Investment Limits

5.1. Introduction

The purpose of this chapter is to delve into the individual limits as prescribed by European Directive 2009/65/EC (also known as UCITS IV[1]). In particular we will explain how these limits are to be checked with an IT/operational focus. Each rule will be described in detail, highlighting any specific data requirements or peculiarities it may have.

Following this we will briefly analyze some of the main differences between the interpretations of various European Union (EU) regulators.

We will also discuss the issue of consistent data provision and steps that can be taken to ensure quality data are available for restriction monitoring.

Finally we will outline the IT/operational process that should accompany the checking of investment limits, both *ex-ante* and *ex-post*.

5.1.1. *Definitions*

In this chapter, I use the following:

– *FDI*: "financial derivative instrument";

Chapter written by Andrew P. WHITE.
1 UCITV IV Directive, available at: http://eur-lex.europa.eu/LexUriServ/LexUriServ. do?uri=OJ:L:2009:302:0032:0096:en:PDF.

– *CIS*: "collective investment scheme";

– *NAV*: "net asset value", i.e. the total value of the fund;

– *asset data*: information pertaining to an asset (e.g. ISIN, issuer, rating);

– *fund data*: information pertaining to the fund (e.g. name, NAV);

– *position data*: information pertaining to a fund's holding of an asset (e.g. market value, quantity);

– *Asset Id*: a unique identifier for every asset. It should remain consistent over time. For a listed security, it can be an ISIN[2]/SEDOL[3]/CUSIP[4]. An identifier such as the alternative instrument identifier (Aii)[5] or similar is recommended for over-the-counter (OTC) derivatives;

– *commitment approach* is used for calculating exposure to derivatives. In this process, each FDI position is converted into the underlying asset of that derivative. For more information on the calculation process, see Chapter 3;

– *counterparty risk* is the calculation of the total risk exposure to a single counterparty. It is reduced by eligible collateral and can be subject to netting if an agreement exists between the fund and the counterparty. For detailed information on this, see Chapter 8;

– *group company* also known as the "ultimate parent issuer". Companies that are included in the same group for the purposes of consolidated accounts, as defined in accordance with Directive 83/349/EEC[6] or in accordance with recognized international accounting rules, shall be regarded as a single body for some rules;

– *union* (denoted by "U"): many of the restrictions work on multiple asset classes/asset selections, therefore we will use U to denote the combination of two asset classes, e.g. TransferableSecurities U MoneyMarketInstuments will return all transferable securities and money market instruments in the fund.

– *Relative complement*, or just *complement* (denoted by "/") of A with respect to a set B, is the set of elements in B but not in A, e.g. Assets/EligibleAssets will list all assets that are not eligible in the fund.

---

2 International Securities Identification Number: http://www.isin.org/.

3 Stock Exchange Daily Official List: http://www.londonstockexchange.com/products-and-services/reference-data/sedol-master-file/sedol-master-file.htm.

4 Committee on Uniform Security Identification Procedures (CUSIP): http://www.cusip.com/cusip/index.htm.

5 http://www.fsa.gov.uk/Pages/Doing/Regulated/Returns/mtr/aii_implementation/index.shtml.

6 Treaty on consolidated accounts, available at: http://eur-lex.europa.eu/LexUriServ/LexUriServ.do?uri=CELEX:31983L0349:en:PDF.

– *assignment* (denoted by ":="): a variable is assigned to by using the ":=" operator. For example, "Total := 5" means the variable "Total" is assigned the value 5.

– *concentration rules*, also known as "Foreach" rules, these rules apply a grouping to the fund's positions before checking;

– *early warning*: all rules have a specific numeric limit (e.g. 10% or 20%), but in order to prevent breaches an early warning is raised when a specific lower threshold is crossed (e.g. 8% or 18%);

– *ex-post check*: normally a daily check (but can also be less frequent) of all positions. (It comes from the Latin "after the fact"); and

– *ex-ante checks* are any checks done before an order is placed on the market (from the Latin "before the fact").

5.1.2. *Structure*

For the purposes of explaining how the rules work, it may be useful to consider a portfolio like a spread sheet. The lines in the sheet represent positions and the columns are the various items of asset and position data that are necessary for checking rules.

AssetName	AssetType	Issuer	PercentNAV
HSBC	Equity	HSBC	4.52
BP	Equity	BP	1.21
Cash	Cash		2.20
UK 2.8% Gilt 2022	Bond	UK	2.45

Table 5.1. *Example portfolio for a simple rule*

For a rule to check only equities, we would apply the filter *AssetType = "equity"*, which would return:

AssetName	AssetType	Issuer	PercentNAV
HSBC	Equity	HSBC	4.52
BP	Equity	BP	1.21

Table 5.2. *Portfolio filtered for equities. All rules need a numeric value to be calculated from the filtered positions. So if, for example, a rule required the total percentage value of these positions, we would use the function SUM of the column PercentNAV (we will abbreviate this to Sum(PercentNAV)). This would return 5.73.*

Most rules require a list of these values to be added/subtracted and for the total value to be compared with a fixed value, such as:

Filter: Assets.Where(AssetType="Bonds") U
Assets.Where(AssetType="Equities")

Breached if: Sum(PercentNAV) > 10

This is a rule which states that the total value of all bonds and equities should be less than or equal to 10% NAV.

5.1.2.1. Concentration rules

Many of the UCITS limits do not directly check at the portfolio level, but require a grouping function to be run first. A concentration rule's phrasing generally begins with something similar to "No single…", e.g. "No single issuer shall be more than 10% NAV" or "No single CIS shall be more than 25% NAV". Algorithmically this works as shown in Table 5.3.

AssetName	AssetType	Issuer	PercentNAV
HSBC, ex1	Equity	HSBC	4.52
BP	Equity	BP	1.21
Microsoft	Equity	Microsoft	5.20
HSBC, ex2	Equity	HSBC	5.65

Table 5.3. *Example portfolio for a concentration rule*

Example: No single issuer shall be more than 10% NAV

Step 1: Use a distinct function on the issuer column to identify the unique list of issuers.

Result: HSBC, BP, Microsoft.

Step 2: For each issuer in the list, sum up all positions of that issuer and check that the total is less than 10% NAV, i.e. we must run the filter *Assets.Where(Issuer = x)* for each issuer in the list, "x" being a placeholder for the issuer.

Result: HSBC: 10.17%, BP: 1.21% and Microsoft: 5.20%.

HSBC is greater than 10% so it would cause a breach. Concentration rules are unusual in the fact that a single rule can cause multiple breaches that need to be remedied.

5.1.2.2. *Concentration rules with a running total*

There is one final type of rule that takes the "foreach" concept one stage further. There are only two examples in UCITS, but these rules require a special type of algorithm. Essentially it is a concentration rule, but rather than causing a breach for every issuer over a limit we keep a running total of all issuers over a limit, and once all issuers have been processed we compare the final running total with a fixed value.

Example: The total value of issuers that are greater than 5% NAV shall be less than 40% NAV.

AssetName	AssetType	Issuer	PercentNAV
HSBC, ex1	Equity	HSBC	4.52
BP	Equity	BP	1.21
Microsoft	Equity	Microsoft	5.20
HSBC, ex2	Equity	HSBC	5.65

Table 5.4. *Example for a concentration rule with running total*

Step 1: Identify a distinct list of issuers, i.e. HSBC, BP and Microsoft.

Step 2: For each issuer, calculate the total value of the issuer, i.e. HSBC: 10.17, BP: 1.21 and Microsoft: 5.20. If the value is greater than 5, update the running total.

Running total after HSBC: 10.17; running total after BP: 10.17; and running total after Microsoft: 15.37.

Step 3: Check whether the final running total is greater than 40, i.e. 15.37 > 40, so this is false. The rule is not breached.

This sums up the various types of rules and algorithms that we must be able to perform in order to calculate whether the UCITS rules are breached or not.

5.2. Investment restrictions

5.2.1. *Permitted investments*

Regulation: Article 50, Paragraph 1.

Description: The main change between the UCITS I legislation (85/611/EEC) and UCITS III (2001/108/EC) was the lengthening of the list of eligible assets. UCITS III opened up the possibility of using derivatives for investment purposes (and not just for hedging), money market instruments and bank deposits. This rule is the cornerstone of the UCITS investment restrictions, as all other restrictions are based upon it. Due to its importance and the relative vagueness of the original legal text (specifically around derivatives and indices), the Eligible Assets Directive (EAD[7]) was published in 2007 and adopted in 2008 clarifying which assets were indeed eligible and which were not. This widening in the scope of eligible assets has been one of the key factors in the rise in popularity of so-called "Newcits" funds – hedge funds that are inserted into a UCITS wrapper. For more information on Newcits, see Chapter 9.

The eligible asset categories for a UCITS are as follows:

1. Transferable securities (TSs). A security is transferable if:

a) the potential loss on the investment is limited to the amount paid to acquire it,

b) there is a reliable valuation for the instrument,

c) appropriate information about it is available,

d) it is negotiable,

e) its acquisition is consistent with the investment objectives of the UCITS, and

f) the risks associated with it must be adequately captured by the risk-management process of the UCITS.

2. Money market instruments (MMIs) are eligible if:

a) they are normally dealt on the money market;

b) the value can be accurately determined at any time;

c) they are liquid; and

d) they are listed on an official stock exchange or traded on a regulated market or the issue/issuer is regulated to protect investors.

Figure 5.1 highlights the decision-making process involved in whether a MMI is eligible or not.

---

7   Eligible   Assets   Directive: http://eur-lex.europa.eu/LexUriServ/LexUriServ.do?uri=CELEX:32007L0016:EN:PDF.

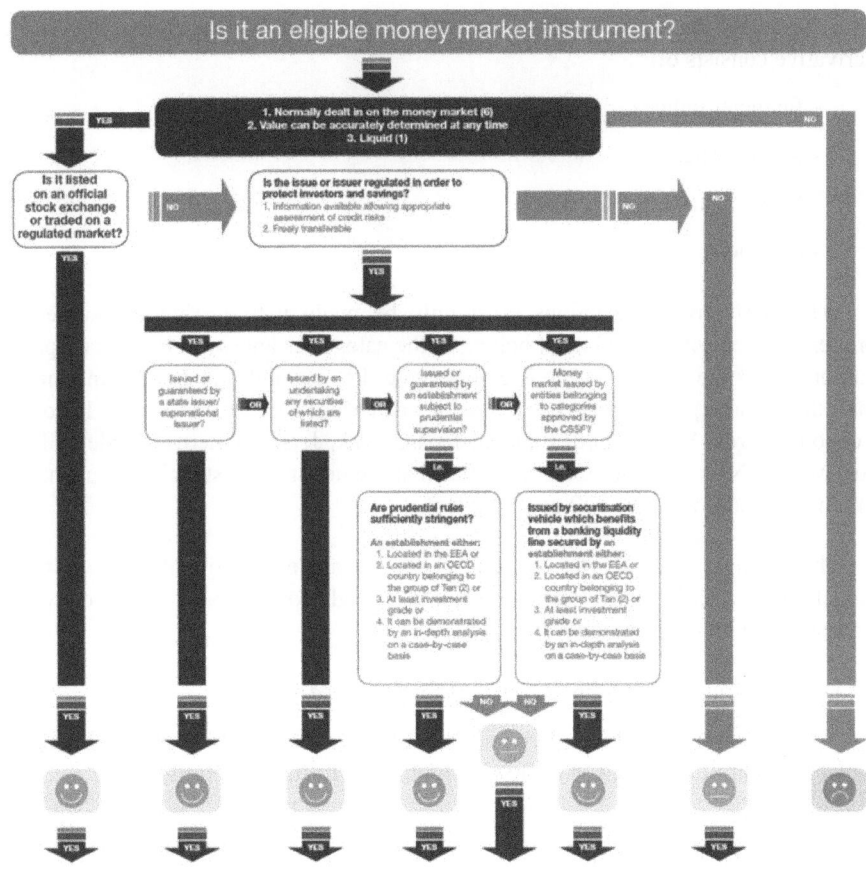

Figure 5.1. *Eligibility of money market instruments (Source: PWC)*

Recently issued TSs and MMIs must contain terms of issue that ensure that an application for official listing will be made within one year.

3. Open-ended collective investment schemes (CISs), provided that the investee CIS limits its own investment in other CISs to 10% NAV;

4. deposits with eligible credit institutions (those with a registered office in a Member State or, if the credit institution has its registered office in a third country, provided that it is subject to prudential rules considered by the competent authorities of the UCITS home Member State as equivalent to those laid down in European Community law), provided that they are repayable on demand (or have the right to be withdrawn) and mature in no more than 12 months; and

5. financial derivative instruments (FDIs), provided that the underlying of the derivative consists of:

- financial indices,

- interest rates,

- foreign exchange rates, or

- currencies.

OTC derivative transactions must only be made with institutions subject to prudential supervision, and must belong to the categories approved by the competent authorities of the UCITS home Member State. For example, in Ireland this means that the counterparty must be a credit institution authorized in the European Economic Area, Switzerland, Canada, Japan, USA, Jersey, Guernsey, Isle of Man, Australia or New Zealand. Counterparties that are not credit institutions must have a minimum credit rating of A-2 or equivalent.

The manager must also ensure that OTCs are subject to reliable and verifiable valuation on a daily basis and can be sold, liquidated or closed by an offsetting transaction at any time at their fair value.

By exclusion the following assets are not permitted:

– commodities (including precious metals or certificates representing them), the typical workaround for this is using Commodity ETFs that are eligible.

– property/real estate;

– private equity; and

– non-financial indices.

This rule requires a pragmatic approach as it would be extremely difficult to (automatically) collect all of the relevant data (especially around information pertaining to liquidity) as mentioned in the EU text and in the advice given by the ESMA[8].

Positions: Assets / (TS ∪ MMI ∪ EligibleFDI ∪ EligibleCIS ∪ EligibleDeposits)

Breached if: Count > 0

---

8 European Securities and Markets Authority, http://www.esma.europa.eu/.

5.2.2. *Maximum of 10% NAV in securities other than those explicitly allowed*

Regulation: Article 50, Paragraph 2 (a).

Text: "A UCITS shall not invest more than 10% of its assets in transferable securities or money market instruments other than those referred to in paragraph 1."

Description: This rule, commonly referred to as the "trash ratio", is one of the rules that differ most widely between different jurisdictions due to its vague wording. It is most commonly interpreted to mean that unlisted TSs and MMIs (or those not traded on a recognized exchange) should not make up more than 10% of the NAV. Some interpretations take the definition further to allow hedge fund indices.

Positions: (TS ∪ MMI) / (EligibleTS ∪ EligibleMMI)

Breached if: Sum(PercentNAV) > 10

5.2.3. *Maximum of 100% NAV global exposure*

Regulation: Article 51, Paragraphs 1 and 3.

Text:

> "*Paragraph 1*: A management or investment company shall employ a risk-management process which enables it to monitor and measure at any time the risk of the positions and their contribution to the overall risk profile of the portfolio."

> "*Paragraph 3*: A UCITS shall ensure that its global exposure relating to derivative instruments does not exceed the total net value of its portfolio."

Description: UCITS III introduced the concept of "sophisticated" and "non-sophisticated" funds. While the concept was never defined very clearly, sophisticated funds were taken to mean those that used a significant number of derivatives or complex investment strategies. Non-sophisticated funds were allowed measured global exposure using the commitment approach, whereas sophisticated funds were to use value at risk (VaR). The sophisticated/non-sophisticated classification has been dropped in UCITS IV and it is now recommended that fund managers monitor the VaR on a daily basis. A fund with a low risk profile may still measure global exposure, however, by using the commitment approach.

There are three compliance rules to be extracted from this:

– the absolute VaR of an UCITS cannot be greater than 20% of its NAV;

– the relative VaR of an UCITS cannot be greater than twice the VaR of a derivative free benchmark (reference portfolio); and

– the sum of the commitment approach for all derivatives must be less than the NAV.

For more information about the risk management process under UCITS and the additional requirements of stress testing and back testing, please see Chapter 5.

5.2.4. *Maximum of 20% NAV in deposits made with the same body*

Regulation: Article 52, Paragraph 1, i (b)

Text: "A UCITS shall invest no more than 20% of its assets in deposits made with the same body."

Description: This is a relatively simple rule to check. The data, however, must be clear on whether the position is ancillary liquidity or an actual bank deposit, which matures in less than a year.

For each: Counterparty of a deposit

Breached if: Sum(PercentNAV) > 20

5.2.5. *Maximum of 10% NAV OTC derivative counterparty risk exposure with approved banks*

Regulation: Article 52, Paragraph 1, ii (a)

Text: "The risk exposure to a counterparty of the UCITS in an OTC derivative transaction shall not exceed 10% of its assets when the counterparty is a credit institution referred to in Article 50(1)(f)."

Description: The credit institutions in Article 50(1)(f) refer to those that have their registered office in a Member State. If the credit institution has its registered office in a third country, then it is eligible provided that it is subject to prudential rules considered by the competent authorities of the UCITS home Member State as equivalent to those laid down in Community law.

Generally those countries that are considered to have prudential rules equivalent to the EU are: the European Economic Area, Switzerland, Canada, Japan, USA, Australia and New Zealand.

For the exact calculation of the counterparty risk exposure, refer to Chapter 8. The counterparty risk is adjusted to subtract any collateral the fund may have received from the counterparty and is subject to quite intricate netting rules. This counterparty risk methodology was the major change between UCITS III and IV.

For each: Counterparty to an OTC where IsCreditInstitution = TRUE AND CounterpartyDomicile IN LIST CountriesWithEquivalentPrudentialRulesList

Breached if: Sum(PercentCounterpartyRiskExposure) > 10

5.2.6. *Maximum of 5% NAV OTC derivative counterparty risk exposure with counterparties other than approved banks*

Regulation: Article 52, Paragraph 1, ii (b)

Text: "The risk exposure to a counterparty of the UCITS in an OTC derivative transaction shall not exceed 5% of its assets, in other cases."

Description: There is a limit of 5% NAV on all counterparties that do not qualify for the 10% limit (presuming they are eligible in the first place, see section 5.2.1 on permitted investments).

For each: Counterparty to an OTC deal Where IsCreditInstitution = FALSE OR CounterpartyDomicile NOT IN LIST CountriesWithEquivalentPrudentialRulesList

Breached if: Sum(PercentCounterpartyRiskExposure) > 5

5.2.7. *Maximum of 10% NAV in securities or money market instruments of the same issuer (except qualified institutions)*

Regulation: Article 52, Paragraph 2, 1st Part (i) and Article 51, Paragraph 3

Text: "A UCITS shall invest no more than 10% (raised from the 5% stated in 51 1(a) in all countries) of its assets in transferable securities or money market instruments issued by the same body."

and "A UCITS may invest, as a part of its investment policy and within the limit laid down in Article 52(5), in financial derivative instruments provided that the exposure to the underlying assets does not exceed in aggregate the investment limits laid down in Article 52."

Description: This and the following rule combined are commonly called the 5/10/40 rule. This first part ensures that no single issuer comprises more that 10% of the portfolio. Article 51, paragraph 3 includes the requirement to add any indirect exposure to the issuer via derivatives to the total exposure, or vice versa, reducing exposure via short derivatives. The rule excludes issuers of government securities and covered bonds that are covered in other specific rules.

Does not apply to: [Quasi-]government securities, covered bonds

For each: Issuer of a security or MMI and underlying issuer (ULIssuer) of a derivative on a single security

Breached if:

- Sum(CommitmentApproachAsPercentNAV[9]) of SecuritiesAndMMI .Where(Issuer = x) +

- Sum(CommitmentApproachAsPercentNAV) of DerivativesIncreasingExposure.Where(ULIssuer = x) –

- Sum(CommitmentApproachAsPercentNAV) of DerivativesDecreasingExposure.Where(ULIssuer = x)

> 10

DerivativesIncreasingExposure, as the name suggests, are all derivative positions that increase exposure to the issuer in question (e.g. long futures, short put/long call options)

For the commitment approach calculation, see Chapter 3.

5.2.8. *Maximum of 40% NAV in securities and derivatives of issuers in which more than 5% is invested in*

Regulation: Article 52, Paragraph 2, 1st Part (ii)

---

9 For the sake of rule brevity for securities and MMIs, CommitmentApproachAsPercentNAV is equal to PercentNAV.

Text: "The total value of the transferable securities and the money market instruments held by the UCITS in the issuing bodies in each of which it invests more than 5% of its assets shall not exceed 40% of the value of its assets."

Description: This rule applies at group level and is a concentration rule with a running total (see section 5.1.2.2) and is broken down into three steps:

– identify all relevant securities and MMIs (e.g. non-government securities), and identify a unique list of ultimate parent issuers;

– for each issuer, if the total issuer exposure is greater than 5% NAV, add to the running total; and

– if running total > 40% NAV, then there is a breach.

An interesting point about this rule is the difficulty in displaying an early warning. Generally we would like to set up an early warning as soon as the value of a rule comes within about 10% (relative) of the investment limit. In the 40% case, this would mean a warning being displayed at 36% NAV. Unfortunately, due to the nature of this rule, imminent breaches can be hard to detect. For example if the fund had five issuers at 6% NAV and two issuers at 4.99% NAV, this rule would have a total value of 30% (nowhere near the early warning limit). Even a tiny upward movement would cause the other two issuers to go above 5%, and in so doing cause the rule to exceed 40%. Therefore this rule requires careful monitoring due to its trigger-like nature.

Does not apply to: [quasi-]government securities, covered bonds

For each: Issuer of a security or MMI and ULIssuer of a derivative

For each issuer:

– IssuerExposure :=

– Sum(CommitmentApproachAsPercentNAV) of SecuritiesAndMMI .Where(Issuer = x) +

– Sum(CommitmentApproachAsPercentNAV) of DerivativesIncreasingExposure.Where(ULIssuer = x) –

– Sum(CommitmentApproachAsPercentNAV) of DerivativesDecreasingExposure.Where(ULIssuer = x)

IF (IssuerExposure > 5) THEN

TotalIssuersOver5Prc := TotalIssuersOver5Prc + IssuerExposure

Breached if: TotalIssuersOver5Prc > 40

Example:

AssetName	AssetType	Issuer	ULIssuer	CommitmentApproachAs PercentNAV
US Treasury Bill	Bond	US		9
Tesco	Equity	Tesco		4
HSBC	Equity	HSBC		4
BP	Equity	BP		9
Microsoft	Equity	Microsoft		7
Long call on HSBC	Option		HSBC	4
Google	Equity	Google		9
Amazon	Equity	Amazon		9

Table 5.5. *Sample portfolio for the 5/40 rule*

Step 1: Calculate the distinct list of issuers for the relevant asset classes, i.e. Tesco, HSBC, BP, Microsoft, Google and Amazon (the US is excluded as it is a government security).

Step 2: Calculate the exposure per issuer, i.e. Tesco: 4, HSBC: 8, BP: 9, Microsoft: 7, Google: 9 and Amazon 9. The HSBC exposure is calculated by adding the equity plus the exposure gained through the long call option.

Those issuers above 5 are summed up, e.g. $8 + 9 + 7 + 9 + 9 = 42$.

Step 3: The rule is breached if the total value is greater than 40, which it is.

Schematically we can represent the rule as in Figure 5.2.

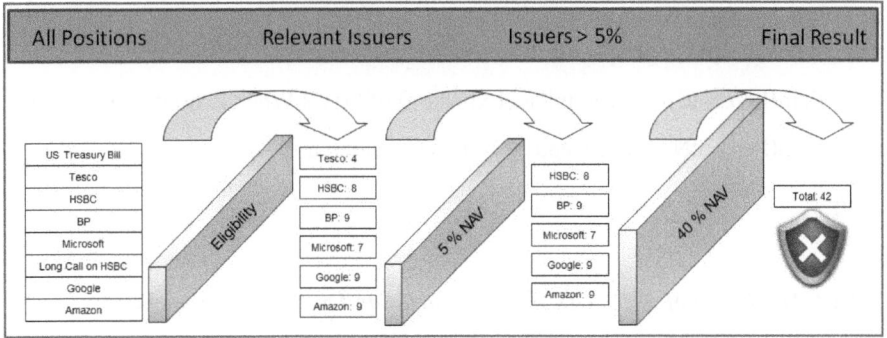

Figure 5.2. *The 5/40 rule logic*

5.2.9. *Maximum of 20% NAV in securities or money market instruments issued by the same body (except qualified institutions)*

Regulation: Article 52, Paragraph 2, 2nd Part

Text: "Notwithstanding the individual limits laid down in paragraph 1, a UCITS shall not combine, where this would lead to investment of more than 20% of its assets in a single body, any of the following:

(a) investments in transferable securities or money market instruments issued by that body;

(b) deposits made with that body; or

(c) exposures arising from OTC derivative transactions undertaken with that body."

Description: Similar to the 10% rule, this rule also adds in any exposures the fund may have in deposits with the body as a bank or with the body as an OTC counterparty. Consistency between the issuer and counterparty information is vital in checking this rule correctly, see 5.5.2. Data .

Does not apply to: [quasi-]government securities, covered bonds

For each: Issuer of a security or MMI, counterparty to a deposit or OTC.

Breached if:

– Sum(PercentNAV) of Securities AndMMI.Where(Issuer = x) +

– Sum(CommitmentApproachAsPercentNAV) of DerivativesIncreasingExposure.Where(ULIssuer = x) –

– Sum(CommitmentApproachAsPercentNAV) of
DerivativesDecreasingExposure.Where(ULIssuer = x) +

  – Sum(PercentCounterpartyRiskExposure) of OTCs.Where(Counterparty = x) +

  – Sum(PercentNAV) of Deposits.Where(Counterparty = x)

> 20

5.2.10. *Maximum of 35% NAV in government and public body securities*

Regulation: Article 52, Paragraph 3

Text: "Member States may raise the 5% limit laid down in the first subparagraph of paragraph 1 to a maximum of 35% if the transferable securities or money market instruments are issued or guaranteed by a Member State, by its local authorities, by a third country or by a public international body to which one or more Member States belong."

Description: Similar to the 10% issuer rule, this rule checks those bodies that are considered government and public securities. By nature, government securities are generally more secure than privately-held securities therefore the 5/10% issuer limit is increased to 35%. In the past it was difficult to find reliable information as to whether the issuer was a government and public securities body, but an increasing number of data providers can now provide this.

Only apply to: [quasi-]government securities

For each: Issuer of a security or MMI.

Breached if:

  – Sum(PercentNAV) of SecuritiesAndMMI .Where(Issuer = x) +

  – Sum(CommitmentApproachAsPercentNAV) of
DerivativesIncreasingExposure.Where(ULIssuer = x) –

  – Sum(CommitmentApproachAsPercentNAV) of
DerivativesDecreasingExposure.Where(ULIssuer = x)

> 35

5.2.11. *Maximum of 25% NAV for bonds issued by EU credit institutions subject by law to special public supervision designed to protect bond holders (covered bonds)*

Regulation: Article 52, Paragraph 4, i

Text: "Member States may raise the 5% limit laid down in the first subparagraph of paragraph 1 to a maximum of 25% where bonds are issued by a credit institution which has its registered office in a Member State and is subject by law to special public supervision designed to protect bond-holders."

Description: This is similar to the 35% rule, but checking covered bonds[10] (Pfandbriefe). Again, reliable data as to whether the bond is covered or not can be difficult to come by.

Only apply to: covered bonds

For each: Issuer of a security or MMI.

Breached if:

   – Sum(PercentNAV) of SecuritiesAndMMI.Where(Issuer = x) +

   – Sum(CommitmentApproachAsPercentNAV) of DerivativesIncreasingExposure.Where(ULIssuer = x) –

   – Sum(CommitmentApproachAsPercentNAV) of DerivativesDecreasingExposure.Where(ULIssuer = x)

> 25

5.2.12. *Maximum of 80% NAV in the covered bonds of issuers in which more than 5% is invested in*

Regulation: Article 52, Paragraph 4, ii

Text: "Where a UCITS invests more than 5% of its assets in the bonds referred to in the first subparagraph which are issued by a single issuer, the total value of these investments shall not exceed 80% of the value of the assets of the UCITS."

Description: This rule is identical to the 5/40 rule (Article 52, Paragraph 2, 1st Part (ii)), except that it only applies to covered bonds and the 40% limit is raised to 80%.

---

10 European Covered Bond Council: http://ecbc.hypo.org/Content/Default. asp?PageID=311.

Only apply to: covered bonds

For each: Issuer of a security or MMI.

For each issuer:

– IssuerExposure :=

– Sum(CommitmentApproachAsPercentNAV) of SecuritiesAndMMI .Where(Issuer = x) +

– Sum(CommitmentApproachAsPercentNAV) of DerivativesIncreasingExposure.Where(ULIssuer = x) –

– Sum(CommitmentApproachAsPercentNAV) of DerivativesDecreasingExposure.Where(ULIssuer = x)

IF (IssuerExposure > 5) THEN

TotalIssuersOver5Prc := TotalIssuersOver5Prc + IssuerExposure

Breached if: TotalIssuersOver5Prc > 80

5.2.13. *Maximum of 20% NAV in respect of investment in the same issuing group*

Regulation: Article 52, Paragraph 4, iii

Text: "Member States may allow cumulative investment in transferable securities and money market instruments within the same group up to a limit of 20%."

Description: This rule applies at group level and in so doing lets individual issuers be up to 10% of NAV, but the group company may not comprise more than 20% NAV. Like the 10% limit, derivatives that indirectly cause exposure to the group company must be added/subtracted to/from the direct exposure. Group company data can be difficult to source, see section 5.5.1. Specific issues.

Does not apply to: [quasi-]government securities, covered bonds

For each: Ultimate issuer of a security or MMI and ultimate ULIssuer of a derivative.

Breached if:

– Sum(PercentNAV) of SecuritiesAndMMI.Where(IssuerGroup = x) +

– Sum(CommitmentApproachAsPercentNAV) of
DerivativesIncreasingExposure.Where(ULIssuerGroup = x) –

– Sum(CommitmentApproachAsPercentNAV) of
DerivativesDecreasingExposure.Where(ULIssuerGroup = x)

> 20

5.2.14. *Index-tracking: maximum of 20% NAV in securities or money market instruments of the same issuer (except qualified institutions)*

Regulation: Article 53, Paragraph 1

Text: "Without prejudice to the limits laid down in Article 56, Member States may raise the limits laid down in Article 52 to a maximum of 20% for investment in shares or debt securities issued by the same body when, according to the fund rules or instruments of incorporation, the aim of the UCITS' investment policy is to replicate the composition of a certain stock or debt securities index which is recognised by the competent authorities, on the following basis:

(a) its composition is sufficiently diversified;

(b) the index represents an adequate benchmark for the market to which it refers; and

(c) it is published in an appropriate manner."

Description: This rule was introduced in UCITS III so that a fund could become an index tracker. Previously, a fund would have breached the 10% rule if it was tracking certain indices (e.g. Siemens constitutes more than 10% of the DAX). The three criteria for index eligibility can be summarized as follows:

– *Sufficiently diversified*: this refers to an index allowing a maximum weighting per issuer of 20% with a capacity for a single constituent to exceed 20% but not exceed 35% of the index.

– *Adequate benchmark*: this implies that the index provider uses a recognized methodology that generally does not result in the exclusion of a major issuer of the market to which it refers.

– *Publication*: this means that the index is accessible to the public and that the index provider is independent from the index replicating UCITS. Note, however, that this second requirement does not stop index providers and the UCITS from forming part of the same economic group, provided that conflict of interest arrangements are in place.

Does not apply to: [quasi-]government securities, covered bonds

For each: Issuer of a security or MMI.

Breached if:

– Sum(PercentNAV) of SecuritiesAndMMI.Where(Issuer = x) +

– Sum(CommitmentApproachAsPercentNAV) of DerivativesIncreasingExposure.Where(ULIssuer = x) –

– Sum(CommitmentApproachAsPercentNAV) of DerivativesDecreasingExposure.Where(ULIssuer = x)

> 20

5.2.15. *Index-tracking: Max 35% NAV in securities or money market instruments of the same issuer (except qualified institutions) for a single issuer*

Regulation: Article 53, Paragraph 2

Text: "Member States may raise the limit laid down in paragraph 1 to a maximum of 35% where that proves to be justified by exceptional market conditions in particular in regulated markets where certain transferable securities or money market instruments are highly dominant. The investment up to that limit shall be permitted only for a single issuer."

Description: This regulation was designed to allow funds to track indices where there is one single dominant constituent. This applied, for example, to the OMX Helsinki Benchmark Index where Nokia was weighted around 40%[11].

For each: Issuer of a security or MMI

For each issuer:

– IssuerExposure :=

– Sum(PercentNAV) of SecuritiesAndMMI.Where(Issuer = x) +

– Sum(CommitmentApproachAsPercentNAV) of DerivativesIncreasingExposure.Where(ULIssuer = x) –

---

11 OMX Helsinki Benchmark Index: https://newsclient.omxgroup.com/cds/Disclosure AttachmentServlet?messageAttachmentId=189080.

– Sum(CommitmentApproachAsPercentNAV) of
DerivativesDecreasingExposure.Where(ULIssuer = x)

IF(IssuerExposure > 20) THEN

NumberOfIssuersGreater20 := NumberOfIssuersGreater20 + 1

Breached if: NumberOfIssuersGreater20 > 1

5.2.16. *Minimum of six issues and maximum of 30% per issuance when more than 35% NAV is invested in a single public issuer*

Regulation: Article 54, Paragraph 1

Text: "By way of derogation from Article 52, Member States may authorize UCITS to invest in accordance with the principle of risk-spreading up to 100% of their assets in different transferable securities and money market instruments issued or guaranteed by a Member State, one or more of its local authorities, a third country, or a public international body to which one or more Member States belong.

"The competent authorities of the UCITS home Member State shall grant such derogation only if they consider that unit-holders in the UCITS have protection equivalent to that of unit-holders in UCITS complying with the limits laid down in Article 52. Such a UCITS shall hold securities from at least six different issues, but securities from any single issue shall not account for more than 30% of its total assets.

"The UCITS [...] shall make express mention in the fund rules or in the instruments of incorporation of the investment company. Each UCITS referred to in paragraph 1 shall include a prominent statement in its prospectus and marketing communications drawing attention to such authorization."

Description: If the fund invests more than 35% in certain government and public securities, then these issuers must be listed in the prospectus. If this is the case, the fund must then hold at least six securities and none of the securities from this issuer may be greater than 30%.

It is unclear from the wording in the regulation whether it is six issues for the issuer in question or any six issues, but the general interpretation is any six securities issued by that or another issuer.

Also note that unless there is an electronic link from the prospectus (i.e. document management system) to the monitoring system, then the list of issuers allowed above 35% must be manually entered into the compliance system.

For each: Issuer of a security or MMI that is specified to be allowed greater than 35% NAV.

Breached if:

– Sum(PercentNAV) of SecuritiesAndMMI.Where(Issuer = x) +

– Sum(CommitmentApproachAsPercentNAV) of DerivativesIncreasingExposure.Where(ULIssuer = x) –

– Sum(CommitmentApproachAsPercentNAV) of DerivativesDecreasingExposure.Where(ULIssuer = x)

> 35 AND (Max(PercentNAV) > 30 OR COUNT < 6)

AssetName	AssetType	Issuer	PercentNAV
US Treasury Bill 1	Bond	US	31
US Treasury Bill 2	Bond	US	1
US Treasury Bill 3	Bond	US	1
US Treasury Bill 4	Bond	US	1
US Treasury Bill 5	Bond	US	1
US Treasury Bill 6	Bond	US	1

Table 5.6. *Sample portfolio breaching the 6/30/35 rule. It is breached as total US > 35 and the US Treasury Bill 1 is 31% NAV*

AssetName	AssetType	Issuer	PercentNAV
US Treasury Bill 1	Bond	US	29
US Treasury Bill 2	Bond	US	2
US Treasury Bill 3	Bond	US	2
US Treasury Bill 4	Bond	US	2
US Treasury Bill 5	Bond	US	2

Table 5.7. *Sample portfolio number 2 breaching the 6/30/35 rule. It is breached as the total US is greater than 35 and the portfolio only contains five issues*

AssetName	AssetType	Issuer	PercentNAV
US Treasury Bill 1	Bond	US	29
US Treasury Bill 2	Bond	US	2
US Treasury Bill 3	Bond	US	2
US Treasury Bill 4	Bond	US	2
US Treasury Bill 5	Bond	US	2
US Treasury Bill 6	Bond	US	2

Table 5.8. *Sample portfolio number 3 not breaching the 6/30/35 rule. This portfolio contains six issues and largest one is less than 30*

5.2.17. *Maximum of 20% NAV in any one CIS*

Regulation: Article 55, Paragraph 1

Text: "A UCITS may acquire the units of UCITS or other collective investment undertakings referred to in Article 50(1) (e), provided that no more than 10% of its assets are invested in units of a single UCITS or other collective investment undertaking. Member States may raise that limit to a maximum of 20%."

Description: This rule ensures no single CIS makes up more than 20% of the fund's NAV. Each CIS can be referenced via its ISIN or AssetId.

For each: CIS

Breached if: Sum(PercentNAV) of CIS.Where(ISIN = x) > 20

5.2.18. *Maximum of 30% NAV in aggregate in non-UCITS CIS*

Regulation: Article 55, Paragraph 2

Text: "Investments made in units of collective investment undertakings other than UCITS shall not exceed, in aggregate, 30% of the assets of the UCITS."

Description: This is a simple rule that can sometimes prove difficult to check due to the lack of data as to whether a CIS is UCITS-compliant or not.

Positions: CIS where IsUCITS = False

Breached if: Sum(PercentNAV) > 30

5.2.19. *Significant influence of voting shares per single issuing body (excluding certain public bodies)*

Regulation: Article 56, Paragraph 1

Text: "An investment company or a management company acting in connection with all of the common funds which it manages and which fall within the scope of this Directive shall not acquire any shares carrying voting rights which would enable it to exercise significant influence over the management of an issuing body."

Description: This rule is to prohibit a fund taking a major shareholding in certain companies. The vaguely worded "significant influence" is normally taken to mean 20% of the total shares. The total value of shares in issue can prove to be tricky to obtain and the accuracy of the figures is also sometimes questionable.

Does not apply to:

   – transferable securities and money market instruments issued or guaranteed by a Member State or its local authorities;

   – transferable securities and money market instruments issued or guaranteed by a third country;

   – transferable securities and money market instruments issued by a public international body to which one or more Member States belong;

   – shares held by a UCITS in the capital of a company incorporated in a third country investing its assets mainly in the securities of issuing bodies with their registered offices in that country, where under the legislation of that country such a holding represents the only way in which the UCITS can invest in the securities of issuing bodies of that country; or

   – shares held by an investment company or investment companies in the capital of subsidiary companies pursuing only the business of management, advice or marketing in the country where the subsidiary is established, in regard to the repurchase of units at unit-holders' request exclusively on its or their behalf.

For each: Issuer of a voting share

Breach If: Sum(PercentOwnership) of Shares.Where(Issuer = x) > 20

5.2.20. *Maximum of 10% of non-voting shares per single issuing body (excluding certain public bodies)*

Regulation: Article 56, Paragraph 2 (a)

Text: "A UCITS may acquire no more than 10% of the non-voting shares of a single issuing body"

Description: This rule ensures that a fund spreads its exposure so that the exposure to any single issuer of a non-voting security does not exceed 10% of the total value of the non-voting securities issued. This and the following three rules (sections 5.2.21 to 5.2.23) have the interesting proviso that if the total value in issue is unknown the rule can be disregarded.

Does not apply to: See Article 56, Paragraph 1

For each: Issuer of a non-voting share

Breached if: Sum(PercentOwnership) of Shares.Where(Issuer = x) > 10

Note: "The limit […] may be disregarded at the time of acquisition if at that time […] the net amount of securities in issue, cannot be calculated."

5.2.21. *Maximum of 10% of the debt securities of any single issuing body*

Regulation: Article 56, Paragraph 2 (b)

Text: "A UCITS may acquire no more than 10% of the debt securities of a single issuing body."

Description: This rule ensures that a fund spreads its exposure so that the exposure to any single issuer of a debt security does not exceed 10% of the total value of the issues of debt securities.

Does not apply to: See Article 56, Paragraph 1

For each: Issuer of a debt security

Breached if: Sum(PercentOfDebtSecurities) of DebtSecurities.Where(Issuer = x) > 10

Note: "The limit […] may be disregarded at the time of acquisition if at that time the gross amount of the debt securities […], cannot be calculated."

5.2.22. *Maximum of 25% of the units of any single CIS (excluding certain public bodies)*

Regulation: Article 56, Paragraph 2 (c)

Text: "A UCITS may acquire no more than 25% of the units of a single UCITS or other collective investment undertaking within the meaning of Article 1(2)(a) and (b)."

Description: This rule ensures that a fund spreads its exposure so that the exposure to any single CIS does not exceed 25% of the total units in issue.

Does not apply to: See Article 56, Paragraph 1.

For each: CIS

Breached if: Sum(PercentOfUnitsInCirculation) of CIS.Where(ISIN = x) > 25

Note: "The limit [...] may be disregarded at the time of acquisition if at that time [...] the net amount of securities in issue, cannot be calculated."

5.2.23. *Maximum of 10% of money market instruments of any single issuing body*

Regulation: Article 56, Paragraph 2 (b)

Text: "A UCITS may acquire no more than 10% of the money market instruments of a single issuing body."

Description: Due to the general lack of information on total MMIs in issue, this rule is normally combined with the 10% debt securities limit

Does not apply to: See Article 56, Paragraph 1.

For each: Issuer of an MMI.

Breached if: Sum(PercentOfMMI) of MMI.Where(Issuer = x) > 10

Note: "The limit [...] may be disregarded at the time of acquisition if at that time the gross amount of the [...] money market instruments [...], cannot be calculated."

5.2.24. *Six-month derogation*

Regulation: Article 57

Text: "While ensuring observance of the principle of risk spreading, Member States may allow recently authorised UCITS to derogate from Articles 52 to 55 for six months following the date of their authorisation."

Description: All UCITS funds are permitted to derogate from the investment restrictions in the above-mentioned articles for a period of six months. This is a necessary rule, as it would nearly be impossible for a fund to start on day one and be perfectly compliant with all restrictions.

5.2.25. *A fund may borrow up to 10% of NAV for temporary purposes*

Regulation: Article 83, Paragraph 2 (a), i

Text: "By way of derogation from paragraph 1, a Member State may authorise a UCITS to borrow provided that such borrowing is on a temporary basis and represents no more than 10% of its assets."

Description: The wording "temporary basis" is rather vague and is usually interpreted to mean that the borrowing may not exceed a certain duration (normally three months) and/or that the number of occasions on which the fund borrows within a specific period of time must be limited.

Breached if: Sum(AbsolutePercentOfNAV) of Borrowings > 10 for 90 consecutive business days

5.2.26. *No uncovered sales of transferable securities, MMIs or other financial instruments*

Regulation: Article 89

Text: "An investment company shall not carry out uncovered sales of transferable securities, money market instruments or other financial instruments referred to in points (e), (g) and (h) of Article 50(1)."

Description: More commonly referred to as naked short-selling, this rule prohibits physical short selling without first borrowing security or ensuring that the security can be borrowed (e.g. via a derivative). It is, however, possible to achieve short selling synthetically (e.g. via a short call and a long put option) or by the use of CFDs.

For each: security or MMI

Breached if: Uncovered quantity of security or MMI > 0

5.3. *Look through*

According to Article 51, paragraph 3 of the directive "When transferable securities or money market instruments embed a derivative, the derivative shall be taken into account when complying with the requirements of this Article."

An instrument that embeds a derivative is one where the derivative element has a different risk and cash flow profile to the host instrument. Common examples are credit-linked notes, convertible bonds and partly paid securities.

In the case of an embedded derivative, we must "look through" the host instrument to the underlying instrument. For all rules the underlying instrument must be accounted for in all exposure calculations.

For example, in the case of a convertible bond we must separate the bond element from the call option on the underlying equity. The exposure to the underlying equity must be added to all other relevant exposures (e.g. issuer exposure to the equity's issuer).

5.4. Market practices and specific cases

One of the main difficulties of UCITS is still the local specifications and varying interpretations between jurisdictions, some illustrative examples are:

– the trash ratio;

– VaR;

– definition of transferable security; and

– borrowing.

5.4.1. *Trash ratio*

Probably the biggest case is in the interpretation of Article 50, Paragraph 2 (a) (the so called "trash ratio" rule). The most flexible country is probably France, as investments in hedge funds and funds of hedge funds are allowed under certain conditions laid down by the regulator (AMF). The Luxembourg regulator (CSSF) has followed the French model, but with some limitations. It is therefore important to check with the regulators, the auditors, professional organizations or any other service providers specialized in UCITS how this particular rule is understood in other jurisdictions.

5.4.2. *VaR*

The introduction of the use of VaR for sophisticated funds came with UCITS III and was initially quite vague. It took various recommendations from CESR (the predecessor to ESMA) to clarify how the VaR was to be calculated. Despite this the national regulators have laid down different parameters to the VaR calculation as illustrated in Table 5.9.

Country Factor	France	Germany	Ireland	Italy	Luxembourg	UK
Level of Confidence	95%	99%	95 or 99%	99%	99%	99%
Holding Period	7 days	10 business days	20 business days	1 month	1 month	1 month
Historical data	-	Min. 1 year	Min. 1 year	Max. 1 year	Max. 1 year	Max. 1 year

Table 5.9. *VaR parameters around the EU*

Some regulators have not defined them at all and have left it up to the individual asset managers.

5.4.3. *Definition of transferable security*

Here we will give a specific example. The Central Bank of Ireland allows a non-UCITS ETF to be classified either as a CIS or as a transferable security. As a TS there is no requirement to look through the ETF to the underlying assets, as diversification is applied at the ETF level and not to the underlyings.

5.4.4. *Borrowing*

Article 83, Paragraph 2 (a) allows for up to 10% NAV in temporary borrowings. The Irish regulator for example does not try to define temporary, the wording being:

An investment company may borrow up to 10% of its assets and a unit trust or a common contractual fund may borrow up to 10% of the value of the fund, provided this borrowing is on a temporary basis.

The UK regulator (Financial Services Authority) is more specific in COLL 5.5.4:

The authorised fund manager must ensure that any borrowing is on a temporary basis and that borrowings are not persistent, and for this purpose the authorised fund manager must have regard in particular to: the duration of any period of borrowing; and the number of occasions on which resort is had to borrowing in any period.

In the next line, the period is set at a maximum of three months.

5.4.5. *Other*

In addition to the rules that vary between countries, there are some extra regulations that have been added in various jurisdictions. For example, in Ireland there is a requirement that derivatives that require physical delivery must have the underlying present in the portfolio at all times (10.6.18, i). Likewise, derivatives that are cash-settled must have sufficient liquid assets to cover the exposure (10.6.18, ii).

Also there are particular limits around repos, reverse-repos and stock lending in certain jurisdictions.

5.4.6. *Summary*

These are some clear examples that show that the compliance officer who is working in multiple jurisdictions should not only be aware of the official EU regulation, but also of the national interpretation and in many cases the market's best practices (e.g. auditor, ESMA guidelines or by asking for direct clarification with the respective regulator).

5.5. Data issues

The absence of reliable high-quality data is one of the key issues in compliance. While all the rules and algorithms can be perfect, if the data input into the checking process is erroneous or missing then the most a compliance monitoring system can do is give a best guess or at least display a visual warning that a specific rule could not be checked due to bad data.

5.5.1. *Specific issues*

UCITS III introduced an entire set of new data item requirements. The most difficult of these to obtain was probably the ultimate parent issuer data (i.e. group company data).

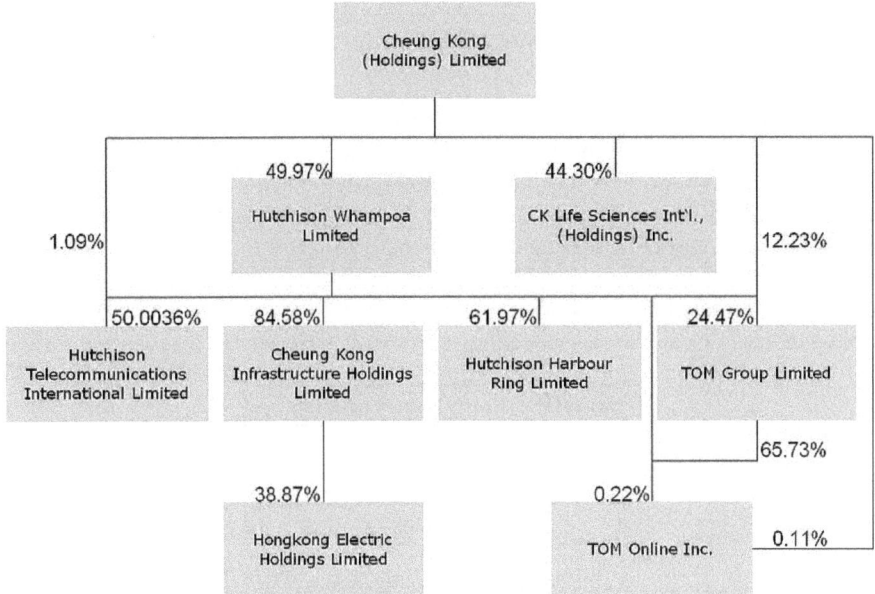

Figure 5.3. *Example group structure chart for Cheung Kong Limited*

With the increasing demand from the UCITS industry, data providers rose to the challenge. Now companies such as Standard & Poor (with their Security to Entity CrossWalk), IDC (with their Business Entity Data Service) and others provide this information.

Other particularly tricky items of data to obtain are the number of shares in issue (Article 56(1)), total CIS units in circulation (Article 56(2c)) and information as to whether a CIS is an UCITS fund or not (Article 55(2)).

5.5.2. *Data consistency*

In a similar area to issuer data, there can also be the onerous issue of consistency between counterparty and issuer information. Consider a portfolio with three positions, as given in Table 5.10.

AssetName	AssetType	IssuerGroup	CounterpartyGroup	PercentNAV
HSBC	Equity	HSBC Ltd.		4.52
Call on BP	OTC Option		HSBC	1.21
GBP Deposit	Deposit		HSBC Bank	2.45

Table 5.10. *Portfolio with different exposures to HSBC*

To calculate our exposure for the 20% group company rule (Article 52(4iii)) we must add all exposures in positions relating to the same entity. This is easy for a human to calculate (all three positions are obviously related to the HSBC group) but practically impossible for an IT system to ascertain (discounting the use of risky fuzzy matching, e.g. using a distance algorithm[12]).

The only solution to this issue is to ensure that there are manually-maintained lookup tables in place that associate the values with each other, e.g.:

EntityID	EntityNameVariation
1	HSBC Ltd.
1	HSBC
1	HSBC Bank

Table 5.11. *Possible entity lookup table*

5.5.3. OTC data

With the exponential uptake in use of OTCs over the past few years, the biggest challenge to emerge is the availability of reliable OTC information. As opposed to exchange-traded instruments whose data can be accessed by any connected IT system, the details of an OTC contract are only known to the two parties. This means an increased burden on the compliance function, as all information must be entered into an IT system before the OTC can be processed. One glimmer of hope in this respect is the recent move towards using Central Clearing with a Central Counterparty (CCP) sitting between buyer and seller. This will more than likely reduce the burden on the individual asset manager as the data will be maintained centrally by the CCP.

---

12 Levenshtein Distance Algorithm: http://www.scribd.com/doc/18654513/levenshtein? secret_password=1aycnw239qw4jqjtsm34#full.

5.5.4. *Technology advances*

Technology is helping to remove some of the difficulties asset managers face in the data management sphere. Traditionally, data warehouses had to be maintained in-house to store all of the relevant asset information. These were cumbersome, expensive beasts that cost vast sums to maintain.

With the widespread adoption of the internet, an increasing number of data providers (whether or not they are true data vendors), stock exchanges are providing so-called APIs[13] (also called "WebServices") that can provide all of the relevant information about an asset via the internet. This means that a compliance system can automatically retrieve any information missing from the original data exported from the accounting system.

5.5.5. *Summary*

The input to the compliance system will come primarily from the accounting system. It must then be enhanced with all the relevant data necessary for UCITS. These may come from external data providers via Web services or from an in-house data warehouse. Consistency of identifiers must be assured and finally there must be a process in place for manually entering missing or incorrect data, as otherwise the compliance check will not be accurate.

5.6. Checking process

Historically, due to various IT and operational constraints, the NAV of the fund was calculated at most once a day. This was therefore the logical point to conduct the UCITS compliance check. Traditionally this is known as the *ex-post* check but it is sometimes also referred to as the batch run or even, erroneously, as the post-trade check.

5.6.1. *Ex-post*

Let us presume that the NAV of the fund is calculated at a certain time every day. As soon as this is done, all relevant data are automatically exported and fed to the compliance monitoring system. In practice this normally means that data from the accounting system (e.g. positions and NAVs) is enhanced with static data from an external data provider (e.g. IDC, Bloomberg, etc.) or from an internal data warehouse.

---

13 Application programming interface (API): http://www.makeuseof.com/tag/api-good-technology-explained/.

5.6.1.1 *Data validation*

The first step that must be carried out before the rules are checked is data validation. Early validation is best practice, as for example a single piece of missing data (e.g. the asset type) could cause nearly every single rule to fail across multiple portfolios.

There are multiple layers of validation:

– *Data type validation*: for example if a numeric value is expected in a certain field (e.g. MarketValue) but a non-numeric value was encountered in it.

– *Expected value validation*: for many data items we have a list of possible values that are accepted (e.g. currencies, countries, asset types). If the data has values that are not in this list, then problems may occur. Therefore it is important to make sure that these fields are checked for consistency.

– *Expected properties*: different asset types have different data items that are necessary for checking (e.g. for cash we need only a few data items and for OTC derivatives we need a lot more). Hence it is necessary to check every asset to see whether we have all the relevant information for it.

– *Other validation*: before actually carrying out the UCITS check, it may be useful to carry out some more advanced validation. One of the most important types of validation involves checking for stale prices, i.e. prices that have not changed since the last check. This could imply that the data export was incorrect or that there has been a processing problem.

Assuming that the checking process is fully automated and no problems were detected, the compliance check can be run. If any validation issues are found, an email will be sent to the compliance officer (among others) outlining any problems.

Import Preview

Uploaded file has errors
- Line 1: AssetType: "Equity" For this asset type the following properties are required: Issuer
- Line 2: IsIndexFund: "NO" Invalid boolean format
- Line 3: NavDate: "yesterday" Invalid date format
- Line 3: MarketValue: "6000000x" Invalid decimal format
- Line 4: AssetCurrency: "XYZ" "XYZ" does not belong to the value set AssetCurrency

N	Name	Nav	NavDate	ParentId	IsIndexFund	AssetCurrency	AssetId	AssetName	Issuer	IssuerGroup	AssetType	MarketValue	Price	Quantity	CallOrPut	C
1	European Equity Fund	100000000	2011-08-11	5	FALSE	EUR	101	Ryanair		Ryanair	Equity	6000000	60	100000		
2	European Equity Fund	100000000	2011-08-12	5	NO	EUR	102	Lufthansa	Lufthansa	Lufthansa	Equity	6000000	60	100000		
3	European Equity Fund	100000000	yesterday	5	FALSE	EUR	16	British Airways	British Airways	British Airways	Equity	6000000x	60	100000		
4	European Equity Fund	100000000	2011-08-11	5	FALSE	XYZ	107	South African Airways	South African Airways	South African Airways	Equity	5500000	55	100000		

The file has 5 invalid cells

Figure 5.4. *Example of a data validation report*

At this stage the compliance officer has two options:

– fix the problems in the master system (i.e. the accounting engine or data warehouse); or

– manually enter the information in the compliance system.

Option one might not be possible for every company, as sometimes the compliance officer is not in a position to remedy the data problems in the master system (or certainly not within a timely manner – especially in large organizations).

Therefore having the second option is vital for any organization. Not only to remedy incorrect or missing data, but also to enter data for which there is no other automatic data source. This information can then be added to the compliance system, so that the user must only enter the missing data once.

Once the data are complete the actual rule-checking process may begin.

5.6.1.2. *Rule checking*

The UCITS rules can be broken down in to two groups – one group for normal funds and one group for index funds. Instead of the normal concentration rules, index funds must comply with the 20%/35% rules.

Every relevant rule is checked and a result saved – OK, warning or breach. For breaches there are two further calculations that must be made:

– is this a new breach?

– is the breach active or passive?

5.6.1.3. *New/existing breaches*

To be in a position to work out whether a breach is new or not, the compliance system must check and save results for there are data every day.

A new breach is one where there was no breach for this rule and portfolio during the last *ex-post* check. If this is not the case, today's breach is a continuation of an existing incident. In this case it is useful to save a "Day Count" total so when a breach is finally closed we can see how long the breach ran for. This can be useful for management statistics and reports (e.g. a report to show the average time to the resolution of breaches).

5.6.1.4. *Active/passive classification*

The classification of a breach into active or passive (also sometimes called advertent/inadvertent) is a requirement for many regulators. Simply put, an active breach is one where an executed trade is the cause of the breach. By reverse definition, a passive breach is one where price movements, or less likely corporate actions, were responsible for the breach.

On first inspection this appears to be a simple enough process. From an *ex-post* perspective (as if an *ex-ante* check is in place, active breaches should *theoretically* be impossible) as long as we know the last quantity for every position in the portfolio from the last check and compare it to the current position we can calculate whether there has been activity. Complications arise in some scenarios:

AssetName	Quantity	Price	MarketValue	PercentNAV
Equity1	100	9 GBP	900 GBP	9.00

Table 5.12. *Positions T-1*

AssetName	Quantity	Price	MarketValue	PercentNAV
Equity1	101	10 GBP	1,010 GBP	10.10

Table 5.13. *Position T*

Here we can see that there has been activity (one share has been bought), but that this purchase was NOT the cause of the breach – one share at either the old price or even the new price would have brought the market value to 909 GBP (or 910 GBP, respectively).

The exact definition of an active breach has not been specified by the regulators; therefore it can be left to the fund manager to decide how to classify what constitutes one.

5.6.1.5. *Result verification*

For any investment manager with multiple funds, the workflow behind processing compliance results is of vital importance.

First of all, the need for a clear compliance overview is of the utmost importance. A heat map or matrix of some sort is essential to give the compliance officer an overview of the current state (see Figure 5.5).

	Bond Fund	DAX Fund	FTSE Fund	Transport Fund
Only eligible assets allowed	OK	OK	OK	✗
Max. 10% NAV in recently is...	OK	OK	OK	OK
Max. 30% NAV in non UCITS CIS	OK	OK	OK	OK
Only eligible deposits	OK	OK	OK	✗
Max. 10% in unlisted securi...	OK	OK	OK	OK
Max. 20% NAV in any one CIS	OK	OK	OK	OK
Max. 10% NAV in trans. secu...	OK	OK	OK	OK
Max. 20% NAV in deposits wi...	OK	OK	OK	OK
Max. 40% NAV in issuers whi...	OK	OK	OK	⚠
Max. 5% OTC counterparty ri...	OK	OK	OK	OK
Max. 10% OTC counterparty r...	OK	OK	OK	OK
Max. 20% NAV in trans. secu...	OK	OK	OK	OK
Max. 25% in covered bonds i...	OK	OK	OK	OK
Max. 35% NAV in government ...	OK	OK	OK	OK
Max. 80% in covered bond is...	OK	OK	OK	OK
Max. 35% NAV exposure to an...	OK	OK	OK	OK
Max. 20% NAV in trans. secu...	OK	OK	OK	OK
Min. 6 Issues if government...	OK	OK	OK	OK
Max. 30% NAV in any issue o...	OK	OK	OK	OK
Max. 20% of the voting righ...	OK	OK	OK	✗
Max. 10% of the non-voting ...	OK	✗	OK	OK

Figure 5.5. *Example of an ex-post compliance overview with UCITS rules in the left column and funds checked across the top*

The traffic light system is the most common paradigm for giving an overview of the results. Green signifies OK, yellow is an early warning and red is a breach. The warning means that a rule is close to being breached (e.g. in the above, the 5/40 rule is close to 40%) and calls for close observation from the compliance officer.

Any new breaches should immediately be visible (e.g. with an additional icon), as should active breaches, which must be resolved as a matter of priority. The ability to filter and analyze the results is extremely important, e.g. to see which breaches are deteriorating, which have been running for more than 30 days, etc.

As the number of portfolios increases, a facility to analyze the underlying reasons behind new breaches is crucial. For example, if we imagine that an OTC counterparty is downgraded overnight – if there are OTCs with this counterparty in multiple portfolios, then a single downgrade could potentially cause tens if not hundreds of breaches (e.g. eligible counterparty rule). The ability to see that that all of these breaches had a single cause would significantly reduce the compliance workload.

5.6.2. *Ex-ante*

In a static world the *ex-post* check would pick up any breaches that had happened during the day (or in the last period if the NAV was not calculated daily). Obviously this does not mesh with the real-world scenario of funds that are actively trading throughout the day. Each of these trades can logically bring the fund into a non-compliant state. One of the most important compliance advances has therefore been *ex-ante* (more commonly known as pre-trade) checking. This involves a proposed trade being checked before it is actually executed.

There are varying reasons for the slow uptake in pre-trade compliance:

– *Lack of straight through processing*: in many buy-side organizations, trades are still executed via phone, email, etc. Therefore it would be impossible for a compliance engine to gain access to information about the trades before they are placed. The solution to this is the installation of electronic front-office/order management systems that route proposed trades to the compliance engine for checking. Only if the compliance engine returns "OK" is the trade actually forwarded for execution, or if execution is still manual, is the end-user given the go - ahead to execute the trade.

– *Lack of centralized IT*: similar to the above, there may be multiple order management system (OMS) in place (e.g. one for bonds, and one for equities), but there is no single point where the current state of the portfolio is known and through which all trades are routed for compliance checking.

– *Speed*: depending on the implementation of a compliance engine, a large or even a medium-sized fund could take too long to pass all the UCITS checks. The number of positions is the main determinant in the algorithmic speed of the compliance check (typically $O(n)$)[14]. Even though funds might be long-term investment vehicles, a delay in execution of a couple of minutes could adversely affect the profitability of the trade. On a purely human note, people in high-pressured jobs are not particularly patient and a pre-trade compliance check that takes longer than a few seconds could hinder the uptake of the system and could result in users reverting to using the telephone again.

With improvements in processor speed and the introduction of straight through processing into many fund managers, pre-trade has become a reality for many. It

---

14 Big O notation: http://rob-bell.net/2009/06/a-beginners-guide-to-big-o-notation/.

still has some hurdles to overcome before it is a standard feature for every asset manager.

Pre-trade checking cannot be seen as a silver bullet. Certain absolute rules (e.g. the eligible assets rule or the eligible counterparties rule) can be checked with confidence, but as few modern accounting systems can provide a real-time NAV any quantitative rule can only be a "best guess".

5.6.2.1. *Ex-ante workflow*

The compliance system will sit somewhere centrally and all systems that need to interact with it are connected (e.g. portfolio management system for "what-if" simulations, order-management systems for pre-trade checks, etc.). It has the current positions for all portfolios and updates them through the day.

Orders can and should be grouped together for compliance purposes as it is possible to be in a scenario where a sell trade is impossible (e.g. as a minimum holding rule would be breached) and so is a buy trade (e.g. the maximum holding rule would be breached or there is not enough cash). Only in combination could the two orders be carried out without failing the compliance check.

Assuming a new order is routed to the compliance system, the workflow is as follows:

1. *Data validation*: as with *ex-post*, it is vital that all pertinent information about the asset that is being traded is available. If it is not the case, the order cannot be checked.

2. *Check*: the portfolio must be updated with the order and all rules being rechecked.

3. *Comparison*: a comparison must be made between the compliance status before the order and the status after.

4. *Result*: The order will fail if:

    a. it causes any new breaches; or

    b. it causes an existing breach to get worse. This is necessary to prevent so-called "healing orders" that improve an existing breach (e.g. reducing the exposure from 45% to 41%) but do not completely clear it.

5. *User input*: the result of the check is returned to the user who sent the order. If the check results in a fail, it is sensible to allow a so-called "override" (e.g. due to data issues, concurrency problems, etc.). Depending on authorization either the user can:

a. directly override the breach themselves and place the order anyway; or

b. they can request an override from a second person/superior who will automatically receive a message asking for an override. It is important that all of these decisions are audited and visible at a later stage.

6. *Update positions*: the positions in the portfolio are updated to include the order:

a. if the order is OK and the user clicks "Place"; or

b. if the order is a "Fail", but it is overridden.

In all other cases, the portfolio's positions are reverted to what they were before the order.

This continues throughout the day until a new NAV is calculated and the *ex-post* check is run for the new day.

5.7. Conclusion

A complete UCITS monitoring solution is the sum of many parts. It is the combination of a set of rules, a data import and management system, a checking engine and a review and resolution management system. Each part is vitally important in its own right.

The European Commission, national regulator and ESMA website must be regularly checked for updates and guidance on the investment limits. The asset and portfolio data must be constantly monitored for consistency and completeness.

For on-going compliance, it is necessary to check *ex-ante* (to prevent any active breaches) as well as *ex-post* (to detect any passive breaches, or any other irregularities) and to audit any changes that have happened.

Finally, overviews of results, analysis functions and advanced management reports are necessary to give the fund manager an accurate and comprehensive overview.

With all this, a compliance officer can confidently claim to be monitoring UCITS as the regulator intended.

Chapter 6

UCITS Distribution

6.1. Introduction and overview

UCITS-complying funds are created to facilitate collective investment by the public and therefore target the full spectrum of potential investors. The overarching objective of an UCITS is to maximize assets under management by reaching the widest range of investors possible, each with their own specific needs and objectives and overall returns to investors. It follows that the process of distribution, both national and cross-border, is a critical component in the life a typical UCITS.

Over the past ten years, the distribution of UCITS has developed into an increasingly complex vertical and horizontal value chain with a multitude of different related and unrelated actors. The most important driver of increasing complexity in UCITS distribution has been the significant level of growth in UCITS sold on a cross-border or international basis. Over the past ten years an increasing numbers of national asset managers, banks and insurance companies have entered the international fund market by launching UCITS to be sold on a cross-border basis, as distinct from a domestic-only sales strategy.

The key objective in launching a cross-border distribution strategy is usually to broaden an existing nationally based fund business by seeking to attract investors (and their assets) in other markets. Often such strategies are launched because the asset manager has been very successful in his domestic market and can see opportunities to replicate that success across multiple jurisdictions simultaneously. Other managers may view foreign markets as a way to "break-out" of a mature domestic market or to transform an existing boutique asset management business

---

Chapter written by Mark EVANS.

onto a larger more profitable footing. Whatever the reason, all such international UCITS promoters or managers seek to target local investors in multiple domestic markets using the same fund structure, generally as a means to extract greater economies of scale and overall efficiencies in operating an UCITS fund.

As the UCITS business model has become more complex and expensive to maintain, greater focus has been placed on international or cross-border distribution as a means to reduce costs relative to additional revenue streams and to seek a greater return on capital in an industry that is increasingly becoming a volume business. Nevertheless, all key stakeholders can and should share the economic efficiencies gained from a operating a cross-border fund strategy. Notwithstanding the significant barriers to initial entry and longer term success, each year waves of former domestic asset managers join the international fund industry. We see no end to this long-term trend, even though it has led to an ultra-competitive market where only a minority are eventually successful and many fail. We will explore the benefits and hurdles related to cross-border distribution further in this chapter.

As many asset managers will attest to, launching and efficiently executing cross-border UCITS distribution strategy is significantly more complex and often riskier than implementing a national or local focus. This complexity arises for a number of reasons. First, to facilitate cross-border distribution, locally-based entities – either part of an international group or independent unrelated third parties – need to be engaged to assist in local marketing or to act as a point of contact with local investors. Further, all host jurisdictions have their own specific investor requirements that should or must be accommodated, their own regulatory and tax frameworks that will influence the distribution of the foreign fund and local sales processes that often means a one size fits all international marketing approach will not work.

Both national and cross-border distribution is complex because in order to facilitate effective distribution, many fund promoters share a part of their management fee, sometimes substantial portions of it, with unrelated local financial entities willing to sell the fund to their local client. This trend, known as guided or open architecture, has led to an increasing number of local banks and other financial entities, even many with their own proprietary fund products, joining the UCITS distribution value chain as a way to generate additional revenue. Many cross-border UCITS engage with multiple local distributors in each domestic market and third party distribution is an increasingly important component.

Moreover, there has been an increase in the both the number of available UCITS distribution channels and the number of actors operating within these channels. This makes for an increasingly competitive and complex value chain from the perspective of both the fund manufacturer and the distributor. It is now common for a single

UCITS fund to have multiple layers of both related and unrelated third party entities involved in and supporting its distribution.

The distribution of an UCITS is increasingly being undertaken by local and international third party financial entities that are separate from the entities responsible for the creation and operation of the UCITS and its asset management. The UCITS distribution value chain in many of the key markets has become markedly divided between entities responsible for the creation and operation of an fund and those that simply sell them. This increasing separation between fund manufacturers and distributors underpins a growing tension over revenue sharing, roles and responsibilities and adds to the complexity of the whole process.

The UCITS Directive has been an important driver of cross-border fund distribution. Changes to the UCITS Directive include enhanced investor protection, product transparency and a broadening of UCITS products available to the global investment community. These enhancements have tended to make the UCITS product more sought-after by investors and local distributors, including those based outside of the European Union (EU), the original target markets for the UCITS concept.

Not only has the process of distribution become more complex, but its interdependence with and reliance on other parts of the UCITS value chain is now critical to the overall success of a UCITS business. In an environment of intense competition, demanding and fickle investors and increasing regulation, efficiently connecting distribution to the market research, product development and fund compliance functions can significantly increase opportunities, gather local investors (and their assets) and secure longer-term success.

There are several distribution methodologies and various channels that can be used by an UCITS (and its management company) to reach local target investors. The use of different channels often occurs where the fund is seeking to attract different investor segments, for example local pension funds, high net-worth individuals or mass retail segments.

Third party distribution has become a critical element in the long-term success of UCITS distribution, especially cross-border and for fund management groups that are not part of multi-national banking or financial groups with local customer bases. However, third party distribution has created a bifurcated UCITS industry with fund manufactures on one side and distributors on the other, together with rising commercial tensions between the two. Moreover, the increasing use of third party distributions requires UCITS and their management companies to properly monitor engaged distributors to ensure that commercial and regulatory compliance is adhered to.

6.2. Domestic distribution

While the purpose of the original UCITS Directive in 1985 was to create a single harmonized market in the EU for the distribution of highly regulated investment funds, i.e. to facilitate cross-border distribution, today a majority of UCITS funds and the assets held continue to be distributed on a domestic basis, i.e. they are for sale in the market where the UCITS is domiciled.

Domestic UCITS distribution processes and channels vary significantly from country-to-country within the EU, reflecting differences in the level of maturity within local asset-management industries, investor preferences, cultural and historic differences between many key UCITS markets. Moreover, domestic tax rules have often played an important role in shaping the development of domestic and cross-border distribution in EU Member States. For many years some EU Member States operated internal tax rules that favored and/or disadvantaged domestic investors in foreign funds as against a similar domestic version as these rules tended to enhance domestic UCITS distribution. Europe contains a number of large asset management markets for the distribution of UCITS and although they have specific differences they each have large domestic only UCITS distribution.

6.2.1. *France*

France is one of the largest European asset management markets but also traditionally one of more nationalistic fund markets. It is difficult for foreign fund groups to successfully access this market. Approximately 90% of all UCITS distribution (and sales) within France is undertaken by French-domiciled UCITSs that are only sold within France. The dominance of locally-based UCITS in the French fund market reflects the way in which UCITSs are sold, the strength of French banking networks as the primary channels of UCITS distribution and the continuing reticence of many French investors to place their capital into foreign domiciled UCITS.

The French market presents the most widespread use of multiple channels of UCITS distribution, with banks, insurance companies, fund-of-funds and corporations all having a significant market share. The large portion of the market represented by institutional investors can be attributed to a 1967 company savings plan (*Plan d'Epargne Entreprise*). The French investment fund market can best be seen as predominately household-investor driven. Representing nearly two-thirds of the investors in institutional investor asset management, these investors are termed "instividuals".

6.2.2. *Germany*

Germany is also a large fund market with varied investor segments, from mass retail through to large corporate, insurance and pension fund investors. Germany has been the most important target market for groups wanting to build assets outside their home domicile. The density of private bank and wealth management operations, as well as the emergence of an independent financial advisor (IFA) or broker-dealer community, provides foreign UCITS with opportunities to distribute their Luxembourg- or Ireland-domiciled UCITS. German investors participated aggressively in the dot.com equity bubble and although they suffered accordingly, they did come back into the market in the mid-2000s. Bank advisers acted as a stabilizing force and investors were persuaded not to materialize their losses.

Germany has a very significant portion of round-trip funds, mainly based in Luxembourg, as a percentage of the total market. This is clearly due to Luxembourg's initiative in embracing UCITS, German-language fluency in Luxembourg and the substantial German cross-border workers in Luxembourg.

6.2.3. *Italy*

The Italian investment fund industry is among the top 10 in Europe, in terms of domiciled fund assets. It is a large investment management market and remains highly attractive for foreign funds. The *Gestioni Patrimoniali in Fondi* (GPF), though expensive for foreign distributors, has been highly effective in attracting investor interest – especially during the tremendous growth during the late 1990s.

The dot.com bubble took its toll on local equity expertise and thus left an opening for foreign groups. MiFID has proven another hurdle for the domestic asset management sector, as the Italian regulator's interpretation of GPF commissions decimated the business incentive. Retail banks dominate.

UCITS distribution and the fact that Italy is very open to market foreign funds has meant that, when coupled with tax regulations that have tended to favor investments in foreign versus domestic UCITS, foreign UCITS now dominate the Italian fund market.

6.2.4. *Switzerland*

Switzerland has a large and open asset management market with multiple channels of distribution available to UCITS from large retail banking networks through to large and smaller niche private banks, fund platforms and brokers. The focus is on selling to mass affluent retail, high-net-worth individuals, foundations and family companies. Such local investors are open to a range of different investment strategies and to foreign funds.

Even though Switzerland is outside the EU, UCITS funds make up the vast majority of funds available for purchase by local Swiss investors. Reciprocity does not extend to Swiss-domiciled investment funds, which do not fall under the UCITS legislation and are unlikely to be distributed abroad. The vast majority of funds distributed in Switzerland are foreign and, mostly, from Luxembourg.

6.2.5. *UK*

The UK is the one of the four largest European markets for the distribution of investment funds, with significant levels of assets available for funds to target. The market is mature, open and competitive in nature, with a broad range of local investor groups ranging from mass retail through to large pension funds, charities, and insurance companies and corporations.

The UCITS segment of the market is large and growing, driven in part by tax advantages that encourage annual investment by retail investors. The majority of UCITS funds distributed are UK-based as the distribution networks are comfortable to sell domestic UCITSs. The penetration of foreign UCITSs has increased over the past five years as local investors and the large IFA networks have become more accustomed to overseas UCITSs. Moreover, the tax regulations have been progressively modified over the past four years to reduce discrimination against foreign funds.

Unlike much of continental Europe, the majority of UCITS distribution to non-institutional or retail investors occurs through IFA channels, brokers, direct sales or through the use of "tax-wrappers" that encourage retail investment. While bank networks are also a viable distribution channel for UCITS, they account for a relatively small proportion of total fund sales. UK institutional investors, like much of the rest of Europe, tend to be targeted directly by UCITS and their sales teams.

6.3. Cross-border distribution

6.3.1. *Introduction*

A growing number of UCITS are distributed on a cross-border basis and the majority of these are known as "true cross-border funds", meaning UCITS that are domiciled in one country and sold in at least two other jurisdictions. Since the creation of UCITS in the late 1980s, both Luxembourg and Dublin have dominated the cross-border fund market. These two key fund domiciles account for approximately 72% and 15% of all true cross-border UCITS, respectively. There are numerous reasons, both tangible and intangible, for the success of both Luxembourg and Dublin as cross-border fund centers. One of the key reasons is that many local distributors and investors view Luxembourgish and Irish UCITS as neutral products.

Notwithstanding the success of these two fund centers, a domestic asset manager in any EU Member State has the opportunity to have a domestically-distributed UCITS registered in another EU jurisdiction for public distribution in that foreign jurisdiction provided the fund complies with the "notification" requirements as set out in the UCITS Directive. In short, as long as the asset manager provides certain information to the host regulatory authority about the UCITS and way in which it proposes to distribute the fund in the target country.

Over the past few years, a small but growing number of French UCITS have successfully entered the cross-border industry, seeking to expand their domestic reach and assets under management. UCITS, from territories other than Luxembourg, Ireland and France, have had very limited success due to the complexity of such distribution activities. These include:

– the different multi-layer distribution channels and relationships that need to be maintained;

– the requirement to appoint local actors from a tax and/or regulatory perspective;

– cross-border flow of documents and monies;

– client servicing requirements; and

– the payment of distribution fees.

In almost all jurisdictions outside the EU, UCITS funds must satisfy local regulations governing public distribution rather than rely on the requirements under the UCITS Directive. Nevertheless, because of the tremendous "brand" reputation that UCITS have developed globally over the past 20 years, many non-EU countries provide different forms of relief from or "fast-track" through their local registration process to distribution publicly. These measures vary from country to country.

6.3.2. Development of the UCITS Directive

The strength of UCITS as a highly valued brand is unquestionable given its ever-increasing popularity on a global basis. Today, UCITS are sold publicly in more than 60 jurisdictions across four different regions: Europe, the Middle East, Asia and Latin America. Non-European investors appreciate and respect the transparency, high regulation, robust risk-management processes and high levels of product variety. This is critical as UCITS promoters are increasingly looking towards additional markets in South America, the Middle East and Asia for new investors (the next stage of growth).

The importance of a coherent EU capital market concept is seen even more clearly as this latest version of UCITS substantially enhances cross-border fund distribution with an "EU passport". The third significant set of amendments to the original UCITS Directive, UCITS IV, is an improvement on UCITS III, and especially the initial cross-border framework envisaged under UCITS I.

The UCITS IV Directive reinforces the fundamental importance of coordinated and consistent protection for unit-holders without impeding obligations or controls unique to a particular Member State yet builds on previous investment-related developments with more flexibility to reduce administrative burdens and improve overall efficiencies.

Importantly for distribution within the EU, UCITS IV streamlines the market entry process by providing for much quicker market entry into host target EU markets.

While the original UCITS Directive was introduced in 1985, it was not until 1988 that the first EU country (Luxembourg) introduced this EU Directive into local regulations to permit the first ever cross-border distributed UCITS. Nevertheless, the growth of cross-border UCITSs was consistent, if modest, from 1988 through to the late 1990s, with a relatively small number of European-wide and globally-based asset managers creating and distributing cross-border UCITSs based in Luxembourg and Ireland.

The strong trend towards equity investment throughout the later part of the 1990s and the accompanying internet bubble fuelled the expansion of UCITS distribution generally, especially on a cross-border basis, as investors across Europe poured their savings into UCITSs. Even greater growth in the number of UCITSs focused on cross-border marketing and the extent of their cross-border footprint and assets held, however, occurred with the introduction of UCITS III in 2002 and its market acceptance from 2004 onwards. Figure 6.1 provides a graphic depiction of the growth in the number of registrations issued to true cross-border funds, almost all UCITSs, during the period through to the end of 2010.

In terms of asset-management firms leading the surge of growth in cross-border UCITS distribution, not surprisingly key firms in the US investment business seeking to enter the European market significantly boosted the UCITS cross-border funds business, especially as their US fund ranges were unable to be distributed outside of the US to any significant extent.

With their wide industry experience, therefore, large business operations and significant assets under management, these managers saw the opportunity to revitalize their AUM numbers by replicating their US fund range in a way that would appeal to European investors. This range was designed with the advantages of the UCITS brand, and the domiciliation country of choice. These funds included Robert Fleming, Franklin Templeton and Fidelity Investments. The UK, Germany, the Benelux countries, Hong Kong and Japan were some of the main distribution countries of these "first-mover" management groups after the dotcom bubble had burst.

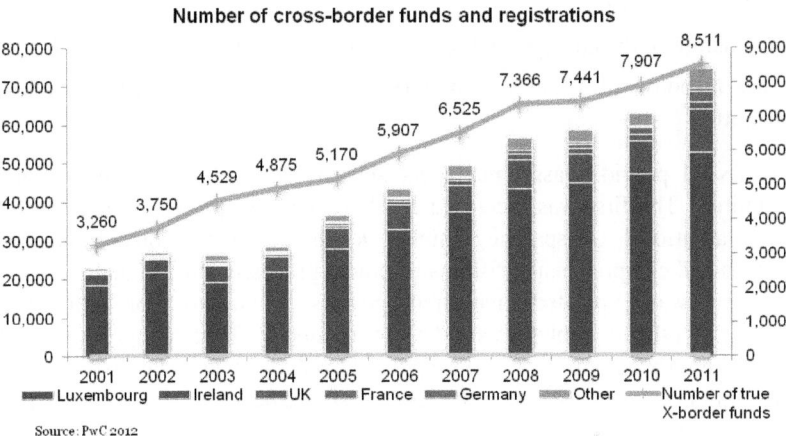

Figure 6.1.

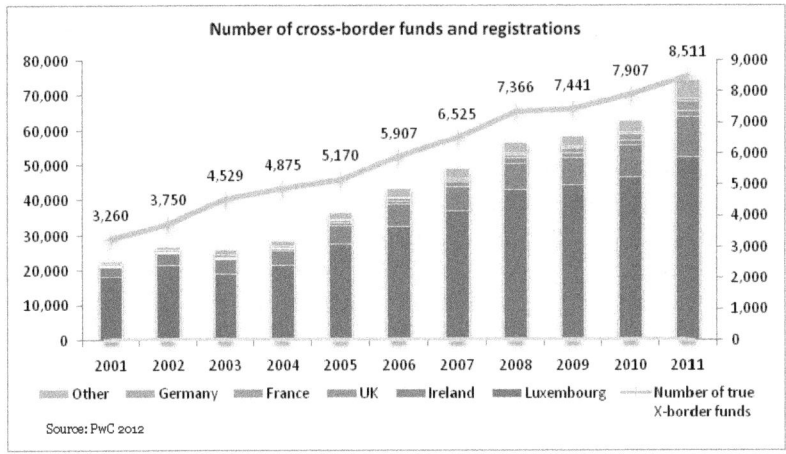

Figure 6.2.

Interestingly, US fund-management groups have consistently maintained a share of UCITS at about 40–50% of the top 10 from 2002 to the present. This very clearly demonstrates the underlying brand value of UCITS to the large US fund industry.

European UCITS manufacturers were slower to begin marketing and designing cross-border funds, as they were more focused on their domestic markets and distribution networks. Nevertheless, as pan-European banking groups have developed so have their cross-border fund distribution strategies.

Why was UCITS III such a catalyst for cross-border fund distribution? The answer lies in two parts:

– the nature of the changes and opportunities bought by UCITS III; and

– the response of UCITS promoters in various European countries to these opportunities.

UCITS III provided asset managers and investors alike with two significant opportunities. The first was increased levels of investor protection and confidence (through additional transparency, higher levels of supervision of management companies and comprehensive risk management processes) in the quality of UCITS. The second was expanded investment powers leading to more attractive and interesting investment strategies and UCITS products. These changes to the UCITS Directive improved product offering and risk management while reducing administration barriers. At the same time it strengthened investor confidence and boosted distribution.

The UCITS III framework enhanced the previous (UCITS I) cross-border sales regime with the condition that investment funds could be domiciled in one country and marketed to all EU Member States. This has encouraged European financial regulators to improve cooperation and speed up some of the administrative processes required to get qualified funds to the market.

Since 2004, Luxembourg UCITS have been strongly marketed across the Asian region. In fact, in many of the key Asian markets, Luxembourg UCITS are the most dominant investment funds sold locally. Although exact data is difficult to extract and rely on, it is generally accepted that the Asian region has recently been supplying between 35-40% of all net sales into cross-border UCITS. Moreover, UCITS are increasingly being sold into the Middle East, especially Bahrain, as well as Latin America, especially Peru and Chile, to feed the large and growing pension fund markets in these countries.

It is too soon to measure the final impact of UCITS IV on the global distribution of UCITS, but new tools such as the master–feeder structure and cross-border fund mergers have been made available to asset managers that enable them to be more efficient in the European market. Time will tell how asset managers will transform these regulatory opportunities into business growth.

6.3.3. Key domiciles of cross-border UCITS

As mentioned, Luxembourg and Ireland are synonymous with cross-border UCITS and their distribution. As of early 2012, according to Lipper, approximately 65% of all cross-border UCITS funds were domiciled in Luxembourg with 15% in Ireland and the remainder roughly split among France, Germany and the UK. This clearly shows the continued dominance of both Luxembourg and Ireland in the UCITS cross-border industry.

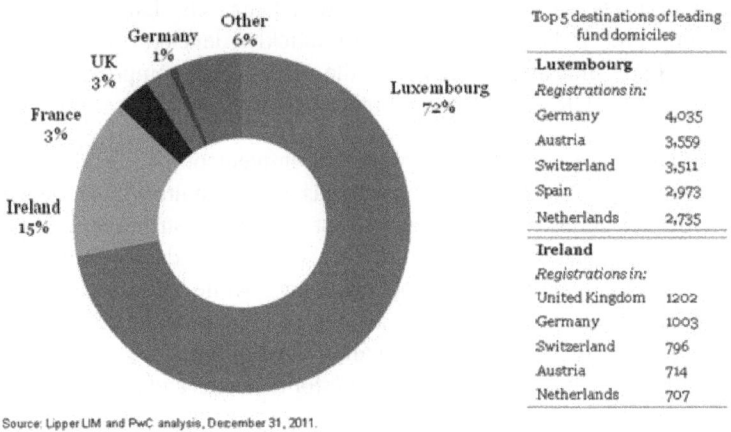

Source: Lipper LIM and PwC analysis, December 31, 2011.

Figure 6.3. *Evolution of cross-border distribution – domicile share of authorizations for cross-border distribution*

It is interesting to note that over the past few years the local fund industries, supported by their governments in the UK, France and Germany, have attempted to refocus on the development of the cross-border offerings of their domestic funds. These measures have met with little success to date. While there are probably numerous reasons for this lack of success, having large internal investment fund markets clearly acts as a significant brake and reduces the ability of these other fund centers to create export-focused, tax, regulatory and commercial policies to support a cross-border industry, as has been the case in Dublin and Luxembourg.

These two leading centers for fund domiciliation have their status due to a number of factors, including but not limited to:

– their reputation for market orientated public policy;

– their regulatory environment;

– stability (economic and political);

– the absence of a domestic market;

– service provider specialization; and

– tax efficiency and neutrality.

These characteristics speak to the common foundation of trust, prudent risk-management and efficient mechanisms for wealth creation.

A small internal market, including that for the distribution of investment products, means that in these countries the focus of tax, regulatory and business policies can be strongly focused on exportation priorities without there being significant impacts on the operation of internal markets. During the 1990s both Luxembourg and Ireland where able to quickly develop very export-focused investment fund industries, free from the limits and compromises that larger economies like the UK, Germany and France suffer from.

Luxembourg was the first country to fully implement the original 1985 UCITS Directive in 1988. Moreover, Luxembourg has a large multi-lingual labor force and this provides an ability to service and assist with the distribution of cross-border funds in multiple jurisdictions. In addition to this, funds receive favorable tax treatment and a regulatory environment that, while accommodating all EU legislation applicable to UCITS (as well as internationally-accepted fund regulations), remains flexible enough to allow fund promoters to quickly launch and modify fund ranges and thus respond to investor demands and market requirements.

The process of developing a mature funds industry began in Luxembourg with its pre-UCITS financial regulator's development of conceptual decisions and structuring procedures to enact the fund registration laws allowing the creation of a variety of investment funds and setting up controls to ensure their proper management. Crucially, the country's geographic advantage, as it is situated between Germany, France and Belgium, has proven instrumental in meeting the challenge of attracting a multi-lingual workforce and training them to be skilled in investment fund management and administration. The presence of large banking groups from Germany and France has enabled Luxembourg to develop the logistical abilities to launch funds, publish the daily Net Asset Value calculations, perform transfer agency procedures, and custody functions.

Ireland has many of the features enjoyed by Luxembourg; a dynamic and growing domiciliation with innovative product development but, also the advantage of native English speakers and a strong international network. Ireland has the natural benefit of its proximity to Britain's very strong financial services sector and this is a considerable advantage as it grows.

The small size of these two countries is certainly an element here too, as they are able to react quickly to market developments and adjust policy as the need arises. Their strong domestic budget management underscores the commitment of their leaders to fiscal propriety and this sends the right signals to investors globally. At the start of 2012, Luxembourg hosted fund promoters from 48 of the 50 top cross-border funds. These promoters are primary domiciled in Luxembourg (42) and Ireland (6).

Economies of scale drive the concentration in both countries. The incremental costs of launching new funds are reduced as more funds are created using the same or similar organizational processes. Many of the noted factors of success of these two jurisdictions tend to perpetuate and reinforce themselves, making it increasingly difficult for other European jurisdictions to enter and/or more successfully compete with Ireland and Luxembourg in the cross-border UCITS market.

6.3.4. *Attractiveness of domestic markets for cross-border distribution*

As mentioned previously, there has been rapid growth in the level and extent of cross-border or international distribution of UCITS over the past ten years. This long-term trend is likely to continue for the foreseeable future as such a strategy looks increasingly attractive for many national asset-management groups in mature domestic markets. One of the key elements in implementing a successful cross-border strategy is to determine which domestic markets will be targeted for distribution and the specific channels or channels that will be utilized to reach potential investors. Usually several factors ultimately determine which domestic markets are targeted and these often include:

– Whether a pre-existing commercial relationship exists with one or more local distributors, for example the UCITS manager may be part of a banking or insurance network with local subsidiaries in various potential target markets or the manager may have an equity stake in a local insurance or banking network. The ability to leverage an UCITS distribution strategy from an associated local distribution network with an existing customer base can often provide an excellent opportunity to sell what would in effect be an "in-house" cross-border UCITS.

– Overall market size and maturity is often a key factor, especially within Europe. It relates primarily to the extent of potential local investors (especially "HNWI private bank clients") and the corresponding depth of available distribution channels.

– The existence and extent of potential local investors, especially institutional investors who may have already made contact with the UCITS sales team or the asset manager by sending a request for proposal having expressed a desire to invest into the UCITS. In these circumstances, distribution to these local investors may be possible through private placement activities rather than by requesting and obtaining local authorization to distribute publicly. In circumstances where initial investor contacts have already been made and opportunities assessed, these jurisdictions will usually be on the target list for distribution.

– Fund originators must have confidence that their funds will attract sufficient investors in order to achieve the fund's strategy in a timely fashion. This presupposes a wider network of promoters, investment advisors and appropriately targeted investors as well as a regulator attentive to market conditions and investor demand.

– Market openness – including architectural and structural aspects. Market openness to foreign UCITSs and particular types of investment strategies can often be a critical factor in determining the eventual target jurisdiction. This is the case especially in the sense of the availability of third party fund distribution networks and their attraction to the type of UCITS that is looking to be marketed, the ease by which market entry can be achieved (which is especially important for markets outside the EU), and the attitude of the local country regulator towards the foreign UCITS.

– Regulation has often played a role in target market development, especially during the earlier days of the UCITS Directive when significant levels of both tax and regulatory discrimination against foreign or cross-border UCITS existed. While these barriers to market entry by foreign UCITS have generally been reduced and/or completely eliminated over the past few years, especially within the EU, they continue to exist in some Asian and Latin American jurisdictions and thus the overcoming of these barriers needs to be considered in determining which markets to target. Within the EU, UCITS IV clearly identifies host country regulators as essential in ensuring a level playing field in administering fund registration, authorization and control. The foundation is being laid whereby regulation (fees, documentation, and timing requirements) should be more harmonized throughout the EU. This could be extended and applied internationally, so that evaluations are made based on the country regulator's registration transparency, fees and documentation requirements as well as the time to approval.

6.3.5. *Key target markets for cross-border UCITS distribution*

6.3.5.1. *In Europe*

Although cross-border UCITS are distributed to more than 60 jurisdictions globally, there tends to be a concentrated core of jurisdictions at the heart of cross-border UCITS distribution in each of the four key regions, (Europe, Asia, Latin America and the Middle East). This core is reflective of the factors that UCITS managers assess when determining target markets. Within Europe, cross-border UCITS distribution tends to be concentrated in 10 key local target markets, as shown in Figure 6.4.

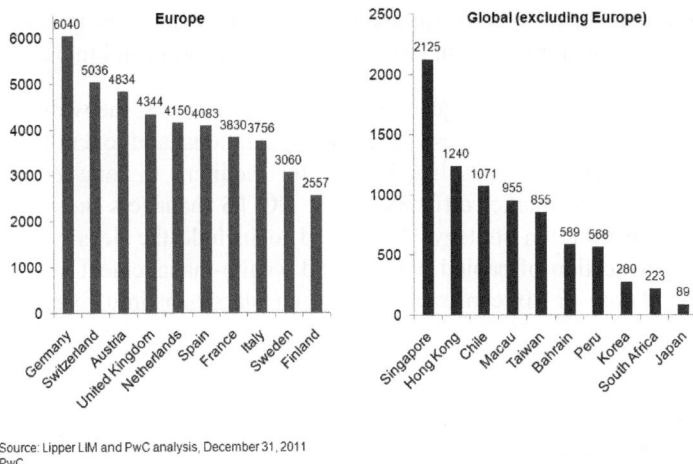

Source: Lipper LIM and PwC analysis, December 31, 2011
PwC

Figure 6.4. *Top 10 target markets for cross-border fund distribution*

As of December 2011, there are six European countries where more than 50% (or 4,000) of cross-border UCITSs are actively distributed. These six jurisdictions are invariably on the target list of most existing and new cross-border promoters as they exhibit many of the factors critical in deciding to launch distribution strategies. Germany has, for many years, been the host jurisdiction most frequently targeted by cross-border or foreign UCITS, with more than 6,000 of the existing 8,500 cross-border UCITSs selling into this large, mature and open host market. Switzerland, Austria, the UK and the Netherlands are also heavily targeted, reflecting the opportunities available to UCITS. In recent years there has been a marked shift in focus towards cross-border UCITS distribution into Northern European jurisdictions, at the same time as the fund industries in a number of Southern European jurisdictions have continued to shrink in size and opportunities to gather assets.

6.3.5.2. *Asia*

The basis for continued growth in the extent of UCITS distribution outside Europe is strong as various analyses anticipate that the gross domestic product of the emerging E7 economies will overtake the G7 economies by 2020, and China may surpass that of the US by the end of the decade.

Asia is the largest UCITS regional market after Europe, as seen in the above figure, where three or four key jurisdictions dominate UCITS distribution. The Asian markets are of particular interest to UCITS fund managers, with especially strong distribution activity in both Hong Kong and Singapore. Astonishingly, 87% of all funds authorized for distribution in Hong Kong are foreign domiciled.

However, a number of large Asian domestic markets remain firmly closed to direct UCITS distribution at the present time, e.g. China, Indonesia and India.

A key aspect of the challenges when marketing to Asia is the wide variability of local cultures, market practices, investor expectations and overall maturity for investment into pooled funds like UCITS for medium- to long-term investment purposes. These are market differences that UCITS managers must assess before launching a distribution strategy. They need to include the density of disposable wealth, sophistication of capital markets and wealth-management requirements, as well as regulatory or tax constraints on wealth placement into foreign investment funds.

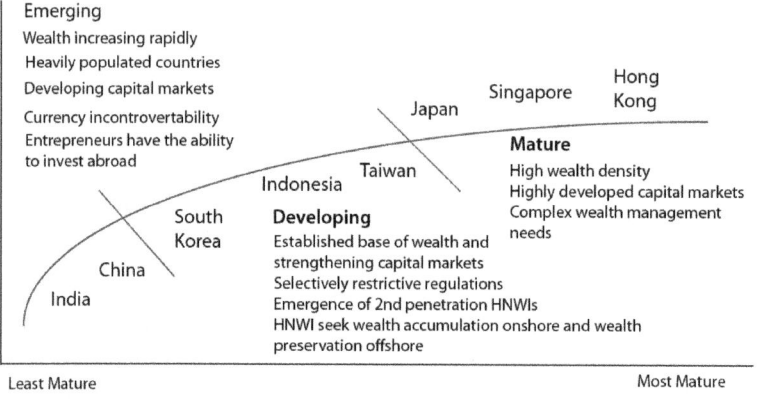

Figure 6.5. *An overview of the maturity levels of Asian markets*

Asian private wealth is growing rapidly and the combined private wealth in this region surpassed that of Europe in 2009 (and it is expected that the region will have more millionaires than the US by 2013). As such, the opportunities are significant for cross-border UCITSs that get their distribution strategy right.

Importantly, the UCITS brand is now recognized throughout much of the Asian region and is seen by many investors, local distributors and regulators alike as a prudent, proven, transparent and low-risk managed investment product. While Hong Kong and Singapore have been the key target markets for the past ten years, Taiwan is also a popular target market and a number of international groups have had very good success in attracting large sales volumes into their Luxembourg UCITS platforms. South Korea permits UCITSs to be distributed locally, although the market is less mature than others. Japan's authorization process for UCITSs is complex and costly, which has deterred many UCITS managers from entry, notwithstanding the size and sophistication of this market, while Malaysian and Thai regulators require UCITSs to be wrapped in local registered funds.

Hong Kong's financial regulator has recently issued a circular to cross-border asset managers regarding client information requirements around liability and client protection. The Securities and Futures Commission notice requires "all licenced corporations to establish and maintain policies and procedures to ensure the proper management of risks if they provide services to clients through overseas counterparties". The companies are also urged to explain the risks associated with such trading activities to clients, the Securities and Futures Commission says.

6.3.5.3. *Latin America and the Middle East*

Outside of Europe – and this is certainly true of the situation in Latin America and the Middle East – the UCITS brand is still developing and a number of large domestic markets remain closed to direct distribution by UCITS, e.g. Brazil and Mexico. Chile and Peru are two countries in Latin America where UCITS has been distributed directly and with significant success over the past seven or eight years, especially in the local pension fund markets that are able to directly invest in highly-regulated foreign funds like UCITSs. The extent of distribution in Latin America is expected to improve, perhaps with the introduction of UCITS IV and other local regulations that encourage the spreading of risk and investment opportunities by local pension funds, corporations and individuals.

6.4. The distribution process

6.4.1. *Public distribution*

Within the EU, UCITS benefit from the "pass-porting" arrangements available under the UCITS Directives and are thus able to be "freely" marketed on a public basis within all Member States without additional authorization from each "host" Member State regulatory authority. This is subject to the successful completion of a "notification" process (registration for marketing) in each Member State as laid out in the UCITS Directive.

While the notification procedures to be followed in each Member State are harmonized and, since UCITS IV, somewhat simplified compared to the previous UCITS regulations, there are significant differences surrounding the local marketing arrangements that must to be complied with, together with various tax reporting requirements in some jurisdictions. The UCITS Directive does not harmonize or include rules regarding the way in which the UCITS should be sold in each Member State and this remains a weakness in creating a true EU "single market" for investment funds. For example, in almost all Member States an UCITS from another Member State must appoint a local paying agent in addition to ensuring that it remains in compliance with each jurisdiction marketing selling rules.

The new UCITS notification procedure, which permits cross-border public distribution, has reduced the time to market (approximately 15 days) and allowed UCITS to more easily compete with other financial products that can be launched and quickly obtain market entry. Under the Directive, the UCITS must submit a range of fund documentation to its home regulator, including details as to how the UCITS will be locally distributed. Within ten working days, the home regulator will then send a notification file prepared by the UCITS, or its representative, to the host regulator. Normally the host regulator has five working days to confirm that the file is complete. The home regulator transmission and confirmation thereof to the UCITS will trigger the right to start marketing in that host EU country without review by the host regulator. However, it is important to note that host regulators can review local marketing information after distribution has started.

Outside the EU, UCITS funds must satisfy local regulations (rather than the UCITS Directive) governing public distribution of foreign funds. These local regulations will vary from country to country but it is fair to say that the registration process to be authorized in order to publicly sell an UCITS outside the EU is usually significantly more complex, time consuming and ultimately costly, than the "notification" process governed by the UCITS Directive for EU Member States. For example, currently the registration process for an UCITS in Hong Kong can take up to 12 months, compared to 15 days for EU cross-border entry! However, in some non-EU jurisdictions, such is the acceptance of the UCITS brand that many jurisdictions UCITS funds have a "lighter" authorization process than the non-UCITS equivalent investment funds.

A public distribution authorized status gives the fund promoter of an UCITS the possibility to target all of the local investors normally and without any restriction. Fully authorized public distribution status is usually sought by cross-border UCITSs when non-institutional investors (retail, mass affluent, high net worth investors) and/or investors through banking networks, financial intermediaries, brokers, direct contact and fund supermarkets are targeted.

6.4.2. *Private placement*

An alternative to authorization for public distribution is by way of private placement. Typically, this means seeking local investors without entering into public marketing arrangements or processes, as they may be defined under the domestic regulatory framework of the host jurisdiction.

Although UCITSs were originally designed as highly-regulated fund products for retail investors and are thus normally distributed on a public basis, private placement has been a viable distribution strategy for many UCITSs that have a narrower distribution strategy. This strategy is typically one that seeks to target a small number of larger institutional investors, because local regulations in many jurisdictions permit such investors to subscribe to shares or units in a foreign UCITSs without the UCITS having been authorized (either via the notification process within the EU or through the local registration process in non-EU jurisdictions) and supervised by the host country supervisory authority. This is often the case when the targeted market segment is institutional, sophisticated and consists of professional investors rather than mass retail or high net wealth individuals.

Distributing UCITS funds into selective jurisdictions via private placement is becoming increasingly common, especially for funds targeting a very narrow category of institutional investors. As mentioned above, however, there are no harmonized rules within the EU surrounding private placement and, thus, fund promoters must contend with the specific local regulations governing private placement (or lack of) in every jurisdiction of intended distribution.

While this form of distribution provides quick market entry, there are drawbacks in the sense that the scope of available investors is quite limited and the rules or market practices are often widely interpreted and subject to change. This leads to increased risks of noncompliance with local regulations.

6.4.3. *Fund wrappers*

Investment funds may also be offered through life insurance wrappers if certain investment restrictions and eligible asset criteria are respected and satisfied. Sold via firms benefiting from the Insurance Mediation Directive, they may be offered throughout Europe in this manner.

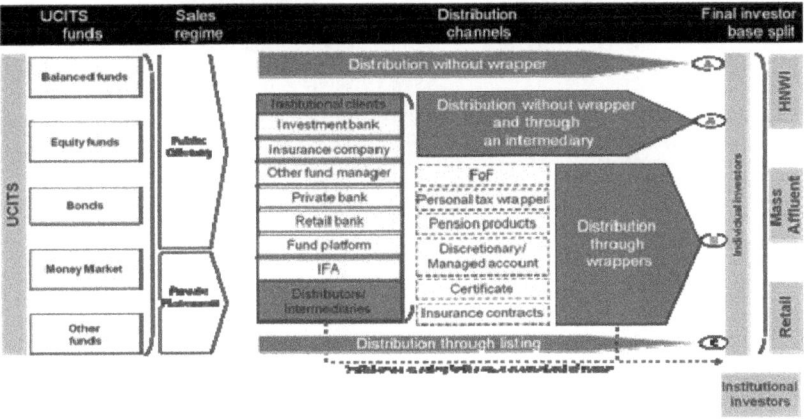

Figure 6.6. *Flow diagram of the various ways in which UCITS funds can be offered through the market*

They may finally be wrapped in structured products, securitized or otherwise included in a distinct mantel rather than the fund one, thereby potentially taking advantage of other EU Directives conferring a passport, like the 2003 Prospectus Directive.

6.5. Distribution channels

6.5.1. *Introduction*

UCITS funds are either distributed directly to local investors or through a large variety of different and often competing channels of financial intermediaries. It has become increasingly uncommon for UCITSs to obtain subscriptions direct from local investors. The vast majority of investors subscribe into UCITS through different local distribution channels. Across most of continental Europe the most common UCITS distribution channel for non-institutional investors is local banking networks, invariably those of large retail banks.

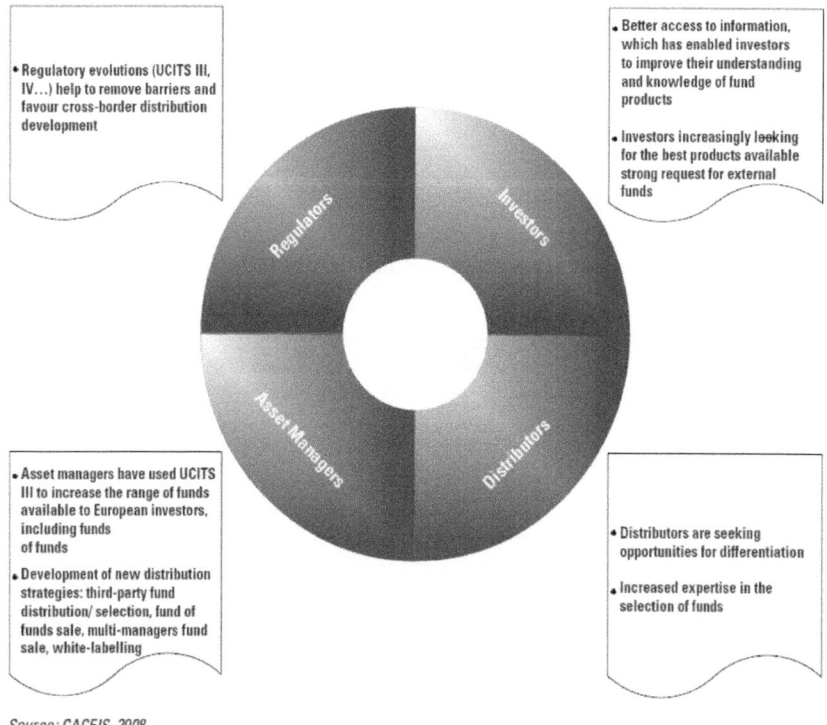

Source: CACEIS, 2008

Figure 6.7.

The most common method of UCITS distribution to these local investors is through investment advisors located within the network of large banking groups, either retail or private banks. In a limited number of jurisdictions, for example the UK, Hong Kong and Germany, IFAs are key distribution channels for cross-border UCITSs. This offers a tremendous variety of options for investors while creating tremendous complexity for fund managers and their counterparties.

The genesis of a fund is the wealth-creation opportunity for both investors and the fund management group, resulting in product innovation within a regulatory framework. It is important to understand that operational and regulatory constraints significantly influence fund originators in UCITS product development. This may include risk profiles, levels of sophistication and eligibility, investment minimums, fund administration costs and the involvement of management (passive and active styles, for example). Fund promoters are keen to reach the fund's target investment level quickly and may resort to a variety of overlapping channels to achieve the immediate minimum for the fund in order to succeed with the given strategy.

6.5.2. *Channel architecture*

There are three types of third party fund distribution: open, closed and guided.

6.5.2.1. *Open architecture*

Distribution channels offer a wide variety of third party funds from competing asset management groups. The advantages of this include a wider pool of potentially attractive investment opportunities for the investor and an opportunity for the distribution channel to increase its revenue without a substantial qualification review of the funds.

This has implications for both domestic and cross-border fund distribution as investors, and investment advisors, have access to larger groups of funds. Some of the implications are positive, such as the chance for some foreign asset managers to enter new markets for some funds. Some are negative, for example captive managers could be concerned that they are seen as being less successful in this broader competitive field. Customer loyalty, and customer perception of their local investment advisor, is central as relationships develop within these changes. The decision that investment managers might take in limiting the extent of "open architecture" is also important as it enables their funds to better compete and hence better advise their clients to create a longer lasting relationship. The data trends show that national, captive channel and market share is slipping to favor third party distribution channels with attendant investment opportunities for the investor.

6.5.2.2. Closed architecture

Investors are offered funds from their investment advisor's own pool of funds; for example, a private banking advisor would solely promote funds from the private bank's network – including that of the parent bank. This has been the case in France, Germany and other European countries. There is an argument from these closed distribution channels to stick with national funds, as they are familiar with them and the fund originators, and there is a greater sense of investor confidence that they know where their money is invested. While this has been very persuasive in the past, investors have shown that they are willing to invest in foreign funds when they have some certainty of transparency and investment returns.

6.5.2.3. Guided architecture

This is regarded as the hybrid scenario whereby fund investment advisers offer funds from a highly selected third party fund management group(s). This has the benefit of the investment advisor's improved knowledge of the funds and a general sense of a controlled risk that is better offered by open architecture with more selection freedom than the closed architecture. German banks have moved to this as a way to stem the growth of IFA. However, offering third party funds can substantially increase operational complexity, given the language and time differences, software challenges and variations in expected levels of service.

Case study: Carmignac – the success of an independent

Founded in 1989 by Eduoard Carmignac, Gestion Carmignac has quickly become one of Europe's leading independent asset management companies and a tremendous example of a successful asset management supported by the efficient implementation of an effective cross-border distribution strategy. With almost €50 billion in assets, Gestion Carmignac has developed a comprehensive range of 19 funds across all asset classes – equities, bonds and multi-strategy, as well as segregated mandate offerings. Its funds are actively marketed in 11 European countries. Its international development includes a subsidiary in Luxembourg, offices in Madrid, Milan and Frankfurt.

The company's success is partly due to a shared purpose of the management and staff as the sole owners of its share capital, underpinning their commitment to long-term profitability and focus on customer service.

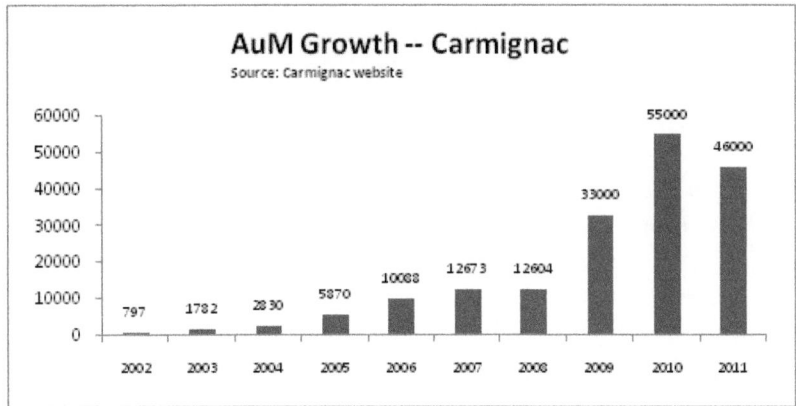

Figure 6.8.

A key component of their success has been the ability to quickly gain subscriptions from investors in target jurisdictions. This was achieved not by paying large levels of distribution commission but through creating bespoke local sales teams that were committed to and extremely knowledgeable of the funds and well rewarded for sales success. These sales groups tended to develop their own local networks of private investors and institutional contacts thereby creating a locally based, intensive and comprehensive sales approach fully supported by excellent client service. The sales strategy of each jurisdiction was "fine-tuned" to reflect the local culture and specific requirements of local investor segments.

6.6. Distribution Channels

6.6.1. *Banking: retail/private*

Banks are the major channel of UCITS distribution throughout continental Europe and in most parts of Asia. The share of UCITS distribution, (net sales or assets), held by banks does vary from country to country reflecting the relative strength and depth of banks as financial institutions in a particular jurisdiction and between the two main banking models, retail and private. Generally speaking, the strength of banking channels for UCITS distribution is due to a variety of reasons but, predominately because of their substantial customer bases and their ability to directly offer a range of financial products and solutions for investors. Moreover, historically many European and Asian investors have placed great faith in large banking institutions and have been unwilling to seek out and pay for independent financial advice as a means to invest their excess savings.

DISTRIBUTION CHANNEL	FRANCE	GERMANY	ITALY	SPAIN	SWITZERLAND	UK
Retail Bank	21.3%	44.4%	54.3%	63.3%	11.6%	2.3%
Private Bank/Discretionary	10.9%	13.5%	13%	8%	51%	6%
Insurance	13.5%	16.4%	13.5%	5%	8%	12.4%
IFA/Advised	8.3%	7.4%	6%	4.3%	6%	55.6%
Supermarket	0.3%	0.5%	0.3%	0.2%	1.5%	1.5%
Direct	0.5%	0.2%	0.2%	0%	1.5%	0.5%
Funds of Funds	11.2%	13.6%	5.1%	7.2%	6.4%	9.2%
Institution/Corporate	34%	4%	7.6%	12%	14%	12.5%
Total	100%	100%	100%	100%	100%	100%

Source: Lipper FMI data digest, 2010

Table 6.1. *European assets by distribution channel*

Retail banks continue to dominate in all of the key large target markets for UCITS, including Spain, Italy, Germany and to a slightly lesser extent in France. Private banks have a market leading position in Switzerland and Singapore. UCITS distribution in the UK, Hong Kong, to a lesser extent continues to be dominated by independent financial advisers, similar to the dominance of broker/dealers in the US. Table 6.1 provides an overview of the share of UCITS distribution held by the major channels in each of the key markets. France is unique with its omnipresent company savings plan (*Plan d'Espargne Entreprise*) and so the banking share is very strong. There is some debate regarding possible changes to French fund distribution to improve transparency, fee clarity, and the product selection process that could translate into regulatory guidance. Given recent financial crises, the banks seem very keen on retaining customers while leveraging their size and frequent contact as key elements of the relationship.

Whilst retail fund supermarkets and on-line platforms have developed as a distinct channel of UCITS distribution in many target jurisdictions, especially across northern Europe, they have not materially threatened the dominance of banking networks. While there has been a slow continuing shift away from banks for UCITS distribution over the past ten years, most noticeably during 2007-2009 crisis period, investor loyalty, (and passiveness), remains strong overall. This also is partially the result of specific strategies implemented by some large bank networks; e.g. *AllFunds* Bank, S.A. that operate as a joint venture with *Banco Santander*, S.A. and *Intesa Sanpaolo* SpA. This precludes cannibalization of customers from *Santander* or third-party distributors in its operational markets. Therefore, banks are keen to use platforms to source additional investors but cautious about allowing other parties to develop contacts with these platform based customers.

The majority of retail UCITS funds are distributed through vast numbers of retail bank branches and private bank offices. The retail and private banks have large numbers of staff and substantial fund selection to offer when they meet and develop relationships with millions of normal Europeans who wish to invest their savings. This is certainly the case in Spain, Italy, France and Germany; especially given the historic nature of large bank groups. The important point is the resiliency of the average investor, who suffered during the dot.com bubble and again more recently; however, the loyalty and sense of relationship with their banks remains very much a dominant force in planning their financial well-being. This speaks to the tremendous brand value enjoyed by banks; despite several unfortunate experiences where it was the banks looking after themselves perhaps a bit more than they did their customers.

6.6.2. *Insurance/Bank-Insurance (bancassurance)*

The insurance industry has long been a key distribution channel for UCITS and has been supported, (protected), through the operation of national based tax incentives and provide various forms of tax relief or advantages if UCITS are acquired via an insurance contract; making it an important driver for fund sales. Very often banking and insurance (assurance) products are co-marketed to facilitate enhanced tax efficiencies and thereby underpinning the dominance of these channels.

6.6.3. *Fund platform growth and the role of intermediaries*

The use of fund platforms to facilitate the sale of UCITS has grown considerably over the past 10 years. These "platforms" are, in reality an intermediate entity linking the UCITS to the end investor as well as being an "execution only" facility that enhances the actual process of investing into a UCITS which typically involves a number of players and benefits greatly from standardization, performance and responsive decision-making. There are two major conduits for fund selection, these are both called platforms but with different users and they can be defined as a fund supermarket or wrap platform dealing with consumers directly or through their advisers. Its core function is generally described as providing access to a diversity of investments but with consolidated administration. Nevertheless, fund managers may also view life assurers as platforms for the distribution of their funds and the service described above can be part of the general service provided by a discretionary investment manager to its clients.

These fund platforms can be identified as:

– Execution only platforms: order routing and settlement;

– Global Platforms: negotiation and execution;

– Negotiation platforms: negotiation & management of dealer agreements and fees.

"Supermarkets" – are in effect websites directed at either pure retail investors or investment professionals which list many UCITS funds for investment and provide the user with the ability to purchase shares or units in the UCITS directly. Retail websites are designed to monetize the fund shopping experience and while offering no investment advice regarding which UCITS funds may offer the most suitable investment strategy for the individual. Some websites do offer some comparative features and similar functionality and the new KIID requirements under UCITS IV will enhance the user experience.

6.6.4. *Boutique Intermediaries*

One type of company that has developed over the past three to four years is that of a third party fund marketing advisory groups targeting professional and institutional investors. Typically, they are experienced industry professionals, knowledgeable in UCITS sales, fund operations, value chain, often from the perspective of large fund groups where they often had a key sales role but now seek to use their UCITS distribution knowledge to assist smaller UCITS funds to sell using a boutique approach. These intermediaries use specific sales processes on behalf of UCITS fund clients, including advising on specific fund structures, sales strategies and targeted fund distribution – even offering individual approaches to asset managers.

6.6.5. *Independent Financial Advisors (IFA)*

6.6.5.1. *The UK*

The more than 20,000 licensed IFA's in the UK dominate the local asset management market and are the main channel for the distribution of UCITS, both domestic and foreign. With relatively strict regulations regarding the provision of investment advice, the UK IFA market contains large networks of IFA's, often comprising hundreds of individual IFA's, smaller boutique style IFA firms through to one man operations.

The pace of development continues with Retail Distribution Review (RDR) rules that forbid commission payments by fund management groups to IFA's in support of the distribution of financial products, including domestic and foreign UCITS, from the end of 2013. To date, IFA payments, similar to distribution fees paid across many European countries and beyond have not been obvious to investors. Investment clients will begin paying for "advice" and services received from their IFA on a fully transparent basis. This is designed to minimize the opportunity for bias due to fund promoter commission payments to IFAs and underpin a level-playing field for all investors. There will be a strong transition period for UK IFAs as investors come to terms with the fees charged for financial advisory and transaction costs.

The extensive success of UK IFA's, and other channels in other markets, clearly points to the trust relationship as critical in retail UCITS distribution; and even more so in cross-border distribution.

Whilst UCITS are heavily distributed throughout continental Europe and Asia through retail and private banking networks and their associated financial entities, IFS's also have a part to play and are expected to become more prominent as an alternative channel of UCITS distribution to banks over the years to come as investors, especially the mass affluent and high net worth individuals increasingly seek more independent and bespoke advice with regards to their investment strategies, especially to fund future retirements. In Germany, where the majority of households hold investment funds, market developments are providing a positive picture for local IFA's. However, continental Europe is without the UK's RDR regulations banning commissions from fund management groups so investors will continue to "pay" for investment advice unknowingly when talking to their local bank or insurance contact. The fees or costs are effectively hidden in "management fees" or processing charges, thus, giving the illusion that the investment advice is free to the bank customer.

Recent surveys are indicating that some bank-dominated countries are showing increasing signs of looking to alternative non-banking distribution channels. Interestingly, the French market was seen as having particular potential for IFA's and fund platforms. Similarly, the IFA's in Italy distinguished themselves in second place, to discretionary placement, as a distribution channel likely to grow market share.

We have previously commented on the relentless growth of cross-border UCITS distribution since 2000, both the number of funds and the extent of their regional and global distribution footprint, in comparison to EU domestic only UCITS distribution. Although there are some current issues that may impede this continuing growth, we believe this growth trend will continue, at least in the short to medium term and expect that, within a few years, assets held in cross-border UCITS will be greater than those of domestic only UCITS.

Given these likely future developments, it is important to identify some of the key principals that determine success in cross-border UCITS distribution. Invariably a number of factors coalesce to drive long-term successful distribution strategies. However, more often than not four key factors tend to often play a significant part of successful cross-border UCITS distribution and we call them the four P's:

– Place: determining the best foreign markets to target;

– Product: local investors are offered a product suitable for their needs;

– Promotion: executing an effective localized marketing and sales strategy;

– Price: the optimum fee payable to local distributors to maximize sales.

6.6.6. *Markets to target*

The starting point in developing a successful cross-border distribution strategy is to determine the target markets. Whilst this seems obvious, given the complexity and costs of implementing cross-border UCITS distribution, the initial selection of local markets to enter is a critical challenge to get right, especially for smaller nationally based asset managers with limited resources and/or knowledge of foreign markets. Even within the so-called "EU single market", cross-border UCITS distribution remains challenging, from defining an effective and specific sales strategy per jurisdiction through to operational processing issues, securing third-party relationships, to fund governance and compliance with local marketing rules and regulations. Moving outside of the EU, selecting target markets may be even more challenging, especially in local markets less familiar with foreign funds, lower levels of investor maturity and less harmonized operational. Whilst the European investment fund market is large and made up of more than 30 individual local markets, cross-border UCITS distribution tends to be concentrated in 10 key target markets that offer, at first glance, the best opportunities for a cross-border UCITS. However, the number of existing UCITS and asset management companies selling into these key markets is especially high meaning there are also significant levels of fierce competition, making it potentially difficult for newcomers.

While an initial view reveals a crowded European cross-border UCITS market, especially at the retail level, many opportunities exist at targeting local institutional investors and new entrants, especially those offering more sophisticated investment policies, often use an institutional investor distribution approach, as this type of sales strategy can be easier to implement and initially maintain.

6.6.7. *Appropriate products*

The preferences for fund products vary considerably across local markets and often between different investor segments in the same market. These preferences can include particular investment strategies and critical product features important to local tastes, for example, specific currency classes, income or capitalization shares or the provision of hedging certain risks. Product features that are critical for one group of local investors, (and thus critical for successful distribution to such groups), may not be at all necessary for other key target investors because, for example, the existence of different local tax rules and market practices. When looking to target multiple jurisdictions considerable thought is necessary in designing a range of products to suit the wide variation of investor preferences whilst at the same time ensuring that the UCITS maintains a level of operational efficiency necessary for long-term success. An appropriate balance needs to be struck between maintaining the efficiency of the cross-border fund and adding additional features in response to every specific investor group. The more features that are added, the more cumbersome and costly the maintenance of the fund structure will become, leading to the need to generate greater assets under management or reduce profits to the asset manager. Getting this balance right will have a significant impact on sales success but, will also become more challenging the wider the distribution footprint of the UCITS.

6.6.8. *An effective marketing strategy*

Each potential target market for the UCITS will have a specific investment culture, tax rules that may favor certain products over others, regulatory requirements and market practices. This usually means that any cross-border promotional strategy for a foreign fund must be sufficiently localized to ensure every chance of success. Language preferences, investor requirements and historical biases regarding fund types, local "wrappers" and specific channels are all factors in which national markets can differ causing asset managers of cross-border UCITS to adopt a level of bespoke local promotion appropriate to each target jurisdiction. Many asset managers rely on the local distributor engaged to sell the UCITS to design and implement a sales strategy approach for the local market.

Large international fund groups often with regional and/or locally based tied sales teams or local offices, implement their own marketing and sales campaigns in addition to the sales process used by their locally engaged distributors. With significant differences across so many local markets it is prudent and commercially justifiable to understand, evaluate and tailor a UCITS sales strategy accordingly. Which specific channels of local distribution will best fit your UCITS and specific product features available and the investors to target. A one-size fits all approach to cross-border UCITS distribution is unlikely to lead to long-term success.

For example in Europe, certain channels tend to dominate UCITS distribution and open architecture in key banking networks often remains a popular distribution approach. Even so, it is important to understand the interests of counterparties in the distribution value chain and to be prepared for amending business and operational plans accordingly. Obtaining a place on a bank's list of funds is one such case. The bank's interests in adding a third party fund can be seen as an added-value service to its customers (normally, where it lacks a competing product) while ensuring that it receives attractive distribution fees. From a fund's perspective, it is important to manage the bank distribution channel carefully to build up larger listings in the future while ensuring that costs are kept in check. In other jurisdictions, including in Asia, local banks and other key UCITS distributor are or already have moved to more of a guided architecture approach to third party fund distribution and this is placing additional challenges and restrictions on a UCITS cross-border strategy.

6.6.9. *Fees to maximize sales*

Another factor often critical to successful UCITS cross-border distribution is the fee or "price" the fund promoter or asset manager is prepared to pay to local distributors contracted to assist in the sale of the UCITS to their clients. Whilst local distributors provide fund manufacturers with a range of "services" in connection with the distribution or sale of the UCITS, providing local distributors with a greater incentive to promote their UCITS may impact the collection of subscriptions into the fund. The fees paid to local distributors ultimately comes from the management fees paid to the management company of the UCITS and so the greater the fees paid to local distributors then the less will remain with the management company and, ultimately the asset manager. This critical issue is further discussed below. Different fee levels are usually requested by local distributors depending on the specific type of fund products to be sold; e.g. equity or bond funds or depending on the level of client service and/or operational involvement requested by the asset manager.

6.7. Distribution agreements, fees and payments

The distribution of a UCITS fund is, under the UCITS Directive, one of the three core functions usually delegated to a management company (except for so-called "self-managed" UCITS that do not utilize a separate management company). If such a delegation of distribution to the management company occurs, then the management company will be primarily responsible for ensuring that the UCITS is appropriately distributed in each target market. This responsibility will include the management company having in place sufficient effective oversight, including robust internal functions to allow for such oversight of each sub-distributor or local entity that has been engaged to market and sell the fund towards local investors according to the strategy designed.

It therefore follows that the cross-border distribution of a UCITS be supported by a domestic operational framework that includes the interaction of the transfer agent, sub- and global custodian and the management company. Specifically, the domestic sales process should be supported and governed by appropriate legal agreements that adequately set-out the specific roles and responsibilities of the local distributor towards the management company and/or the UCITS and ensure the mitigation of commercial and regulatory risks of distribution.

Typically the local distribution agreement should state:

– The regulatory status and local approval of the third party distributor to undertake such activities (i.e. bank license, insurance company, etc.);

– The circumstances in which the third party distributor is permitted and authorized to represent the fund or its global distributor and indicate the specific restrictions on such activity;

– Whether the distributor may appoint sub-distributors without prior authorization of the fund or what type of authorization is required;

– That the distributor is obliged to provide the prospectus/KIID/other marketing material to investors prior to subscription and to inform investors about investment risks etc;

– That the distributor adheres to selling restrictions set out in the agreement;

– Clauses ensuring that the management company of the UCITS is not in breach with its obligations (e.g. AML, complaints escalation, delivery of marketing documents (no manipulation), delivery of legal documents (KIID));

– The periodical reporting (e.g. fund volumes) that is required to be made by the distributor and to which entity such information must be transmitted, including the manner in which transmission must occur;

– Appropriate escalation processes for key events that may occur during the life of the contract;

– The framework in which the third party distributor can operate (i.e. use of marketing material prepared by the distributor itself, data protection, etc.);

and to ensure that EU Directives and other regulations pertaining to AML are appropriately complied with by the distributor at all time by including:

– Detailed description of the due diligence measures which the third party has to carry out in accordance with the Luxembourg AML Law;

– Description of the information and documents that the third-party has to request and verify from the investor and beneficial owner;

– Terms and conditions relating to the communication of information and documents required by Luxembourg professionals (required information must be made available upon request and without delay);

– Control of the good application of the contractually defined tasks (i.e. agreement about regular testing visits).

Once distribution agreements are executed, they need to be operationally implemented into the necessary back office processes, especially in relation to the payment of fees and charges to local distributors by the UCITS or the management company on its behalf as a delegated function. The distribution agreement processes should also involve the transfer agent of the UCITS and also the sub-custodian and global custodian. The calculation of commissions or fees payable to local distributors can be exceedingly complex the wider the distribution footprint of the UCITS is, especially if the UCITS is utilizing multiple local distributors in each of the markets in which it is promoted. In these circumstances the calculation and payment processes are highly fragmented often with a significant level of manual calculation and intervention. It is therefore necessary to have strict procedures for transposition of new/updated/terminated agreements into the back office system. Manual intervention in distribution fee calculation, reporting and payment due to complex fee agreements or limited system capabilities significantly increases commercial risks.

Given the power of some large local distribution networks, it is not uncommon to find small asset managers, looking to initially create rather modest cross-border UCITS strategies, at a commercial disadvantage in seeking to locally distribute their product. Major distributors often require to enter the agreement on behalf of a group of companies – whose participants may be disclosed or undisclosed – which leads to the risk that the fund can be distributed in countries where it should not be distributed (i.e. no authorization for public distribution). The wider the distribution network becomes the more the management company will need to maintain multiple non-standard agreements and therefore will need to implement robust and efficient control environments, both from commercial and regulatory perspectives.

There is a large diversity of distribution related fees paid throughout Europe, Asia and Latin America for the distribution of UCITS, based on the type of distributor, the type of product, the relationship with the asset manager and/or the specific way in which the asset manager wishes the fund to be sold. In Southern European jurisdictions, there is a greater concentration of available distributors and this has been a factor in UCITS having to pay higher levels of distribution commission, (or rebates) compared to Northern European countries where local banking networks have less of a share of total net sales into investment funds for the same type of product.

As mentioned previously, distribution or trailer fees are paid by the UCITS or, more commonly, the management company, to the local distributor to facilitate the local promotion or sales process, including the provision of "advice" to end investors, (typically clients of the distributor). The fees also act as a financial incentive for the distribution company and network so they understand the UCITS product and the sales strategy created by the management company of the UCITS and also to ensure access to the distributors clients, (investors). Such fee payments must also be in compliance with EU Directives regarding the provision of investment services. One must also distinguish between rebates paid to a distributor to those paid to an institutional investor. Usually the rebate paid to the distributor will exclusively benefit him/her and the final client may not benefit at all from such payments whereas the institutional investor, as a final client, will benefit directly of such advantage.

The distribution fee rates, the manner of their calculation and payment frequency, usually monthly or quarterly, are agreed between the promoter/UCITS management company or its representatives and the distributor. These fees effectively constitute a re-distribution part of the management fees to the local distributor. These fees are usually calculated based on the holdings of the distributor during a specific period and can be aged, tiered and scaled.

Generally speaking, over the past ten years, the commercial alignment of UCITS distributors, especially across Europe, with that of UCITS promoters has tended to diverge creating somewhat of a power struggle between these two parties over the revenue derived from the UCITS business. On balance, the commercial strength of distributors relative to that of UCITS promoters has increased during this period, meaning that most UCITS promoters or asset managers have needed to provide distributors with increasingly larger fees to facilitate third party distribution. Larger international fund groups clearly have more leverage and have been able to better withstand the growth in power of the distributors. Medium sized and smaller UCITS managers have tended to fare less well and are being squeezed by many large distribution networks. These trends are having long term implications for the funds industry.

This commercial realignment over the past ten or more years has been due to a multitude of factors including the increasing business volumes on distribution platforms, the concentration of successful distribution networks in many key jurisdictions that UCITS tend to target, the continued dominance of banking groups across continental Europe and much of Asia, the slow development of alternative distribution channels, the increasing complexity and difficulty of cross-border fund distribution, the strong relationships that many local distributors have with their clients who are also potential targets for foreign UCITS and the increasing number of cross-border UCITS wishing to competing for "shelf space" in popular distribution channels. Strong distributors place increasing demands on UCITS if they wish to be locally promoted, especially UCITS promoters lacking international brand recognition. These demands include higher fees but, also comprehensive training of sales staff, high quality marketing material that is constantly updated and high levels of effective customer assistance and support. Large international distribution networks have found it easier to meet these demands but others have found it more difficult, often with material impacts on their distribution objectives.

However, and especially within the EU, political pressure is rising, with support from regulatory authorities, for requiring greater levels of transparency, especially in connection with fees charged to investors for financial products, including UCITS. Increased transparency and new rules will impact the payment of fees to local distributors in an effort to increase transparency towards end investors and reduce, eliminate or manage conflicts of interest.

It is likely that in many jurisdictions and across the entire EU, the present way in which distributors are remunerated will change over the next few years as both regulators and investor groups are looking to reduce conflicts of interest, increase product transparency and improve investor confidence in the financial services industry in general. For example, in the UK, new rules will totally prohibit the payment of distribution fees by UCITS, (and other financial products), to the distributor and as such the distributor, as an adviser, will need to be remunerated by the investor instead. Denmark and the Netherlands have proposed similar rules. At the European level, the MiFID II directive, which was published in October 2011, includes proposals on banning inducements for independent advisers.

As well as an increasing trend towards greater transparency, complex cross-border strategies tend to generate commercial and regulatory risks both for the UCITS and the distributor directly facing investors. Distribution risks can be grouped into three broad areas; distribution strategy (what to sell, where to sell it and how to sell it to ensure success), strategy implementation (selecting distributors, creating compliant marketing materials, achieving market entry), and operations (AML, KYC, accurate fee calculations, ongoing regulatory and tax reporting). As cross-border distribution continues to expand these, associated risks become more critical to the UCITS business and therefore is being more closely monitored and evaluated for their impact.

6.8. Future thoughts: UCITS in transition

A tried and tested product, vetted at both European and international levels, the UCITS brand is more than 25 years old and accepted as the only globally distributed investment fund product. UCITS as a brand has proved worthy of the high level of trust it has amongst the global investor community, local distributors the world over and regulators from key markets in every region. Unique amongst global investment products, the short and medium term future continues to look positive for UCITS, especially given the lack of substantive competition. However, in the longer term UCITS face a less certain future, if only because we live in an increasing competitive, nationalistic and fast changing financial world.

The global finance crisis of 2007-2010, the various regulatory and investor changes that followed and the current persistent financial instability are all likely to weigh heavily on the future success of all types of investment products, including UCITS, especially in some key markets where UCITS distribution has traditionally been strong. Current UCITS distribution models will need to continue to adapt to the continuing lack of investor confidence, current and future demographic changes, the increasing variety of competing products, the emergence of new markets and the continuing decline of others and finally, an increasing shift towards private savings for long-term retirement.

Current distribution models will be impacted by new rules and regulations requiring greater product transparency, limiting, changing and/or prohibiting the use of fees to support distribution in ways that create conflicts of interest, the continuing rising tension between product manufacturers and distributors and the increasing use of technology which is likely to further support and enhance the globalization of financial products.

In the short-term to medium-term, new and proposed transparency requirements and rules surrounding the use of commission payments to facilitate distribution, will force many distributors to alter radically their existing distribution models and shift the balance towards investors. Furthermore, there will be an additional wave of regulations within Europe including AIFMD, UCITS V, MiFID II and FATCA, that will significantly alter many existing distributions across Europe and throughout the world.

Farther afield, markets in the Middle East and Asia will continue to mature offering UCITS even greater opportunities to distribute locally, while new markets will continue to expand and open up in South America. Nevertheless, products competing directly with UCITS are likely to emerge in Asia, the proposed "Asia Fund Passport" being one current initiative designed to directly compete with UCITS sold into the Asian region. These changes will require UCITS to innovate in order to maintain their existing significant penetration in this region. Africa may, over the next 20 years provide UCITS with a number of key target markets especially if their middle-class and institutional investor segments grow strongly.

In the longer term, significant demographic shifts in many markets currently targeted by UCITS together with an increasing reliance on individuals funding their own retirement will provide UCITS with a unique opportunity to promote themselves as long-term retirement savings vehicles within the EU, and potentially other markets outside of Europe. This opportunity would require further regulatory changes to the UCITS Directive but also adaptations to existing distribution models. It is likely that we will see new financial products aggressively competing with UCITS both in and outside of Europe. It is difficult to imagine a situation where, in the longer term, UCITS remain without significant competition in the cross-border marketplace. Moreover, the growing trend of increasing nationalistic and protectionist tendencies ignited by the recent financial crisis may not stop and if it continues to grow, cross-border UCITS sold outside of the EU may find increasing difficulties to quickly enter foreign markets at ease. A failure to constantly adapt the UCITS Directive to these significant global demographic and commercial shifts may leave the brand open to a gradual decline in the long term from its current pinnacle of success.

Chapter 7

The UCITS Management
Company and Delegation

7.1. Introduction

7.1.1. *Overview of chapter coverage*

This chapter will look at the UCITS organizational structure, with a particular emphasis on delegated roles and responsibilities. It will concentrate on the different roles and responsibilities that are outlined in implementing Directive 2010/43/EU[1] (the "Organization Directive") on the organizational requirements, conflicts of interest and rules of conduct for a UCITS management company.

As with any regulatory framework, practice evolves within it. It is important to note that while the Organization Directive does not refer to the rules and responsibilities of the main fund service providers directly, we outline the high-level roles and responsibilities detailed in the Organization Directive and provide suggestions as to the service providers these roles maybe delegated to. This chapter will also look at the reporting within the Organization Directive and consider the best practice to be applied to UCITS.

Chapter written by Killian BUCKLEY and Ciara O'SULLIVAN.
1 Commission Directive 2010/43/EC of 1 July 2010 implementing Directive 2007/65/EC of the European Parliament and of the Council as regards organizational requirements, conflicts of interest, conduct of business, risk management and content of the agreement between and depositary and a management company.

In preparing this chapter we have concentrated on the details of the directives themselves. We note that certain countries will interpret provisions differently and practice will have evolved separately in other countries. We believe, however, that an analysis of the underlying directives is the most appropriate form for this chapter in order to give an overarching European view.

7.1.2. *History of the organizational structure of a UCITS*

As we know from previous chapters, the original UCITS Directive – Directive 85/611/EEC ("*UCITS Directive*") – established the UCITS product as a European collective investment scheme. It set out the legal forms that a UCITS could take, the investment and borrowing rules permitted, liquidity requirements, prospectus disclosure rules, and rules relating to the role and obligations of the UCITS depositary/custodians and manager.

One of the aims of the UCITS Directive was to create a fund passport. A fund passport allowed an UCITS authorized in one EU Member State to be sold throughout the other Member States without the requirement to register the UCITS in each Member State, subject to the local market rules of the country the UCITS was marketing into. Although, the UCITS fund itself benefited from an EU passport, the UCITS Directive required that the UCITS, its management company and its depositary were located in the same Member State. This meant that the activities related to collective portfolio management (the management and administration of the UCITS) were subject to the law of one Member State (i.e. the Member State in which the management company is situated). Promoters (the originator and decision maker of a UCITS) who wanted to set up a UCITS in one country had to create an UCITS and locate its management company in the same country, even if the promoter already had a UCITS management company located in another Member State.

A number of inefficiencies that were in the original UCITS Directive were addressed when UCITS III was implemented. UCITS III consisted of two directives:

– the Product Directive (Directive 2001/108/EC); and

– the Management Company Directive (Directive 2001/107/EC).

The Management Company Directive attempted to give a European passport to the management company of a UCITS and to enable it to operate throughout Europe as well as introducing more organizational-type rules and capital adequacy requirements to be met by the management company. This directive also introduced a simplified prospectus that was to aid the cross-border marketing of funds and enhance investor understanding of UCITS products through a shorter, more user-friendly document that detailed the salient points of an offering. However, despite management company passporting being foreseen in the directive, this did not materialize and led to an inefficient product and increased costs for the management company that were ultimately borne by the investor. Similarly, the introduction of the simplified prospectus did not lead to a more comprehensible offering document, as its production became mired in disclaimers and ever more complex jargon.

The Product Directive 2001/108/EC expanded the type of eligible investments for an UCITS and it also required the management company to employ a risk-management process that enabled it to monitor and measure the risk of derivative positions and their contribution to the overall risk profile of the UCITS at any time.

7.1.3. Evolution to UCITS IV

Figure 7.1. *A flow diagram of the evolution and application of UCITS IV*

In July 2005, a European Commission Green Paper identified a number of shortcomings within the existing UCITS regulatory framework. One of the shortcomings identified was the fact that only the fund could be passported, preventing the management company from availing of the single EU market.

Following detailed consultation, the European Commission proposed, a series of targeted amendments to the UCITS III framework in November 2006 in a White Paper titled *Enhancing the Single Market Framework for Investment Funds*. These enhancements ultimately became Directive 2009/65/EC (*"UCITS IV Directive"*). The purpose of the UCITS IV Directive was to enhance market efficiencies while ensuring investor protection at all times. One of the key amendments was the introduction of an effective management company passport.

This evolution is important in that it is helpful to understand the regulatory drivers that created the UCITS IV environment. If Member States were to agree to a management company passport, it was necessary that management company rules and regulations were adopted and implemented in a reasonably harmonized manner across Europe.

This chapter will deal with the organizational structure and the roles and responsibilities of the different parties. The section on the implementation of the Organization Directive contains MiFID-like requirements around:

– organizational and internal control;

– conflicts of interests; and

– rules of conduct and risk management for management companies.

The Organization Directive seeks to align the MiFID and UCITS regulations with the aim of achieving equivalent standards between MiFID firms and UCITS funds.

7.1.4. *UCITS IV organizational structure, conflicts of interest and rules of conduct*

The Organization Directive sets out a comprehensive new legal framework applicable to all management companies (whether they avail of the passport of not), for their organization, conflicts of interest and rules of conduct. The Organization Directive is prescriptive, setting out specific controls and requirements that must be put in place to ensure investor protection.

Although the principles outlined in the Organization Directive are applicable to all management companies, they are flexible enough to ensure that their application is proportionate, taking into account the nature, scale and complexities of the management company in what is often referred to as the principle of proportionality. This principle gives some flexibility to the management company depending on the structure and organizational arrangement of the management company and the nature of the different UCITSs that it manages. However, the minimum standards of the UCITS IV Directive need to be satisfied.

Investment companies that do not designate a management company (self-managed investment companies or SMICs) are subject to the same rules of conduct and provisions regarding conflicts of interest and risk management as management companies.

Figure 7.2 provides a summary of the UCITS IV management company's organization, conflicts of interest, rules of conduct, and supervision of delegates' requirements. It also gives an outline of the contractual agreement that is entered into with the depositary where the UCITS is located in a different jurisdiction to the management company. This chapter does not specifically deal with the agreement between the depositary and the management company.

As a final comment, to avoid any possible confusion that may arise where the management company's and the fund's competent authority are located in different Member States, the UCITS IV Directive sets out the appropriate split of regulatory responsibilities between the competent authority of the management company's home Member State and the competent authority of the fund.

The rules in force in the management company's home Member State will apply relating to the organization of the management company including delegation arrangements, risk-management procedures and the conduct of business rules. The rules in place in the UCITS home Member State will apply to the set-up and functioning of the UCITS.

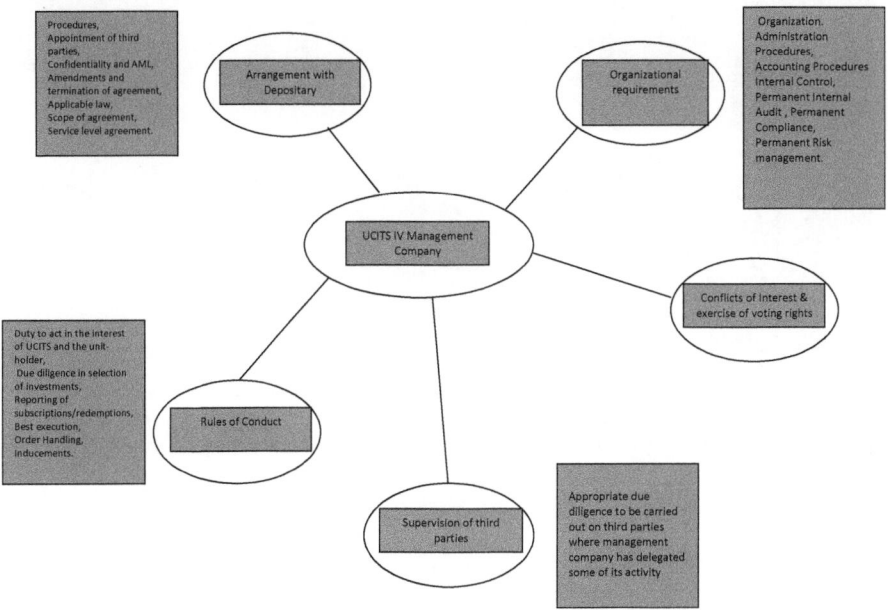

Figure 7.2. *Summary of the role of management companies in UCITS IV, as set out in the Organization Directive*

7.1.4.1. *Roles and responsibilities of the board, senior management and permanent functions*

The board of directors has ultimate responsibility for the activities of the management company and ensures that the management company meets its legal and regulatory obligations.

The senior management consists of the person(s) who conduct the business of the management company. The Organization Directive specifically sets out responsibilities for the senior management.

In addition to this, the management company will have a permanent compliance function, permanent risk-management function and permanent internal audit function. The responsibilities of these functions are outlined in Figure 7.3.

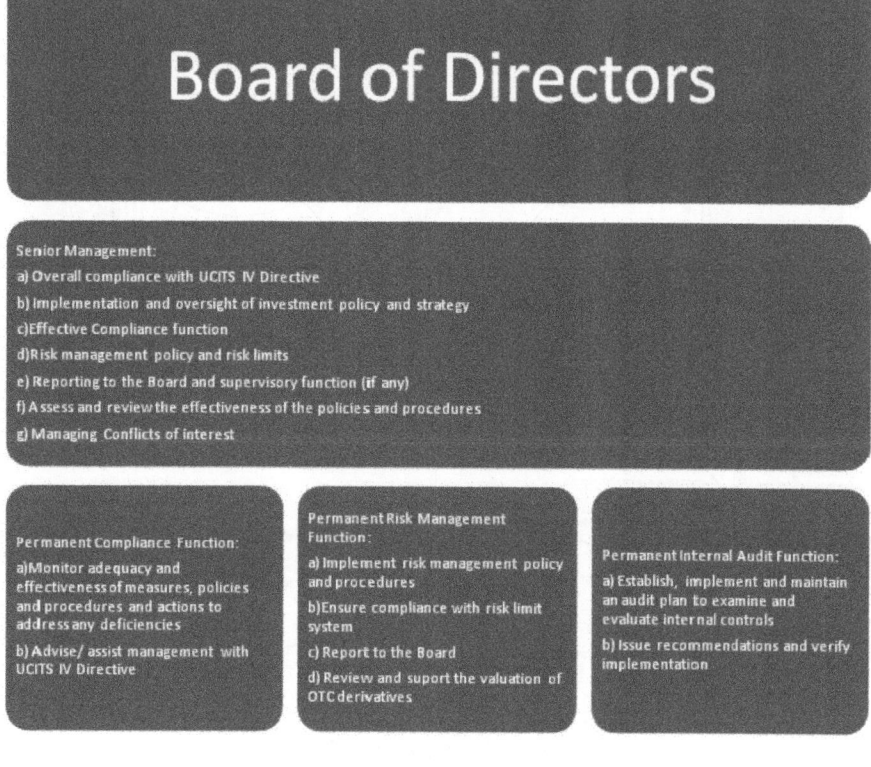

Figure 7.3. *Responsibilities of the board of directors, senior management, and their permanent functions*

The Organization Directive also sets out the structure and resources of the permanent compliance, internal audit and risk function. It notes that SMICs are required to have a risk management function, but while it is considered good practice to have a permanent compliance and internal audit function for a SMIC, it is not obligated in the Organization Directive.

	Permanent compliance function	Permanent internal audit function	Permanent risk function
Independent	Yes; proportionality can be taken into account	Yes	Yes; proportionality can be taken into account
Resources required	Appoint a Compliance officer Proportionality can be taken into account	Proportionality can be taken into account	Proportionality can be taken into account
Applies to the management company	Yes	Yes	Yes
Applies to the SMIC	Good practice not obligated	Good practice not obligated	Yes

Table 7.1. *Structure and resources of permanent functions*

7.1.4.2. *Delegations*

In practice, management companies (or SMICs, as appropriate), may consider delegating one or more of these functions to third parties for the purpose of more efficient conduct of the management companies' business. They may delegate if the laws in their home Member State allows delegation. The delegation is subject to certain obligations outlined in the UCITS IV Directive, e.g. the management company must inform the competent authorities of its Home Member State. In relation to delegated functions it is important that the party to whom the functions are delegated is qualified and capable of undertaking the functions in question and that the management company oversees the party's performance of the functions that have been delegated. The management company should document this oversight to illustrate that it continues to evaluate the performance of the delegates on a periodic basis.

For example, a management company will often delegate the performance of the risk-management activities including the valuation of over-the-counter (OTC) derivatives to third parties. Before entering into such arrangements, management companies must take the necessary steps to verify that the third party has the ability and capacity to perform the risk-management activities reliably, professionally and effectively and carry out on-going assessment of the performance of the delegate.

7.1.4.3. *Organizational structure – general principles*

As mentioned, the Organization Directive details the conflicts of interest provisions and the new rules of conduct for UCITS management companies. The matrix in section 7.2 summarizes the general principles for the organization and rules of conduct for management companies and outlines suggested service providers that the activities maybe delegated to. However it is important to note that, ultimately, the legal and regulatory requirements of the management company are the responsibility of the board of directors.

Management companies are required to have a documented organizational structure with clearly-assigned reporting lines and allocation of responsibilities, an adequate internal control mechanism, effective internal reporting and communication and orderly records. Firms are also required to have an adequate business continuity policy and systems to safeguard the security and processing of information and the maintenance of accounting policies and procedures. Management companies must regularly monitor and evaluate their systems and internal control mechanisms.

While the above requirements are intuitive and sensible, it is advisable that the management company think practically about how the requirements will be implemented. It is recommended that a party, potentially senior management, take "ownership" of the maintenance of this organizational structure in a documented matrix that is easily understandable and, perhaps more importantly, flexible. Like any business, the business of running a management company is subject to many stresses and strains, both internally and externally. It is advisable therefore that the structure in place is prescient and appropriate and that each party understands its responsibilities.

Equally important is a clear policy at management company level about what actions should be taken "when things go wrong". It is important that each service provider is on board as to when, how, and to whom issues will be raised. An efficient escalation procedure, be it to senior management or the board of directors, is vital for adequate reaction to events.

As mentioned in section 7.1.4.1 the Organization Directive outlines the role and the responsibilities of the permanent compliance, permanent risk management and permanent internal audit functions.

In addition, management companies will need to have policies in the following areas:

– *Resources*: management companies are required to employ personnel with the relevant skills, knowledge and expertise to carry out their function and to monitor the activities of third parties.

– *Electronic data processing*: management companies are required to have suitable electronic systems to permit a timely and proper recording of each portfolio transaction or subscription/redemption order. Management companies are required to have a high level of security during the electronic processing and for the maintenance of confidentiality and integrity of data.

– *Accounting procedures:* UCITS accounting procedures shall be maintained for the UCITS so that all of the assets and liabilities of the UCITS can easily be identified. The accounting policies and procedures in place should ensure the protection of unit-holders.

– *Complaints handling*: management companies are required to establish, implement and maintain effective and transparent complaints-handling procedures. The complaints-handing procedures must be available to investors free of charge. It is important that a documented procedure is in place, irrespective of where the complaint originates. The procedure should include regular interaction with the complainant and a finite time frame for resolution.

– *Control by senior management*: senior management is responsible for the management company's adherence with the UCITS IV Directive obligations. The Organization Directive refers to control by a senior manager of:

- the implementation of the investment policy,

- the approval of investment strategies,

- compliance function,

- ensure that the risk limits are implemented and complied with,

- review the adequacy of the investment decisions and that they are in line with the strategies, and

- review and approve the risk management policy.

The senior management and, where appropriate, its supervisory function, shall assess and periodically review the effectiveness of policies, arrangements and procedures relevant to the UCITS IV Directive and take measures to address any deficiencies identified.

Not surprisingly, the interaction between senior management and the investment manager is especially important here. Senior management must be comfortable with the investment manager's ethos and rationale on managing the fund's assets and how risk is interpreted and managed both within the portfolio and from an operational perspective. The communication with the board of directors is also relevant. While senior management will control the process on a day-to-day basis, the board of directors must be comfortable (and understand) the methodology involved in portfolio management.

– *Personal transactions*: the management company is required to establish, implement and maintain adequate arrangements and reporting of personal transactions.

– *Recording of portfolio transactions and subscription and redemption orders:* a management company is required to ensure that for each portfolio transaction relating to the UCITS, a record of information that is sufficient to reconstruct the details of the order and the executed transaction is available without delay. UCITS subscription and redemption orders must be centralized and recorded immediately after receipt of the order. The Organization Directive sets out details of what must be recorded for portfolio transactions and subscriptions and redemptions orders. These are detailed provisions (e.g. the name of the person transmitting the order). The investment manager often delegates these functions to specialized service providers. Therefore, it is important prior to engaging with the delegate that the management company has satisfied itself that the delegate can adhere to these provisions.

7.1.4.4. *Conflicts of interest*

The conflicts of interest policy must:

– identify the circumstances when potential conflicts will arise; and

– establish procedures to be followed and measures to be adopted to manage these conflicts.

7.1.4.5. *Exercise of voting rights*

Management companies are required to develop adequate and effective strategies for determining when and how voting rights attached to instruments are to be exercised to the exclusive benefit of the UCITS. A summary description of this should be available to investors as well as details of the actions taken.

7.1.4.6. *Rules of conduct*

The rules of conduct can be divided into six main areas:

– *Duty to act in the best interests of the UCITS and their unit holders*. Management companies are required to ensure that unit holders are treated fairly. They must also apply appropriate policies and procedures for preventing malpractice. Fair, correct and transparent pricing models and valuation systems are to be used for UCITS and the management company must act so that no undue costs are charged to the UCITS.

– *Due diligence requirements on the selection and on-going monitoring of investments.* Management companies are to ensure that there is a high level of diligence in the selection and ongoing monitoring of investments and they are required to have adequate knowledge and understanding of the assets in which the UCITS are invested. Written policies and procedure on due diligence must be in place and arrangements must be implemented to ensure that investment decisions on behalf of the UCITS are carried out in compliance with the objectives, strategies and risk limits.

– *Reporting obligations in respect of execution of subscription and redemption orders.* When a subscription or redemption order is carried out, the management company must confirm execution of the order and this must contain specific information.

– *Best execution.* Best execution rules will be applied to a UCITS following the implementation of UCITS IV. These are similar to MiFID rules. Management companies must take all reasonable steps to obtain the best possible result for the UCITS, taking into account price, costs, speed, likelihood of execution and settlement, order size and nature. The best execution policy should be available to investors and the management company must regularly monitor the effectiveness of it arrangement and policy for the execution of orders.

– *Order handling.* The Organization Directive contains detailed rules on the handling of orders and the management company is required to establish and implement procedures and arrangements that provide for the prompt, fair and expeditious execution of portfolio transactions on behalf of an UCITS.

– *Inducements.* Management companies must act honestly, fairly and professionally in accordance with the interests of the UCITS. In order to ensure this, a UCITS management company is prohibited from paying or providing certain fees, commission or non-monetary benefit (in relation to the activities of investment management and administration) except if they are:

- paid or provided to or by the UCITS or on behalf of the UCITS;

- paid or provided to or by a third party if;

    i) it is disclosed appropriately,

    ii) the payment of the fee enhances the quality of the service provided,

- proper fees that enable or are necessary for the provision of the relevant service and which by their nature cannot give rise to conflicts with the management company's duty to act honestly, fairly and professionally in accordance with the interest of the UCITS.

7.2. Roles and responsibilities within the organizational structure

The general principles for the organization of management companies have been outlined in section 7.1.4. The Organization Directive acknowledges that the management company may want to delegate some or all of its activities to third parties. Where the activities are delegated, due diligence checks as outlined in section 7.1.4.2 should be carried out by the management company on the third party. The third party should fulfill all the organizational and conflicts of interest requirements in relation to the activity to be undertaken. The management company should also verify that the third party has taken appropriate measures to comply with the requirements and should effectively monitor compliance by the third party with these requirements.

Where the delegate is responsible for applying the rules governing the delegated activities, equivalent organizational and conflict of interests requirements should apply to the activity of monitoring the delegated activities. The management company should be able to take into account in the due diligence process the fact that the third party to whom activities are delegated will often be subject to MiFID.

UCITS management companies will often meet their obligations with regards to determining that the third party satisfies the requirements to fulfill the organizational and conflicts of interest requirements by having service-level agreements, side letters and other forms of agreements in place. Responsibility for ensuring that the third party complies with its obligations rests with the management company and, ultimately, the legal and regulatory requirements of the management company are the responsibility of the board of directors.

Tables 7.2 and 7.3 summarize the general principles for the organization, conflicts of interest and rules of conduct for management companies and outlines suggested service providers that the activities may be delegated to. The matrices indicate which of the rules apply to SMICs. As mentioned above, SMICs are required to comply with the rules of conduct and provisions regarding conflicts of interest and risk management. SMICS are invited, but not obliged, to comply with the administrative and accounting provisions and the internal control provisions, taking into account the principle of proportionality. Management companies are required to comply with all of the provisions.

Organizatioal rules		Senior Management*	Compliance*	Internal Audit*	Risk Management Function*	Administrator**	Investment Manager**	Distributor**	SMIC
Administrative and Accounting Procedures	Documented organisational structure with clearly assigned responsibilities					√	√	√	
	Effective internal reporting and communication of information (incl to third parties)					√	√	√	
	Maintenance of adequate and orderly records of business and suitable electronic data processing systems					√	√	√	
	Systems and procedures to safeguard security, integrity and confidentiality of information					√	√	√	
	Adequate Business Continuity Plan					√	√	√	
	Control and safeguard arrangements for electronic data processing					√	√	√	
	Effective accounting policies and procedures					√			
	Procedures for handling of investors' complaints					√	√	√	
	Necessary resources with adequate skills, knowledge and expertise					√	√	√	
Internal Control Mechanism	Timely and proper recording of portfolio transactions, subscription and redemption orders					√		√	
	Compliance with Directive 2009/65/EC	√				√	√	√	
	Adequate control by senior management	√				√	√	√	
	Regular reporting to senior management and supervisory function	√				√	√	√	
	Establish permanent compliance function	√	√						
	Establish permanent internal audit function			√					
	Establish permanent risk management function	√			√		√		√
	Arrangements and recording of personal transactions					√	√	√	
Conflicts of Interest	Identify conflicts of interest and establish policy					√	√	√	√
	Strategies for the exercise of voting rights						√		√

*Specific roles and responsibilities as outlined in Directive 2010/10/EU for senior management, compliance, intern al audit, and risk management functions

**Tasks that are outlined in Directive 2010/10/EU that may be delegated by the management company to the service providers mentioned

Table 7.2. *Organizational rules and suggested parties for delegation*

Rules of Conduct

		Senior Management*	Compliance*	Internal Audit*	Risk Management Function*	Administrator**	Investment Manager**	Distributor**	SMIC
Duty to act in interest of UCITS and unitholders	Treat unit holders fairly					√	√	√	√
	Procedures and policies to prevent malpractices					√	√	√	√
	Use of fair, correct and transparent pricing models and valuation systems					√			√
Due diligence requirements	High level of diligence in the selection and on going monitoring of investments						√		√
	Adequate knowledge and understanding of invested assets						√		√
	Investment decisions are in compliance with UCITS objectives/strategies/risk limits						√		√
Reporting of dealing orders	Report subscription/redemption orders to unit-holders					√		√	√
	Information on status of order					√		√	√
Best Execution	Establish and implement best execution arrangements						√		√
	Monitor effectiveness of best execution policy						√		√
Order Handling	Procedures and arrangements for prompt, fair and expeditious execution of portfolio transactions						√		√
	Policy for order allocation						√		√
Inducements	Prohibition on certain fees, non-monetary benefit or commission paid by or to management company						√		√

* Specific roles and responsibilities as outlined in the Directive 2010/43/EU for senior management, compliance function, internal audit function and risk management function.

** Tasks that are outlined in Directive 2010/43/EU that maybe delegated by the management company to the service providers mentioned.

Table 7.3. *Rules of conduct and suggested parties for delegation*

7.2.1. *The evolving role of the depositary*

The depositary keeps safe the UCITS assets and provides a supervisory oversight on certain of the activities of the fund. The depositary remains in the same domicile as the fund and continues to be a separate legal entity to the management company. Following the financial crisis and Madoff's investment fraud, a number of gaps in investor protection were identified in the existing UCITS IV model. Consequently the European Commission has begun to engage with the public regarding amending the UCITS IV Directive to enhance the regulation and supervision of the depositary. This work is on-going and is not yet complete, but will include enhancements to the UCITS IV Directive, named UCITS V. These amendments will further clarify the

UCITS depositary function, including the liability and eligibility requirements, and ensure consistency between the legislation applicable to depositaries of UCITSs and alternative investment funds.

The Organization Directive sets out additional requirements that should apply to the relationship between the management company and the depositary when they are located in different Member States. Particular focus is placed on the written agreement to be drawn up between the management company and the depositary. Details on the procedures to be followed by the parties, exchange of information and obligations on confidentiality and money laundering, appointment of third parties and provisions for amendment of the agreement are outlined in the Organization Directive. The depositary agreement should be governed by the law of the UCITS' home Member State.

7.3. Reporting matrix – how parties interact for reporting

The Organization Directive mentions specific reports that must be made to the competent authority, senior management and board of directors. Details of the reports that are outlined in the Organization Directive together with details of whom the report should be sent to are outlined in Table 7.4.

Interestingly, depending on the jurisdiction of the senior management of the UCITS, the reporting provided to the senior management is in fact provided to the board of directors.

Area	Report	Competent authority	Board of directors	Senior management
Accounting	Financial report that reflects a true and fair view of the management company's financial position and that complies with accounting standards and rules	√		
Investment Strategies	- Implementation of investment strategies, policies and risk limits - Internal procedures for taking investment decisions			√

Table 7.4. *Reporting matrix*

Compliance	Compliance report indicating appropriate remedial measures taken where deficiencies are identified			√
Risk management	Risk-management report indicating appropriate remedial measures taken where there are deficiencies identified			√
Risk management	- Consistency between the current levels of risk incurred and the risk profile of the UCITS - The compliance of each managed UCITS with relevant risk limit systems - Adequacy and effectiveness of the risk-management process, indicating appropriate remedial measures that have been taken where deficiencies are identified		√	
Internal audit	Internal audit report indicating appropriate remedial measures taken where deficiencies are identified			√
Risk levels	The current level of risk incurred by each managed UCITS and any actual or foreseeable breaches to their limits			√
Risk-management process	- Material changes in the risk-management process - Types of derivative instruments used, underlying risks, quantitative limits and the methods that are chosen to estimate the risks associated with a derivative	√		
Conflicts of interest	Situations where organizational or administrative arrangements made for the management of conflicts of interest are not sufficient to ensure risks of damage to UCITS/unit-holder will be prevented			√

Table 7.4. Continued *Reporting matrix*

In practice in addition to the reporting mentioned above, the management company will receive reports from a number of its delegates, namely the investment manager, administrator, depositary and distributor. Examples of the types of reports received from various service providers are:

– Additional investment manager report, which may include:

- reporting on the fund performance;

- exceptions to the investment borrowing, strategies and prospectus investment objectives and policies and any remedial action that has been taken;

- exceptions to the risk limits, profile and contributions;

- maintenance of logs for investment breaches, complaints and compensation payments;

- details of changes in investment objectives, policies and restriction;

- temporary suspension of the Net Asset Value calculations.

– Creation/termination of a UCITS including sub funds:

- details of internal audit findings; and

- business plan reporting.

– Additional administrator report, which may include:

- information on price accuracy, static security prices, stock reconciliations, reconciliations;

- pricing errors and shareholder transaction errors and details of any remedial action taken;

- expense budgeting;

- annual and semi-annual accounts;

- authorized signature list;

- profit and loss account;

- information on capital monitoring;

- details of internal audit findings;

- approval of dividends;

- details of complaints; and

- maintenance of error logs and compensation payments.

– Additional distributor reporting may include:

- sales and redemptions;

- distribution channels;

- new markets and compliance requirements with these markets; and

- complaints handling.

– Additional depositary reporting, which may include:

- depending on the fund structure, information on pricing errors or breaches of the investment policies, strategies and objectives, pricing errors, details that assets of the fund are safely kept; and

- investor complaints.

7.4. UCITS IV organizational framework – applying best practice

7.4.1. *Driving best practice*

The new UCITS organizational and conduct of business rules have the overarching principle of investor protection and supervision at their core. To ensure that an effective management passport was implemented, the Commission considered it necessary to have robust organizational, conflict of interest and conduct of business rules in place that would apply to all management companies, whether they used the passport or not. This is essential to ensure that investors in funds that are managed cross-border are adequately protected and are not exposed to additional operational or lower standards of investor protection compared to funds managed locally. The principle of proportionality has been applied in order to avoid excessive administrative or procedural burdens on either the management company or the competent authority. UCITSs may be constituted as an investment company or a SMIC, therefore the Organization Directive requirements can be adjusted as appropriate.

As previously mentioned, the law of the management company's home Member State regulates the management company's organization and conduct of business rules.

The UCITS IV organizational, conflict of business and conduct of business rules apply to management companies and as a matter of good practice, apply to SMICs (subject to proportionality).

7.4.2. *MiFID-like requirements*

The Organization Directive seeks to ensure as much consistency as possible with the MiFID regulations, bearing in mind the specific nature of UCITS collective investment management. This creates consistency between UCITS managers and MiFID investment firms. It also avoids duplication and unjustified burdens for management companies providing individual portfolio management services.

As accounting is one of the key areas of the UCITS' administration and is considered part of the organization of the management company, it is important that some principles concerning the organization of accounting is noted, over and above that of MiFID. The UCITS accounting should be kept so that all assets and liabilities of UCITS are identifiable and accounting processes and procedures are maintained to ensure the calculation of the NAV and the accurate valuation of assets and the NAV. The organizational provisions of MiFID are also enhanced to make the senior management of the UCITS responsible for implementing and monitoring the investment policy of the UCITS.

The conflicts of interest section has been enhanced in the Organization Directive. Management companies are required to apply effective strategies to define how and if the voting rights attached to instruments are voted for to the exclusive benefit of unit-holders.

7.4.3. *Typical UCITS IV structure*

UCITS funds can be set up as investment funds or common funds. The UCITS directives have never mandated how the UCITS funds should be set up but have left this decision to the management company to determine, depending on the promoters' preferences.

An UCITS set up as a common fund has no legal personality and must be managed by a management company. An investment company, however, has its own legal personality and can either appoint a management company or designate itself as a SMIC. As we have already mentioned, whether or not an investment company has a management company will determine the level of organizational rules that apply to it.

The role of a management company under the UCITS Directive is much broader than the investment management of a fund. It includes valuation and pricing, regulatory compliance monitoring, maintenance of a unit-holder register, record keeping and marketing. It is common for the management company to delegate these functions (where permitted by local regulations) and to oversee the operation of the delegated functions. A common structure has developed that is outlined in Figure 7.4.

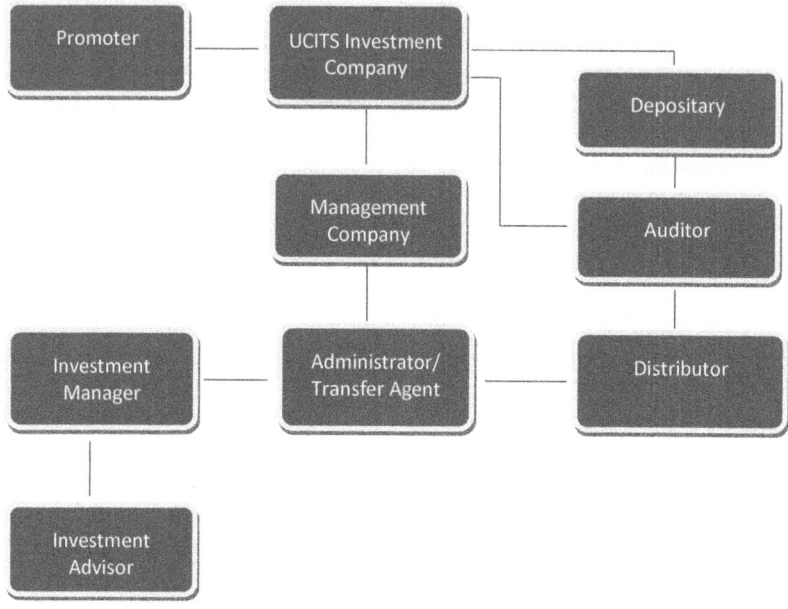

Figure 7.4. *A common UCITS investment company structure*

Within this structure:

– Depositary: an UCITS must appoint a credit institution as a depositary bank. The depositary is responsible for both the safekeeping of assets and the supervision of the fund.

– *External auditor*: the fund or its management company prepares an annual and half-yearly report. The annual report is audited by an authorized external auditor with appropriate professional experience.

– Investment manager: the management company is responsible for investment management. This is often delegated to an expert investment advisor. The investment manager makes investment decisions for the UCIT, in accordance with the UCITS' objectives, polices and strategies. It is important that the management company ensures that the investment manager carries out its duties in line with the Organization Directive requirements, e.g. best execution, due diligence of investments, order handling, proxy voting and inducements.

– *Administration/transfer agent*: part of the role of the management company is administrative, e.g. accounting services, valuation and pricing (including tax matters), maintenance of a unit-holder register, distribution of income, unit issues and redemptions and record keeping. It is becoming increasingly evident that the management companies are delegating these functions (where permitted) to an administrator. An administrator is typically a specialist in accounting, NAV calculation, keeping of the register of shareholders/unit holders, handling of subscriptions and redemptions, communication with investors and preparation of financial statements.

– *Distributor*: a distributor typically markets and sells the UCITS to investors for the management company. As a distributor will often receive fees for selling the UCITS, it is important that the management company ensures that the distributors treat unit-holders fairly and equally. A distributor will often be required to carry out anti-money-laundering checks on potential investors prior to enabling them to invest in the fund.

– *Investment advisor*: often an investment manager will seek the expert advice from an investment advisor. An investment advisor makes investment recommendations or conducts securities analysis in return for a fee.

7.4.3.1. *New entrants to UCITS – what to watch out for*

The amount of time, cost and effort required from a new entrant to the UCITS arena will depend on the extent to which the promoter is aware of MiFID and its implications on the organization and conduct of the business rules of a company. To a large extent, where a promoter has knowledge of the MiFID environment, the UCITS organizational and conflict of interest rules and rules of conduct should ensure that consistent regulation is applied across group companies.

The new organizational rules may prove more challenging to a non-MiFID firm as the organizational requirements and conflicts of interest are detailed and significant costs may have to be incurred prior to the required structure being implemented.

New entrants need to consider a number of factors, some of which include:

– *Jurisdiction of choice*: previously, UCITS management companies had to be set up in the same location as the fund, but now with the UCITS IV management company passport these limitations do not apply. Therefore, it is easier for a new entrant to set up funds in multiple jurisdictions but manage the fund from one jurisdiction. This makes the process more cost-effective for the management company. Management companies are free to consider the best country for them to locate to, the governance structure in place in each location, and the type of entity that they would like to be set up as.

– *Distribution network*: ultimately, each management company will need to satisfy the investors of the fund that the fund and the management company satisfy investor requirements. Therefore, if potential investors have a jurisdiction of choice for the location of the fund or the management company, these considerations must be considered.

– *Tax*: UCITS IV did not harmonize tax across Europe; therefore it is important for the management company to consider its own tax liability and that of the fund when looking at the different jurisdictions and structures. As the management company does not have to be located where the fund is located, the fund tax authority may challenge the domicile of the fund. Each jurisdiction will have to be considered carefully. The management company may need to consider transfer pricing and also any implications that VAT would have for these service flows. Access to double taxation treaties by the UCITS, may also be a factor of where the fund should be domiciled.

– *Delegation*: when a management company wants to delegate some of its activity to another service provider, the rules regarding delegation are subject to the management company's home State competent authority's obligations.

– *Proportionality*: UCITS IV introduces challenges that funds need to meet in the guise of appropriate organizational, conflicts of interests and conduct of interest rules. The proportionality principle applied to some of the Organization Directive provisions gives the management company some discretion on how to apply the rules to suit their organization. However, there are minimum requirements that must be applied.

– *Internal organization of management company/investment manager*: if the new entrant is an existing MiFID firm, it will be familiar with a number of UCITS IV requirements. However, where the entrant is not familiar with MiFID or wishes to delegate some if its activities to a non-MiFID firm, the new organizational and rules of conduct could prove challenging and may lead to changes in how the management company carries out its existing distribution.

Therefore internal organization procedures of management company or the investment manager where the management company chooses to delegate the investment management will need to be reviewed in light of the extensive UCITS IV rules. A robust organizational, conduct of business and risk management process will need to be implemented and put in place.

Clear decision-making procedures and clear assignment of responsibilities need to be put in place along with procedures on record keeping and business continuity. Conflicts of interests and the exercise of voting rights need to be in place together with procedures for personal transactions. A permanent internal audit function, compliance function and risk-management function may need to be established depending on the fund type (SMIC may be excluded, depending on the jurisdiction).

Robust breach reporting, risk management and due diligence in the selection and on-going monitoring of assets need to be implemented. Pricing models that are accurate and fair will need to be implemented. Best execution, handling of orders and inducements will also need to be implemented.

7.5. Conclusion

UCITS IV has provided detailed MiFID-like organizational and code of conduct rules. The management companies should be able to delegate some of their activities to third parties provided that sufficient due diligence is carried out to ensure that the third party is capable and qualified to carry out the delegated activity. These rules of delegation are subject to the rules of the Member State of the management company and management companies can continue to delegate their activities to other service providers. This ensures an effective UCITS operating model that draws on the European experience of MiFID firms.

It is vital that promoters that are new to Europe consider the most efficient model for them, particularly in terms of the delegation of roles and responsibilities. All parties need to be very clear on what is expected of them, both from a regulatory perspective and also depending on how that manifests itself on a day-to-day operational basis.

Chapter 8

UCITS Taxation

8.1. Introduction

Luxembourg UCIs (Undertakings for Collective Investment) enjoy a favorable *ad hoc* tax regime compared to other resident entities.

The UCIs' regime aims to achieve relative neutrality between those investing directly in the market and those going through a collective investment scheme. This is explained by the original intent that collective investment schemes should serve to democratize access to capital markets to a wider range of investors by allowing them to get an exposure to a diversified portfolio of assets, thanks to the mutualization of their investment capabilities.

Over the past few years, Luxembourg has created new types of collective investment schemes offering alternative tax treatment, but all of them allow tax neutrality (SV, Sicar, Sepcav/Assep). In this chapter, we will concentrate on typical UCIs.

However, the effective tax treatment of UCIs cannot be properly apprehended without taking consideration of external taxation factors such as:

– the taxation of income derived from the UCIs' investments; and

– the taxation occurring at the investor level.

Chapter written by André PESCH, Romain JACQUES and Ludovic DEFLANDRE.

The following chapter will address the major tax issues surrounding the Luxembourg UCIs. In order to explain these tax issues, we take an approach whereby we look at several "levels" of a fund (investments, the fund itself, investors in the fund). Furthermore, we will analyze the tax issues relating to the different actor-players surrounding UCIs (such as advisory and management companies).

Before tackling taxation at the different levels of a fund, a major difference has to be outlined between Luxembourg UCIs depending on their corporate/contractual form. Luxembourg UCIs can have different forms from a corporate/contractual law perspective. The main distinction in this respect has to be made between the contractual form and the corporate form.

8.1.1. *The contractual form: the Fonds Commun de Placement*

FCP stands for the French expression *Fonds Commun de Placement*, which means a common investment fund. Like a unit trust in the UK, a FCP is set up in the form of a contract between the fund manager and the investors, in a similar way to a partnership, and is not a separate legal entity in its own right. Instead, the legal entity is the management company setting up the fund. Investors hold units in a FCP.

8.1.2. *The corporate form: investment company with variable or fixed share capital*

SICAV stands for *Société d'Investissement à Capital Variable*, or open-ended investment company, whose ownership is in the form of shares. With SICAVs, the fund itself is a stock corporation and is thus a legal entity. The company's capital depends on the amounts paid in by investors. As with a FCP, shares in a SICAV are bought and sold on the basis of the value of the fund's assets, or net asset value. In accordance with applicable laws and regulations, a SICAV can either appoint a separate management company or can be self-managed. A SICAF is almost identical to a SICAV with one major difference being that the share capital is fixed.

From a Luxembourg tax perspective, there are no relevant differences between a SICAV and a SICAF (*Société d'Investissement á Capital Fixe*). Also, no major differences should exist from an international tax perspective. For this reason, we will use the term SICAV in this chapter to cover both the SICAV and SICAF.

Table 8.1 details the main differences between FCPs and SICAVs from a Luxembourg tax perspective.

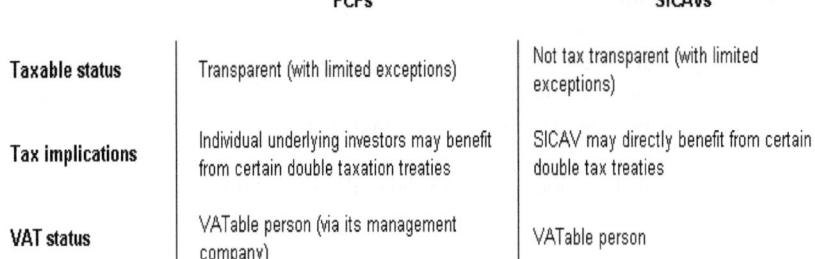

	FCPs	SICAVs
Taxable status	Transparent (with limited exceptions)	Not tax transparent (with limited exceptions)
Tax implications	Individual underlying investors may benefit from certain double taxation treaties	SICAV may directly benefit from certain double tax treaties
VAT status	VATable person (via its management company)	VATable person

Table 8.1. *The differences in taxation between FCPs and SICAVs*

The fact that a FCP is a tax-transparent entity while the SICAV/SICAF benefits from a tax personality (and is opaque) has many impacts that will be explained in the following pages.

From a VAT point-of-view, most of the financial services benefit from a VAT exemption. The complexity and evolution of financial markets have, however, resulted in different interpretations of the rules initially laid out in the VAT legislation across different Member States.

The new UCITS IV directive, which enables investment funds to be managed by a management company established in another EU Member State, brings additional queries from a VAT perspective. These queries may potentially lead to distortions of competition between taxable entities performing the same activity. In addition, as service flow becomes increasingly international, involving cross-border transactions, it becomes increasingly easy to incur additional VAT cost, which is often irrecoverable for the fund management actors.

The impacts of the new UCITS IV Directive will also be analyzed from an international tax law perspective, since it should entail fund structures and restructurings that prior to its entry into force were not achievable but induced important tax issues.

8.2. Taxation of the fund

8.2.1. *Corporate income and net worth tax*

Resident Luxembourg corporate entities are, in principle, subject to corporate and municipal business and net worth tax in Luxembourg. However, SICAVs are exempt by law from income and corporate tax. FCPs are equally exempt from corporate tax.

8.2.2. *Registration duty*

A fixed registration duty of €75 must be paid by a SICAV at incorporation, in the case of modification of the articles of incorporation and in the case of transfer of the effective place of management or registered office to Luxembourg.

This registration duty does not vary depending on the number of compartments of the SICAV.

FCPs are not subject to this registration duty.

8.2.3. *Annual subscription tax*

8.2.3.1. *General tax rate*

An annual subscription tax of 0.05% is due by the UCIs. In practice, this tax is calculated quarterly based on the UCIs net asset value (or each sub-fund net asset value) at the end of each quarter. The mentioned tax corresponds to ¼ of 0.05% of the UCIs net asset value at the end of each quarter, which is payable quarterly.

A practical example:

	Net asset value	Subscription tax (1/4 of 0,05%)
First quarter	100	0,0125
Second quarter	200	0,025
Third quarter	250	0,03125
Fourth quarter	300	0,0375
Total tax due		*0,10625*

8.2.3.2. *Reduced tax rate of 0.01%*

UCIs governed by the SIF (specialized investment fund) Law[1] and institutional sub-funds or other UCI types and classes of shares reserved to institutional investors in such UCIs might benefit from a reduced subscription tax of 0.01% applicable on their total net assets.

---

1 The law of February 13, 2007 relating to SIFs.

Other UCIs benefit from a reduced tax rate of 0.01% in the following cases:

– undertakings or sub-funds whose sole object is the collective investment in money market instruments[2] or the placing of deposits with credit institutions; and

– undertakings or sub-funds whose sole object is the collective investment in deposits with credit institutions.

8.2.3.3. *Exemption*

Subscription tax exemption is applicable in relation to:

– the value of the assets represented by units held in other Luxembourg UCIs, to the extent that such UCIs have already been subject to effective subscription tax;

– SIFs as well as individual compartments of SIFs:

- the exclusive object of which is the collective investment in money market instruments and the placing of deposits with credit institutions,

- the weighted residual portfolio maturity that does not exceed 90 days, and

- that have obtained the highest possible rating from a recognized rating agency.

– SIFs whose securities are reserved for:

- institutions for occupational retirement provision, or similar investment vehicles, set up on one or more employers' initiative for the benefit of their employees, and

- the companies of one or more employers investing the funds they own in order to provide their employees with retirement benefits;

– SIFs which:

- benefit from the microfinance label[3] of the Luxembourg Fund Labelling Agency,

---

2 According to Article 1 of the Grand-Ducal Regulation of April 14, 2003, such money market instruments are deemed to include any notes and instruments representing claims, whether or not they may be characterized as securities, including bonds, certificates of deposit, treasury bills and any other similar instruments provided that at the time of their acquisition their residual maturity does not exceed 12 months, taking into account any related hedging financial instruments. In addition, floating rate notes with a residual maturity exceeding 12 months are permitted, provided the interest rate is adjusted to market conditions at least annually. In certain cases, an UCI whose portfolio has an average remaining maturity not exceeding 12 months may also qualify for the reduced rate.

- SIFs whose investment policy rules that 50% of the assets are invested in one or more microfinance institutions, as defined by the Grand Ducal Decree of July 14, 2010; and

– exchange traded funds.

Foreign UCIs are not subject to the subscription tax, even in the case where they are managed by a Luxembourg management company or have their effective place of management in Luxembourg[4].

8.2.4. *Tax on dissolution*

The different restructurings involving the dissolution of UCIs, such as mergers and demergers, can generally be achieved in a tax-neutral way from a Luxembourg tax perspective.

However, such restructuring may trigger tax issues at the level of the assets as well as at the level of the investors. Indeed, income derived from foreign assets invested by Luxembourg UCIs may be taxable in the source country (capital gains taxes, stamp taxes, etc.).

In addition, such restructurings might result in a withholding tax liability if they fall within the scope of the EU Savings Directive.

Similarly, the transformation of a SICAV into a common fund and, inversely, the transformation of a common fund into a SICAV can be done in a tax-neutral way from a Luxembourg tax perspective. Impacts of the EU Savings Directive should, however, be carefully taken into account.

8.2.5. *Indirect taxation*

8.2.5.1. *Position of the Luxembourg VAT administration before the BBL case*

In the BBL (Banque Bruxelles Lambert) case, the European Court of Justice (hereafter the "ECJ") had to give its opinion on the question as to whether a Luxembourg SICAV had to be regarded as a taxable entity for VAT purposes. The ECJ looked at the activities carried out by such a vehicle, which involved collective

---

3 Microfinance includes all financial operations other than consumer loans, the objective of which is to support poor populations excluded from the traditional financial system by financing small revenue-generating activities, and whose value does not exceed €5,000.
4 Assets and profits of the Luxembourg management company are, however fully, subject to tax in Luxembourg (see the section 8.5.1 the taxation of the management company).

investment in transferable securities of capital raised from the public. With the capital provided by investors when they subscribe for shares, a SICAV assembles and manages portfolios consisting of transferable securities on behalf of the subscribers and for a fee. The ECJ was of the opinion that such activities go beyond the mere acquisition and sale of securities and seeks to produce income on a continuing basis. Based on these elements, the ECJ concluded that the activities performed by investment funds qualified as economic activities for VAT purposes, conferring on investment funds the status of a taxable entity.

Before the decision of the ECJ in the BBL case, the Luxembourg VAT administration had always considered that SICAVs did not perform economic activities in the sense of European and Luxembourg VAT legislation. This was because their activities consisted of collective investment in transferable securities. In consequence, similarly to passive holding companies, SICAV/F/Rs were not considered taxable entities for VAT purposes.

This implied that SICAVs were generally exempt from administrative obligations linked to VAT in Luxembourg (i.e. VAT registration, VAT returns, etc.), but also that all the VAT paid within the framework of their activity represented a definitive burden.

The fact that investment funds were not considered taxable entities for VAT purposes also had an impact on the localization of the services received from suppliers established outside Luxembourg. Indeed, since the position of the Luxembourg VAT administration was that the investment funds did not qualify as taxable entities, services rendered by foreign suppliers (i.e. not established in Luxembourg) were deemed to be located where the suppliers were established from a Luxembourg VAT point of view. This situation resulted in a higher VAT burden for investment funds receiving services from a supplier established in an EU country other than Luxembourg (where no exemption applies) since these services were subject to the VAT applicable in the country of the supplier. This was at a rate higher than the Luxembourg standard rate (i.e. 15%), which is the lowest standard VAT rate applicable within the EU Member States. This situation was favorable, however, for investment funds when receiving services from suppliers established outside the EU, for instance a US supplier, since no VAT was incurred by investment funds in that case.

8.2.5.2. Circular 723 – change in the Luxembourg VAT administration's position

While Luxembourg investment funds were not considered taxable entities, and hence were treated as final consumers from a VAT point of view, since October 21, 2004 the decision of the ECJ in the BBL case has recognized them as taxable. This status had to be taken into account by the Luxembourg VAT administration.

Following the ECJ decisions in the BBL and Abbey National cases, the Luxembourg VAT administration issued Circular 723 (the "Circular") on December 29, 2006 expressing its interpretation of the ECJ decisions regarding the taxable status of investment funds and the scope of the VAT exemption on the management services relating to investment funds.

The Circular allotted a taxable status to investment vehicles whose management is VAT-exempt by virtue of article 44, 1, d) of the Luxembourg VAT law.

Article 44, 1, d) of the Luxembourg VAT law exempts the management of UCIs – including SICAR and specialized investment funds, as well as pension funds – from VAT subject to the supervision of the CSSF[5] or to the *Commissariat aux Assurances* and the management of securitization vehicles located in Luxembourg.

Based on the above, investment funds qualify as taxable entities for Luxembourg VAT purposes.

In the specific case of common funds (FCPs), the taxable status is conferred on the management company, as it is deemed to perform the activity of constituting and managing the portfolio of securities of the funds; the fund having no legal personality itself. Furthermore, the individual compartments within the investment fund will not be considered individually for VAT.

8.2.5.3. *Impact of the Circular on Luxembourg investment funds*

A positive outcome of the ECJ decision is that investment funds are now in a position to avoid foreign VAT on intangible services received, but benefit from the lower Luxembourg VAT rate or from the Luxembourg exemption of UCI management services which is, generally, still wider in scope than in other EU Member States.

According to the place of supply rules, services rendered between two taxable entities are deemed to be located at the place where the taxable recipient is established. Hence, services rendered to Luxembourg investment funds, now being qualified as taxable entities, are located in Luxembourg and no longer in the country of establishment of the supplier. Therefore, Luxembourg investment funds no longer have to pay the VAT applicable in the supplier's country but will benefit from the Luxembourg standard VAT rate, when an exemption is not applicable.

The recognition of the taxable status of investment funds might, however, result in additional VAT cost for Luxembourg investment funds receiving services from suppliers established outside the EU. While such services were in principle not

---

5 *Commission de Surveillance du Secteur Financier.*

subject to VAT in the past situation, Luxembourg investment funds might now incur Luxembourg VAT when a VAT exemption is not applicable.

8.2.5.4. *VAT administrative obligations for Luxembourg investment funds*

Currently the Luxembourg VAT administration considers that activities carried out by investment funds are VAT exempt. This does not entitle investment funds to deduct the VAT they incur on the purchase of goods and services in relation to these activities. The situation is different in other EU Member States, such as the UK or Ireland, which are more favorable for investment funds in respect of their input VAT deduction right.

On this basis, since SICAVs are considered to carry out activities that are fully exempt without a right to input VAT deduction, they are relieved from the obligation to register for Luxembourg VAT purposes, unless they would be liable for VAT:

– on services received from abroad; or

– on intra-EU acquisitions of goods for an annual amount higher than €10,000 (exclusive of VAT).

Investment funds required to register for VAT are required to fill out a simplified annual VAT return in which they will report the services they have received from abroad and for which they are liable to pay the Luxembourg VAT based on the reverse charge mechanism.

The legal deadline for the filing of the annual simplified VAT return is March 1 of the following year.

Up to now, an automatic filing extension of eight months has been granted by the Luxembourg VAT administration for the filing of an annual VAT return. The annual simplified VAT return due for 2012 should therefore be filed with the Luxembourg VAT administration by November 1, 2013 at the very latest.

Although an extension may be granted for the filing of the VAT return, the same is not true for the payment of the VAT due, which should be paid by the expiration of the legal filing deadline at the latest.

Therefore, the VAT authorities could well request the payment of a provisional installment. This provisional installment will of course offset the amount of VAT due based on the annual VAT return and the excess will be reimbursed to the fund if the amount of the installment exceeds the VAT due based on the VAT return.

With regard to the FCP, as mentioned above, the FCP does not have any legal personality itself. Therefore, invoices issued to the FCP should be received by the management company and reported in the VAT return due from the FCP's management company.

8.2.5.5. *VAT exemption: non-exhaustive lists of services covered*

Article 44, 1, d), of the Luxembourg VAT Law exempts the management of UCIs from VAT, including SICAR and specialized investment funds, as well as pension funds that are subject to the supervision of the CSSF or to the *Commissariat aux Assurances* as well as the management of securitization vehicles located in Luxembourg.

The Circular issued by the Luxembourg VAT administration provides further clarification on the scope of the VAT exemption applicable to management services provided to investment funds.

The Circular confirms that portfolio management and administration services fall within the scope of the VAT exemption provided for by Article 44, 1, d) of the Luxembourg VAT Law.

The Circular also confirms that portfolio management and administration services remain exempt from VAT, even when they are supplied by a third party, indirectly to the funds. This is providing that they form a distinct whole, and are specific to and essential for the management of the funds.

The VAT authorities have provided further clarification with regard to services rendered by a third party in their Circular 723bis issued on April 30, 2010. The VAT authorities added that the supply of one single isolated service delegated to a third party is not covered by the VAT exemption of Article 44, 1, d) of the Luxembourg VAT law. There have been several discussions about Circular 723bis, which has been released in the absence of any new legal or jurisprudential evolution. It is generally accepted that this circular does not really change the situation and that it should not negatively impact VAT exemption as long as the services are specific to and essential for the management of the funds.

Depositary services, whose aim is to ensure that the management complies with the law, fall within the framework of the control and supervision functions of the funds, rather than qualifying as management services. Hence, although certain services rendered by depositary banks can remain VAT exempt, since April 1, 2007, these control and supervision functions have been subject to VAT at the rate of 12%.

The notion of management remains undefined in the Luxembourg legislation. However, the following non-exhaustive list of services also falls within the scope of the VAT exemption applicable to fund management services, as confirmed by the Luxembourg VAT administration in the Circular[6]:

– investment management;

– administration:

- legal and fund management accounting services,

- customer inquiries,

- valuation of portfolio and pricing of the shares or units, including tax returns,

- regulatory compliance monitoring,

- maintenance of shareholder or unit holder register,

- distribution of income,

- share of unit issues and redemptions,

- contract settlements, including certificate dispatch, and

- record keeping.

8.3. Taxation of investments made by UCIs

Income derived from foreign assets invested by Luxembourg UCIs may be taxable in the source country. The source country may levy withholding taxes, capital gain taxes, stamp taxes, etc.

The taxable basis and the rate of the tax will depend on the tax legislation of each state the UCI invests in.

Luxembourg has signed many treaties aiming to avoid double taxation, i.e. in the source country and in Luxembourg.

The avoidance of double taxation by application of a DTT (double tax treaty) may operate either through an exemption at the level of the investors provided certain requirements are met or through a reduction (or exemption) of WHT (withholding tax).

Although UCIs are not subject to corporate income tax in Luxembourg (hence no legal double taxation occurs, strictly speaking), Luxembourg has negotiated that such treaties apply within a series of countries in relation to income paid to SICAVs.

---

6 The Luxembourg VAT administration, as well as the ECJ in the case of Abbey National, referred to Annex II of the UCITS Directive, which provides a non-exhaustive list of services falling within the VAT exemption.

With FCPs, due to their lack of legal personality they are precluded from the benefits of treaties but in turn might enjoy transparency under circumstances that will enable their investors to make use of the double tax treaties entered into between the country of residence and the country of investment of the fund.

Due to the fact that Luxembourg UCIs are not subject to income tax, when foreign (withholding) tax has been levied on the income generated by the UCI, these taxes are neither creditable nor refundable in Luxembourg.

SICAVs and SICAFs should, according to the official Internet site of the Luxembourg tax authorities, be able to benefit from the double tax treaties[7] listed in Table 8.2.

Armenia	Moldova	Trinidad and Tobago
Austria	Monaco	Tunisia
Azerbaïjan	Mongolia	Turkey
Bahrain	Morocco	United Arab Emirates
China	Poland	Uzbekistan
Denmark	Portugal	Vietnam
Finland	Qatar	
Georgian Republic	Romania	
Germany	San Marino	
Hong Kong	Singapore	
Indonesia	Slovakia	
Ireland	Slovenia	
Israel	South Korea *	
Malaysia	Spain	
Malta	Thailand	
* Under discussion		

Table 8.2. *Countries in which SICAVs and SICAVs should be able to benefit from tax treaties*

The full benefit of tax transparency for FCPs is subject to many conditions and, in particular, will depend on the recognition of the transparency by both the country of the investment and the country in which the investor is based. It also involves

---

7 With the double tax treaty between Luxembourg and South Korea, discussions as to the applicability of the treaty have been "resurrected" and no final decision has been taken at the time when this chapter was written. The application of the Luxembourg–Chinese double tax treaty to Luxembourg SICAVs/SICAFs also seems to be in the process of being re-analyzed by the Chinese authorities.

complex implementation procedures in the case of investors from different jurisdictions.

Recently, many transnational pension pooling projects have been envisaged or implemented in order to achieve very important economies of scale. It should be noted that Luxembourg FCPs can be a very attractive solution for pension pooling projects whereby a Luxembourg FCP pools the assets that are part of one or more pension programs in a group if the relevant DTT should remain applicable. In other words, given the transparency of the FCP, the double tax treaties that were applicable prior to the pooling should remain applicable notwithstanding the fact that a FCP has been interposed.

If a Luxembourg UCI invests in shares in a Luxembourg-based fully taxable Luxembourg corporation, a withholding tax at a rate of 15% should apply to dividend payments made by the corporation to a Luxembourg UCI. In case the UCI is a FCP, relevant double tax treaties or the European Parent-Subsidiary Directive may allow a reduction or avoidance of this withholding tax. This is in principle not possible in the case that the recipient is a SICAV or SICAF.

However, it should be noted that Luxembourg WHT is – for Luxembourg resident taxpayers – an advance payment of the income or corporate tax due. Since SICAV are arguably subject to corporate tax but exempt, one may claim that since WHT is an advance payment. One could argue that it has to be reimbursed.

Luxembourg does not levy WHT on capital gains, interest payments (except on profit participating bonds and when applying the savings directive) and liquidation bonuses.

On an Organisation for Economic Co-operation and Development level, initiatives have been taken and possible solutions discussed that aim for UCIs or their investors to benefit from the relevant double tax treaties between the country of the UCI or the investor and the source country, with the aim of achieving tax neutrality.

8.4. Taxation at the level of the UCI investor

8.4.1. *Withholding tax*

Dividends paid by/capital gains derived from the sale of shares/units in a Luxembourg investment fund are not subject to any Luxembourg withholding tax. Such distributions might, however, be subject to withholding tax in the case of application of the EU Savings Directive.

8.4.2. *Luxembourg individual investor*

The income derived from investments in UCIs by Luxembourg resident individuals is, in principle, taxable. However, they are not subject to tax on capital gains on the disposal of UCI shares or units, except in the case of speculative gains (i.e. sale of the shares or units of the UCI within six months of their acquisition) or a gain upon disposal of an important participation. A participation is important if the investor (which includes his partner and minor children) holds more than 10% of the capital in a SICAV (the 10% is computed by taking into consideration the capital of the whole fund and not the capital of the possible sub-fund (compartment). A gain realized by an individual investor on an important participation is taxable whether the participation has been held for more or less than six months.

8.4.3. *Foreign investors*

Since January 1, 2011, with the adoption of the 2010 Law, non-resident investors (individuals and corporations) in a Luxembourg UCI are not subject to tax in Luxembourg on capital gains realized upon the disposal of their shares/units in a Luxembourg UCI. This is irrespective of the whether or not they held a substantial shareholding of more than 10% in the UCI.

8.4.4. *EU Savings Directive*

8.4.4.1. *Main characteristics of the Directive/Law*

The main aim of the Directive is to ensure that savings income in the form of interest payments generated in an EU Member state in favour of individuals being resident of another EU Member state are effectively taxed in accordance with the fiscal laws of their state of residence.

As it would have been easy for individuals to circumvent the Directive by investing in UCIs that would have distributed such income (instead of investing directly in debt claims, etc), the scope of the Directive covers also (certain) UCIs.

For a transitional period, however, Austria and Luxembourg have obtained that a withholding tax can apply (instead of an exchange of information). Therefore, if a Luxembourg-based paying agent makes an interest payment to an investor who does not want to have relevant information exchanged with his/her country of residence. The withholding tax of 35% will apply during a transitional period.

The transitional period will end once agreements on the exchange of information relating to such payments are concluded with certain third countries[8].

8.4.4.2. *Main concepts*

"Interest" payments falling within the scope of the EU Savings Directive have received a wide interpretation, including notably:

– Income distributed by, or income realized upon the redemption, sale or refund of shares or units of UCITS recognized in accordance with the UCITS Directive may potentially qualify as interest in the meaning of the Law.

– For Luxembourg UCIs, a distinction has to be made according to the type of income derived from the UCIs. The following rules apply:

  - for distributions, Luxembourg has opted for the "15% threshold rule", i.e. distributions of UCITS that directly or indirectly hold more than 15% of their assets in the form of in-scope debt claims are within the scope of the EU Savings Directive; and

  - for redemptions, the sale or refund of shares of Luxembourg UCIs directly or indirectly investing more than 25% as of January 1, 2011 (previously the threshold was 40%) of their assets in in-scope debt claims are in scope.

The term "indirectly" used above is here to avoid structurings with the main purpose of avoiding the Directive to be applied. However, only the part of the dividends or capital gains that is related to the underlying interest income should be subject to the withholding tax. When this information is not available, all of the dividend distribution or capital gain is considered to be derived from interest income. If the information is missing for capital gains, all of the gain is considered to be derived from the underlying interest income, where the amount of the gain cannot be determined and all of the sales proceeds are considered to be derived from interest income.

---

8 Also with effect from July 1, 2005, a number of non-EU countries (Switzerland, Andorra, Liechtenstein, Monaco and San Marino) and certain dependent or associated territories (the Cayman Islands, Jersey, Guernsey, the Isle of Man, the British Virgin Islands, the Turks and Caicos Islands, Gibraltar, Anguilla, Montserrat, Aruba and the Netherlands Antilles [hereafter "the Territories"]) have agreed to adopt similar measures. These involve either the provision of information or transitional withholding in relation to payments made by a paying agent (within the meaning of the EU Savings Directive) established within such countries or Territories to, or collected by such a paying agent for, an individual resident or a "residual entity" established in an EU Member State. In addition, Luxembourg has entered into the reciprocal provision of information or transitional withholding arrangements with these Territories in relation to payments made by a paying agent established in Luxembourg to, or collected by such a paying agent for, an individual resident or a "residual entity" established in one of these Territories.

A "residual entity" is defined as an entity established in a Member State that does not have a legal personality, is not subject to general rules of business taxation, is not an UCITS, and has not opted to be treated as an UCITS for the purpose of the law.

According to Luxembourg law, all entities established in Luxembourg that would otherwise have qualified as residual entities must be considered as having opted to be treated as an UCITS. Therefore, no Luxembourg common funds (e.g. FCPs) and income distributed by, or income realized upon the redemption, sale or refund of shares or units of such common funds which are always potentially in scope are residual entities according to the Luxembourg law implementing the directive.

8.4.4.3. *Paying agent*

The paying agent is the economic operator who pays interest to or secures the payment of interest for the immediate benefit of the beneficial owner.

To be considered a Luxembourg resident paying agent, the following apply:

– the paying agent is an individual or entity resident in Luxembourg;

– the agent either pays the interest directly or ensures that it is paid for the benefit of an individual who is the beneficial owner of the interest; and

The paying agent is personally responsible for levying this withholding tax. Any failure to do so will leave the paying agent to settle the withholding tax and therefore bear the cost directly together with a penalty of 0.5% on the amount of the tax.

Withholding tax paid in Luxembourg pursuant to the law must give rise to a tax credit; this is taken into consideration in the country of residence of the beneficial owner. If the withholding tax deducted exceeds the total amount of income tax due in the country of residence, the excess must be reimbursed by the beneficial owner's country of residence.

A Luxembourg paying agent may have to withhold tax on income distributed by an UCITS or UCI registered in countries other than Luxembourg, in cases where such income falls within the scope of the law.

8.4.5. *Directors' fees*

Directors' fees are subject to a withholding tax at a rate of 20% of the gross amount (25% if the tax is withheld from the net amount) that is levied by the company paying the fees.

Such a withholding tax may satisfy in full the tax liability on fees received by a non-resident director earning less than €100,000 per tax year, assuming the latter has no other income source from Luxembourg.

The withholding tax must be paid within eight days of the distribution.

8.5. Management and advisory companies

8.5.1. *Corporate taxation*

8.5.1.1. *Registration duty*

Luxembourg management and advisory companies are subject to a fixed registration duty of €75 in the following cases:

– at incorporation;

– if the articles of incorporation are modified; and

– if the effective place of management or registered office to Luxembourg is transferred.

The registration duty due by the management company of a single FCP is in principle payable by the management company but may be charged to the FCP.

8.5.1.2. *Annual taxation*

Management companies are fully taxable entities subject to Luxembourg CIT (corporate income tax) and MBT (municipal business tax) at the overall tax rate of 28.8% from January 1, 2011 (in Luxembourg city).

Management companies are also subject to NWT (net wealth tax) levied annually at a rate of 0.5% and calculated on the basis of the unitary value of the company as of January 1 of each year.

As of January 1, 2011, an annual minimum taxation of €1,500 (€1,575 including a 5% unemployment surcharge) may apply to management and advisory companies under certain circumstances.

The Luxembourg tax authorities have clarified that all Luxembourg management companies, including management companies managing a single FCP, are considered to be fully taxable entities.

8.5.1.3. *Dividends and interest*

A withholding tax of 15% is in principle levied on dividends paid by management and advisory companies. This rate might, however, be reduced on the basis of the DTT or on the basis of the EU Parent–Subsidiary Directive.

Management or advisory companies are allowed to pay interim dividends under the normal authorization procedures (which include a specific authorization in the company's by-laws and the preparation of interim financial accounts) and are also required to create a legal reserve (5% of net profit until the accumulated reserve equals 10% of subscribed capital). The interim dividend authorization procedures include specific authorization in the articles of association and the preparation of interim financial statements, under the control of the auditor.

No Luxembourg withholding tax is due on interest payments except where EU Savings Directive is applied.

8.5.1.4. *Tax on dissolution*

Liquidation proceeds distributed by Luxembourg management and advisory companies to their shareholders are not subject to withholding tax in Luxembourg.

Nevertheless, unrealized capital gains resulting from the liquidation profit are subject to CIT and MBT, as all the assets of the Luxembourg management and advisory company are deemed to be realized upon their liquidation.

8.5.2. *Indirect taxation*

8.5.2.1. *Management company*

The management of investment funds qualifies as an economic activity for VAT purposes, conferring the status of a taxable entity on the management company.

Management services provided to investment funds, which are supervised by the CSSF, benefit from the VAT exemption according to article 44, 1, d) of the Luxembourg VAT Law.

This VAT-exempt activity does not open a deduction right to management companies. Hence, like investment funds, management companies are in principle relieved from the obligation to register for Luxembourg VAT purposes unless they would be liable for VAT:

– on services received from abroad; or

– on intra-EU acquisitions of goods for an annual amount greater than €10,000 (exclusive of VAT).

Up until recently, the interpretation made by the Luxembourg VAT authorities was that the management of funds not subject to the supervision of the CSSF (for instance, non-Luxembourg established funds not distributed in Luxembourg) could not benefit from the VAT exemption granted by article 44, 1, d) of the Luxembourg VAT Law. Being considered taxable, the management of funds not supervised by the CSSF was therefore treated as an activity giving a VAT deduction right to the management companies and to the different providers of the non-supervised funds.

However, it appears that the Luxembourg VAT authorities changed their interpretation in this respect in the middle of 2010, which has been confirmed by a communication from the ALFI (Association for the Luxembourg Fund Industry) in February 2011. According to this new position, the Luxembourg VAT authorities consider that the management of funds not subject to the supervision of the CSSF but subject to prudential control in their home country, similar to the control exercised by the CSSF, would constitute an exempt activity. The result of this new interpretation is that the input VAT incurred in relation to this activity is no longer deductible, as being linked to an exempt activity not giving a VAT deduction right.

Compared to the past position of the Luxembourg VAT authorities, this new interpretation negatively impacts the VAT deduction right of banks, management companies and other financial sector professionals when rendering services to funds not supervised by the CSSF.

We could raise the objection that this new position goes against the text of article 44, 1, d) of the Luxembourg VAT Law, which is pretty clear and does not give rise to interpretation in the sense that the VAT exemption is only granted to investment funds subject to supervision by the CSSF. This issue is actually the object of a pending case with the Luxembourg Tribunal, but the decision has not yet been released at the time of writing this chapter. In the meantime, the VAT authorities have confirmed their intention to apply this interpretation.

Discussions will take place shortly between the professionals of the financial sectors to evaluate the consequences and the actions to be taken further to this decision.

8.5.2.2. *Advisory company*

8.5.2.2.1. Taxable status and related VAT administrative obligations

The advisory services of investment funds qualify as an economic activity for VAT purposes, giving the advisory company the status of a taxable entity.

The VAT situation of advisory companies is pretty similar to that of management companies.

Indeed, investment advisory services benefit from the VAT exemption granted by article 44, 1, d) of the Luxembourg VAT Law.

Therefore, advisory companies are performing an exempt activity that does not entitle them to deduct the input VAT incurred on the purchase of goods and services in relation to that activity.

Like investment funds and management companies, the advisory companies of investment funds are in principle relieved from the obligation to register for Luxembourg VAT purposes, unless they would be liable for VAT:

– on services received from abroad; or

– on intra-EU acquisitions of goods for an annual amount greater than €10,000 (exclusive of VAT).

8.5.2.2.2. VAT treatment of investment advisory services: case referred to the ECJ

On June 3, 2011 an important case was referred to the ECJ by a German court concerning the VAT treatment of investment advisory services.

In the case referred to the ECJ, the referring court asked the ECJ whether investment advisory services rendered to the fund manager are exempt from VAT.

The question raised by the German court has been defined as follows:

"For the purpose of interpreting the term 'management of special investment funds', is the service provided by the third- party managers of a special investment fund sufficiently specific and hence exempt from taxation only if:

(a) The manager performs a management function and not only an advisory function.

(b) The service differs in nature from other services by reason of a characteristic feature that qualifies for tax exemption under this provision.

(c) The manager operates on the basis of a delegation of functions under Article 5g of Directive 85/611/EEC1, as amended."

Currently investment advisory services benefit from the VAT exemption applicable to fund management services as per article 44, 1, d) of the Luxembourg VAT Law. Even though the term "management" is not defined in the Luxembourg VAT Law, it is accepted that services provided by an external manager in the form of an advisory position within the scope of its management of investment funds are in principle covered by the VAT exemption provided for in article 44, 1, d). This would be the case even if the service is limited to the advisory function. This position has so far been approved by the Luxembourg VAT administration. However, this VAT treatment is not harmonized within EU countries where such services might not be VAT exempt when they are limited to the advisory function.

Considering the impact that a taxation of such services would have in investment funds, the position of the ECJ will be of the highest importance to the Luxembourg fund industry.

8.6. Impact of UCITS IV

8.6.1. *General considerations*

UCITS IV encourages the development of cross-border set-up and operations.

In particular, the UCITS Directive now authorizes master-feeder structures. It also provides for a minimum harmonized legal framework for cross-border fund mergers and grants for a management company. This allows a Luxembourg fund to be managed by a management company that is a resident of another Member State, or conversely, it enables a Luxembourg management company to manage a UCI located in another Member State.

Although aimed at enhancing flexibility and fair competition between EU Member states, making use of these possibilities will raise additional tax issues which are not directly solved by EU regulations.

Hereafter, we have focused on a series of situations illustrating these difficulties.

8.6.1.1. *Cross-border fund mergers*

The merger of a Luxembourg UCI into a foreign UCI does not trigger relevant tax consequences at the level of the Luxembourg fund.

However, at the level of the investor, fund mergers are often treated by local tax authorities as a disposal of shares, which may trigger capital gains taxes, withholding taxes, the application of the EU Savings Directive and other issues.

Also, at the time of the merger, the transfer of assets to the absorbing fund may lead to transfer taxes (stamp duties) in the country out of which assets are transferred as well as in the country of investment.

8.6.1.2. *Master-feeder*

Typically, in the master-feeder UCI structure, a master fund may be created in one domicile with investors from other Member States investing in this fund via a locally domiciled feeder fund.

Changing from a single-tier structure into a master-feeder structure does, from a tax perspective, trigger issues very similar to those involved in a merger, i.e. potential capital gains and Savings Directive issues at the level of the investor and transfer taxes at the level of the assets.

The implementation of a master-feeder structure should not entail major tax issues at the level of the Luxembourg UCI itself, whether the UCI is a master (receiving the assets) or a feeder (transferring the assets).

8.6.1.3. *Management company passport*

Under some circumstances, the use of a management company resident of another Member State might trigger issues in relation to establishing the tax residence of the Fund.

In particular, a UCI set-up in the form of a FCP might be considered by the state of residence of the management company as being resident in the country of such management company from a tax perspective. It may also happen that the tax authorities of the investors take a similar view.

Or, even if the fund is not considered to be resident of the country where the management company is located, the country of the management company or its investor may still be considered as having a permanent establishment in the country where the management company is located. As far as Luxembourg management companies are concerned, the Luxembourg legislation explicitly states that such is not the case; in other words the fact that a foreign fund is managed by a

Luxembourg management company will not mean that the fund will have a permanent establishment (tax presence) in Luxembourg.

Depending on circumstances, these situations can lead to ineligibility treaties benefits or may involve the risk that the fund is considered a taxable resident in both countries (i.e. in the country of its management company and in the country of the UCI).

Indicators of the tax effectiveness of using a pan-European management company include the corporate tax rate, the method of computation of the taxable basis of the management company, transfer pricing rules, VAT and, last but not least, the taxation of the fund itself. Setting up a pan-European management company in the right country, with well analyzed service and fee flows, can offer very attractive opportunities from a tax perspective.

8.6.2. *Additional queries and open points from a VAT point of view*

Considering the lack of harmonization within the EU Member States as well as their divergence in the interpretation of VAT exemption, particular attention should be paid to VAT, in order to avoid the restructuring envisaged to lead to significant irrecoverable VAT costs for the actors.

The UCITS directive raises additional uncertainties and several issues will have to be considered:

– the localization of the services,

– the application of input VAT deduction right,

– the localization of the funds in a favorable country, etc.

The above issues are of particular interest with regards to FCP.

As already mentioned, the actual position of the Luxembourg VAT administration is to consider that a FCP cannot be treated as a taxable entity for VAT purposes by itself, with the consequence that a FCP cannot have a VAT number in its own name. The taxable status is conferred to its management company. This position is not shared by all EU Member States; some of them consider that a FCP is a taxable entity by itself and can be granted a VAT number independently from that of its management company.

As of July 1, 2011, a management company established in Luxembourg might be entitled to manage FCPs established in Luxembourg and in other EU Member

States. A Luxembourg resident FCP, however, might be managed by a management company established in an EU Member State other than Luxembourg.

All these situations permitted by the new UCITS Directive might lead to the following situations:

– taxation of the services in the country where the FCP is established;

– taxation of the services in the country where the management company is established;

– taxation of the services in the country where a third party is established.

– non-taxation of the services;

– double taxation of the services.

These situations can be illustrated with the following examples:

– In the case where a Luxembourg-established supplier performs a taxable service to a FCP established in France[9] but is managed by a Luxembourg management company, where would the services rendered by the Luxembourg supplier deemed to be located and taxable? In France, where the FCP is established, or in Luxembourg, where the management company is established?

– In the case where a third party established in Spain performs a taxable service to a French FCP managed by a Luxembourg management company, where would the services rendered by the Spanish supplier deemed to be located and taxable? In Luxembourg, where the management company is established, or in France, where the FCP is established?

Questions also arise as to where services provided by a foreign management company to its FCPs will be located and potentially taxable. When a management company established in a country where a FCP is treated as a taxable entity and renders services to a Luxembourg FCP, would the management company charge its local VAT due to the fact that it cannot be provided with the VAT number of the Luxembourg FCP?

The Luxembourg VAT administration has not yet given its view in such situations. In order to obtain additional clarification from the Luxembourg VAT administration and thus decrease the legal uncertainty of these situations, meetings are scheduled between the professionals of the financial sector, advisory companies and the Luxembourg VAT administration.

If we rely on the Circular 723 stating that a FCP has no legal personality in itself and therefore that the taxable status is conferred to its management company, we

---

9 Where a FCP might be treated as a taxable entity and have its own VAT number.

might argue that services rendered to the FCP should be deemed to be rendered to its Luxembourg management company. The place of supply of such services should then be Luxembourg, where the management company would be liable to pay Luxembourg VAT unless the services qualify for the VAT exemption according to the local Luxembourg VAT legislation.

Similarly, services rendered to a Luxembourg FCP managed by a management company established outside Luxembourg should be deemed to be located in the country where the management company is established, i.e. outside Luxembourg.

As Luxembourg is the EU country that applies the lowest standard VAT rate (15%) and has a wide interpretation of the VAT exemption applicable to fund management services and to the common funds that might benefit from this exemption, Luxembourg should be an attractive jurisdiction for the implementation of management companies managing funds established in different EU Member States.

At the time of writing this chapter, informal discussions were actually going on between professionals in the financial sector regarding the opportunity to amend Circular 723 in the sense that in the future a FCP will be treated as a taxable entity itself and be entitled to receive a Luxembourg VAT number.

The issue should be less relevant for investment funds organized under the form of SICAV, SICAF and SICAR, as these funds already have a recognized tax status. Hence, services provided to such funds will be located in the country where these funds are established.

The decision of the place in which to establish the management company might also be influenced by the national legislation of each EU country with respect to the determination of the VAT deduction right. Member States that grant an input VAT deduction right to management companies managing foreign funds will have a competitive advantage compared to Member States that do not grant such a right, like Luxembourg based on the current interpretation of the Luxembourg VAT administration.

The same consideration is true for Member States allowing a partial VAT deduction right to investment funds. For instance, in the case of a cross-border merger between two funds established in different Member States, the decision regarding which fund will absorb the other might be influenced by the fact that one of the two Member States will grant a deduction right to the fund. In that case, having the absorbing fund in the country allowing such a right might limit the VAT burden of the restructuring.

Chapter 9

Alternative UCITS

9.1. Introduction

The year 2012 may prove a turning point for alternative funds that conform to the Undertakings for Collective Investments in Transferable Securities or UCITS format. The structuring of hedge fund strategies as UCITSs has become very popular since the 2007 financial crisis. Alternative fund managers are choosing to replicate alternative strategies under UCITS in order to access assets from retail and institutional investors that are not comfortable investing through less regulated structures for various reasons.

From an alternative manager's point of view, the primary upside of UCITS can be summarized in one word: distribution. Being a European Union (EU)-regulated investment product, UCITSs can be sold throughout the EU to both institutional and retail investors. This automatic passport is particularly attractive. It is therefore not surprising that the market for alternative UCITS has grown dramatically in the past five years and it is now estimated that there are over 900 alternative UCITS funds with assets in excess of $150 billion. This amount is still small relative to the total of $2 trillion invested in hedge funds, yet this is developing as the new growth area in Europe.

Assets under management, as well as the number of funds trying to replicate hedge fund strategies are increasing. This latest development in the UCITS fund industry can be explained in a number of different ways. Uncertainty surrounding

Chapter written by Christian SZYLAR.

the directive on alternative investment fund managers[1] (AIFMs) is one of the key drivers of this development but it is not the sole reason. Packaging hedge fund strategies as UCITSs is not straightforward and it raises a lot of challenges for the managers as well as for the UCITS brand. An important question is can we determine whether structuring hedge fund strategies as UCITSs will compromise these strategies and provide the same level of returns, considering the constraints under UCITS regulations such as investment restrictions, liquidity requirements, operational requirements and risk management? Is the hedge fund industry sufficiently aware of all these requirements that can challenge deliveries? Leverage, short-selling, financial derivatives and alternative asset classes are the key tools at the disposal of hedge-fund managers in their quest for top performance. Restrictions on techniques to achieve short exposure and the prohibitions of certain asset types point to a serious downside of UCITS: lower investment returns. Achieving returns that are not correlated to any index can prove to be more difficult in a regime intended for long-term retail products. This entails another serious drawback of UCITS: lower fees. While this is good news for investors, a manager who is not achieving the kind of returns possible in a non-UCITS model will not be able to command the same level of fees. So, while the traditional "2 and 20" fee structure is theoretically possible in an UCITS, the reality is that a manager will be charging significantly lower fees.

Distribution is the key element for hedge fund strategies packaged under the UCITS label. An alternative manager launching an UCITS fund for the first time expects to attract a new type of investor and money that would not otherwise be available. The investor base is wide and includes private investors, pension funds, insurance companies, funds platforms, fund-of-funds (funds of alternative UCITS funds), private banks, private wealth managers and retail banks. Formulating alternative strategies under UCITS allows some institutional investors, such as pension funds, to invest higher allocations into UCITSs compared to other investment vehicles, such as unregulated funds. The quest to gather assets is one of the most important objectives of those managers tempted by UCITSs. Raising assets is generally the primary driver for an asset manager choosing to launch a new product. Other drivers include diversifying the types of investor and meeting investors' demands for a particular product. Readers will find it useful to read the chapter on UCITS distribution in this book.

Will institutional and retail investors be interested in this new investment vehicle if these strategies offer a lower return than their original strategies or less than a traditional long-term only UCITS? The answer to this question is crucial for the longevity of this new segment within the UCITS offering. It is also very important

---

1 A proposal for an AIFM directive was announced by the European Commission in April 2009. http://ec.europa.eu/internal_market/investment/alternative_investments_en.htm.

to answer another question: should the regulators allow these products under UCITS? Is there a potential risk that the UCITS brand may be challenged by managers entering into a new environment such as UCITS? What is the real risk at the end for investors and for the UCITS brand? Some regulators, in Asia for example, are worried that, without controls, there is the potential for an unsophisticated investor in one of these programs to end up owning a sophisticated UCITS.

When the first hedge fund strategies were replicated under UCITS they were, and sometimes still are, referred to as "Newcits". The main risk in naming them "Newcits" is that it introduces a sub-category of products into UCITS that can appear to be confusing for investors. We need to avoid creating segmentation in the market. We believe that it is dangerous to introduce a different semantic within a harmonized framework such as UCITS. UCITS is not only a European brand but it is also a globally recognized product and UCITS funds are distributed all around the world including Asia, the Middle East and South America. Introducing a distinction within UCITS may cause damage as it creates confusion about whether it is a real UCITS or not. UCITS funds only exist as long as they all comply with the applicable rules and regulations. EFAMA (European Fund and Asset Management Association), the European Fund Association, also made clear that using the term "Newcits" was not appropriate for the reasons mentioned above. As such, the term "Newcits" should be avoided and we will not make any further reference to it in this chapter. Nevertheless it is fair to admit that it constitutes another type of fund under UCITS. For the benefit of this chapter, we will refer to such funds as alternative UCITS.

We also have to be extremely cautious about replicating hedge fund strategies under UCITS – they do not equate to hedge funds. The risk is in thinking that those strategies under UCITS will deliver the same level of return as pure hedge funds and, consequently, that they will appear to be "miracle" products when everyone is in quest of strong and persistent returns. So the risk is in believing that by investing in alternative UCITS the investor is making the perfect deal: getting typical hedge fund typical with the liquidity of an UCITS and lower risk. Gaining liquidity and reducing risk come at a cost. Coming to this conclusion will disappoint more than one investor. It should also be made clear that not all hedge fund strategies can be replicated under UCITS. Some strategies may require too high a level of leverage to come under UCITS and some strategies may also face illiquidity problems.

Ultimately the long-term success of the alternative UCITSs will be derived from their performance in terms of net returns combined with a successful distribution network. Setting an alternative UCITS without thinking about the distribution network will be the wrong approach, as assets will not materialize merely because an alternative UCITS is launched by an alternative manager. Some participants had thought that money would flow once the product had been UCITS branded – some alternative managers may well be disappointed.

The increase in UCITS funds replicating hedge fund strategies justifies the presence of a specific chapter on the topic in this book. The latest developments suggest that hedge fund UCITSs are gathering momentum and we are seeing a persistent trend towards packaging hedge fund strategies under an UCITS umbrella. Currently investors may also have access to funds that only invest in alternative UCITSs. Specific indices have been developed by the industry to track their performance.

In this chapter we will try to explain the motivations behind the structuring of hedge fund strategies under UCITS as a result of the 2007 financial crisis and its implications. We will then try to understand why some alternative managers have considered launching UCITS products and the objectives behind their decisions. We will also discuss which hedge-fund strategies can be replicated under UCITS and whether all of them can easily be replicated. As the management of an UCITS fund requires a strong operational structure and compliance with strict rules, we will also discuss the key points and challenges to be considered before launching an alternative UCITS. We will try to get an idea about the performance of these new products and whether they are worth launching. Finally, we will also introduce some of the most commonly used financial instruments allowed under UCITS, as they can be used to get synthetic short exposure as well as generating leverage.

9.2. The main drivers for packaging hedge fund strategies under UCITS

Before 2007 the investment world was relatively simple: on one side you had the traditional "long-only" managers mainly running UCITSs or the US-equivalent mutual funds; and on the other side you had the world of hedge funds. To phrase it differently, you had regulated and unregulated investment. There was little interaction between long-only managers and hedge fund managers. Each side was attending its own conferences, its own events, etc. The financial crisis has changed that.

The 2007 financial crisis started in the US when the subprime mortgage market in the US began to display an increasing rate of mortgage defaults. Collateralized mortgage obligations (CMOs), a type of collateralized debt obligation (CDO), allowed these problems to spread from the mortgage market to other sectors of the economy, having especially widespread effects on financial markets as a whole. These "toxic" assets heavily impacted the balance sheets of the major market makers in investment banking. As a result, confidence in the markets disappeared, resulting in a freezing of credit in the credit market. As trust – the most important foundation in the financial markets – had gone, the consequence was the liquidity crisis, as no private financial institutions were willing to lend scarce cash to another. This was because the former could not trust that the latter was correctly revealing the extent of its CMO holdings, and neither could be sure what those holdings were worth. According to 2007 news reports, financial firms and hedge funds owned more than $1 trillion in securities backed by these now-failing subprime mortgages – enough to start a global financial tsunami if more subprime borrowers started defaulting. By June 2007, Bear Stearns stopped redemptions in two of its hedge funds and Merrill Lynch seized $800 million in assets from two Bear Stearns hedge funds. Even this move was a small affair in comparison to what was to happen in the months ahead. These liquidity problems turned to insolvency in September of 2008, when private lending froze completely in a number of important credit markets, such as commercial paper. As a result, non-financial businesses were unable to get access to the financing they required to function normally, leading to problems in the real economy. Recession was the logical consequence, starting in the US and almost immediately being followed by recession in Europe. Lehman Brothers filed for bankruptcy on September 15, 2008 and this event had major consequences as it was the largest bankruptcy filing in US history – Lehman holding represented over $600 billion in assets. This created a real panic on the markets and furthered the liquidity crisis. This event also had other consequences on the hedge fund industry in that it revealed the dependency on prime brokers for hedge funds. Lehman provided prime brokerage services to a large number of hedge funds. As part of these prime brokerage relationships, hedge funds placed investment assets with Lehman's broker-dealer units in different jurisdictions. These assets, posted as collateral for funding activities, could then be reused by Lehman to meet its own obligations in a process called re-hypothecation. Given its insolvency, many of Lehman's prime brokerage clients suddenly lost access to (and, potentially, part of their claims on) their collateral assets for the duration of the administration process. They were thus forcibly locked into positions of changing value whose future accessibility would depend on different legal proceedings and contractual arrangements in various jurisdictions. This event also revealed that the lack of segregation of assets at Lehman meant that leverage funds were unable to immediately recoup their assets. This lesson has been learnt and explains why the AIFM directive is placing a lot of emphasis on custodian responsibilities. This is not the only reason, however, why the regulators have imposed additional rules on custody for hedge fund managers.

Another event damaged the hedge fund industry: Bernard Madoff and his Ponzi scheme. We do not think that we have to explain who Bernard Madoff is and what happened as he entered in the history books as being behind the biggest fraud organized by one sole individual. On December 10, 2008, Madoff's sons told authorities that their father had confessed to them that the asset management unit of his firm was a massive Ponzi scheme. He was arrested by the FBI the day after and on June 29, 2009 he was sentenced to 150 years in jail. This affair can simply be summarized as a failure of institutional investors (and also high net worth individuals who gave their money directly to him based on trust) to have conducted proper due diligence before investing their clients' money as well as a failure to return assets after the fraud became public. This fraud led to further scrutiny of the depositaries' responsibilities and most of the civil actions are hinged on this central issue. A number of hedge funds lost money as a result of Madoff, and as a direct consequence they in turn lost some investor confidence. Redemptions within fund-of-hedge funds became important and some hedge funds lost a lot of assets even though some of them were still showing acceptable performance in 2008. For many hedge funds whose assets were mainly coming from funds-of-hedge funds, this event forced them to evaluate their dependency on such funds and to consider how they could diversify the source of their assets.

The 2007 financial crisis and its surrounding effects – the failure of Lehman as a prime broker, the Madoff affair and the depositary problems, the quest for liquidity – had major consequences on the hedge fund industry. This has led to a number of post-crisis expectations, mainly from institutional investors:

– investors are looking for greater transparency;

– investors want to reduce operational risk when considering hedge fund strategies;

– investors are focusing on strong risk-management capabilities;

– investors want less "exotic" fund domiciliation and are looking for well-regulated countries with better regulatory oversight – onshore versus offshore;

– investors are looking for liquidity and proper valuation;

– investors are less confident in complex strategies and financial derivatives and UCITS offers strict criteria for financial eligibility, leverage and risk management;

– as assets under management decreased, the hedge fund managers had to find alternative sources of assets rather than solely relying on funds-of-hedge funds or high net worth individuals;

– hedge fund managers are trying to get access through pan-European markets and institutional investors[2];

– many hedge fund managers suffered from the lack of performance in 2008, seeing high levels of redemptions; and

---

2 Around 40% of UCITS funds are distributed outside Europe.

– a proposal for an AIFM directive was issued by the European Commission in April 2009 to regulate the European alternative industry (hedge funds and also private equity).

Moving into UCITS appeared to be a reasonable decision for some alternative managers if we consider the uncertainties created by the first AIFM draft directive. It is interesting to note that the liabilities of depositaries in AIFM go further than those in UCITS IV. UCITS V should align the two regimes with regards to the depositary roles, responsibilities and liabilities. In 2009 the largest hedge funds had UCITS offerings such as Blue Crest, RWC Partners and Marshall Wace for their long-short equity strategies. At the same time, the industry was also offering an increasing number of solutions to those alternative managers tempted by UCITS and a lot of banking or private platforms are now available to set up and distribute alternative UCITSs. For some alternative managers UCITS appeared to be a "lifebelt". It is difficult to get an accurate idea of how many of these products exist under UCITS, as this will depend on the criteria used to select them. According to HFR (Hedge Fund Research Inc.) there are now about 700 UCITS-compliant hedge funds with total assets under management of $70 billion to $75 billion.

9.3. Alternative strategies under UCITS and challenges

What are we talking about here? How many of these products are currently available on the market? What is an alternative UCITS and what does it try to achieve? Which hedge fund strategies can be replicated under UCITS and which would appear to be harder to replicate? Where are the challenges for an alternative manager in packaging a strategy in an UCITS format? Where are the limitations for alternative UCITSs? In this section we will try to answer these important questions.

9.3.1. *What is an alternative UCITS?*

An alternative UCITS is a concept grouping funds that follow a hedge fund-type strategy aiming to generate an absolute return or absolute performance. Alternative UCITSs are simply UCITSs that take advantage of certain investment techniques allowed by the UCITS regulations that enable them to pursue strategies that were previously more common in the alternative investment sector – in particular, the hedge fund sector. They tend to invest in a range of financial derivative instruments and use such instruments to enable them to have both long and synthetic short exposures. Some may also use a certain degree of leverage (this may be embedded in the range of derivatives used).

In theory, the current UCITS framework (with synthetic derivatives used to get short exposure, leverage level, and financial derivatives for investment purposes) should allow most of the alternative strategies to be replicated. Nevertheless, UCITS will not be the appropriate label for certain alternative strategies due to the liquidity of underlying strategies/holdings. Some asset classes are not authorized under UCITSs. There are also investment limits and borrowing rules, as well as rules governing the usage of financial derivatives. Barriers to conversion need to be fully reviewed and assessed before launching any UCITS product. There are some excellent expert advisors on UCTIS who can aid in this review before deciding on entering the UCITS world.

The following is a non-exhaustive list of the main alternative strategies that can be structured within an UCITS. Not all of them can easily be replicated due to UCITS constraints.

9.3.1.1. *Long/short equity*

The long/short managers attempt to identify both the most undervalued and the most overvalued companies. They go long the undervalued and short the overvalued companies' equity. The use of short-selling in general serves two main purposes. First, it can represent a view on an overvalued asset. Second, it can be used to hedge the market risk of the long position. The advantage of holding both long and short positions is that the portfolio should make money in most market environments.

Short selling involves the sale of a security not owned by the seller, a technique used to take advantage of an anticipated price decline. The short sellers use all available techniques for shorting securities, including outright securities shorting, uncovered put options, and occasionally futures shorting. A short seller must generally pledge to the lender other securities or cash as collateral for the shorted security in an amount at least equal to the market price of the borrowed securities.

9.3.1.2. *Equity market neutral*

The strategy seeks to be beta neutral, and only generate return from the relative out-performance of the long versus the short positions, regardless of how the market moves. The neutral position can refer to beta, sector, country, currency, industry, market capitalization, style neutral, or any combination of these factors.

9.3.1.3. *Convertible arbitrage*

The convertible arbitrage strategy, as the name implies, is associated with convertible securities. The managers attempt to profit from three different sources: coupon return and short rebate, gamma trading, and mispricing.

A convertible security is a fixed income instrument that can later be converted into a fixed number of shares. Holding a convertible is therefore equivalent to holding a bond position and a call option on the specified amount of underlying stocks. Until maturity, the bond holder will receive a coupon payment and will thus have a stable income source. The bond holder will receive a coupon payment from the interest payment of the convertible bond, unless s/he decides to convert before maturity. The coupon payments, however, are usually low compared to normal bond coupons, and the managers therefore often use leverage.

Additionally, a manager can receive an income from shorting the underlying stock and, much like the short selling strategy, receive an immediate income from the sale, which can be re-invested. Depending upon the negotiated short rebate, a convertible bond manager can often generate a higher return on the re-investment than the short lending fee.

9.3.1.4. *Global macro*

The global macro strategy is one of the oldest and most successful of all hedge fund strategies, but the strategy is in fact a departure from the literal meaning of the term "hedge fund" as most of the global macro hedge funds do not hedge their investments. Instead, the managers make very large directional bets that reflect their forecasts of market directions, as influenced by major economic trends and/or particular events. The managers trade interest rates, equity securities, currencies, and commodities and use leverage and derivatives extensively to hold large market exposures and to boost returns.

9.3.1.5. *CTA/managed futures*

A commodity trading advisor (CTA) or managed futures strategy uses the future markets for trades including commodities, interest rates, equity indices and occasionally currency futures. The individual managers may specialize within a certain range of different futures. The strategy can be further broken down to two main sub-strategies: systematic and discretionary.

Managers who follow a systematic strategy use a proprietary trading model with a particular trading technique, such as trend-following, counter-trend or spread trading. Systematic managers normally have a well-diversified portfolio across different markets, where they methodically abandon their losing trades while allowing their winning trades to run.

The discretionary managed futures strategy is very similar to the global macro strategy. The main differences are that the managers of discretionary managed futures exclusively make bets with futures. The managers make directional long-term positions based on fundamental forecasts and/or short-term bets based on specific information.

9.3.1.6. *Event-driven strategies*

Event-driven managers attempt to capitalize on company news events, such as earnings releases, spin-offs, carve-outs, mergers, chapter 11 filings, re-structures, bankruptcy reorganizations, recapitalizations and share buybacks. The portfolio of some event-driven managers may shift in majority weighting between risk arbitrage and distressed securities, while others may take a broader view. Instruments include long and short common and preferred stocks, as well as debt securities and options. Leverage may be used by some managers.

The replication of alternative strategies under the UCITS format implies a certain number of adaptations, such as the limitation of leverage and the fact that physical shorting is not allowed under UCITS, which means that short exposure can only be achieved using synthetic derivatives. For hedge fund managers, these very attributes of an UCITS product introduce challenges. There is also the need to register with another regulator, most often in Luxembourg[3] or Ireland. Luxembourg is the destination of choice for fund domicile; at 49.92%, it accounts for nearly half of all alternative UCITS funds. Together with Ireland (at 18.84%) and France (at 11.90%), these nations represent the countries of domicile for four out of every five funds.

In addition, more parties are needed to manage an onshore fund (notably the custodian as well as the administrator), while there are also increased burdens on operations, compliance (such as getting a pre-trade monitoring system[4]), marketing and, to some extent, the investment staff of the investment advisor.

Three other constraints may also constitute an obstacle.

The first one is the ineligibility of certain types of assets, such as physical commodities, credit and distressed securities, but it does not constitute a definite blocking point for the majority of alternative strategies. An UCITS can only invest in "eligible assets". Eligible assets include:

– transferable securities admitted to or dealt in on a regulated market, including structured financial instruments if they meet the transferable securities criteria;

---

3 Refer to Chapter 1 on setting up an UCITS fund.
4 Chapter 5 on investment limit details all kinds of challenges raised by UCITS investment limits. It is particularly important in the case of alternative managers launching an UCITS product, as in their capacity of investment manager they will have a pre-trade compliance responsibility. This requires strong technology or the appropriate tools to monitor trades and their potential impact on an UCITS limit.

– money market instruments;

– deposits;

– closed-ended funds; and

– open-ended funds.

No more than 10% of net assets (the so-called "trash ratio") maybe invested as non-core investments in transferable securities and money market instruments that are not listed on a stock exchange or dealt in on another regulated market.

The second constraint is the liquidity requirement under UCITS. As most of hedge funds offer monthly or quarterly liquidity, the requirement for at least fortnightly liquidity may be a strong limitation for alternative managers. An UCITS fund must re-purchase or redeem its shares/units at the request of any unit holder. UCITS funds can operate via daily, weekly or twice-monthly dealing. An UCITS can require that UCITS funds comply with investment diversification, such as the 10% limit and 5/40 rule as explained in Chapter 5.

The third constraint is linked with exposures to OTC (over-the-counter) counterparties. Exposures to OTC counterparties must be kept within the UCITS limits. Risk exposure to an OTC counterparty may not exceed 5% Net Asset Value or 10% (in the case of EU or equivalent credit institutions). All of these limitations are explained in detail in Chapter 4 on counterparty risk.

With regards to these potential limitations of UCITS, the easiest alternative strategy that can be replicated under UCITS seems to be the equity hedge (including 130/30), mainly because of the eligibility of assets ("vanilla") and the liquidity they provide. Although the eligible asset rules – which preclude exposure to physical commodities and property, and typically restrict any other investment to a 10% NAV limit – restrict strategies available to an UCITS product. As a practical matter, it is the liquidity requirements that present the greatest limitations on a manager's ability to implement hedge fund strategies in an UCITS product.

The UCITS structure suits some strategies better than others. It is therefore logical that the first alternative UCITS were equity hedge (long/short and equity market neutral). Long/short equity represents more than 25% of the entire hedge fund industry[5]. They constitute a favored investment for investors searching for exposure to equities and benefiting at the same time from alpha resulting from stock picking carried out by the alternative managers.

---

5 PerTrac, *The Coming of Age of Alternative UCITS Funds*, January 2012. http://www.pertrac.com/resources/pertrac-research/the-coming-of-age-of-alternative-ucits-funds/.

Other strategies have followed, including global macro (a top-down approach), emerging markets, event-driven and fixed-income strategies.

The following graphs give some indication about how alternative UCITSs are split between strategies.

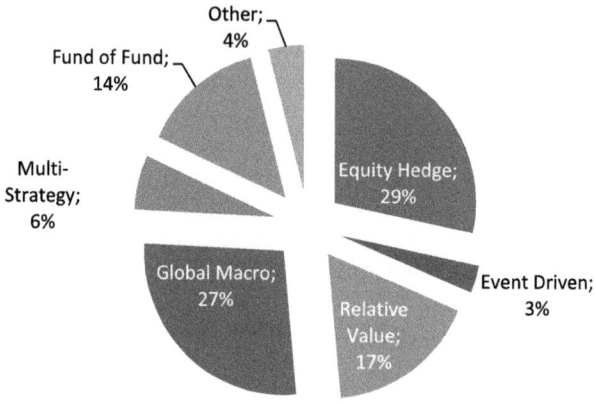

Figure 9.1. *An alternative UCITS split by the number of funds.*
Source: Seeds Finance Morningstar, June 2011

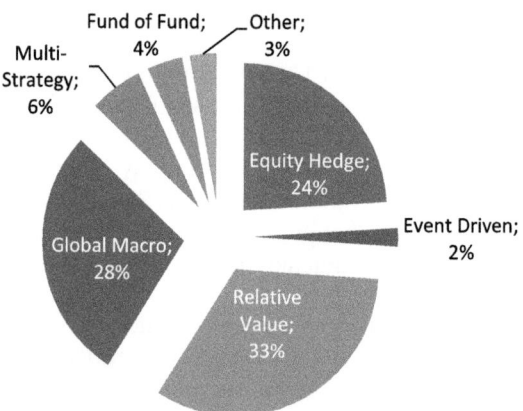

Figure 9.2. *Alternative UCITS split by assets under management.*
Source: Seeds Finance Morningstar June 2011

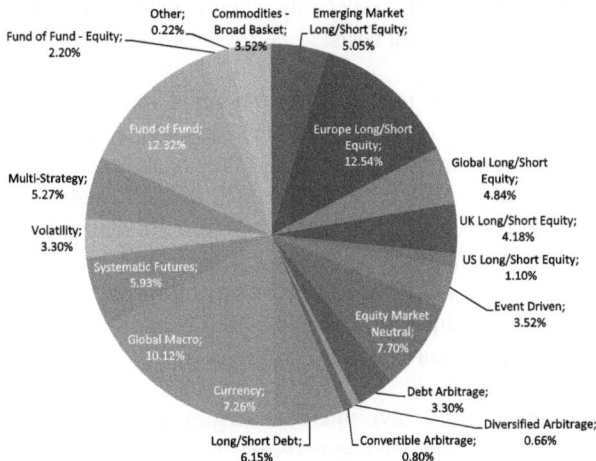

Figure 9.3. *Alternative UCITS split by detailed strategies.*
Source: Seeds Finance Morningstar June 2011

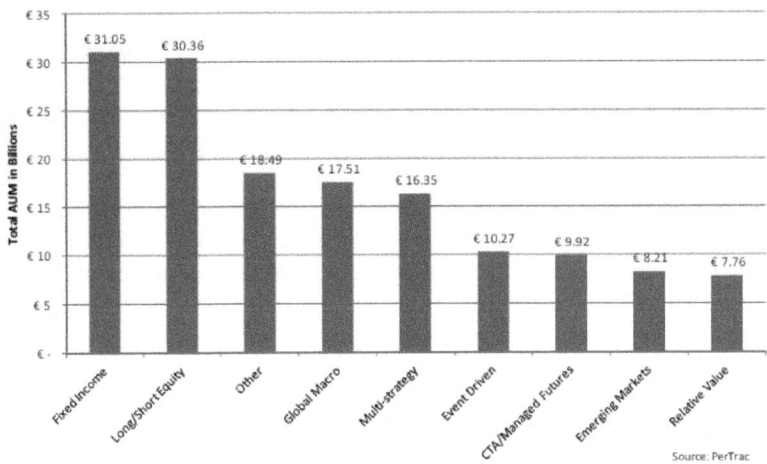

Figure 9.4. *Total assets under management (AUM) of*
alternative UCITS funds by strategy as of October 2011

Concentrated strategies and illiquid ones, such as distressed strategies, would be difficult to replicate under the UCITS format. Equity long/short strategies fit the investment constraints better than most. There are certainly advantages in an onshore vehicle, but they are not a catch-all solution for everyone. Managers need to assess all of the factors carefully, especially when considering the high set-up costs as well as the ongoing operational costs.

As the alternative UCITS is a growing market it has attracted some big new entrants to help managers cope with UCITS requirements as well as helping alternative managers to distribute their funds. For details of companies offering a UCITS platform, readers can refer to the 2012 UCITS hedge platform survey published by *The Hedge Fund Journal*[6]. It details all platforms offered on the market. Using an UCITS platform can be a convenient decision for those alternative managers that do not have all of required structures in place as well as distribution knowledge for UCITS products. Entering the UCITS world with a partner who is fully aware of all UCITS requirements is a wise decision.

Managers of hedge fund investment strategies are accustomed to advising lightly-regulated offshore funds. In comparison, the legal and custodial structures for the onshore hedge fund strategies via UCITS can appear to be much more complex. There are now around 20 UCITS third party platforms promoting their services. Managers can profit from the distribution, administration, risk management, and investment bank platforms with the additional reputational status behind.

Benefits for investors depend on the platform model, especially relating to asset management and investment banking platforms, and the pre-selection of a hedge fund manager. A big name or an outstanding track record is no guarantee of better returns but it can give investors some comfort in the fund selection.

Platforms charge a platform fee, however, and managers might be bound to execute their trades through the investment bank trading desk. Consequently, there is a great deal of learning and adaptation required to tap into the emerging investor appetite for UCITS compliant investing. Some managers are helped by third party marketers to develop their distribution networks.

9.4. The cost of liquidity on alternative UCITS returns

A recent survey by Serge Darolles of Lyxor Asset Management compares alternative UCITSs to off-shore hedge funds[7]. The main findings are:

– that UCITS regulations have a higher impact (in terms of costs) on global macro/CTA strategies;

---

6   http://www.thehedgefundjournal.com/magazine/201202/research/UCITS-hedge-platform-survey.php.

7 http://www.ucitsindex.com (Newsletter 11/2011).

– skilled managers (defined as the UCITS managers that leverage on hedge fund expertise) perform better;

– alternative UCITS funds have lower risk return profiles; and

– the alternative UCITS universe has a very high level of performance dispersion, meaning that it is very important to select the firm, strategy and fund. Investors still need to do their due diligence work.

Barclays Capital has also made an interesting study of the alternative UCITSs[8]. Its key findings are:

– Assets under management in alternative UCITS funds have experienced significant growth in the past couple of years and currently stand at $113 billion.

– 90% of assets are in funds offering daily liquidity. This share of assets attributable to funds offering daily liquidity is not only large, but also growing (it was up by 79% last year).

– Charging investors a performance fee is not a problem in the alternative UCITS world. Instead, it is management fees where managers might feel the squeeze: only 8% of assets are in alternative UCITS are charging 2%+ in management fees.

– Investors in alternative UCITS can be classified as one of three types:

- dedicated funds of alternative UCITS funds (FoAUF), currently representing only 4% of the total alternative UCITS asset base;

- traditional hedge fund investors, but mostly private investors. Institutional investors by and large have been faithful to the traditional hedge fund model and are currently marginal investors in alternative UCITS; and

- retail investors (mostly reached via distributors like fund platforms, retail banks, independent financial advisors and defined contribution pension providers) represent a large share of the alternative UCITS funds' asset base. Among the managers interviewed, they represented on average over 60%, although we would be uncomfortable using this number for the whole market, given the small size of our sample.

– There are three types of managers active in alternative UCITS:

- traditional asset managers which manage about 75% of the AUM in alternative UCITS;

- independent alternative boutiques, which manage 14% of the AUM in alternative UCITS; and

---

8 Barclays Capital, Prime Services, *Hedge Fund Pulse – UCITS: to be or not to be*, November 2011.

- hedge-fund managers, which manage only about 10% of the AUM in alternative UCITS.

– The key success factors (in asset raising) in the alternative UCITS space are both product and manager-related:

- product-related factors include daily liquidity, low volatility, simplicity of strategy and track record (note that only one product in the top 10 by AUM has less than a three-year track record); and

- manager-related success factors include distribution capabilities (both size and skill), solid operational infrastructure, multiple products and a recognizable brand.

Comparing the relative performance of alternative UCITS against hedge fund performance is not an easy exercise. It depends first of all on how the alternative UCITS universe is determined and how funds are split by strategies. Following the development of these products under UCITS, some providers have created specific benchmarks to measure their performances. Depending on the benchmark selected, the relative performance may not appear to be the same. For example, in the Kepler UCITS annual review of 2011 it stated in its summary page that[9]:

> "UCITS hedge funds in our universe had a reasonable first half of the year but were generally unable to protect capital in the volatility of the late summer. As a group they delivered a relatively poor result for 2011 in absolute terms. In relative terms, however they outperformed offshore peers. The Absolute Hedge Global Index fell by -4.58% whilst offshore hedge funds (the HFR Index) fell by -5.02%. Not a bad result considering the vastly better liquidity terms that UCITS funds offer."

Strategy	Performance 2011 (%)		
	AH UCITS Index	Equivalent HFRI Indices	Difference
AH Global Index	-4.58	-5.02	0.44
AH Credit Index	-0.48	n/a	n/a
AH Long/Short Equity Index	-6.85	-8.25	1.40
AH FX Index	-2.15	n/a	n/a
AH Macro Index	-4.09	-3.78	-0.31
AH Managed Futures Index	-10.10	-3.58	-6.52
AH Market Neutral Index	0.83	-1.99	2.82

Source: Hedge Fund Research, www.hedgefundresearch.com; Kepler Partners, www.absolutehedge.com

Table 9.1. *Absolute Hedge Global Index versus Hedge Fund Research Indices fund weighted index*

9 Kepler/Absolute Hedge, *Annual Review: UCITS Review of 2011*, February 12, 2012, see http://www.absolutehedge.com/.

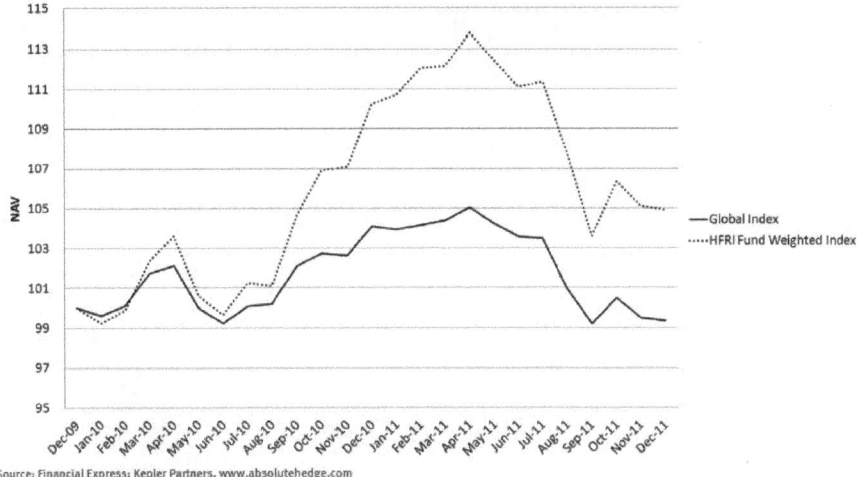

Source: Financial Express; Kepler Partners, www.absolutehedge.com

Figure 9.5. *Absolute Hedge Global Index versus Hedge Fund Research Indices fund weighted index*

To represent alternative UCITS performance we also measured their relative performance versus the offshore hedge fund index (Hedge Fund Research) using the UCITS HFS Index. The UCITS HFS Index was created by the Freienbach-based Swiss 2n20.com AG in order to provide a performance overview of all hedge funds that are UCITS III compliant. Therefore all UCITS III funds that apply strategies normally used in hedge funds (also known as absolute return strategies) that have more than €10 million of assets under management and offer at least weekly liquidity are tracked. The UCITS HFS Index currently tracks €90 billion of assets under management[10].

We first started to build a correlation matrix (from February 2010 to January 2012) showing the correlation between each HFS index and HFR index as well as NewEdge (for the CTA strategy). For each index we have summarized a key number of statistics, such as cumulative return, annualized return, annualized Sharpe and annualized volatility. We then report the difference between the UCITS indices and the relative hedge fund indices. We have also plotted the time series for each UCITS index against the relative hedge fund index[11].

---

10 Founded in 2009, the Freienbach-based Swiss 2n20.com AG is a financial service provider specialized in internet-based services tailored for the hedge fund industry, http://2n20.com/relaunch/index.php and http://www.ucitsindex.com/.
11 There is an element of currency to be considered as HFS index are in Euros and HFR indices are in US dollars.

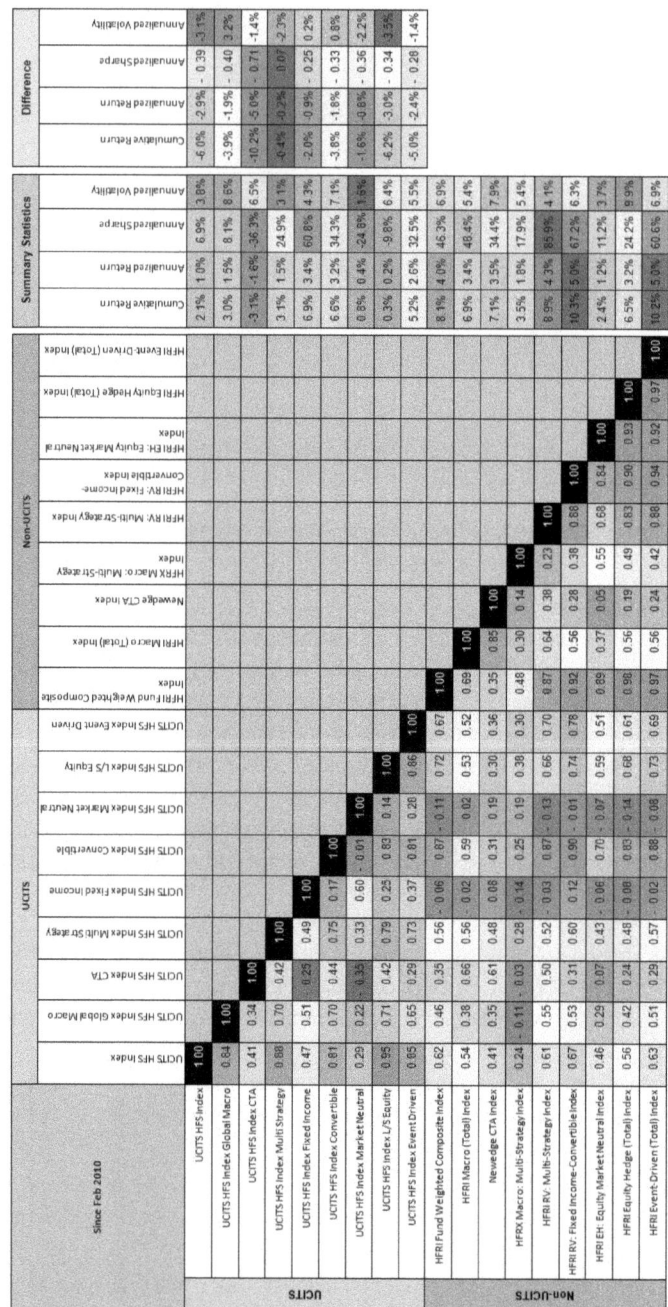

Table 9.2. *Alternative UCITS and hedge funds: correlations and performance*

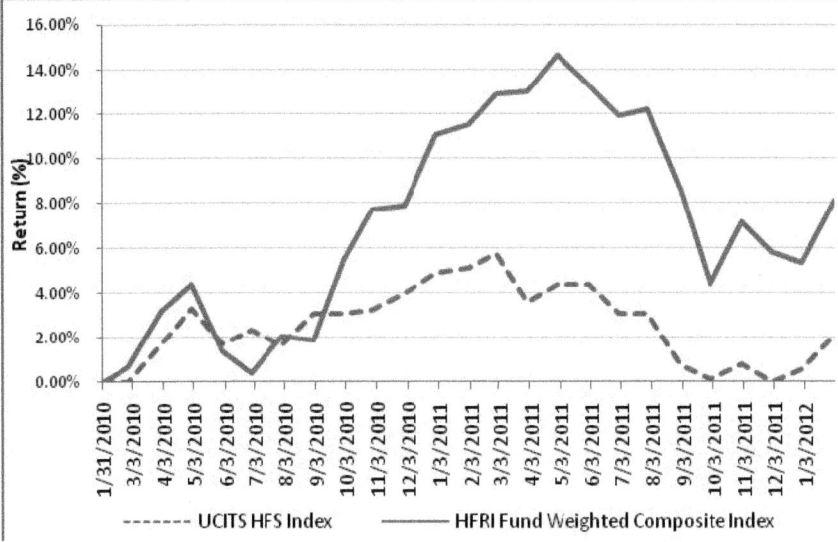

Figure 9.6. *Comparison of the performance of UCITS HFS Index and HFRI fund weighted composite index*

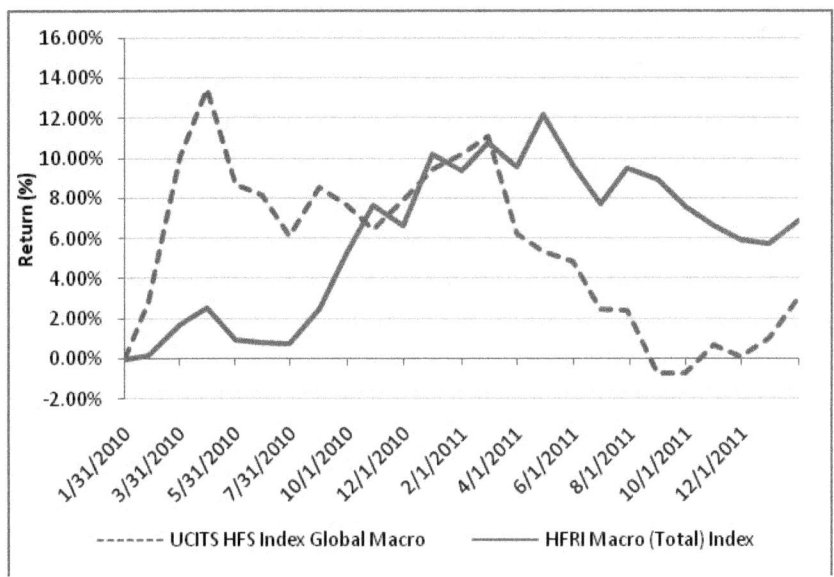

Figure 9.7. *Comparison of the UCITS HFS Index global macro versus HFRI macro (total) Index*

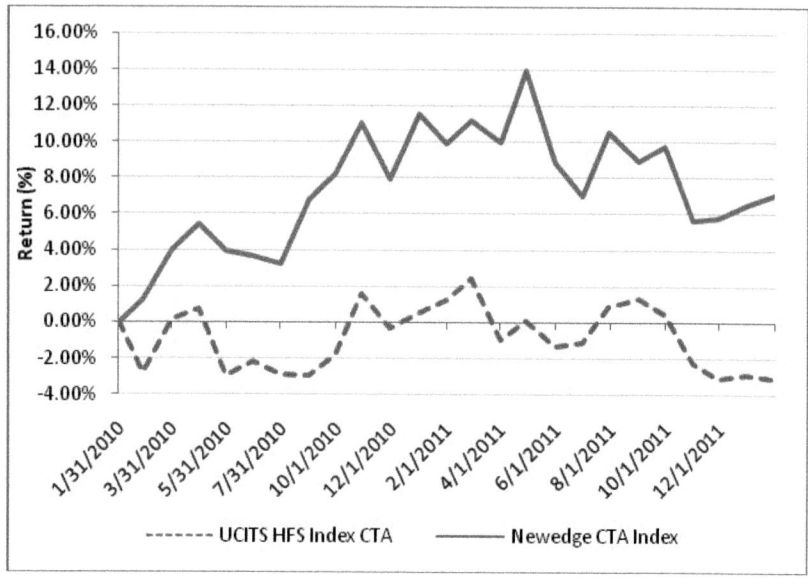

Figure 9.8. *Comparison of the performance of UCTS HFS Index CTA and the NewEdge CTA Index*

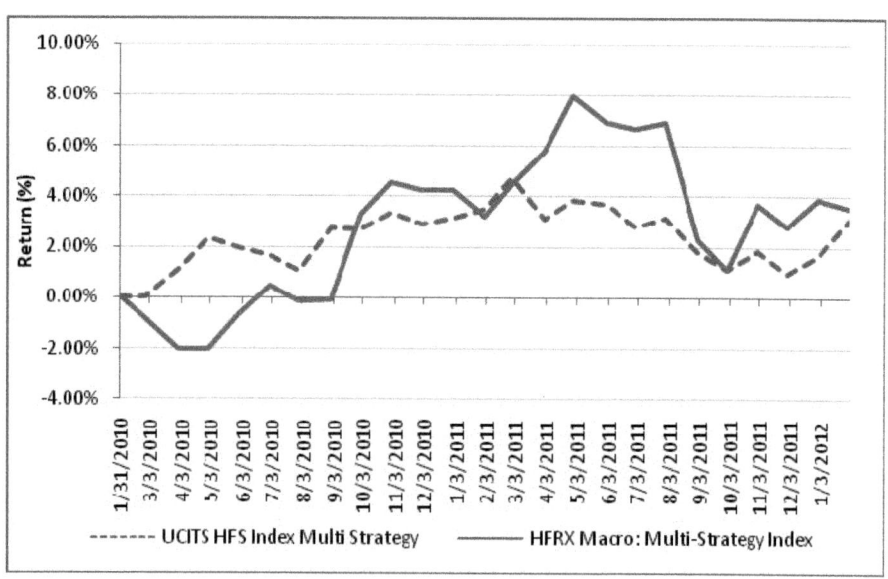

Figure 9.9. *Comparison of the performance of UCITS HFS Index Multi Strategy and HFRX macro: multi-strategy index*

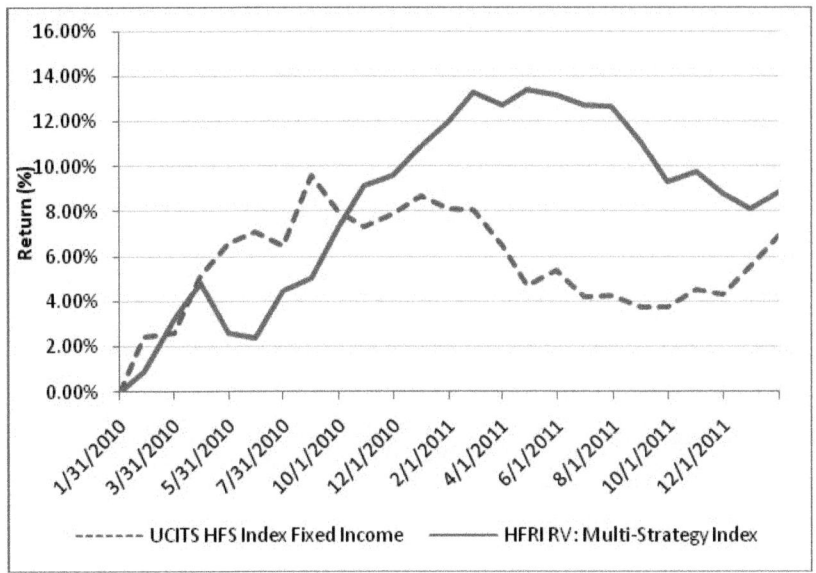

Figure 9.10. *Comparison of the performance of UCITS HFS index fixed income and HFRI RV (relative value): multi-strategy index*

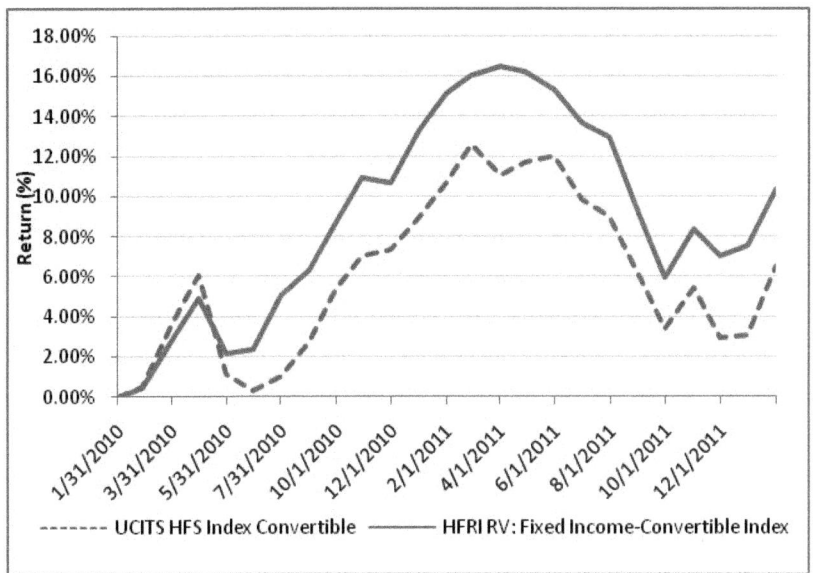

Figure 9.11. *Comparison of the performance of UCITS HFS index, convertible, and HFRI RV: fixed income – convertible index*

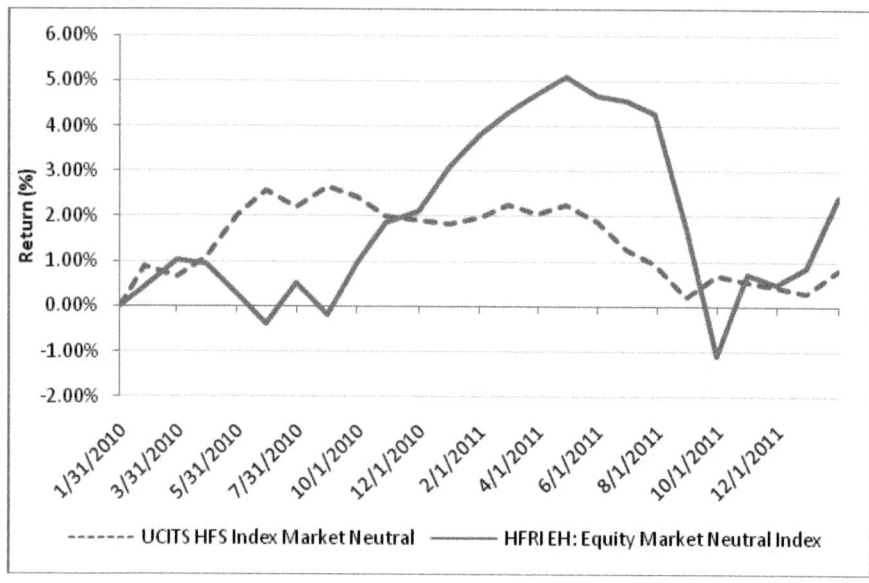

Figure 9.12. *Comparison of the performance of the UCITS HFS Index, market neutral, and HFRI Equity Hedge: equity market neutral index*

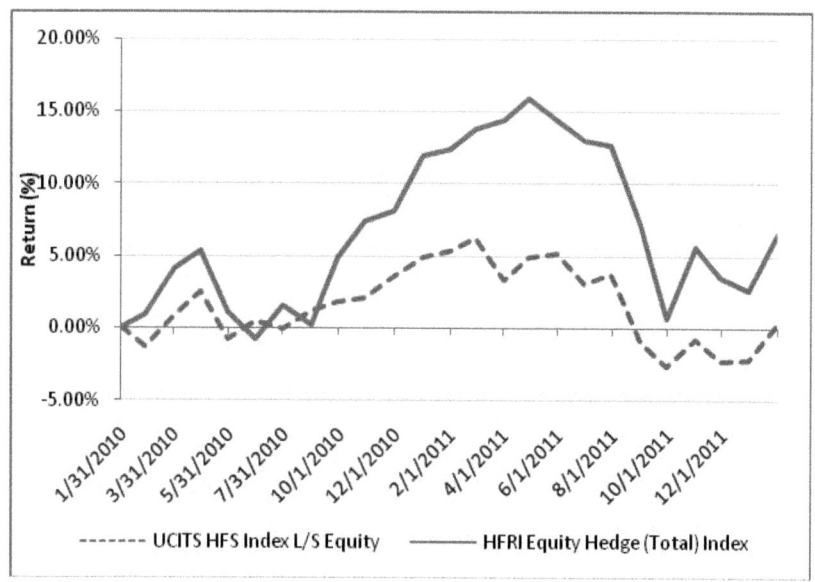

Figure 9.13. *Comparison of the performance of the UCITS HFS index L/S Equity and HFRI equity hedge (total) index*

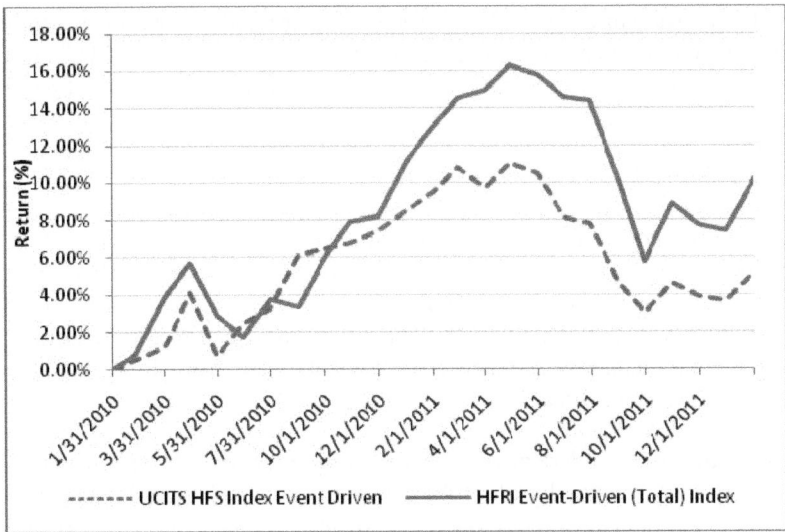

Figure 9.14. *Comparison of the performance of the UCITS HFS index, event driven and HFRI event-driven (total) index*

According to this analysis, it clearly appears that UCITS alternatives are not performing as well as their hedge fund counterparts. This is not really a surprise. Looking at cumulative returns, for example, the UCITS HFS Index CTA has a -10.2% difference in terms of return compared to the NewEdge CTA index. The UCITS HFS Index L/S equity is showing a difference of -6.2% over that period compared to its hedge fund peer index.

UCITS investment offers high levels of regulation and greater liquidity, but has tended to provide lower returns than non-UCITS funds, due to limitations on exposure. Some alternative UCITSs can now perform better than their equivalent hedge fund peers, however, and it will be up to investors to find the right ones to invest in. It is important in the end that the level of tracking errors in the spread between the alternative UCITS and hedge funds (for long/short equity, for example) are acceptable for investors and within the tolerance band, if one has been defined. This is fundamental for investor acceptance of the liquidity premium they pay.

Nevertheless, we have to be cautious when mentioning the relative performance of alternative UCITSs for several reasons:

– the lack of long historical data so we cannot compare the long term track records; and

– the variety of databases and methods used to select alternative UCITS.

With time we will get a much better idea of their relative performance compared to their hedge funds peers and the increased number of alternative UCITSs will help to provide a better understanding of what drives the difference in terms of returns.

9.5. Financial derivative instruments

One of the most attractive points for alternative managers under UCITS is its more liberal scope for the use of derivatives – listed or OTC derivatives. The following pages present the most popular financial derivatives (see Table 9.3) being used in funds managed under UCITS. This list is not exhaustive but constitutes the most commonly employed financial instruments that also allow replication of alternative investment strategies.

Listing all financial derivatives including very complex OTC instruments would be a hard task. We cannot list all of the exotic derivatives that can be used as part of the UCITS investment strategy here, so we have limited ourselves to the most common derivatives that allow us to develop alternative strategies under UCITS.

9.5.1. *Swap*

9.5.1.1. General definition

A swap is a form of derivative in which two parties agree to exchange streams of payment at fixed intervals according to terms specified by the contract. The payments are either at fixed rates of return or indexed rates of return relative to a notional value. The most common type of swap is an *interest rate swap*.

In an interest rate swap, one party agrees to pay a fixed rate of interest in return for receiving a floating rate from the other party. Swaps can be used to hedge existing portfolio positions (by exchanging the return of an asset for a less risky rate of return) or to speculate on the return spread between the return of two payment streams. Other types of swaps that are commonly used are:

– *currency swaps*, where the parties exchange cash flows denominated in different currencies;

– *total return swaps*, where one party exchanges a cash flow indexed to a non-money market asset, i.e. an equity index in exchange for an interest rate; and

– *swaptions*, which are an option on a swap – typically giving the holder the right to enter into swap at a future point in time at a pre-specified level of interest on both payment streams of the swap.

Forwards	Currency forward
Difference	Contracts for difference
Futures	General
	Equity future
	Equity index futures
	Bond index futures
	Currency futures
	Interest rate futures
	Bond futures
Options	Currency options
	Equity index options
	Bond index options
	Equity options
	Bond options
	Interest rate options
	Options on bond futures
	Options on interest rate futures
Swaps	Currency swaps
	Interest rate swaps
	Inflation swaps
	Total return swaps
	Asset swaps
	Index swaps
	Swaptions
	Credit default swaps (also considered a credit derivative)
	Spread lock
Others	Other credit derivatives
	Collateralized debt obligation
Warrant	Equity warrants
	Bond warrants
	Fixed index warrants
Convertible	Convertible equity
	Convertible bonds

Table 9.3. *A list of the main financial derivatives*

9.5.1.2. *Different types of swaps*

9.5.1.2.1. Total return swap

A total return swap is a contract in which one party receives interest payments on a reference asset plus any capital gains and losses over the payment period. The other party receives a specified fixed or floating cash flow unrelated to the credit-worthiness of the reference asset, especially where the payments are based on the same notional amount. The reference asset may be any asset, index or basket of assets.

A total return swap allows one party to derive the economic benefit of owning an asset without putting that asset on its balance sheet, and allows the other party (that does retain that asset on its balance sheet) to buy protection against a loss in its value.

The essential difference between a total return swap and a credit default swap (CDS) is that the latter provides protection not against loss in asset value but against specific credit events. In a sense, a total return swap is not a credit derivative at all, in the way that a CDS is. A total return swap is funding-cost arbitrage.

Total return swaps are most commonly used with equity indices, single stocks, bonds and defined portfolios of loans and mortgages.

9.5.1.2.2. Credit default swap

The ability to take outright short positions has an important implication for asset managers of credit, in particular, due to the emergence of a specific class of credit derivative called a CDS in the past few years. A CDS allows managers to:

– take advantage of their analysts' ability to identify deteriorating credit and generate positive returns where previously their only option was not to own the issue and thereby not incur a loss;

– protect the portfolio against volatility and potential spread widening by buying protection on index products; and

– use of a variety of additional strategies, such as selling protection against one index and buying protection against another.

A CDS is a swap designed to transfer the credit exposure of fixed-income products between parties. It is the most widely used credit derivative. It is an agreement between a protection buyer and a protection seller, whereby the buyer pays a periodic fee in return for a contingent payment by the seller upon a credit event[12] (such as a certain default) happening in the reference entity. Most CDS contracts are physically settled, where upon a credit event the protection seller must pay the par amount of the contract against the protection buyer's obligation to deliver a bond or loan of the name against which protection is being sold.

---

12 Default payments are triggered by "credit events". Credit events are strictly defined by an International Swaps and Derivatives Association agreement (2003). The standard credit events for corporate names are: bankruptcy, obligation acceleration, obligation default, failure to pay, repudiation/moratorium, and restructuring.

A CDS is often used like an insurance policy or hedge for the holder of the debt, though because there is no requirement to actually hold any asset or suffer a loss, a CDS is not actually a form of insurance. The typical term of a CDS contract is five years, although being an OTC derivative almost any maturity is possible.

Family	Type	Index Name	Number of entities	Description
Europe	Benchmark Indices	iTraxx Europe	125	Most actively traded names in the six months prior to the index roll
		iTraxx Europe HiVol	30	Highest spread (riskiest) names from iTraxx Europe index
		iTraxx Europe	50	Sub-investment grade names
	Sector Indices	iTraxx Non-Financials	100	Non-financial names
		iTraxx Financials Senior	25	Senior subordination financial names
		iTraxx Financials	25	Junior subordination financial names
		iTraxx TMT	20	Telecommunications, media and technology
		iTraxx Industrials	20	Industrial names
		iTraxx Energy	20	Energy industry names
		iTraxx Consumers	30	Manufacturers of consumer products
		iTraxx Autos	10	Automobile industry names
North America	Benchmark Indices	CDX North America Investment Grade	125	Most actively traded names in the six months prior to the index roll
		CDX North America High Yield	100	Highest spread (riskiest) names from iTraxx Europe index
		CDX North America Crossover	35	Sub-investment grade names
Asia	Benchmark Indices	iTraxx Asia ex-Japan	70	50 Investment grades and 20 non-investment grade entities
		iTraxx Japan	50	Most liquid traded investment grade entities
		iTraxx Australia	25	Most liquid traded investment grade entities on the Australian Stock Exchange

Table 9.4. *CDS index list*

9.5.1.2.3. Example [FAB 02]

> XYZ plc credit spreads are currently trading at 120 bps over the benchmark government bond for 5-year maturities and 195 bps over for 10-year maturities. A portfolio manager hedges a $10 million holding for 10-year paper by purchasing the following credit default swap, written on the 5-year bond. This edge protects for the first five years of the holding, and in the event of XYZ's credit spread widening, will increase in value and may be sold on or before expiry at a profit. The 10-year bond holding also earns 75 bps over the short-term paper for the portfolio manager.
>
> Term: 5 years
>
> Reference credit: XYZ plc 5-year bond
>
> Credit event: The business day following occurrence of specified credit event
>
> Default payment: Nominal value of bond x (100 – price of bond after credit event)
>
> Swap premium: 3.35%

Assume that midway into the life of the swap there is a technical default on XYZ plc.

9.5.1.3. *Some other credit derivatives*

9.5.1.3.1. First to default [JOR 04]

The protection buyer is covered against the first default among a basket of issuers (typically the basket ranges between five and 10). First to default (FTD) is also sometimes called a basket default swap. FTD offers investors enhanced returns on the credit risk of a basket of corporate institutions. A simple explanation of the mechanics of FTDs is given below and expanded on using some recent examples. FTD notes are similar in structure to credit-linked notes. The key difference is that instead of taking the credit exposure of a single company, here the investor takes the credit exposure on the first company to default within a specified basket of companies (as defined by an underlying reference portfolio). In exchange for taking this credit risk, the investor receives regular coupon payments.

The holder of a FTD contract buys protection against the credit risk on a basket of several entities for a notional (N) and a certain time frame until maturity. Investors buying such securities pay a premium on a regular basis until maturity of the contract or the first default on one of the reference entities. In exchange, the seller of the protection guarantees until maturity that the buyer will recover the notional of the contract if there is a default on the reference entity. In the case of a default, the buyer stops paying the premium and the seller of the protection either delivers $(1 - R)*N$, where R is defined as the recovery rate (cash settlement), or receives a notional N of individual deliverable obligation from the buyer of the defaulted reference entity (a physical settlement).

9.5.1.3.2. Pricing

Pricing models for basket-based products are continually evolving. The underlying pricing model for FTDs is based on the impact that time has on the implicit default probability. This model carries out Monte Carlo simulations against different risk scenarios to arrive at the most appropriate spread for the basket. The scenarios are represented by the number and timing of defaults.

In simple terms, the premium to buy protection using a FTD basket is a percentage of the sum of the five individual credit default swap spreads. Underpinning FTDs is the notion that since it is extremely unlikely that all five names in one basket will default, an investor can buy protection on five names with a FTD basket for less than using individual CDS trades.

As a result, the more closely correlated the names within the FTD, the smaller the percentage of the total sum. For example, a basket of five Korean credits, which are considered strongly correlated, may cost 40% of the sum of the spreads because if one defaults the others are likely to follow and so the protection is less effective than for an uncorrelated basket.

9.5.1.3.3. Collateralized debt obligation

The protection buyer is protected on a tranche of loss among a CDS portfolio (typically between 50 and 100 names) [TAV 03]. Each tranche has its own risk and each one is subject to a rating [STA 03]. For example, a collateralized debt obligation (CDO) might issue four classes of securities designated as:

(1) senior debt;

(2) mezzanine debt;

(3) subordinate debt; and

(4) equity.

Each class protects those more senior to it from losses on the underlying portfolio. The sponsor of a CDO usually sets the size of the senior class so that it can attain triple-A ratings. Likewise, the sponsor generally designs the other classes so that they achieve successively lower ratings. In a way, the rating agencies are really the ones who determine the sizes of the classes for a given portfolio.

Historically, CDOs were created to provide greater liquidity in the economy. They allow banks and corporations to sell off debt, which frees up more capital to invest or loan. The creation of CDOs is one reason why the US economy has been so robust in the past five years, but at the same time also one of the main reasons for the 2007 financial crisis. However, the downside of CDOs is that they allow the originators of the loans to avoid having to collect on them when they become due, since the loans are now owned by other investors. This may make them less disciplined in adhering to strict lending standards.

Another downside is that CDOs are so complex that the buyers are rarely sure of exactly what they are buying. They often rely on their trust in the bank selling the CDO without doing enough personal research to be sure the package is really worth the price they are paying.

The opacity and complexity of CDOs can cause a market panic if something happens to make sellers lose their trust in the product. This then makes the CDOs difficult to resell. This helped cause the 2007 banking liquidity crisis.

A synthetic CDO is a transaction that transfers the credit risk on a reference portfolio of assets. The reference portfolio in a synthetic CDO is made up of credit default swaps.

9.5.1.3.4. Credit spread option

The buyer protection again covers variances in the increase or decrease of a CDS price. He or she buys the right to enter in a CDS if a certain level of spread is reached.

9.5.1.3.5. Credit-linked note

A credit-linked note is issued under the form of a bond. It is a funded credit derivative. As opposed to an unfunded credit derivative, such as a default swap, credit-linked notes imply an investment in the cash instrument. These are notes given by one issuer (usually a bank), which has a credit risk exposure to a second issuer (often a corporation, which is known as the "reference issuer"). These notes pay an enhanced coupon, typically linked to LIBOR (the London interbank offered rate), to the investor for taking on the added credit risk of the second reference issuer. If the note defaults, the investor stands to lose some or all of his or her coupon income and principal. In this case, the investor is the protection seller and the bank is the protection buyer.

9.5.1.3.6. Currency swap

A currency swap is a foreign exchange agreement between two parties to exchange a given amount of one currency for another and, after a specified period of time, to return the original amounts swapped.

Currency swaps can be negotiated for a variety of maturities up to at least 10 years. Unlike a back-to-back loan, a currency swap is not considered to be a loan by US accounting laws and thus it is not included on a company's balance sheet. A swap is considered to be a foreign exchange transaction (short leg) plus an obligation to close the swap (far leg) that is a forward contract.

Currency swaps are often combined with interest rate swaps. For example, one company would seek to swap a cash flow for their fixed-rate debt denominated in US dollars for a floating-rate debt denominated in Euros. This is especially common in Europe, where companies "shop" for the cheapest debt regardless of its denomination and then seek to exchange it for the debt in the desired currency.

Box 9.1. Example

Company A and company B, a US firm and a European firm, respectively, enter into a five-year currency swap for $50 million. Let us assume the exchange rate at the time is $1.25 per euro (i.e. the dollar is worth €0.80). First, the firms will exchange principals. So, company A pays $50 million, and company B pays €40 million.

Let us say the agreed-upon dollar-denominated interest rate is 8.25% and the euro-denominated interest rate is 3.5%, and both companies make payments annually, beginning one year from the exchange of the principal.

Company A therefore pays €40 million * 3.50% = €1,400,000 to company B, which will pay company A: $50 million * 8.25% = $4,125,000.

If, at the one-year mark, the exchange rate is $1.40 per euro, company B's payment equals $1,960,000 and company A will pay the difference ($4,125,000 – $1,960,000 = $2,165,000).

Finally, at the end of the swap, the parties re-exchange the original principal amounts. These principal payments are unaffected by exchange rates at the time.

9.5.1.3.7. Swaption

Definition

A swaption is a financial instrument granting the owner an option to enter into an interest rate swap. A swaption gives the buyer the right but not the obligation to enter into a swap. There are two types of swaption contracts: a payer swaption or a receiver swaption. A payer swaption gives the owner of the swaption the right to enter into a swap where he or she pays the fixed leg and receives the floating leg. A receiver swaption gives the owner of the swaption the right to enter into a swap where he or she will receive the fixed leg and pay the floating leg.

The buyer and seller of the swaption agree on:

– the strike rate;

– length of the option period (which usually ends on the starting date of the swap if swaption is exercised);

– the term of the swap;

– notional amount;

– amortization; and

– frequency of settlement.

Properties

Unlike ordinary swaps, a swaption not only hedges the buyer against downside risk; it also lets the buyer take advantage of any upside benefits. Like any other option, if the swaption is not exercised by maturity, it is worthless when it expires.

If the strike rate of the swap is more favorable than the prevailing market swap rate, then the swaption will be exercised as detailed in the swaption agreement.

It is designed to give the holder the benefit of the agreed-upon strike rate if the market rates are higher, with the flexibility to enter into the current market swap rate if they are lower. The converse is true if the holder of the swaption receives the fixed rate under the swap agreement.

Swaption styles

There are three styles of swaptions. Each style reflects a different timeframe in which the option can be exercised:

– in *American swaption* the owner is allowed to enter the swap on any day that falls within a range of two dates;

– in *Bermudan swaption* the owner is allowed to enter the swap on a sequence of dates; and

– in *European Swaption* the owner is allowed to enter the swap on one specified date.

9.5.1.3.8. Variance swap

A variance swap is a financial derivative whose payoff is equal to the difference between the square of annualized realized volatility (that is, the actual annual variance), σ^2 realized, of returns on the underlying price over that period and a fixed quantity, σ^2 strike, sometimes known as the variance strike, i.e. in the above notation, the payoff is σ^2 realized – σ^2 strike. Effectively, it is a forward contract on the actual variance.

The actual annual variance is calculated based on a pre-specified set of sampling points over the period. It does not coincide with the classic statistical definition of variance, but follows the usual market convention of not subtracting the mean.

The variance swap may be hedged and hence priced using a portfolio of European call and put options with weights inversely proportional to the square of strike. The advantage of variance swaps is that they provide pure exposure to the variability of the underlying price, as opposed to call and put options that carry directional risk (delta).

The payout of a variance swap is often capped. It is market practice to determine the number of contract units as $\dfrac{\text{VegaNotational}}{2\sigma_{\text{strike}}}$ to approximate the payoff of a volatility swap.

Closely related contracts include volatility swap, correlation swap and gamma swap.

9.5.2. Contracts for difference

9.5.2.1. *General definition and general risks*

A contract for difference (or CFD) is a contract between two parties – buyer and seller – stipulating that the seller will pay the buyer the difference between the current value of an asset and its value at the contract time (if the difference is negative, then the buyer pays the seller). Such a contract is an equity derivative that allows investors to speculate on share price movements without the need for ownership of the underlying shares.

CFDs allow investors to take long or short positions and, unlike futures contracts, have no fixed expiry date or contract size. Trades are conducted on a leveraged basis with margins typically ranging from 1% to 30% of the notional value for CFDs on leading equities. CFDs are currently available in listed and/or OTC markets.

As with any leveraged product, maximum exposure is not limited to the initial investment; it is possible to lose more than you put in. These risks are typically mitigated through use of stop orders and other risk reduction strategies (for the most risk averse, guaranteed stop-loss orders are available at the cost of an additional one-point premium on the position and/or an inflated commission on the trade).

CFDs allow a trader to go short or long on any position with a variable margin (set by the brokerage) that allows him or her to trade on margins of up to 5% (and sometimes 1%). Lack of appreciation for the sort of exposure that can occur after taking full advantage of such financing is therefore a crucial reason that many CFD traders lose. A solid money management strategy, however, can allow a trader to take full advantage of CFDs to his or her benefit. The CFD broker or principal will always be required to mirror the underlying market valuation and, as a result, when risk management is applied CFDs can be a solid trading tool.

Therefore, anyone approaching CFDs should analyze what they could lose, as opposed to simply focusing on what they could gain.

Box 9.2. Long trade example

A long trade is a position that is opened with a buy in the expectation that the share price will rise.

Vodafone is currently trading at 140.5 pence. Investor A believes that Vodafone is going to rise and places a trade to buy 10,000 shares as a CFD at 140.5 pence. The total value of the contract would be £14,050 but he would only need to pay an initial 10% deposit (initial margin) of £1,405.

A week later, investor A's prediction is correct and Vodafone rises to 145.0 pence, and he decides to closes his position. By selling 10,000 Vodafone CFDs at 145.0p, he will make a profit on the trade of:

Opening level: 140.5 pence

Closing level: 145.0 pence

Difference: 4.50 pence

Profit on trade: $4.5 \times 10,000 = £450.00$

9.5.3. *The forward contract*

9.5.3.1. *General definition*

A forward contract is a form of OTC that obliges one party to purchase a good from another party at a fixed future date for a price and currency specified in the terms of the contract. This is in contrast to a spot contract, which is an agreement to buy or sell an asset today. Forwards are frequently used to hedge positions against price fluctuations in the underlying security, or to speculate on the price movement of that security. Initiating a position in a forward does not require any financial outlay, so it allows for leveraged positions to be taken. Forward contracts are very similar to futures contracts, except they are not taken to market, exchanged, traded, or defined on standardized assets.

Box 9.3. Example

Microsoft goes to JP Morgan Chase and asks for a quote on a currency forward for €12 million in three months. JP Morgan Chase quotes a rate of $0.925, which would enable Microsoft to sell euros and buy dollars at a rate of $0.925 in three months' time. Under this contract, Microsoft would know it could convert its €12 million to $11,100,000 (12,000,000 × 0.925 = 11,100,000). The contract would also stipulate whether it will settle in cash or will call for Microsoft to actually deliver the euros to the dealer and be paid $11,100,000.

Now let us say that three months later, the spot rate for euros is $0.920. Microsoft is quite pleased that it locked in a rate of $0.925, as with the new spot rate they would receive 12,000,000 × 0.920 = $11,040,000. Microsoft made a profit of $60,000 by entering into the forward currency contract.

However, had rates risen in the three-month period, Microsoft would have a made a loss (e.g. at a spot rate of $1.00, Microsoft would have received $12,000,000, but would still have to deliver the euros and accept a rate of $0.925, and therefore make a potential loss of $900,000).

9.5.4. *The futures contract*

9.5.4.1. *General definition*

This contract is an agreement to buy or sell an asset at a certain time in the future for a certain price. Futures are traded in exchanges and the delivery price is always such that today's value of the contract is zero. Therefore, in principle, we can always engage in futures without the need for initial capital: the speculator's heaven!

Although similar in nature, futures and forwards exhibit some fundamental differences in the organization and the contract characteristics (see Table 9.5).

	Forwards	Futures
Primary market	Dealers	Organized exchange
Secondary market	None	Primary market
Contracts	Negotiated	Standardized
Delivery	Contracts expire	Rare delivery
Collateral	None	Initial margin, mark-the-market
Credit risk	Depends on parties	None [clearing house]
Market participants	Large firms	Wide variety

Table 9.5. *Differences between forwards and futures contracts*

9.5.4.2. *Different types of futures*

9.5.4.2.1. Currency future

A currency future contract is a transferable futures contract that specifies the price at which a currency can be bought or sold at a future date.

Currency future contracts allow investors to hedge against foreign exchange risk. Since these contracts are marked-to-market daily, investors can – by closing out their position – exit from their obligation to buy or sell the currency prior to the contract's delivery date.

9.5.4.2.2. Interest rate futures

These are contracts where the holder agrees to take delivery of a given amount of the related debt security at a later date (usually no more than three years). Futures may be in treasury bills and notes, certificates of deposit, commercial paper, or Government National Mortgage Association certificates, etc. Interest rate futures are stated as a percentage of the value of the applicable debt security.

The value of interest rate futures contracts is directly tied to interest rates. For example, as interest rates decrease, the value of the contract increases. As the price or quote of the contract goes up, the purchaser of the contract gains, while the seller loses.

A change of one base point in interest rates causes a price change. Those who trade in interest rate futures do not usually take possession of the financial instrument. In essence, the contract is used either to hedge or to speculate on future interest rates and security prices. For example, a pension fund manager might use interest rate futures to hedge the bond portfolio position. Speculators find financial futures attractive because of their potentially large return on a small investment due to the low deposit requirement. Significant risks exist, however.

9.5.4.2.3. Bond futures

A bond future is a contractual obligation for the contract holder to purchase or sell a bond on a specified date at a predetermined price. A bond future can be bought in a futures exchange market and the prices and dates are determined at the time the future is purchased.

Bond contracts are standardized and are overseen by a regulatory agency that ensures a certain level of equality and consistency. However, this form of derivative can be risky because it involves trading at a future date with only current information. The risk is potentially unlimited for either the buyer or seller of the bond because the price of the underlying bond may change drastically between the initial agreement and the exercise date.

9.5.5. *Options*

9.5.5.1. *General definition*

An option is a derivative contract that conveys to its purchaser the right (but not the obligation) to buy or sell the underlying security at a pre-specified price (strike price) over a period that is defined within the terms of the contract.

If the option is exercised, the writer of the contract is obliged to fulfill the terms and conditions of the contract through transfer of the underlying (or its cash equivalent, if so defined). If the option is not exercised, then it expires worthless. The only transfer of the underlying cash would have been the premium paid by the purchaser at the time that the contract was written.

Options exist as calls (the right to buy the underlying) and puts (the right to sell the underlying).

Calls and puts can either be purchased or written to achieve a desired exposure to the underlying security without the capital constraint of physically purchasing that security.

Similarly to future contracts, an option contract provides exposure to an underlying asset but offers increased liquidity, the ability to take either long or short positions, the ability to take positions in baskets of stocks (i.e. indexes), and the ability to introduce leverage through only minimal outlay, which would not be available through trading the underlying itself. Unlike futures contracts, option contracts require an initial premium, for which they confer the right to pass up exercise if that remains within the purchaser's interests. An out-of-the money option would expire worthless (with the loss of the premium) while an in-the-money-option would be exercised under contractual terms. There are no offsetting margin payments under option contracts.

Similarly to futures contracts, the underlying can be any of a wide variety of securities or even other contracts, such as futures or swaps. From a strategic perspective, fund managers may combine different option contracts to achieve a variety of low-risk exposures. For example, buying a call and a put with the same exercise price (known as a straddle) allows the fund to benefit (due to less premium outlay) by either a rise or fall in the price of the underlying. If the fund manager expects the underlying price to be volatile then this (or a similar strategy) may be employed. Options, contrary to popular press, can offer timely, low risk and highly liquid solutions to previously unattainable portfolio rebalancing requirements.

9.5.5.2. *Different types of options*

9.5.5.2.1. Currency option

A currency option is a contract that grants the holder the right, but not the obligation, to buy or sell currency at a specified exchange rate during a specified period of time. For this right, a premium is paid to the broker, which will vary depending on the number of contracts purchased. Currency options are one of the best ways for corporations or individuals to hedge against adverse movements in exchange rates.

Investors can hedge against foreign currency risk by purchasing a currency option put or call.

9.5.5.2.2. Equity option

An equity option is an option in which the underlier is the common stock of a corporation, giving the holder the right to buy or sell its stock at a specified price, by a specific date. It is also called a stock option.

The specific stock on which an option contract is based is commonly referred to as the underlying security. Options are categorized as derivative securities because their value is derived in part from the value and characteristics of the underlying security. A stock option contract's unit of trade is the number of shares of underlying stock that are represented by that option. Generally speaking, stock options have a unit of trade of 100 shares. This means that one option contract represents the right to buy or sell 100 shares of the underlying security.

9.5.5.2.3. Interest rate option

Interest rate options are European-style, cash-settled options on the yield of US treasury securities. Options on short-, medium-, and long-term rates are available to meet your needs. These options give you an opportunity to invest based upon your views of the direction of interest rates.

In general, when yield-based options are purchased, a call buyer and a put buyer have opposing expectations about interest rate movements. A call buyer anticipates that the interest rates will go up, increasing the value of the call position. A put buyer anticipates that rates will go down, increasing the value of the put position. A yield-based call option buyer will profit if, by expiration, the underlying interest rate rises above the strike price plus the premium paid for the call. Alternatively, a yield-based put options buyer will profit if, by expiration, if the interest rate has declined below the strike price less the premium paid. Of course, taxes and commissions must be taken into account in all transactions.

9.5.5.2.4. *Asset swapped convertible option transactions*

An asset swapped convertible option transaction (ASCOT) is an option on a convertible bond. Typically, hedge funds that have large convertible bond portfolios may wish to reduce their exposure to the market value of a bond. They can do so by selling their convertible bond to a broker or third party and simultaneously buying an option on the bond.

9.5.6. *Warrant*

9.5.6.1. *General definition*

Warrants are a type of option issued by a corporation giving the holder of the option the right to buy shares in the corporation for a pre-specified price. When exercised, the corporation is obliged to issue new shares of its stock and deliver these to the holder of the warrant in exchange for the strike price. The main conceptual difference between a standard exchange traded option and a warrant is that the exercise of a warrant results in the issuance of new stock, whereas the writer of an exchange-traded option delivers previously-issued stock upon exercise. This can result in a drop in the price of the underlying stock when the warrant is exercised (known as the dilution effect). Typically, warrants have a much longer lifespan than regular options.

A wide range of warrants and warrant types are available. The reasons you might invest in one type of warrant may be different from the reasons you might invest in another.

9.5.6.2. *Different types of warrants*

9.5.6.2.1. Equity warrants

Equity warrants can be either call or put warrants:

– call warrants give you the right to buy the underlying securities; and

– put warrants give you the right to sell the underlying securities.

9.5.6.2.2. Basket warrants

As with a regular equity index, warrants can be classified at an industry level, for example. Thus, basket warrants mirror the performance of the industry.

9.5.6.2.3. Index warrants

Index warrants use an index as the underlying asset. Your risk is dispersed – using index call and index put warrants – just like with regular equity indexes. It should be noted that they are priced using index points.

9.6. Conclusion

Funds compliant with UCITS are of growing attraction to alternative managers. UCITS as a global brand was the answer to the post-2007 financial crisis. For hedge funds, whose assets were severely depleted by the crisis of 2007, UCITS-compliant products have been seen as an opportunity to reach out to a new and diversified base of investor. At the same time investors were looking for robust regulation as an additional safeguard and comfort blanket for hedge fund investment and UCITS provides this high level of comfort.

The 2007 financial crisis was the main catalyst for change and institutional investors understood the benefits of having liquidity when retail investors saw the benefits of diversifying away from pure long-only strategies. Even if UCITS has greater restraints in terms of eligible assets, leverage, risk management, shorts via synthetic derivatives, and investment limits, it is still possible to replicate most of the alternative strategies under an UCITS format. Hedge fund managers were also helped by UCITS third party platforms offering the set-up of the fund, distribution, administration and risk management with the additional reputational status behind.

Will this trend continue in the future? It is difficult to answer that question and there is currently certainly a demand for alternative UCITSs. As we have tried to explain in this chapter, the UCITS-compliant versions of alternative strategies are not performing as well as the hedge funds. This is the liquidity premium. It is important that in the end investors are satisfied with the level of tracking error measuring the spread between the alternative UCITS and hedge funds (for long/short equity for example) and that the difference in terms of return remains in the tolerance band. Investors will not have access to the full alpha that pure hedge funds are able to generate.

Since 2007 due diligence on hedge funds for capital allocations has also increased. Today, hedge funds have to face in-depth due diligence before getting a mandate. The increased due diligence process over hedge funds has also helped to restore trust in investing with alternative managers. We also note that investors' appetite for hedge funds have recently increased. The case in 2007–2011 may have changed today. If this starts to indicate fewer inflows for alternative UCITS, this creates the next question... *sine die*!

Bibliography

[COM 07] COMMISSION DE SURVEILLANCE DU SECTEUR FINANCIER, Rules of Conduct to be Adopted by Undertakings for Collective Investment in Transferable Securities with Respect to the Use of a Method for the Management of Financial Risks, as well as the Use of Derivative Financial Instruments, CSSF Circular 07/308, CSSF, 2007.

[COM 10a] COMMISSION DE SURVEILLANCE DU SECTEUR FINANCIER, Règlement CSSF N° 10-4 Portant Transposition de la Directive 2010/43/UE de la Commission du 1er Juillet 2010 Portant Mesures d'Exécution de la Directive 2009/65/CE du Parlement Européen et du Conseil en ce qui Concerne les Exigences Organisationnelles, les Conflits d'Intérêts, la Conduite des Affaires, la Gestion des Risques et le Contenu de l'Accord Entre le Dépositaire et la Société de Gestion, Loi du 17 décembre 2010, Règlement 10-4, CSSF, 2010.

[COM 11a] COMMISSION DE SURVEILLANCE DU SECTEUR FINANCIER, CSSF Circular 11/498, CSSF, 2011.

[COM 11b] COMMISSION DE SURVEILLANCE DU SECTEUR FINANCIER, Nouvelles Dispositions Applicables aux Sociétés de Gestion de Droit Luxembourgeois Soumises au Chapitre 15 de la loi du 17 Décembre 2010 Concernant les Organismes de Placement Collectif et aux Sociétés d'Investissement qui n'ont pas Désigné une Société de Gestion au sens de l'Article 27 de la loi du 17 Décembre 2010 Concernant les Organismes de Placement Collectif, CSSF Circular 11/508, CSSF, 2011.

[COM 11c] COMMISSION DE SURVEILLANCE DU SECTEUR FINANCIER, CSSF Circular 11/512, CSSF, 2011.

[COM 09a] COMMITTEE OF EUROPEAN SECURITIES REGULATORS, CESR's Technical Advice to the European Commission on the Level 2 Measures Related to the UCITS Management Company Passport, CESR/09-963, CSSF, 2009.

[COM 09b] COMMITTEE OF EUROPEAN SECURITIES REGULATORS, CESR's Technical Advice at Level 2 on Risk Measurement for the Purposes of the Calculation of UCITS' Global Exposure, CESR/09-489, CESR, 2009.

[COM 09c] COMMITTEE OF EUROPEAN SECURITIES REGULATORS, Risk Management Principles for UCITS, CESR/09-178, CESR, 2009.

[COM 10b] COMMITTEE OF EUROPEAN SECURITIES REGULATORS, CESR's Guidelines on Risk Measurement and the Calculation of Global Exposure and Counterparty Risk for UCITS, CESR/10-788, CESR, 2010.

[DOW 02] DOWD K., *An Introduction to Market Risk Measurement*, Wiley Finance, 2002

[JOR 02] JORION P., *The New Benchmark for Managing Financial Risk: Value at Risk*, Second edition, McGraw-Hill, 2002.

[JOR 07] JORION P., *Financial Risk Manager Handbook*, Fourth edition, Wiley Finance, 2007.

[NAS 07] NASSIM N.T. , *The Black Swan: the Impact of the Highly Improbable*, Penguin, 2007.

[NEW 09] NEW YORK TIMES, NOCERA J., "Risk mismanagement", *New York Times*, January 2, 2009. Available at: http://www.nytimes.com/2009/01/04/magazine/04risk-t.html?pagewanted=1&_r=1, accessed 4.4.12.

[OFF 09] OFFICIAL JOURNAL OF THE EUROPEAN UNION, Directive on the Coordination of Laws, Regulations and Administrative Provisions Relating to Undertakings for Collective Investment in Transferable Securities (UCITS), Directive 2009/65/EC, EU, 2009.

[RÉG 10] BOURDONNAIS R., TERRAZA M., *Analyse des Séries Temporelles – Applications à l'Économie et à la Gestion*, 3rd edition, Dunod, 2010.

[SOP 09] SOPRANO A., CRIELAARD B., PIACENZA F., RUSPANTINI D., *Measuring Operational and Reputational risk – A Practitioners' Approach*, Wiley Finance, 2009.

[YOU 09] YOUNG B., COLEMAN R., *Operational Risk Assessment – The Commercial Imperative and Transparent Approach*, Wiley Finance, 2009.

List of Authors

Romain BERRY
Citigroup
London
UK

Killian BUCKLEY
Kinetic Partners
Dublin
Ireland

Ludovic DEFLANDRE
Baker & McKenzie Luxembourg
Luxembourg

Mark EVANS
PricewaterhouseCoopers
Luxembourg

Benjamin GAUTHIER
PricewaterhouseCoopers
Luxembourg

Romain JACQUES
Baker & McKenzie Luxembourg
Luxembourg

Thierry LÓPEZ
PricewaterhouseCoopers
Luxembourg

Ciara O'SULLIVAN
Kinetic Partners
Dublin
Ireland

André PESCH
Baker & McKenzie Luxembourg
Luxembourg

Christian SZYLAR
Marshall Wace
London
UK

Andrew P. WHITE
FundApps
London
UK

Jérôme WIGNY
Elvinger, Hoss & Prussen
Luxembourg

Céline WILMET
Elvinger, Hoss & Prussen
Luxembourg

Index